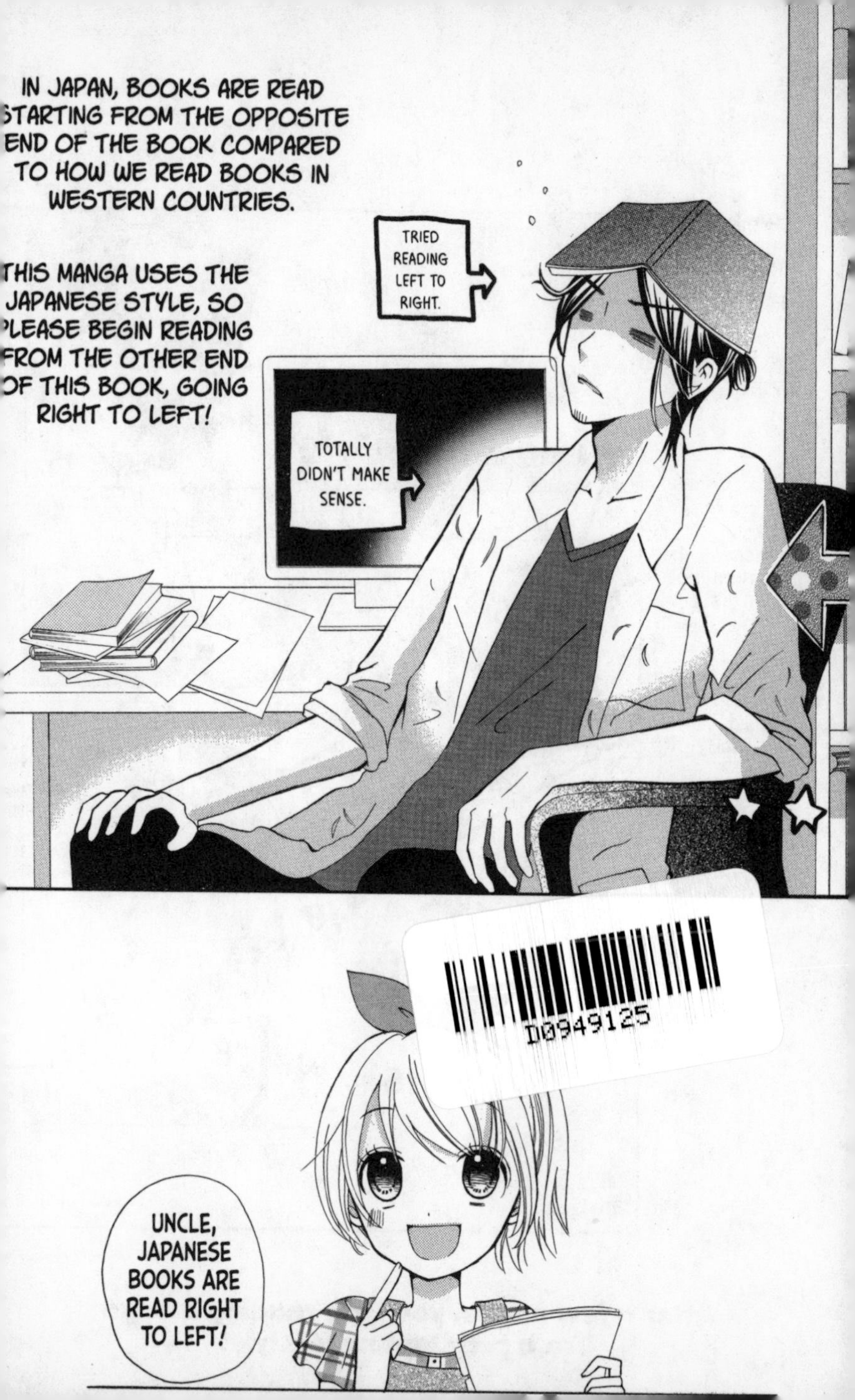
IN JAPAN, BOOKS ARE READ STARTING FROM THE OPPOSITE END OF THE BOOK COMPARED TO HOW WE READ BOOKS IN WESTERN COUNTRIES.
THIS MANGA USES THE JAPANESE STYLE, SO PLEASE BEGIN READING FROM THE OTHER END OF THIS BOOK, GOING RIGHT TO LEFT!
TRIED READING LEFT TO RIGHT.
TOTALLY DIDN'T MAKE SENSE.
UNCLE, JAPANESE BOOKS ARE READ RIGHT TO LEFT!

Page 25

On this page, the top two panels are read first.

This panel is the top right-most after the first two, so it's next.

This panel is the next top right-most, so it is read next.

This is the bottom left-most panel and is read last.

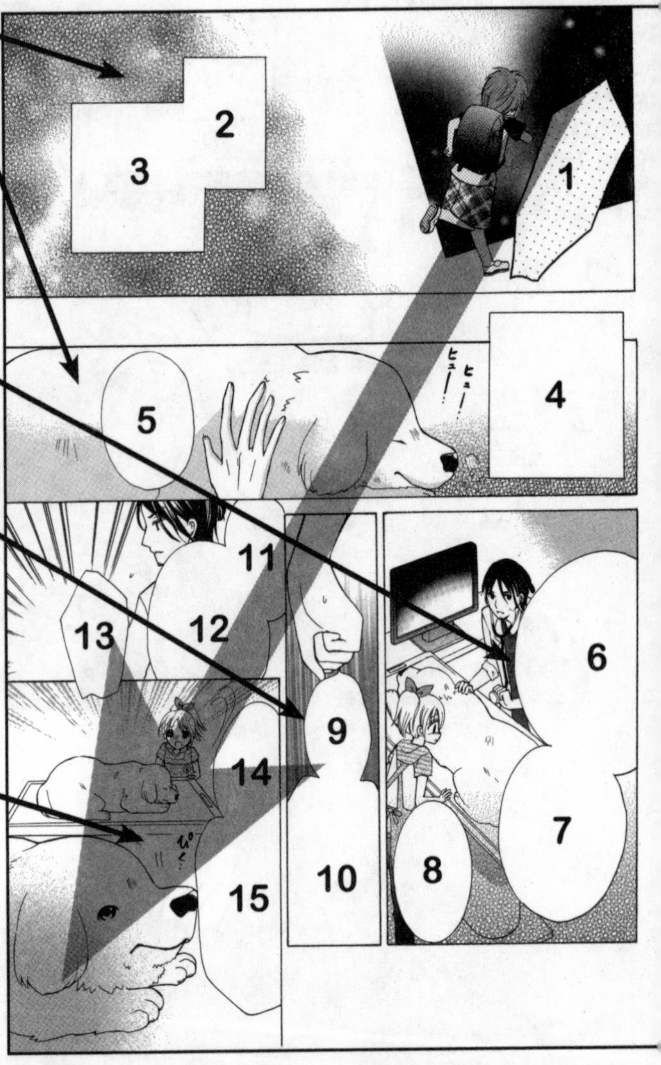

1
2
3
4
5
6
7
8
9
10
11
12
13
14
15

After a few pages, you'll be reading manga like a pro–Japanese-style!

HOW TO READ MANGA

Japanese is written right to left and top to bottom. This means that for a reader accustomed to Western languages, Japanese books read “backwards.” Since most manga published in English now keep the Japanese page order, it can take a little getting used to—but once you learn how, it’s a snap. Here’s a handy guide!

Here you can see pages 24-25 from volume 1. The speech balloons have been numbered in the order you should read them in.

Page 24—read this one first!

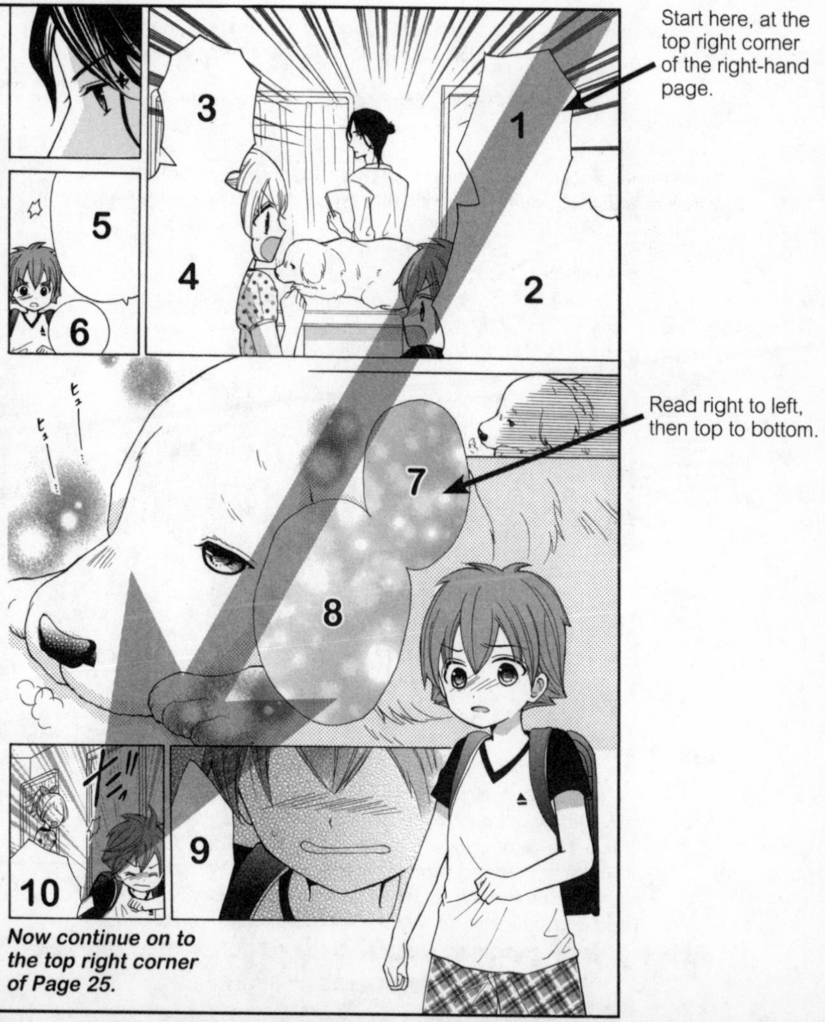
Start here, at the top right corner of the right-hand page.
1
2
3
4
5
6
Read right to left, then top to bottom.
7
8
9
10
Now continue on to the top right corner of Page 25.

Yuzu the Pet Vet 5 is a work of fiction. Names, characters, places, and incidents are the products of the author's imagination or are used fictitiously. Any resemblance to actual events, locales, or persons, living or dead, is entirely coincidental.

A Kodansha Comics Trade Paperback Original
Yuzu the Pet Vet 5 copyright © 2018 Mingo Ito © 2018 NIPPON COLUMBIA CO., LTD.
English translation copyright © 2021 Mingo Ito © NIPPON COLUMBIA CO., LTD.

Published in the United States by Kodansha Comics, an imprint of
Kodansha USA Publishing, LLC, New York.

Publication rights for this English edition arranged through
Kodansha Ltd., Tokyo.

First published in Japan in 2018 by Kodansha Ltd., Tokyo
as *Yuzu no Doubutsu Karute ~Kochira Wan Nyan Doubutsu Byouin~*, volume 5.

ISBN 978-1-64651-081-8

Original cover design by Tomoko Kobayashi

Printed in the United States of America.

www.kodanshacomics.com

9 8 7 6 5 4 3 2 1
Translation: Julie Goniwich
Lettering: David Yoo
Kodansha Comics edition cover design by Matthew Akuginow

Publisher: Kiichiro Sugawara

Director of publishing services: Ben Applegate
Associate director of operations: Stephen Pakula
Publishing services managing editor: Noelle Webster
Assistant production manager: Emi Lotto, Angela Zurlo
Logo and character art ©Kodansha USA Publishing, LLC

YUZU THE PET VET

Welcome to the Bow Meow Animal Hospital

5

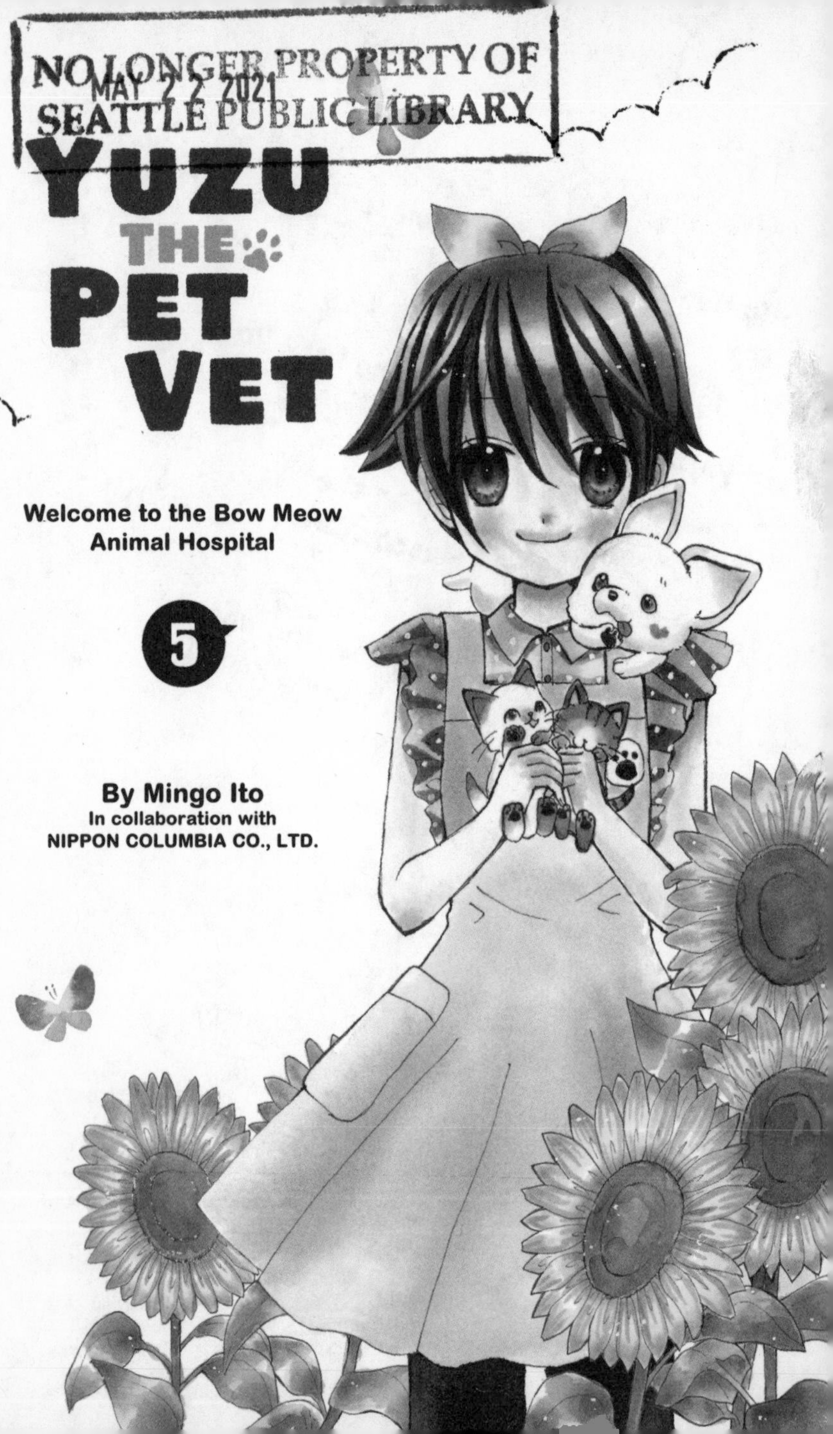

By Mingo Ito
In collaboration with
NIPPON COLUMBIA CO., LTD.

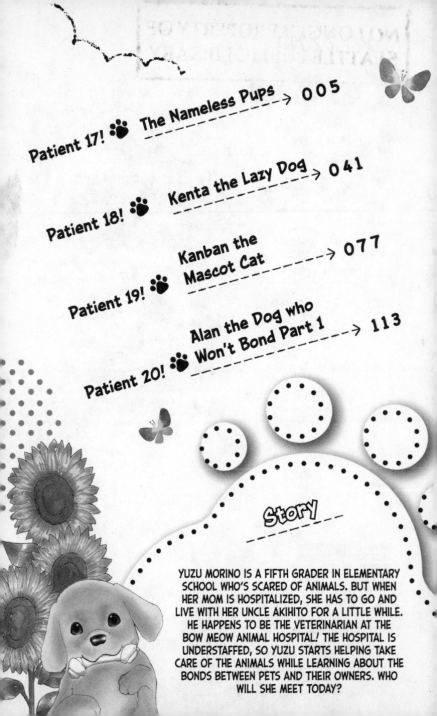

Story

YUZU MORINO IS A FIFTH GRADER IN ELEMENTARY SCHOOL WHO'S SCARED OF ANIMALS. BUT WHEN HER MOM IS HOSPITALIZED, SHE HAS TO GO AND LIVE WITH HER UNCLE AKIHITO FOR A LITTLE WHILE. HE HAPPENS TO BE THE VETERINARIAN AT THE BOW MEOW ANIMAL HOSPITAL! THE HOSPITAL IS UNDERSTAFFED, SO YUZU STARTS HELPING TAKE CARE OF THE ANIMALS WHILE LEARNING ABOUT THE BONDS BETWEEN PETS AND THEIR OWNERS. WHO WILL SHE MEET TODAY?

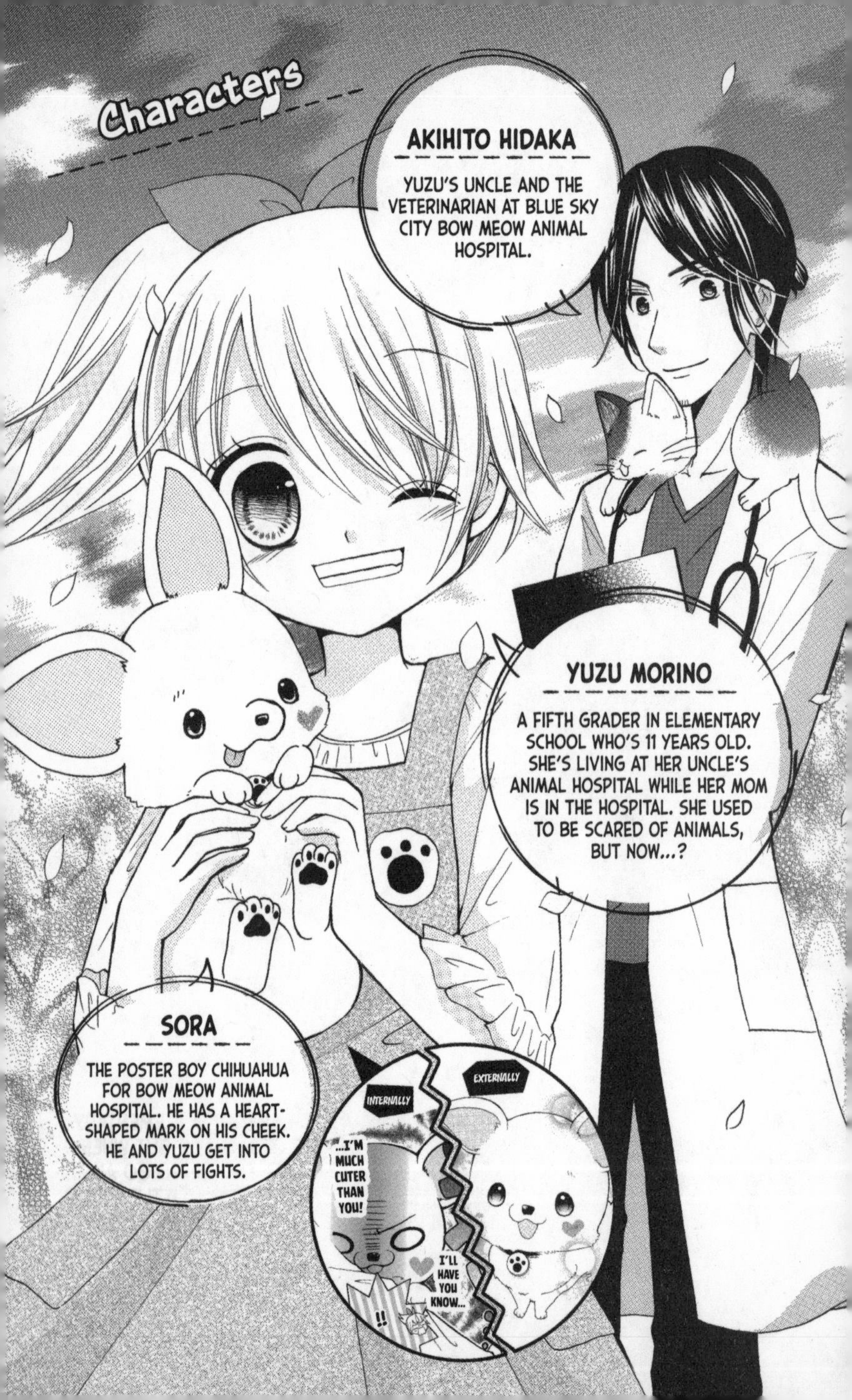
Characters
AKIHITO HIDAKA
YUZU'S UNCLE AND THE VETERINARIAN AT BLUE SKY CITY BOW MEOW ANIMAL HOSPITAL.
YUZU MORINO
A FIFTH GRADER IN ELEMENTARY SCHOOL WHO'S 11 YEARS OLD. SHE'S LIVING AT HER UNCLE'S ANIMAL HOSPITAL WHILE HER MOM IS IN THE HOSPITAL. SHE USED TO BE SCARED OF ANIMALS, BUT NOW...?
SORA
THE POSTER BOY CHIHUAHUA FOR BOW MEOW ANIMAL HOSPITAL. HE HAS A HEART-SHAPED MARK ON HIS CHEEK. HE AND YUZU GET INTO LOTS OF FIGHTS.
EXTERNALLY
INTERNALLY
...I'M MUCH CUTER THAN YOU!
I'LL HAVE YOU KNOW...
!!

YUZU THE PET VET

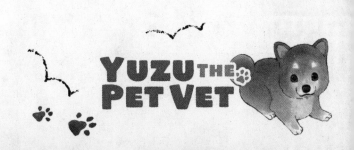

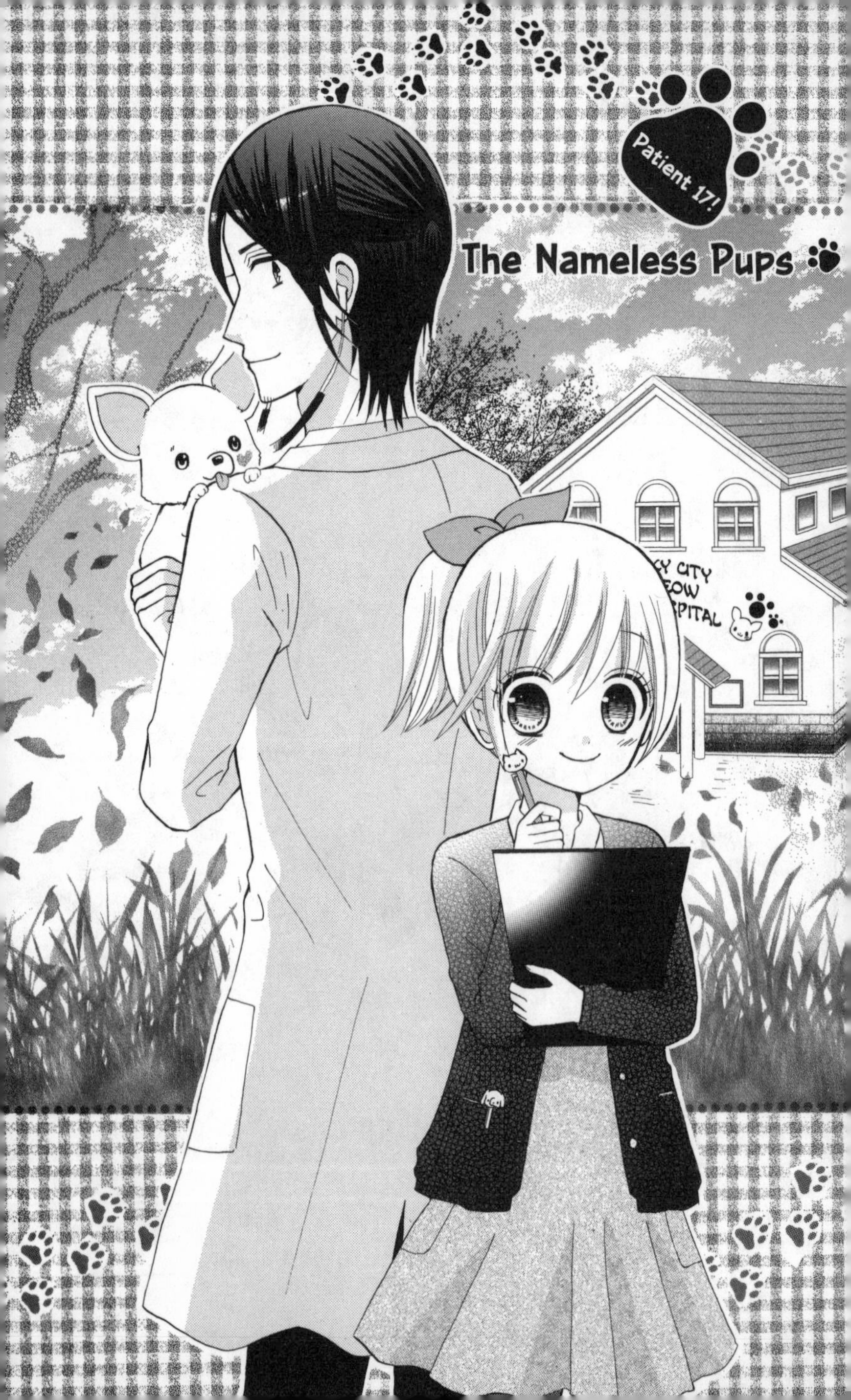
Patient 17!
The Nameless Pups

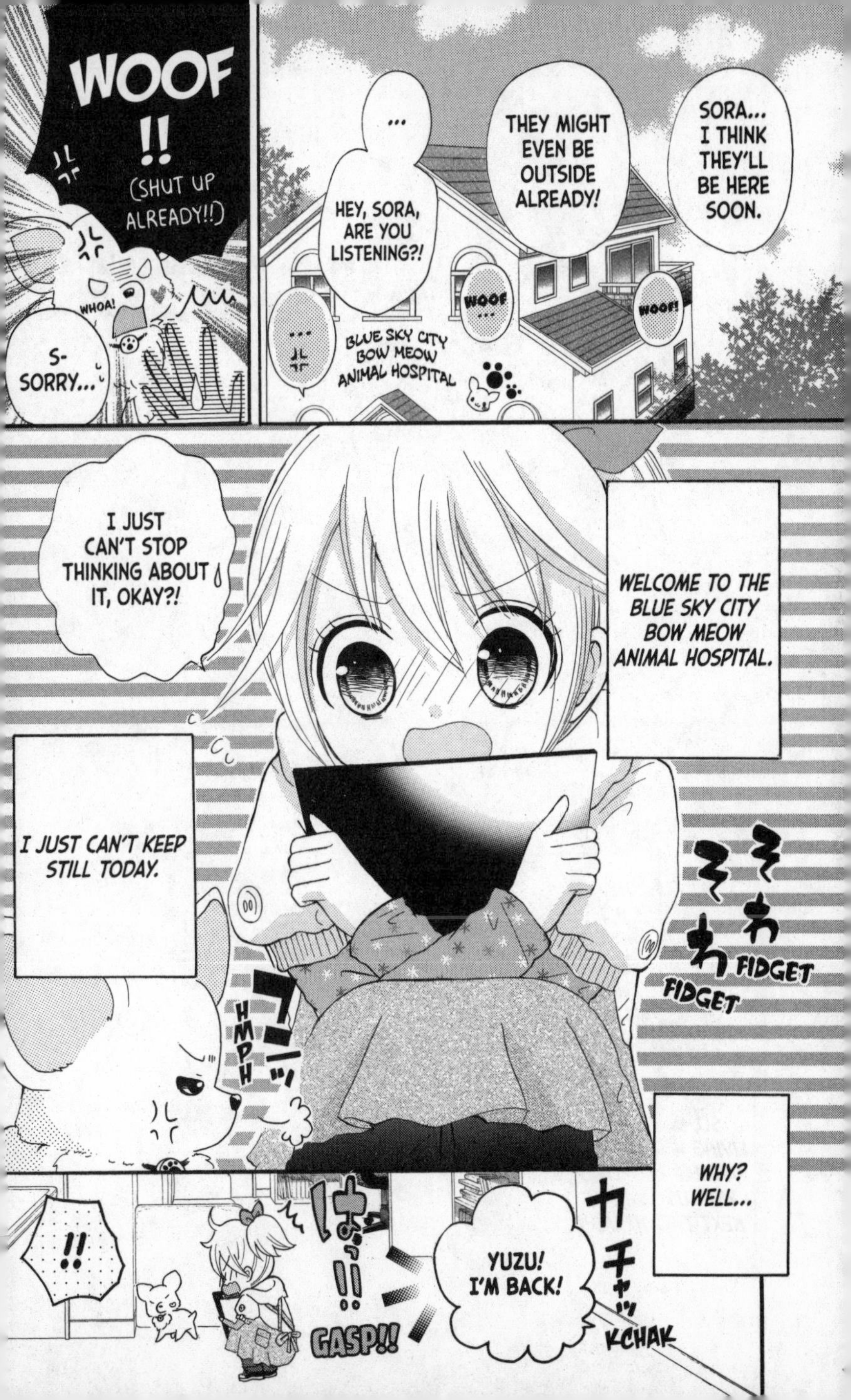
SORA... I THINK THEY'LL BE HERE SOON.
THEY MIGHT EVEN BE OUTSIDE ALREADY!
...
HEY, SORA, ARE YOU LISTENING?!
WOOF!
WOOF ...
...
BLUE SKY CITY BOW MEOW ANIMAL HOSPITAL
WOOF!!
(SHUT UP ALREADY!!)
WHOA!
S-SORRY...
WELCOME TO THE BLUE SKY CITY BOW MEOW ANIMAL HOSPITAL.
I JUST CAN'T STOP THINKING ABOUT IT, OKAY?!
I JUST CAN'T KEEP STILL TODAY.
そわそわ
FIDGET FIDGET
HMPH
WHY? WELL...
カチャッ
KCHAK
YUZU! I'M BACK!
はっ!!
GASP!!
!!

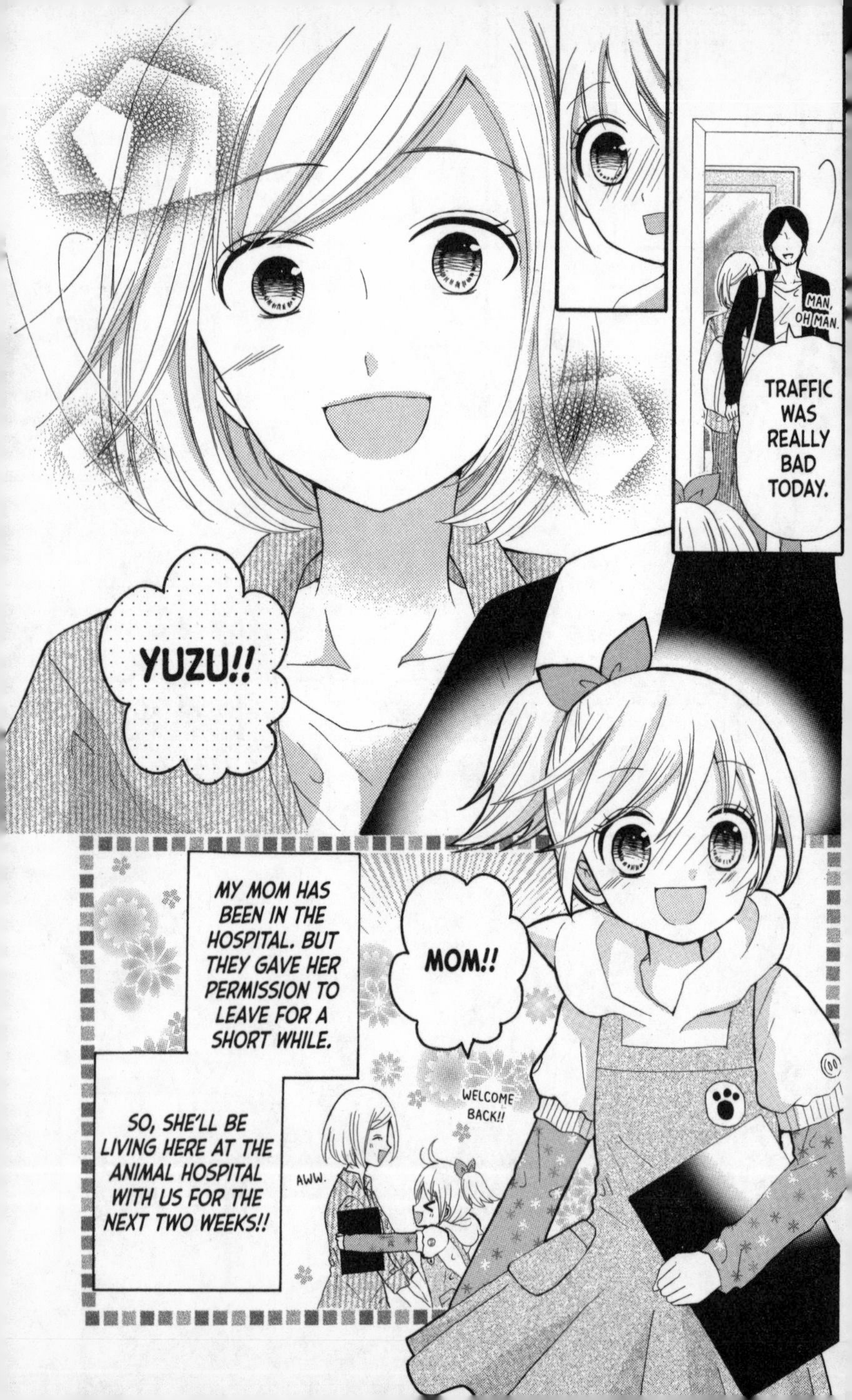

MAN, OH MAN.
TRAFFIC WAS REALLY BAD TODAY.
YUZU!!
MOM!!
MY MOM HAS BEEN IN THE HOSPITAL. BUT THEY GAVE HER PERMISSION TO LEAVE FOR A SHORT WHILE.
WELCOME BACK!!
AWW.
SO, SHE'LL BE LIVING HERE AT THE ANIMAL HOSPITAL WITH US FOR THE NEXT TWO WEEKS!!

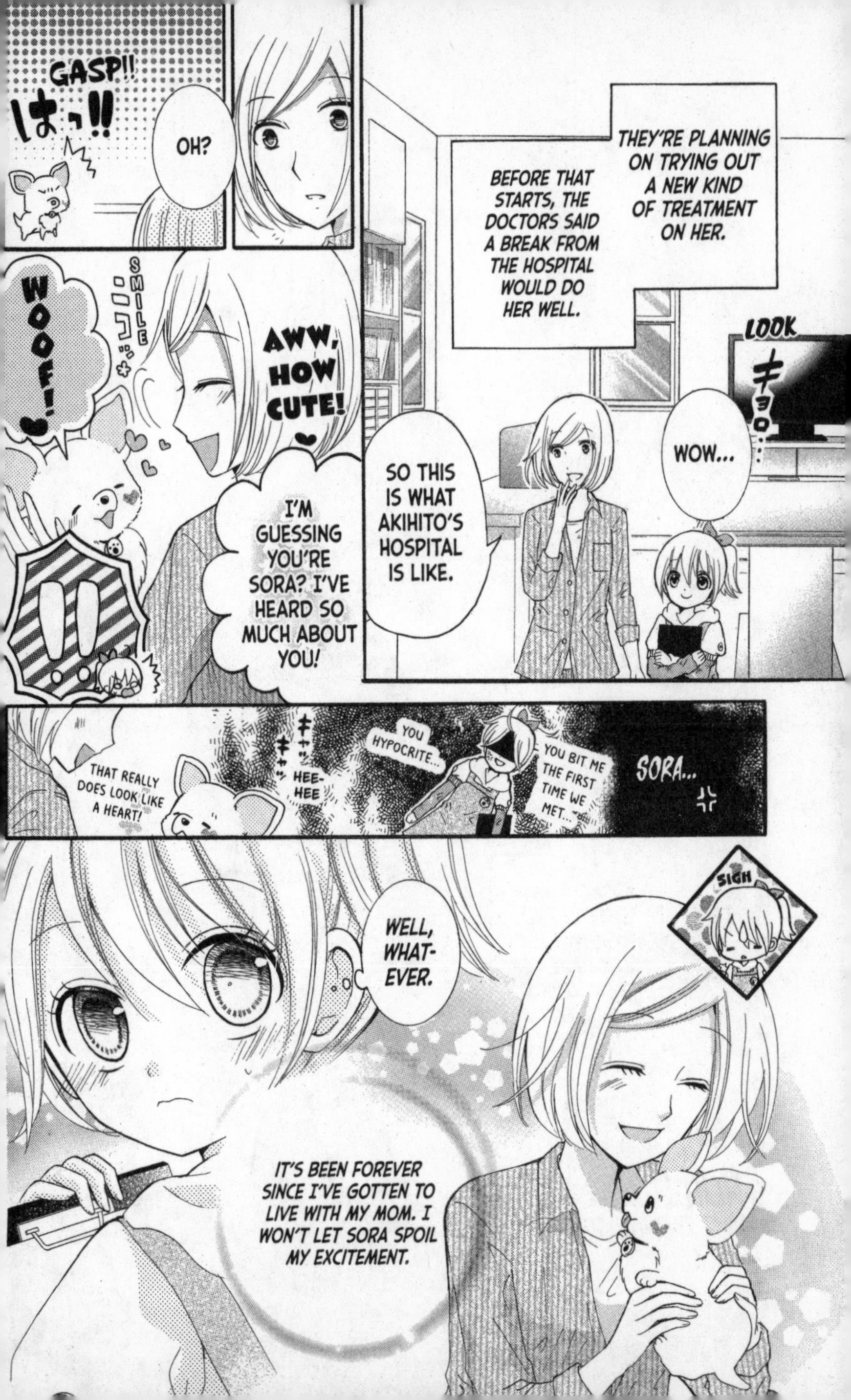
THEY'RE PLANNING ON TRYING OUT A NEW KIND OF TREATMENT ON HER.
BEFORE THAT STARTS, THE DOCTORS SAID A BREAK FROM THE HOSPITAL WOULD DO HER WELL.
LOOK
キョロ
WOW...
SO THIS IS WHAT AKIHITO'S HOSPITAL IS LIKE.
OH?
GASP!!
はっ!!
AWW, HOW CUTE!
I'M GUESSING YOU'RE SORA? I'VE HEARD SO MUCH ABOUT YOU!
SMILE
ニコッ
WOOF!!
SORA...
YOU BIT ME THE FIRST TIME WE MET...
YOU HYPOCRITE...
HEE-HEE
キャッキャッ
THAT REALLY DOES LOOK LIKE A HEART!
SIGH
WELL, WHAT-EVER.
IT'S BEEN FOREVER SINCE I'VE GOTTEN TO LIVE WITH MY MOM. I WON'T LET SORA SPOIL MY EXCITEMENT.

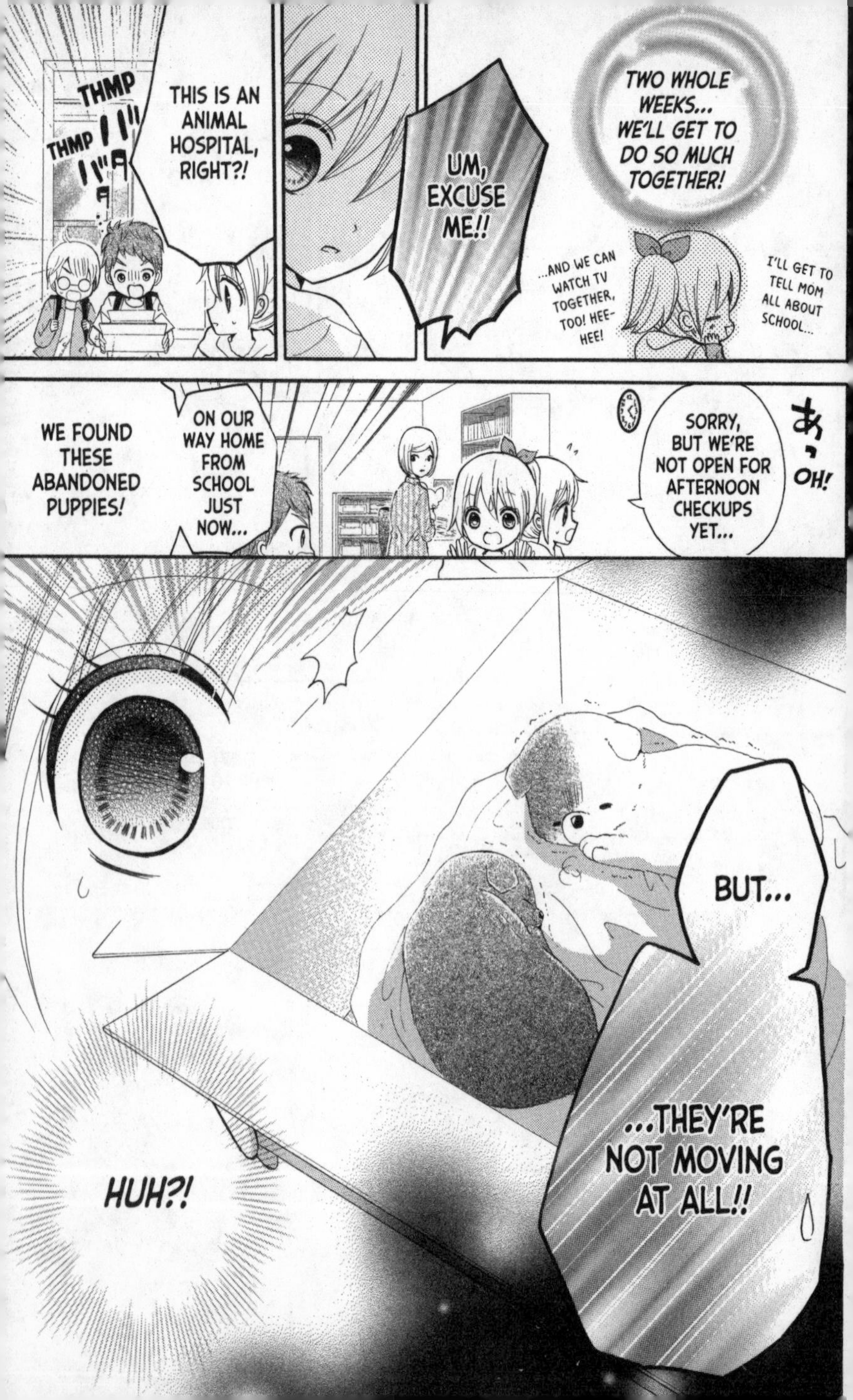
TWO WHOLE WEEKS... WE'LL GET TO DO SO MUCH TOGETHER!
I'LL GET TO TELL MOM ALL ABOUT SCHOOL...
...AND WE CAN WATCH TV TOGETHER, TOO! HEE-HEE!
UM, EXCUSE ME!!
THIS IS AN ANIMAL HOSPITAL, RIGHT?!
THMP THMP
あっ OH!
SORRY, BUT WE'RE NOT OPEN FOR AFTERNOON CHECKUPS YET...
ON OUR WAY HOME FROM SCHOOL JUST NOW...
WE FOUND THESE ABANDONED PUPPIES!
BUT...
...THEY'RE NOT MOVING AT ALL!!
HUH?!

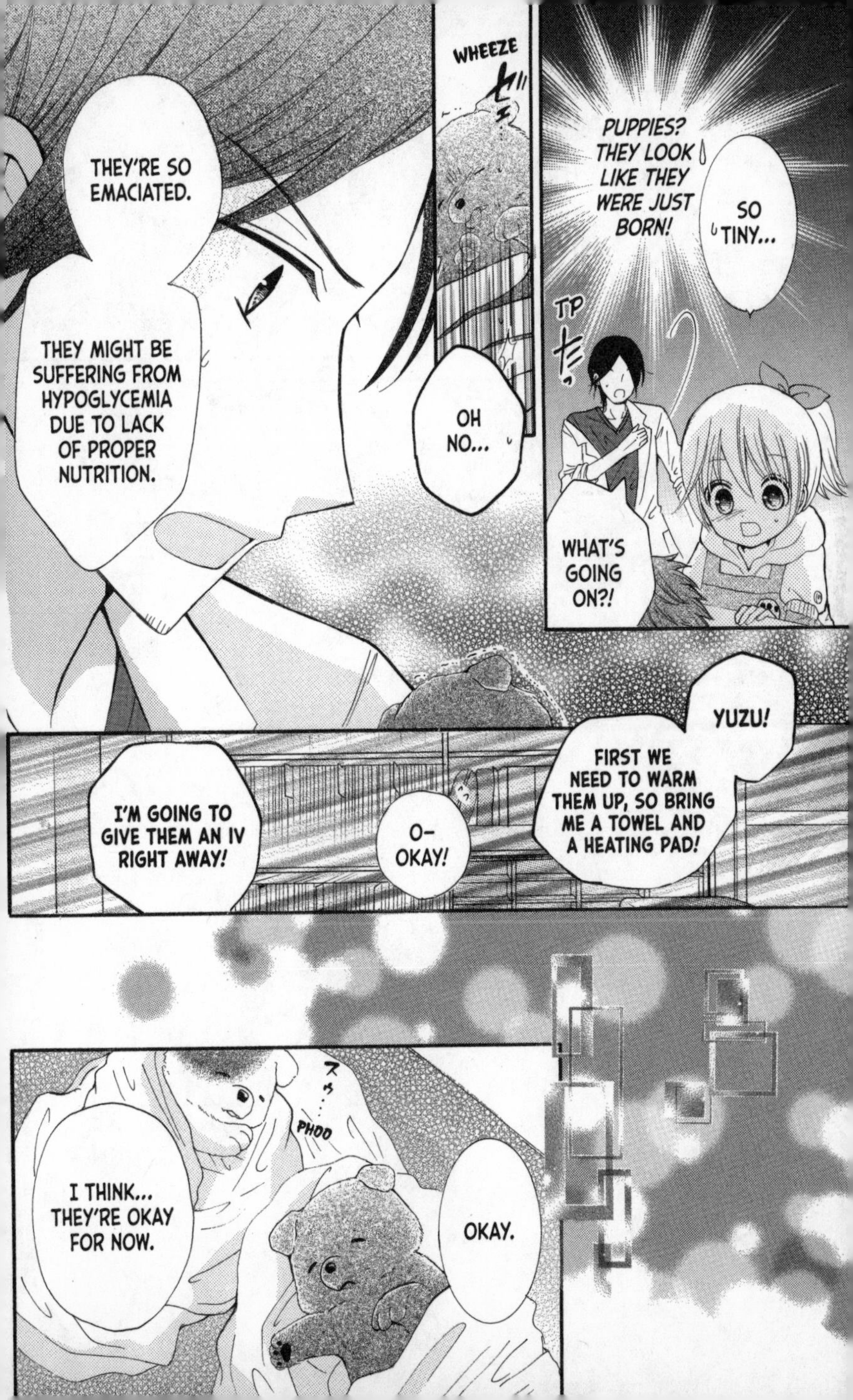
SO TINY...
PUPPIES? THEY LOOK LIKE THEY WERE JUST BORN!
TP
WHAT'S GOING ON?!
WHEEZE
OH NO...
THEY'RE SO EMACIATED.
THEY MIGHT BE SUFFERING FROM HYPOGLYCEMIA DUE TO LACK OF PROPER NUTRITION.
YUZU!
FIRST WE NEED TO WARM THEM UP, SO BRING ME A TOWEL AND A HEATING PAD!
O-OKAY!
I'M GOING TO GIVE THEM AN IV RIGHT AWAY!
OKAY.
PHOO
I THINK... THEY'RE OKAY FOR NOW.

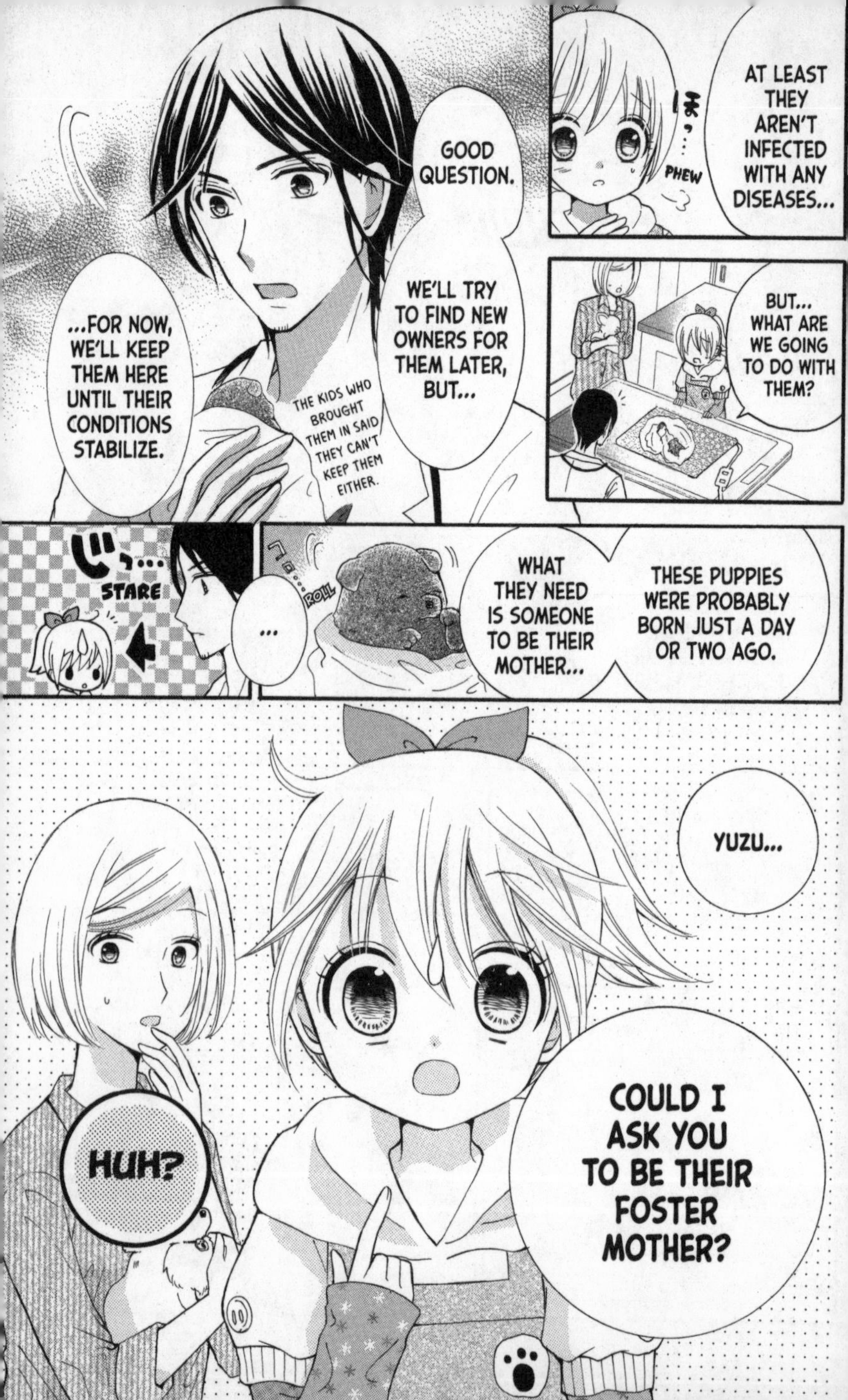
AT LEAST THEY AREN'T INFECTED WITH ANY DISEASES...
ほっ…
PHEW
BUT... WHAT ARE WE GOING TO DO WITH THEM?
GOOD QUESTION.
WE'LL TRY TO FIND NEW OWNERS FOR THEM LATER, BUT...
THE KIDS WHO BROUGHT THEM IN SAID THEY CAN'T KEEP THEM EITHER.
...FOR NOW, WE'LL KEEP THEM HERE UNTIL THEIR CONDITIONS STABILIZE.
THESE PUPPIES WERE PROBABLY BORN JUST A DAY OR TWO AGO.
WHAT THEY NEED IS SOMEONE TO BE THEIR MOTHER...
ROLL
...
じっ…
STARE
YUZU...
COULD I ASK YOU TO BE THEIR FOSTER MOTHER?
HUH?

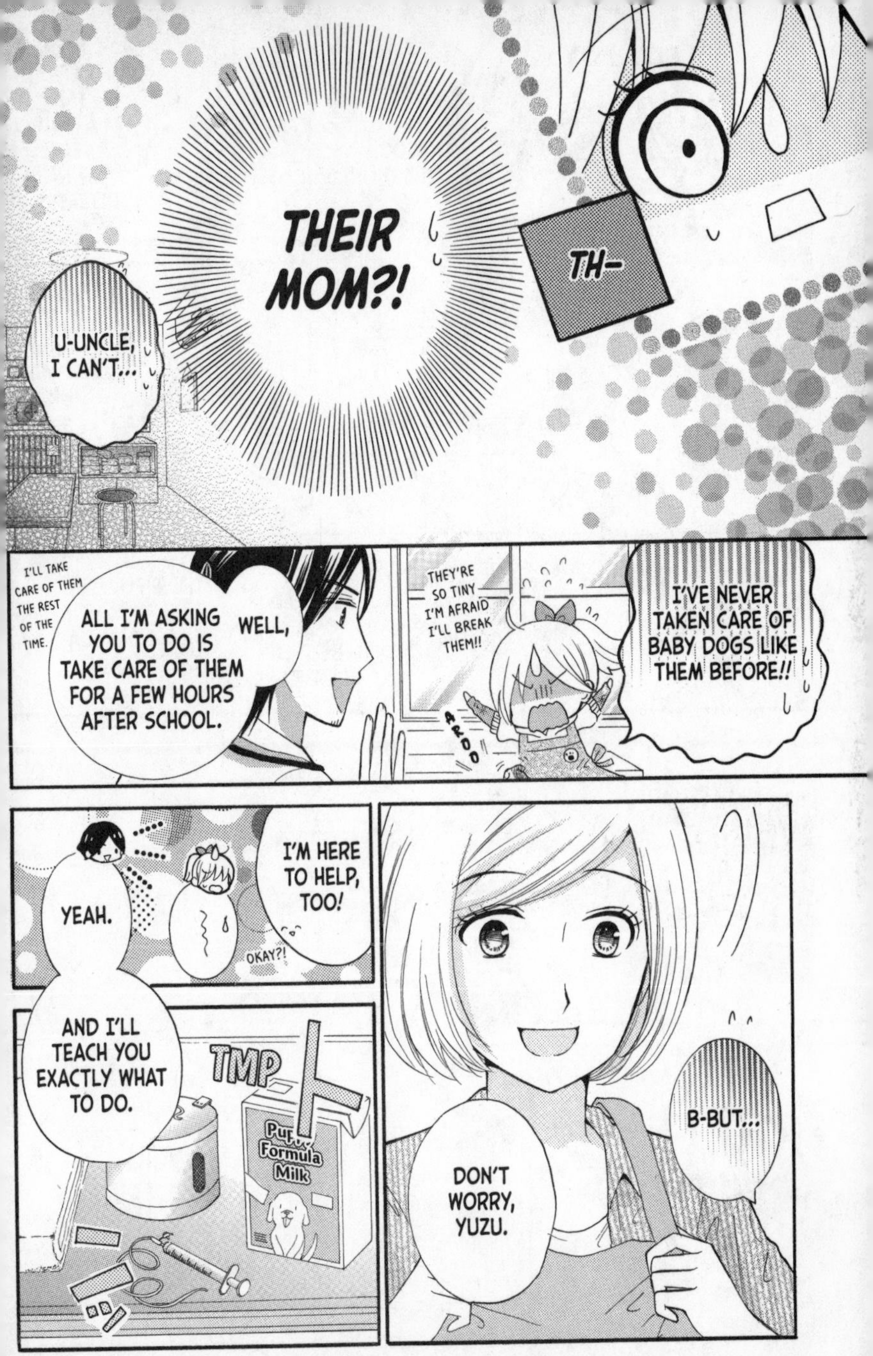
TH-
THEIR MOM?!
U-UNCLE, I CAN'T...
I'VE NEVER TAKEN CARE OF BABY DOGS LIKE THEM BEFORE!!
THEY'RE SO TINY I'M AFRAID I'LL BREAK THEM!!
WELL,
ALL I'M ASKING YOU TO DO IS TAKE CARE OF THEM FOR A FEW HOURS AFTER SCHOOL.
I'LL TAKE CARE OF THEM THE REST OF THE TIME.
B-BUT...
DON'T WORRY, YUZU.
I'M HERE TO HELP, TOO!
OKAY?!
YEAH.
AND I'LL TEACH YOU EXACTLY WHAT TO DO.
TMP
Puppy Formula Milk

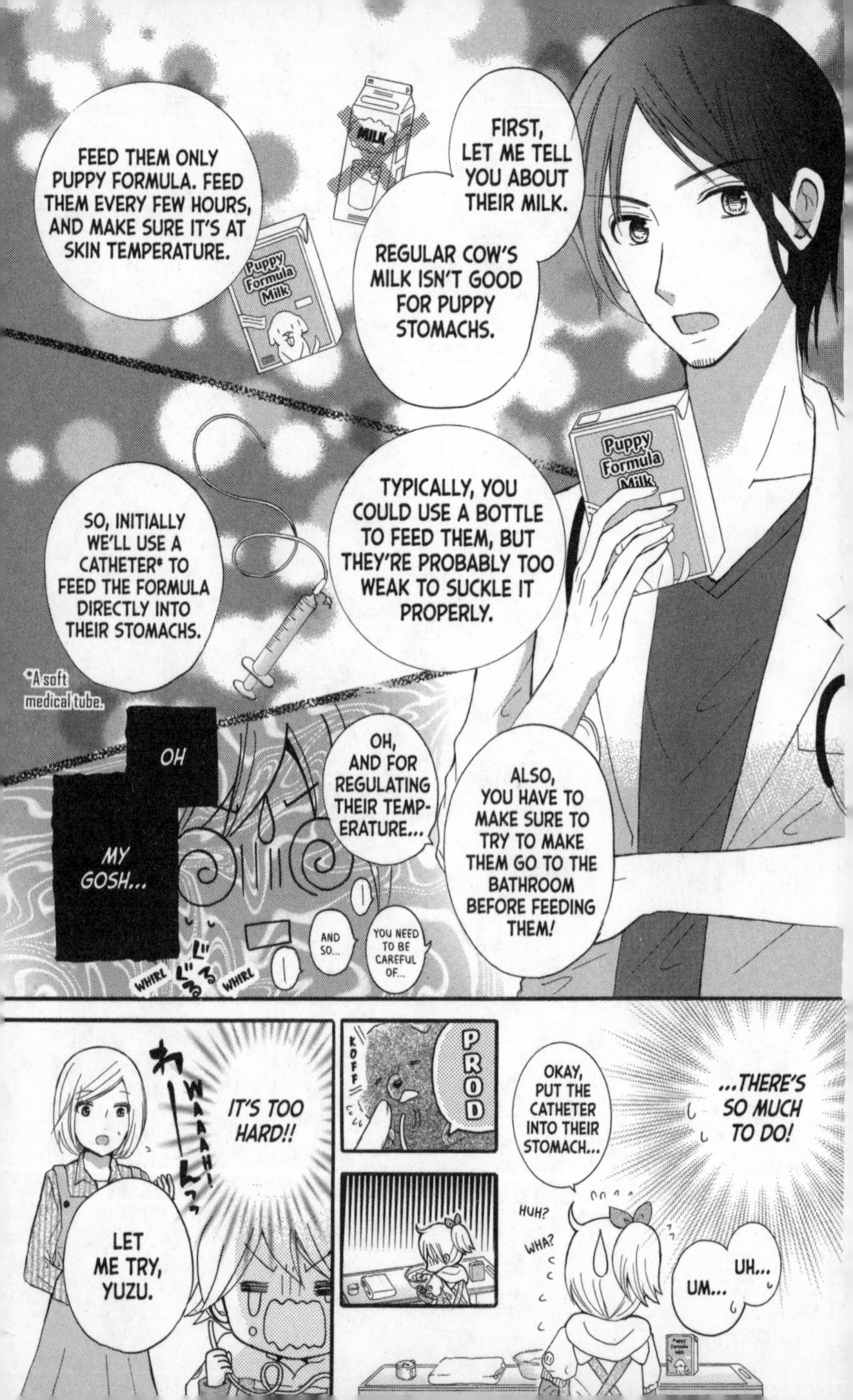
FIRST, LET ME TELL YOU ABOUT THEIR MILK.
MILK
REGULAR COW'S MILK ISN'T GOOD FOR PUPPY STOMACHS.
FEED THEM ONLY PUPPY FORMULA. FEED THEM EVERY FEW HOURS, AND MAKE SURE IT'S AT SKIN TEMPERATURE.
Puppy Formula Milk
Puppy Formula Milk
TYPICALLY, YOU COULD USE A BOTTLE TO FEED THEM, BUT THEY'RE PROBABLY TOO WEAK TO SUCKLE IT PROPERLY.
SO, INITIALLY WE'LL USE A CATHETER* TO FEED THE FORMULA DIRECTLY INTO THEIR STOMACHS.
*A soft medical tube.
ALSO, YOU HAVE TO MAKE SURE TO TRY TO MAKE THEM GO TO THE BATHROOM BEFORE FEEDING THEM!
OH, AND FOR REGULATING THEIR TEMPERATURE...
YOU NEED TO BE CAREFUL OF...
AND SO...
OH
MY GOSH...
WHIRL
WHIRL
OKAY, PUT THE CATHETER INTO THEIR STOMACH...
...THERE'S SO MUCH TO DO!
HUH?
WHA?
UH...
UM...
PROD
KOFF
IT'S TOO HARD!!
WAAAH!
LET ME TRY, YUZU.

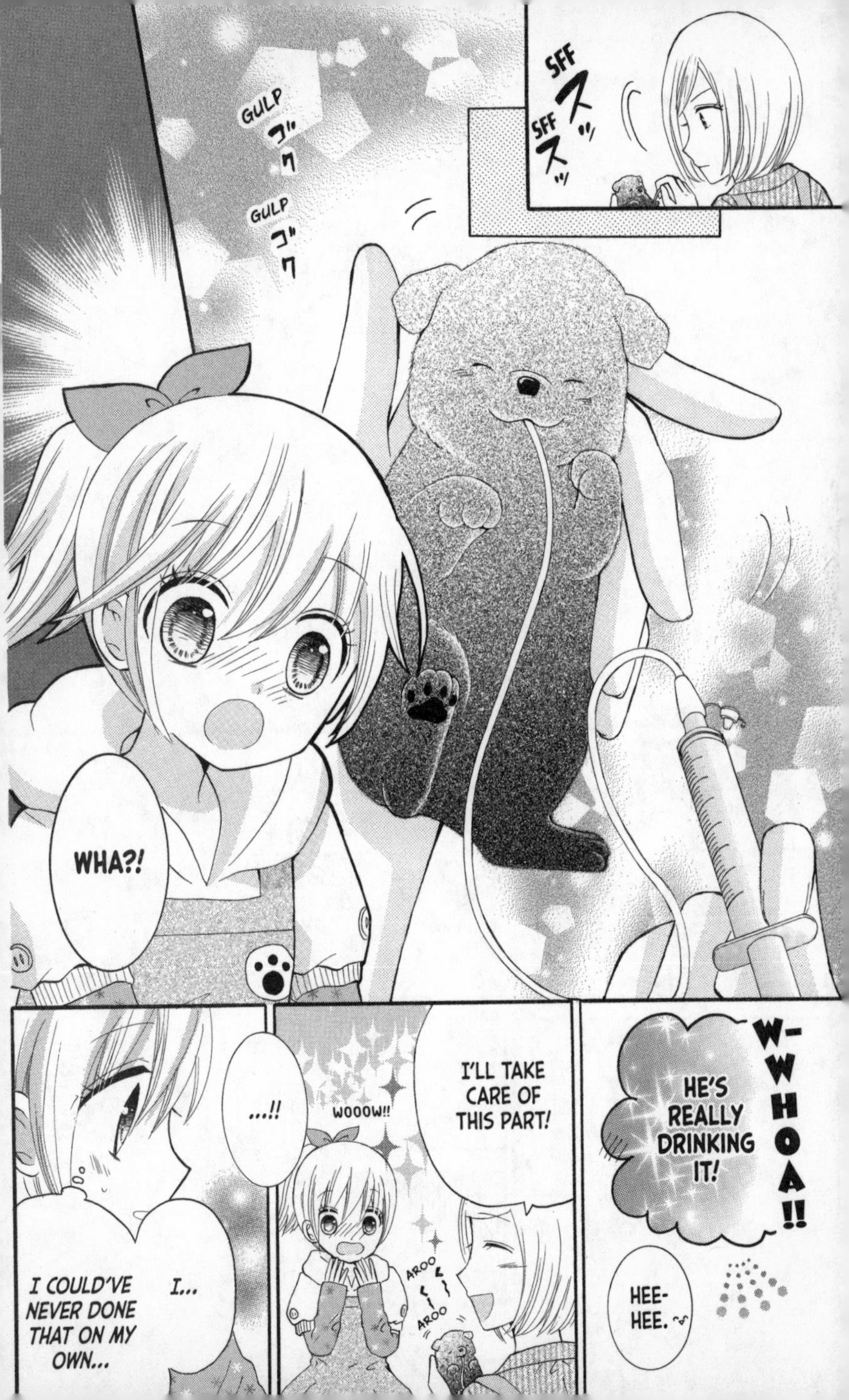
SFF
スッ
SFF
スッ
GULP
ゴク
GULP
ゴク
WHA?!
W-WHOA!!
HE'S REALLY DRINKING IT!
HEE-HEE.
I'LL TAKE CARE OF THIS PART!
...!!
WOOOW!!
AROO
AROO
I...
I COULD'VE NEVER DONE THAT ON MY OWN...

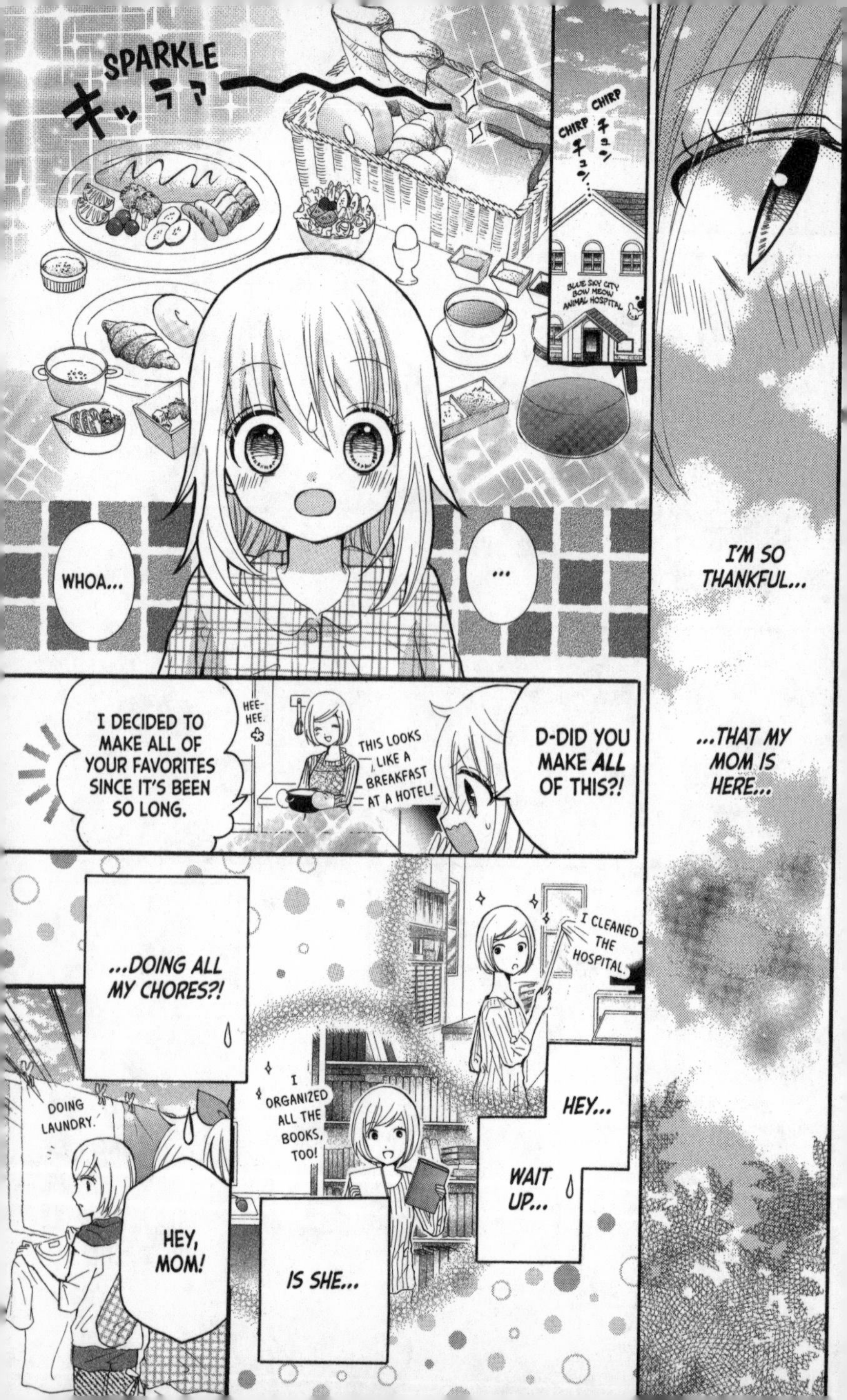
I'M SO THANKFUL...
...THAT MY MOM IS HERE...
CHIRP CHIRP
チュンチュン...
BLUE SKY CITY BOW MEOW ANIMAL HOSPITAL
SPARKLE
キッラァ
...
WHOA...
D-DID YOU MAKE ALL OF THIS?!
THIS LOOKS LIKE A BREAKFAST AT A HOTEL!
HEE-HEE.
I DECIDED TO MAKE ALL OF YOUR FAVORITES SINCE IT'S BEEN SO LONG.
I CLEANED THE HOSPITAL.
HEY...
WAIT UP...
I ORGANIZED ALL THE BOOKS, TOO!
IS SHE...
...DOING ALL MY CHORES?!
DOING LAUNDRY.
HEY, MOM!

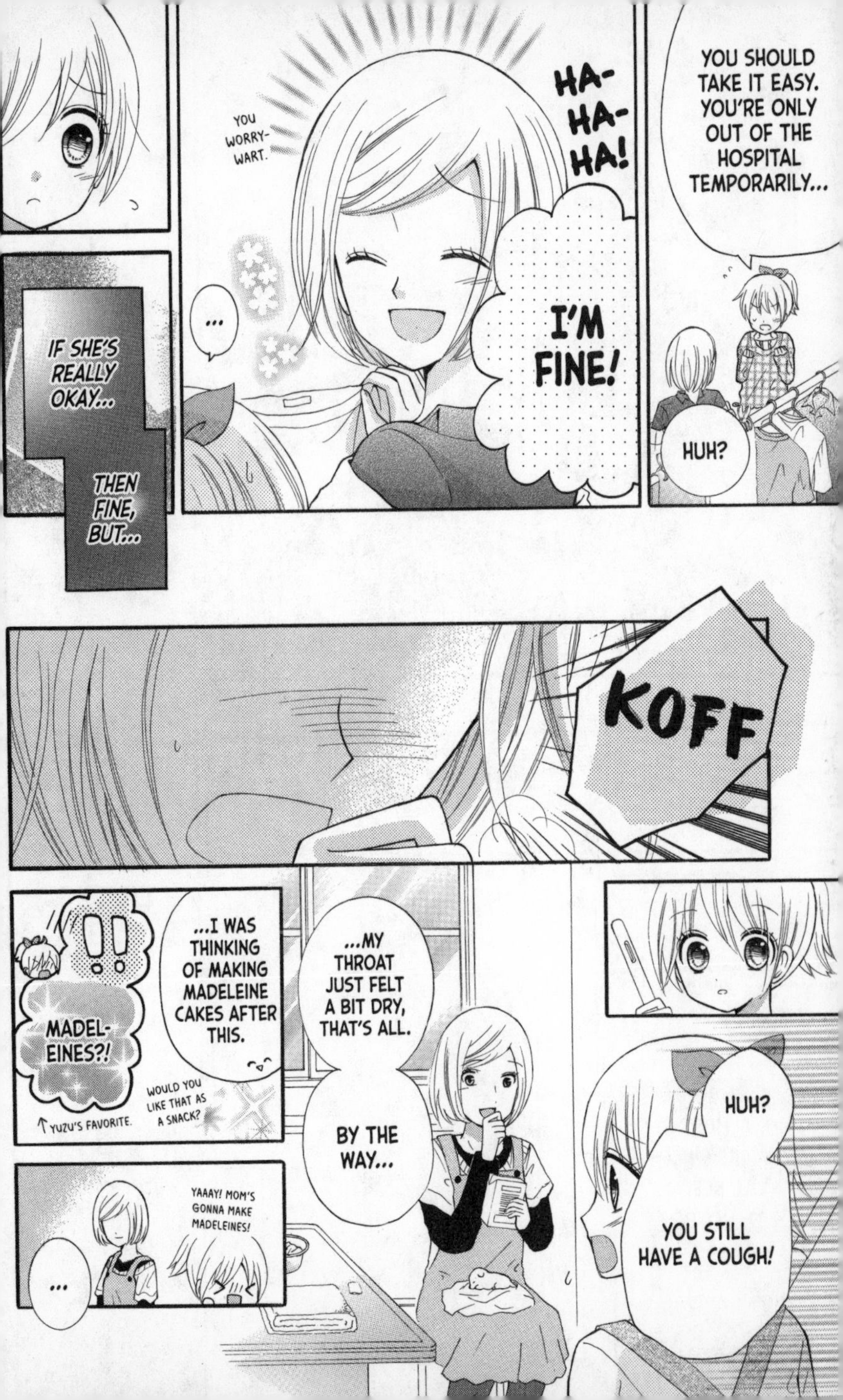
YOU SHOULD TAKE IT EASY. YOU'RE ONLY OUT OF THE HOSPITAL TEMPORARILY...
HUH?
HA-HA-HA!
I'M FINE!
YOU WORRY-WART.
...
IF SHE'S REALLY OKAY...
THEN FINE, BUT...
KOFF
HUH?
YOU STILL HAVE A COUGH!
...MY THROAT JUST FELT A BIT DRY, THAT'S ALL.
BY THE WAY...
...I WAS THINKING OF MAKING MADELEINE CAKES AFTER THIS.
WOULD YOU LIKE THAT AS A SNACK?
!!
MADEL-EINES?!
↑YUZU'S FAVORITE.
YAAAY! MOM'S GONNA MAKE MADELEINES!
...

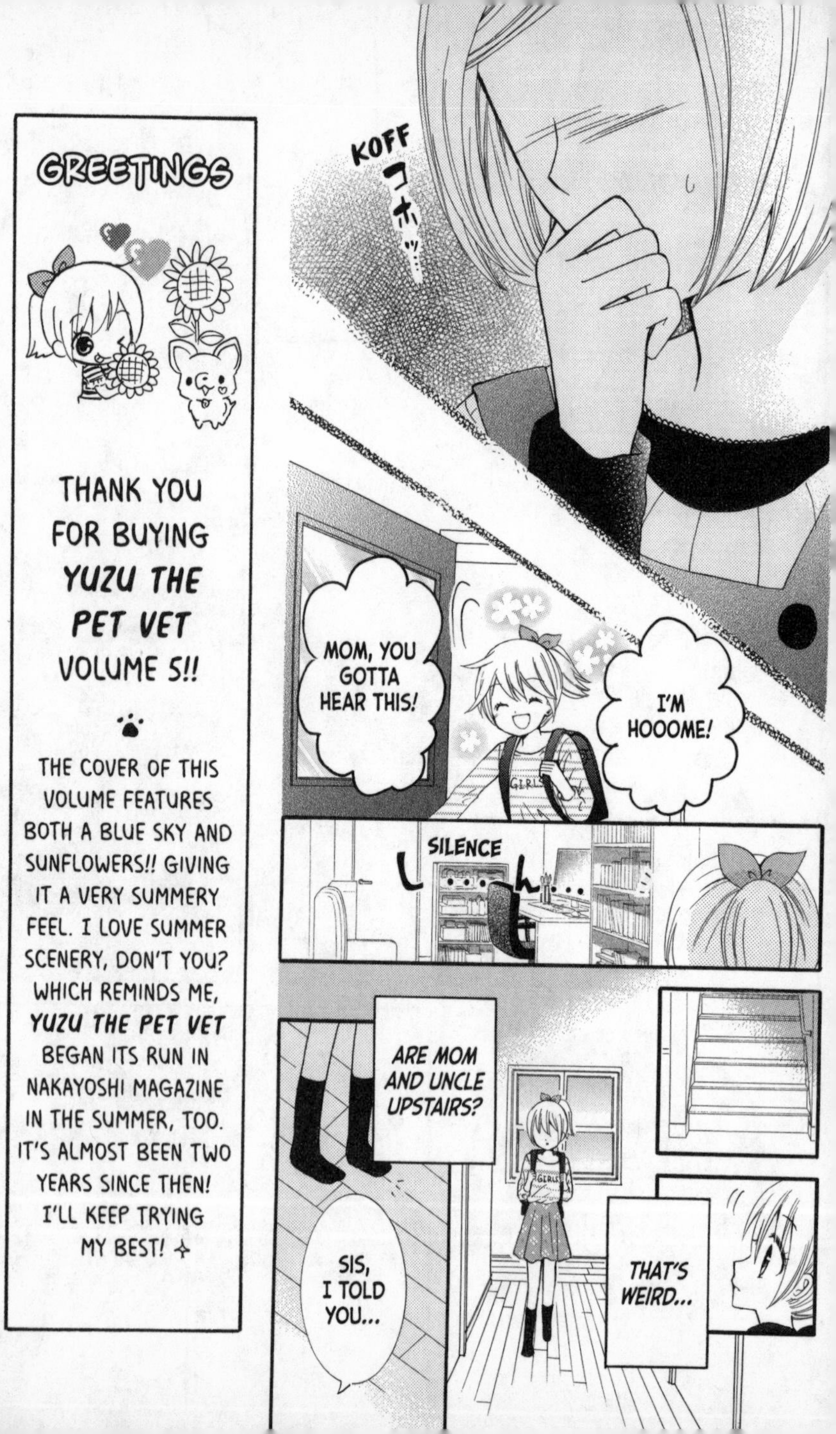
KOFF
コホッ…
I'M HOOOME!
MOM, YOU GOTTA HEAR THIS!
SILENCE
しーん…
THAT'S WEIRD...
ARE MOM AND UNCLE UPSTAIRS?
SIS, I TOLD YOU...

GREETINGS

THANK YOU FOR BUYING ***YUZU THE PET VET*** VOLUME 5!!

THE COVER OF THIS VOLUME FEATURES BOTH A BLUE SKY AND SUNFLOWERS!! GIVING IT A VERY SUMMERY FEEL. I LOVE SUMMER SCENERY, DON'T YOU? WHICH REMINDS ME, ***YUZU THE PET VET*** BEGAN ITS RUN IN NAKAYOSHI MAGAZINE IN THE SUMMER, TOO. IT'S ALMOST BEEN TWO YEARS SINCE THEN! I'LL KEEP TRYING MY BEST! ✧

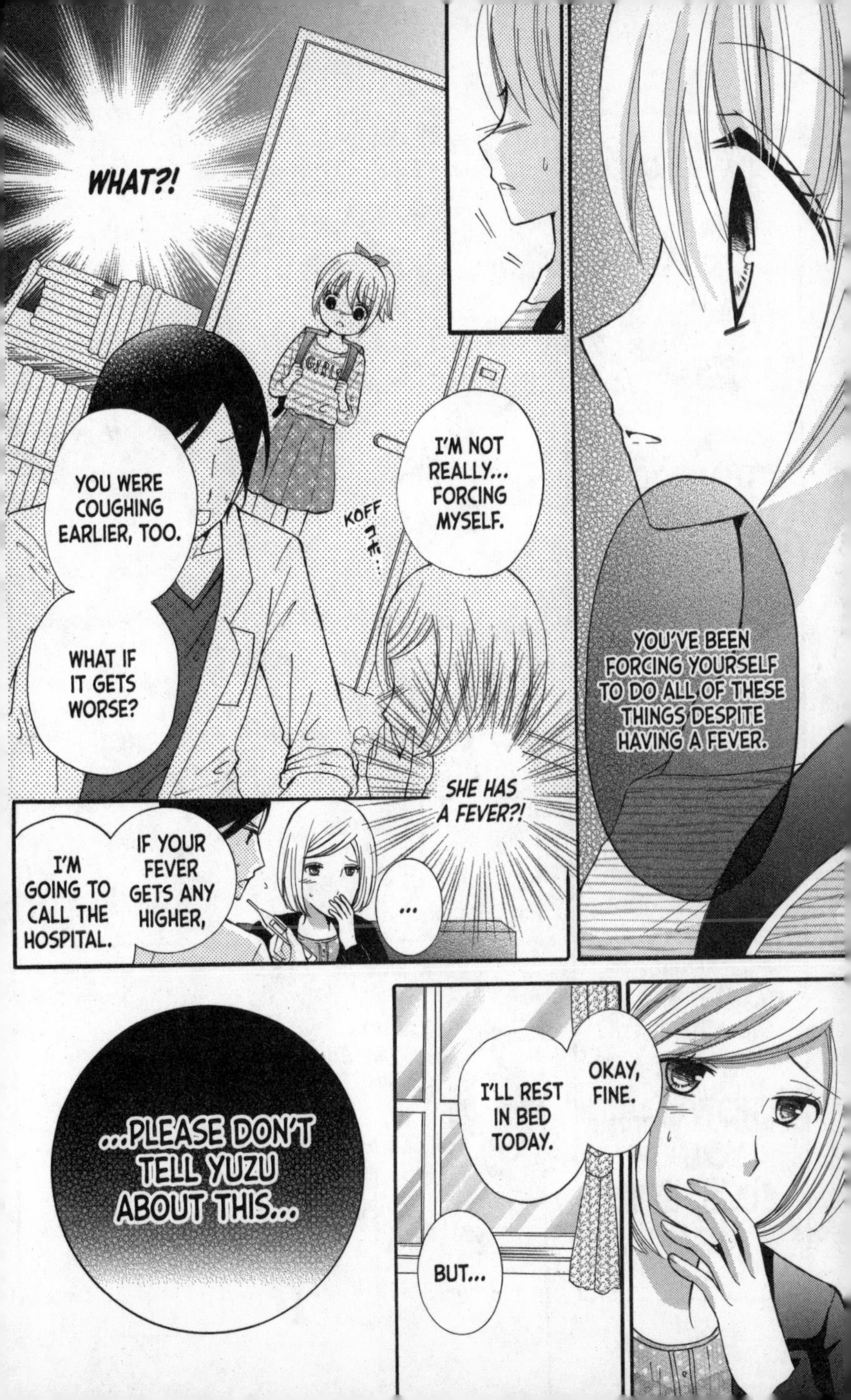
YOU'VE BEEN FORCING YOURSELF TO DO ALL OF THESE THINGS DESPITE HAVING A FEVER.
WHAT?!
I'M NOT REALLY... FORCING MYSELF.
KOFF
YOU WERE COUGHING EARLIER, TOO.
WHAT IF IT GETS WORSE?
SHE HAS A FEVER?!
...
IF YOUR FEVER GETS ANY HIGHER,
I'M GOING TO CALL THE HOSPITAL.
OKAY, FINE.
I'LL REST IN BED TODAY.
BUT...
...PLEASE DON'T TELL YUZU ABOUT THIS...

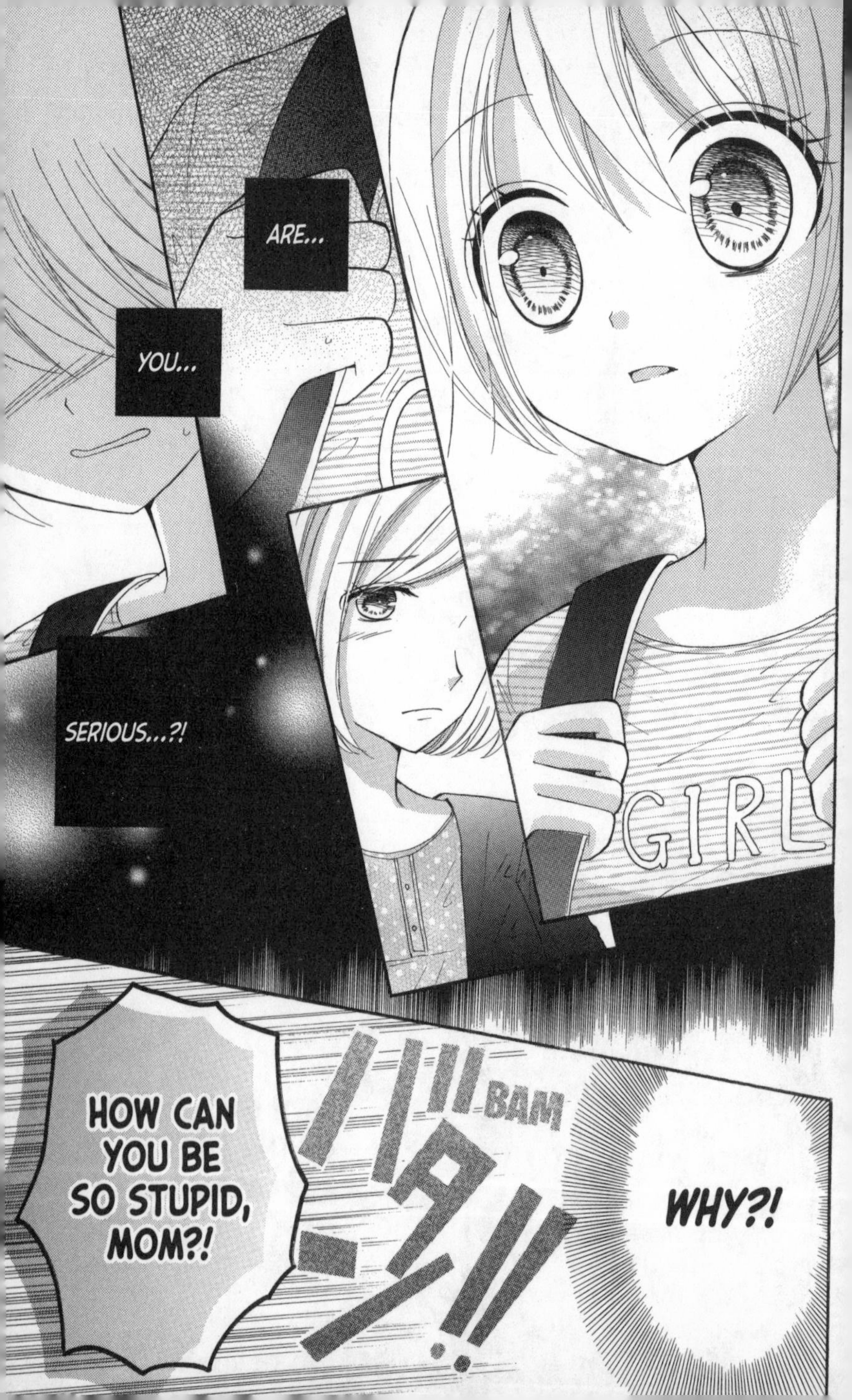
ARE...
YOU...
SERIOUS...?!
GIRL
WHY?!
BAM
HOW CAN YOU BE SO STUPID, MOM?!

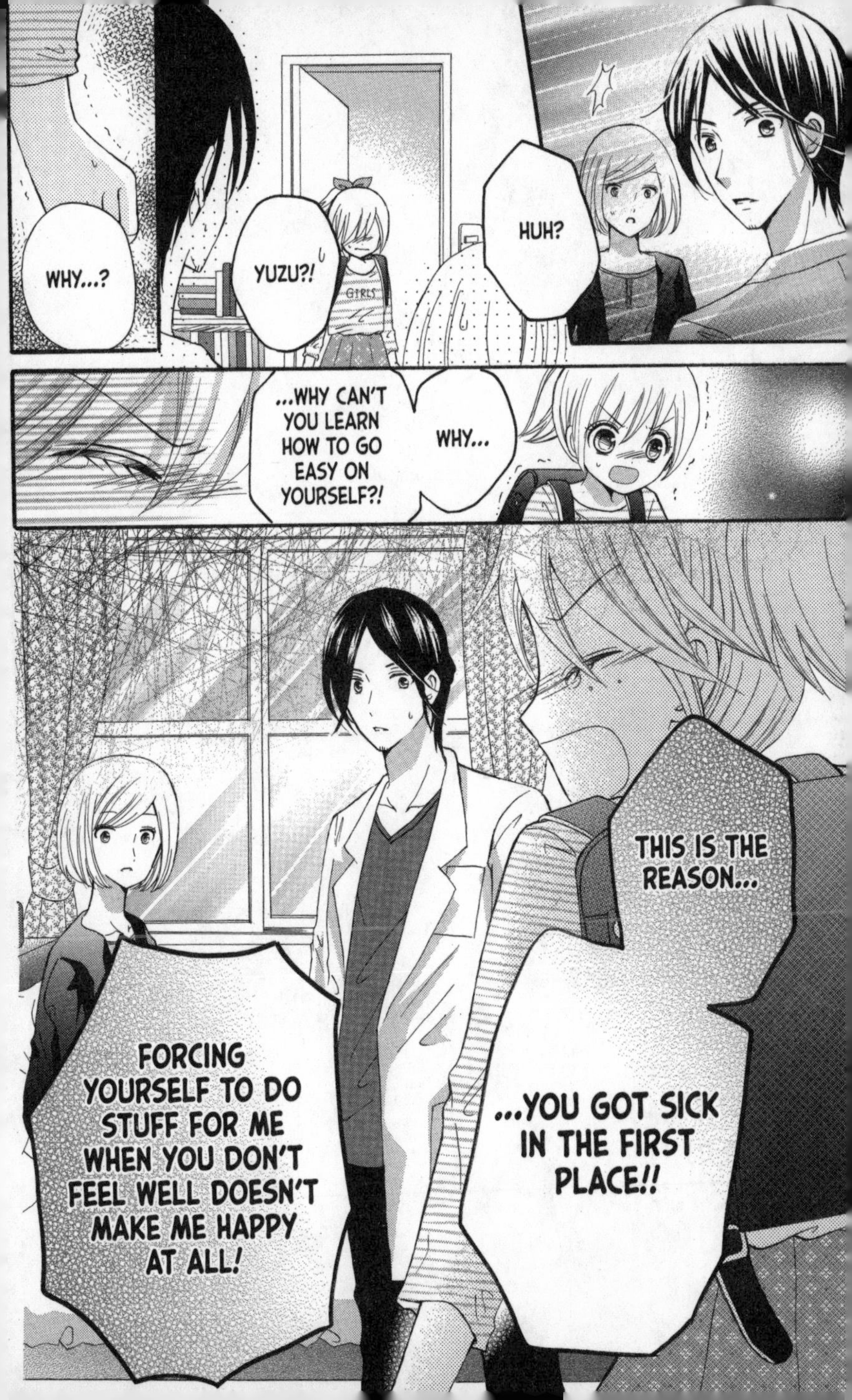
HUH?
YUZU?!
WHY...?
WHY...
...WHY CAN'T YOU LEARN HOW TO GO EASY ON YOURSELF?!
THIS IS THE REASON...
...YOU GOT SICK IN THE FIRST PLACE!!
FORCING YOURSELF TO DO STUFF FOR ME WHEN YOU DON'T FEEL WELL DOESN'T MAKE ME HAPPY AT ALL!

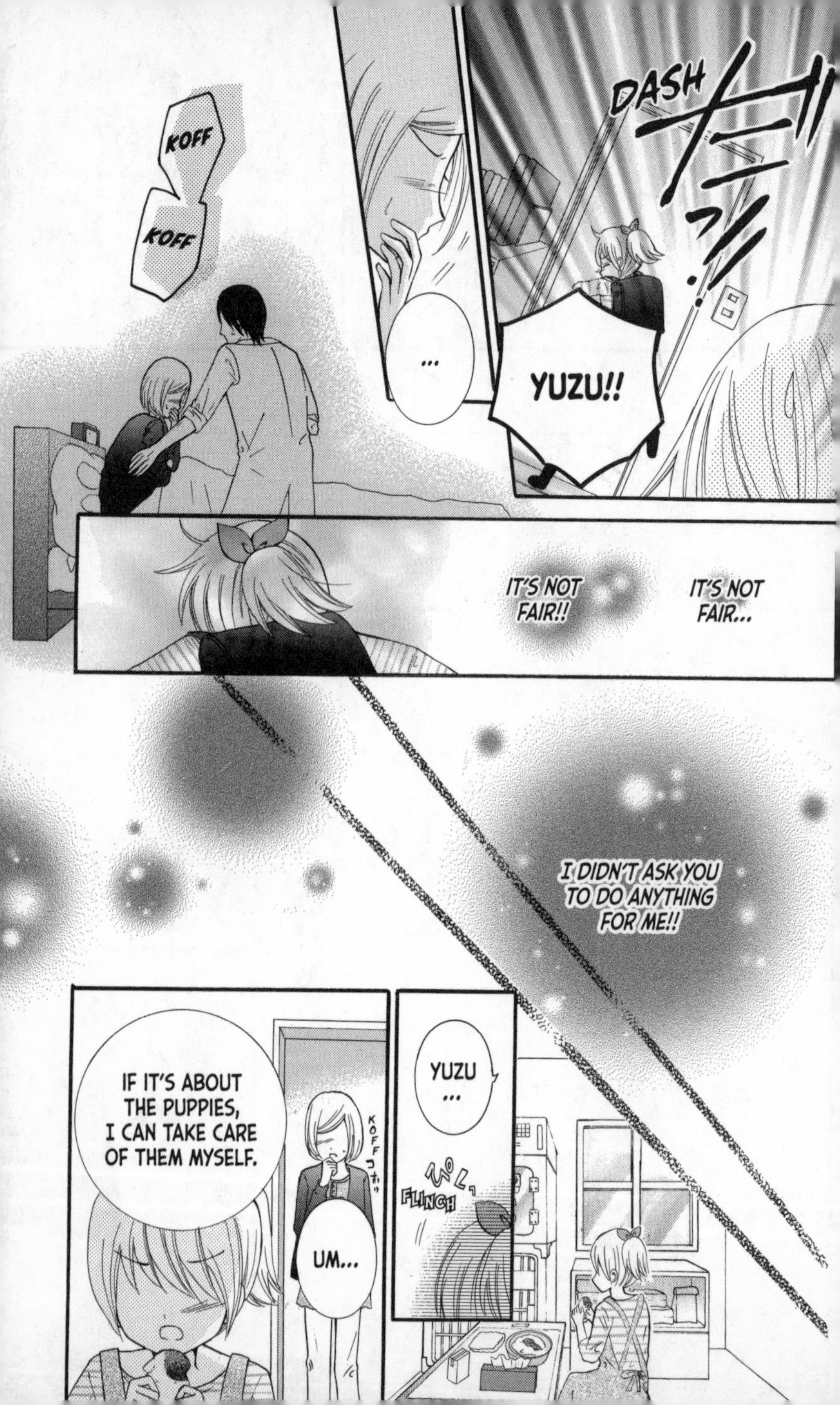
DASH
YUZU!!
...
KOFF
KOFF
IT'S NOT FAIR...
IT'S NOT FAIR!!
I DIDN'T ASK YOU TO DO ANYTHING FOR ME!!
YUZU...
FLINCH
KOFF
UM...
IF IT'S ABOUT THE PUPPIES, I CAN TAKE CARE OF THEM MYSELF.

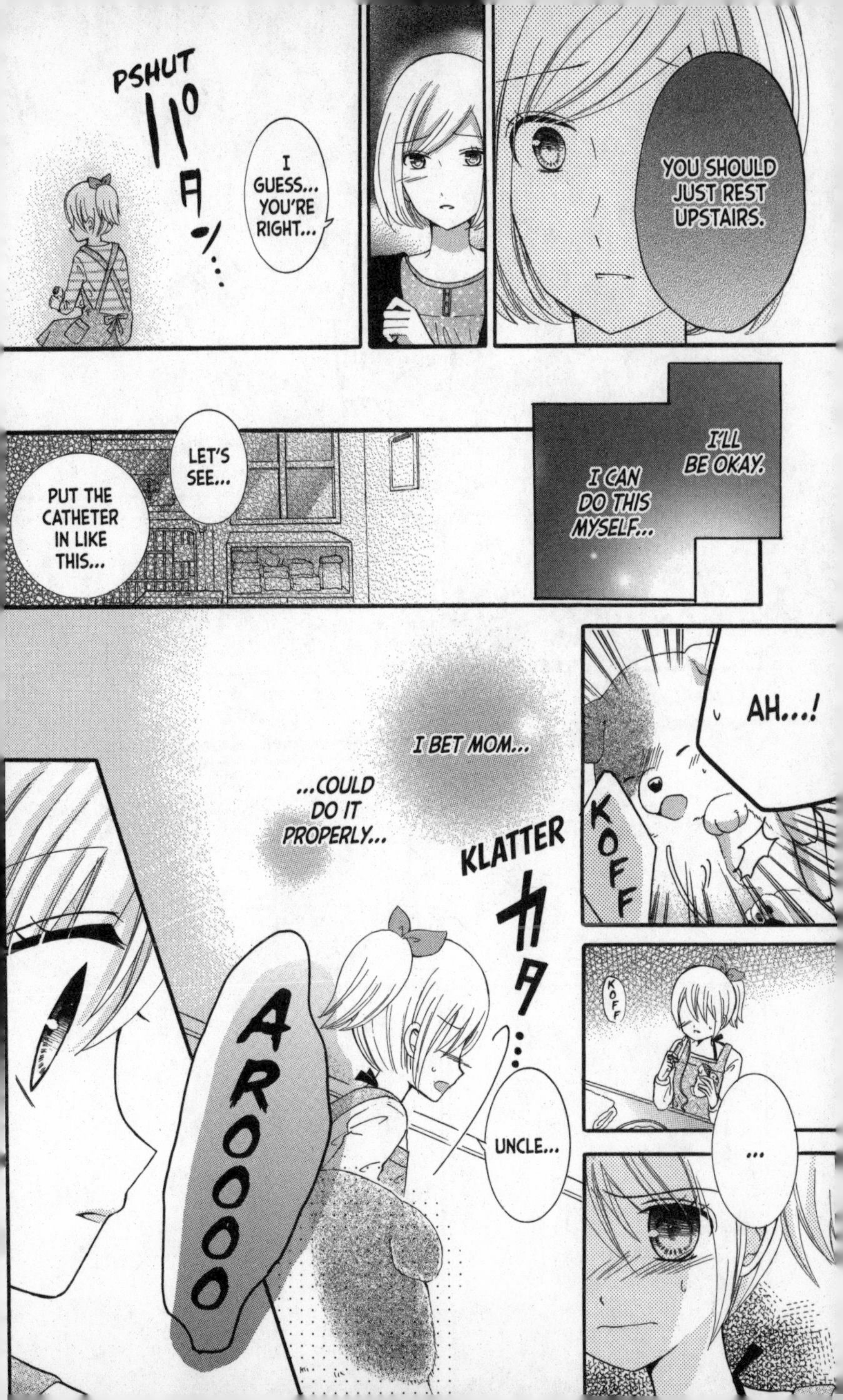
YOU SHOULD JUST REST UPSTAIRS.
I GUESS... YOU'RE RIGHT...
PSHUT
I'LL BE OKAY.
I CAN DO THIS MYSELF...
LET'S SEE...
PUT THE CATHETER IN LIKE THIS...
AH...!
KOFF
KOFF
...
I BET MOM...
...COULD DO IT PROPERLY...
KLATTER
カタ...
UNCLE...
AROOOOO

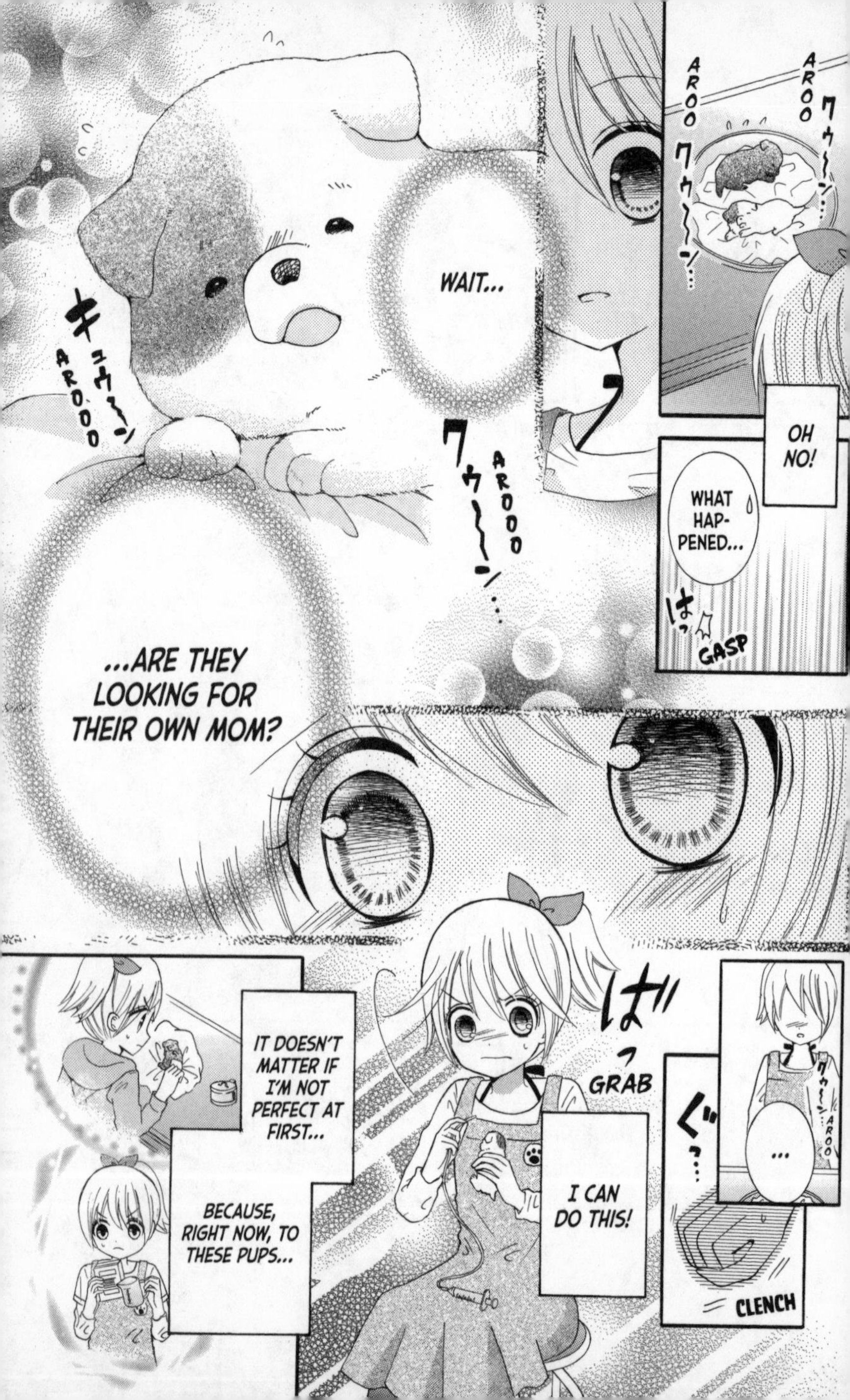
AROO
AROO
OH NO!
WHAT HAPPENED...
GASP
WAIT...
AROOO
AROOO
...ARE THEY LOOKING FOR THEIR OWN MOM?
AROO
...
CLENCH
GRAB
I CAN DO THIS!
IT DOESN'T MATTER IF I'M NOT PERFECT AT FIRST...
BECAUSE, RIGHT NOW, TO THESE PUPS...

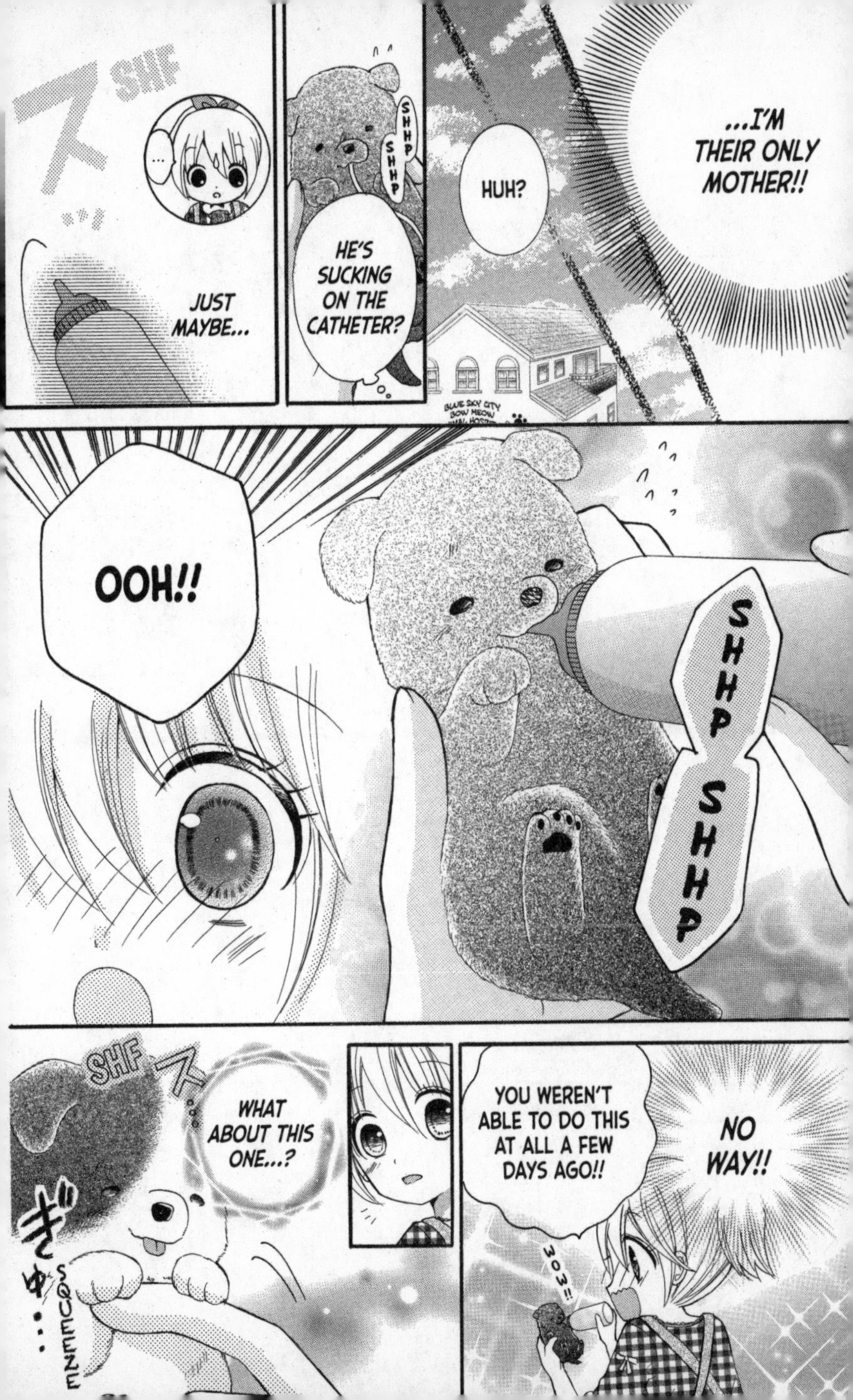
...I'M THEIR ONLY MOTHER!!
HUH?
BLUE SKY CITY
BOW MEOW
SHHP SHHP
HE'S SUCKING ON THE CATHETER?
SHF
...
JUST MAYBE...
SHHP SHHP SHHP
OOH!!
NO WAY!!
YOU WEREN'T ABLE TO DO THIS AT ALL A FEW DAYS AGO!!
WOW!!
WHAT ABOUT THIS ONE...?
SHF
SQUEEZE

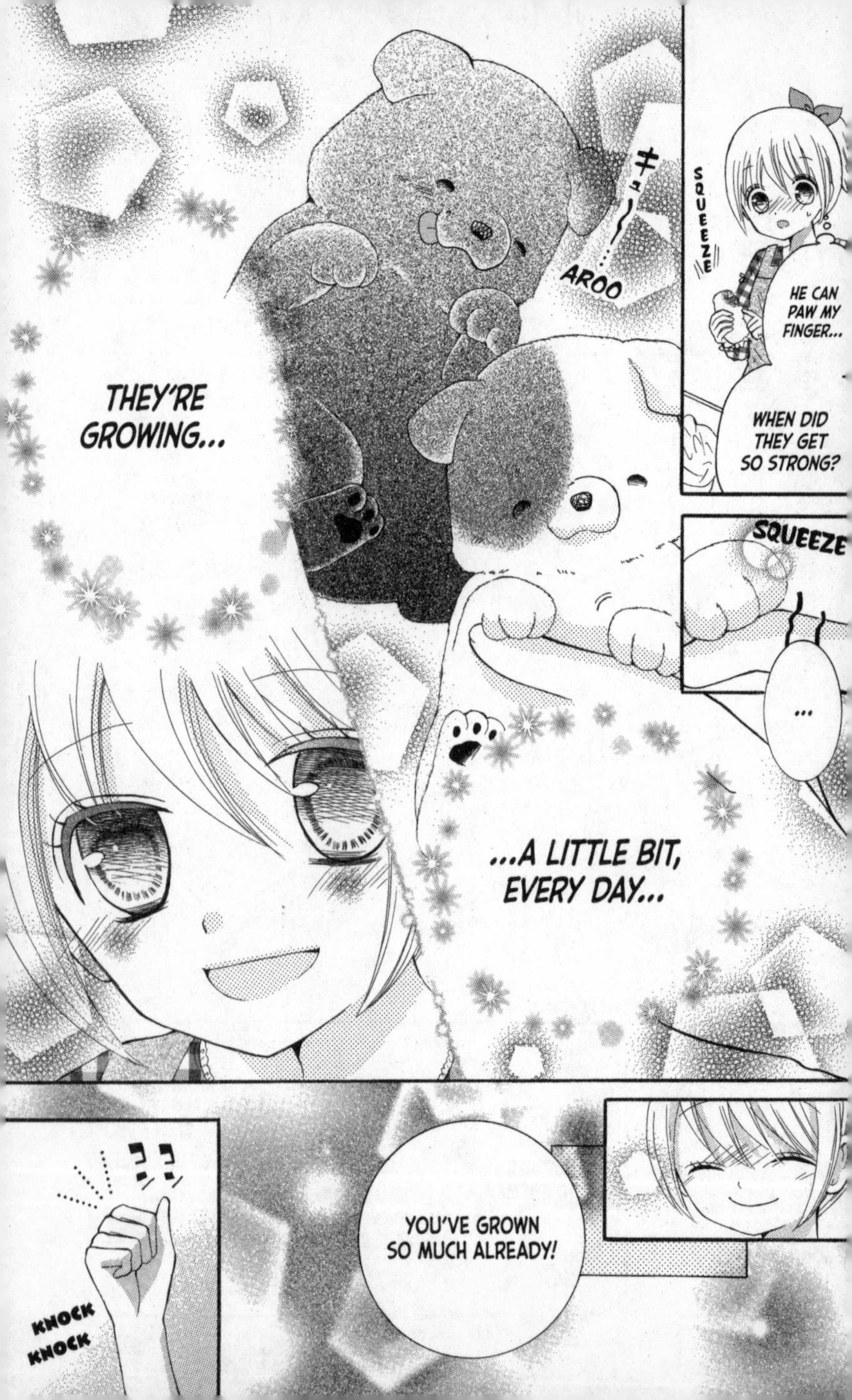
SQUEEZE
HE CAN PAW MY FINGER...
WHEN DID THEY GET SO STRONG?
SQUEEZE
...
キュ~...
AROO
THEY'RE GROWING...
...A LITTLE BIT, EVERY DAY...
YOU'VE GROWN SO MUCH ALREADY!
KNOCK KNOCK

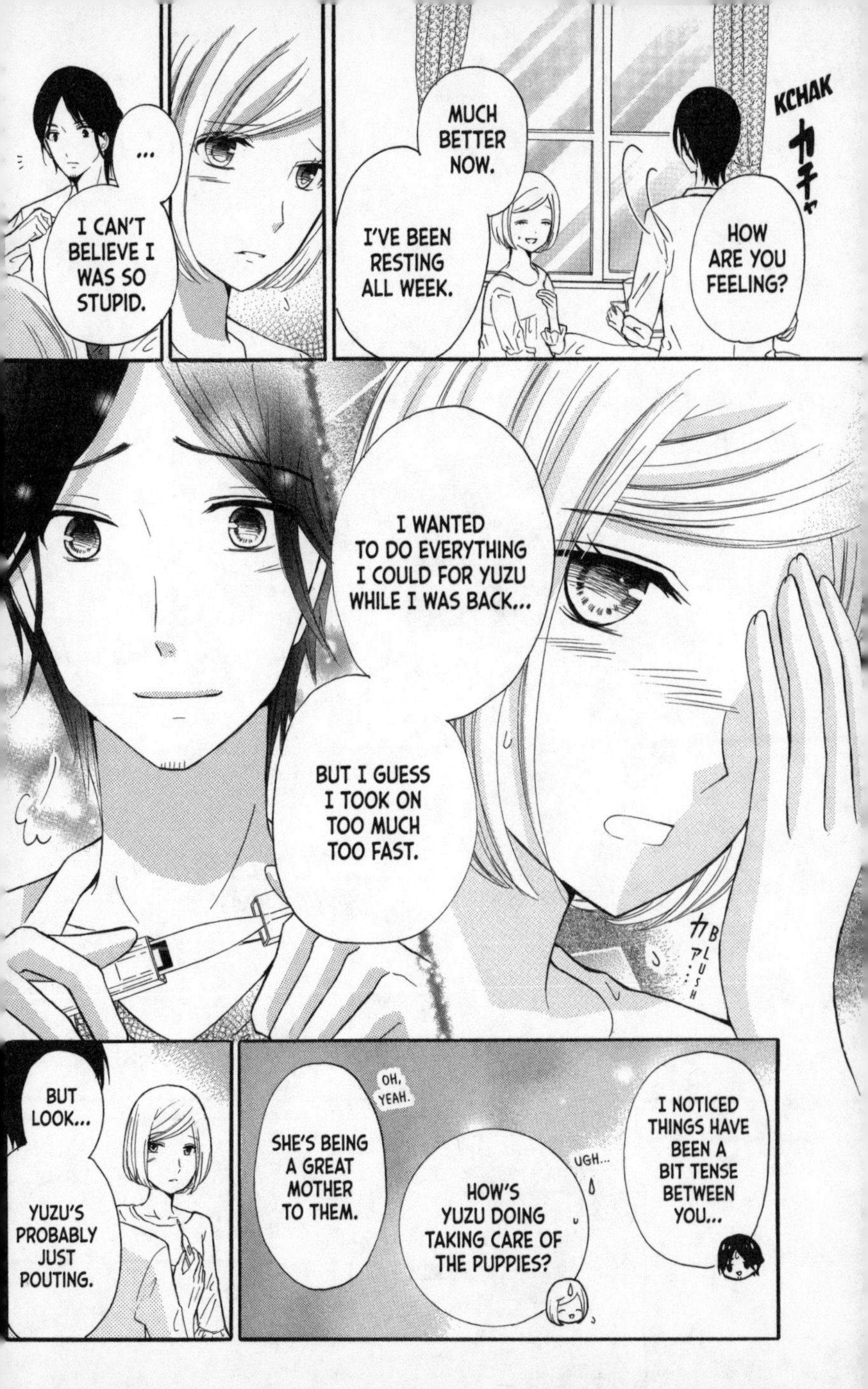
KCHAK
カチャ
HOW ARE YOU FEELING?
MUCH BETTER NOW.
I'VE BEEN RESTING ALL WEEK.
...
I CAN'T BELIEVE I WAS SO STUPID.
I WANTED TO DO EVERYTHING I COULD FOR YUZU WHILE I WAS BACK...
BUT I GUESS I TOOK ON TOO MUCH TOO FAST.
カァ...
BLUSH
I NOTICED THINGS HAVE BEEN A BIT TENSE BETWEEN YOU...
UGH...
HOW'S YUZU DOING TAKING CARE OF THE PUPPIES?
OH, YEAH.
SHE'S BEING A GREAT MOTHER TO THEM.
BUT LOOK...
YUZU'S PROBABLY JUST POUTING.

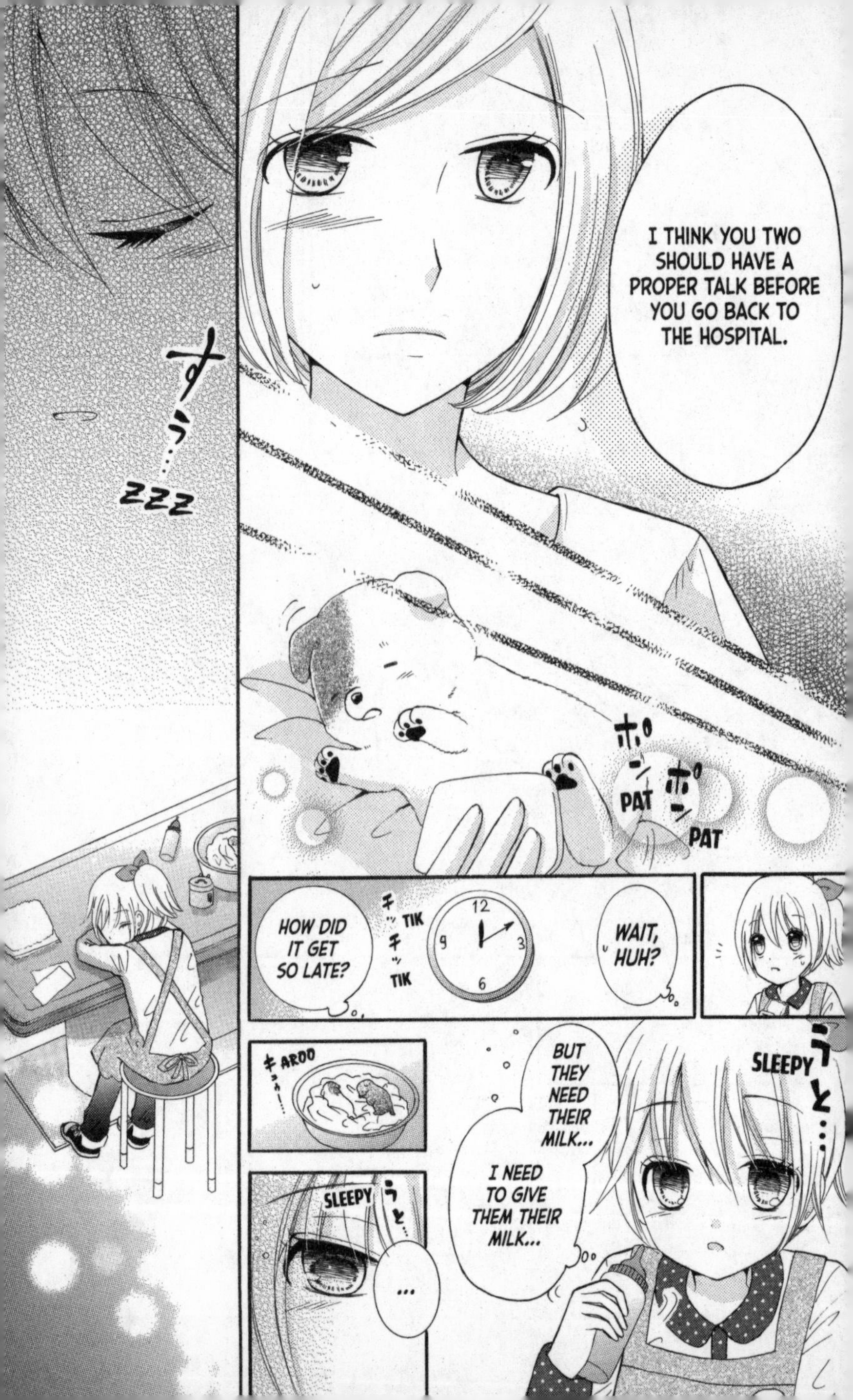

I THINK YOU TWO SHOULD HAVE A PROPER TALK BEFORE YOU GO BACK TO THE HOSPITAL.
PAT
PAT
WAIT, HUH?
TIK
TIK
HOW DID IT GET SO LATE?
SLEEPY
BUT THEY NEED THEIR MILK...
I NEED TO GIVE THEM THEIR MILK...
AROO
SLEEPY
...
ZZZ

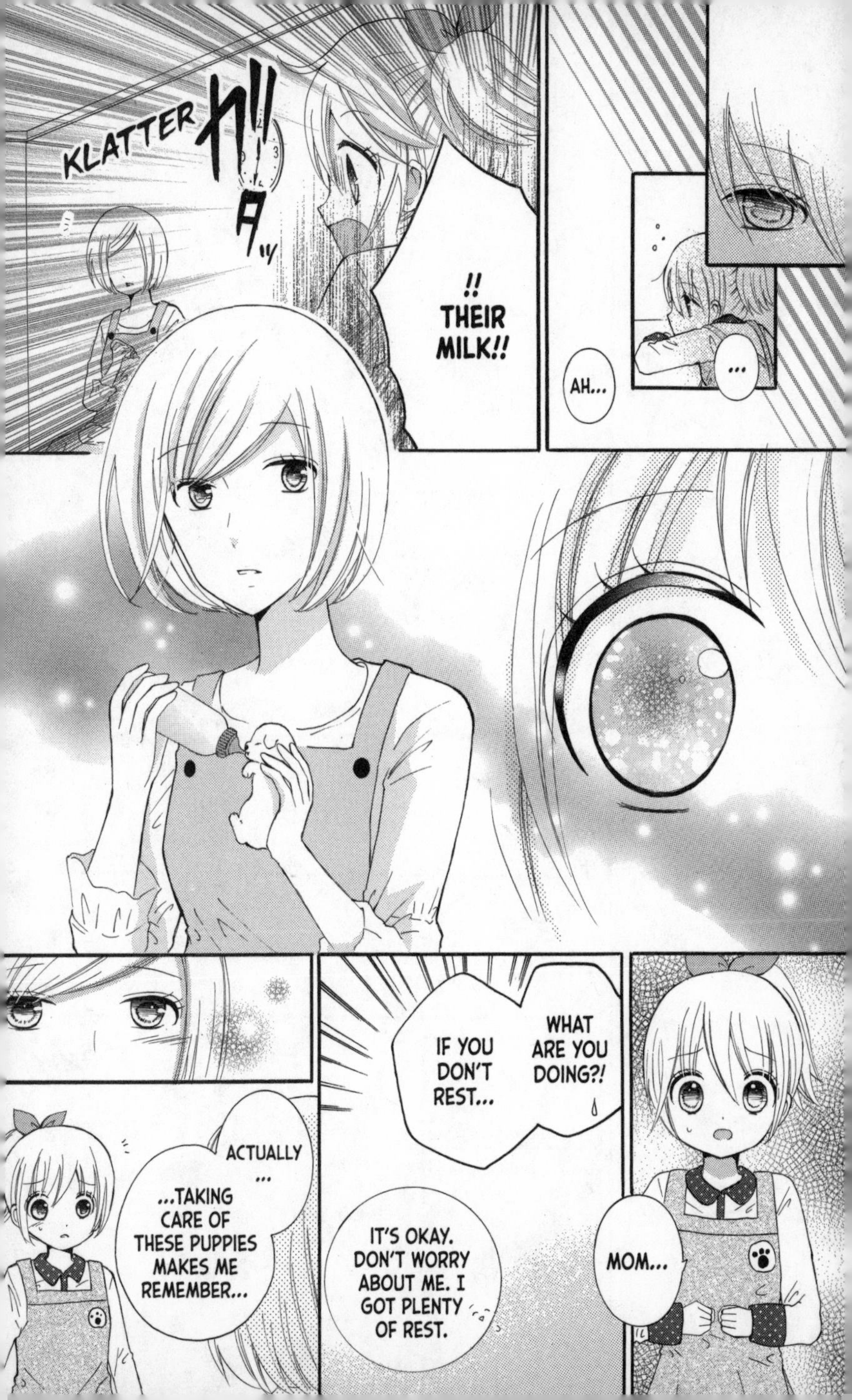
...
AH...
KLATTER
!! THEIR MILK!!
MOM...
WHAT ARE YOU DOING?!
IF YOU DON'T REST...
IT'S OKAY. DON'T WORRY ABOUT ME. I GOT PLENTY OF REST.
ACTUALLY ...
...TAKING CARE OF THESE PUPPIES MAKES ME REMEMBER...

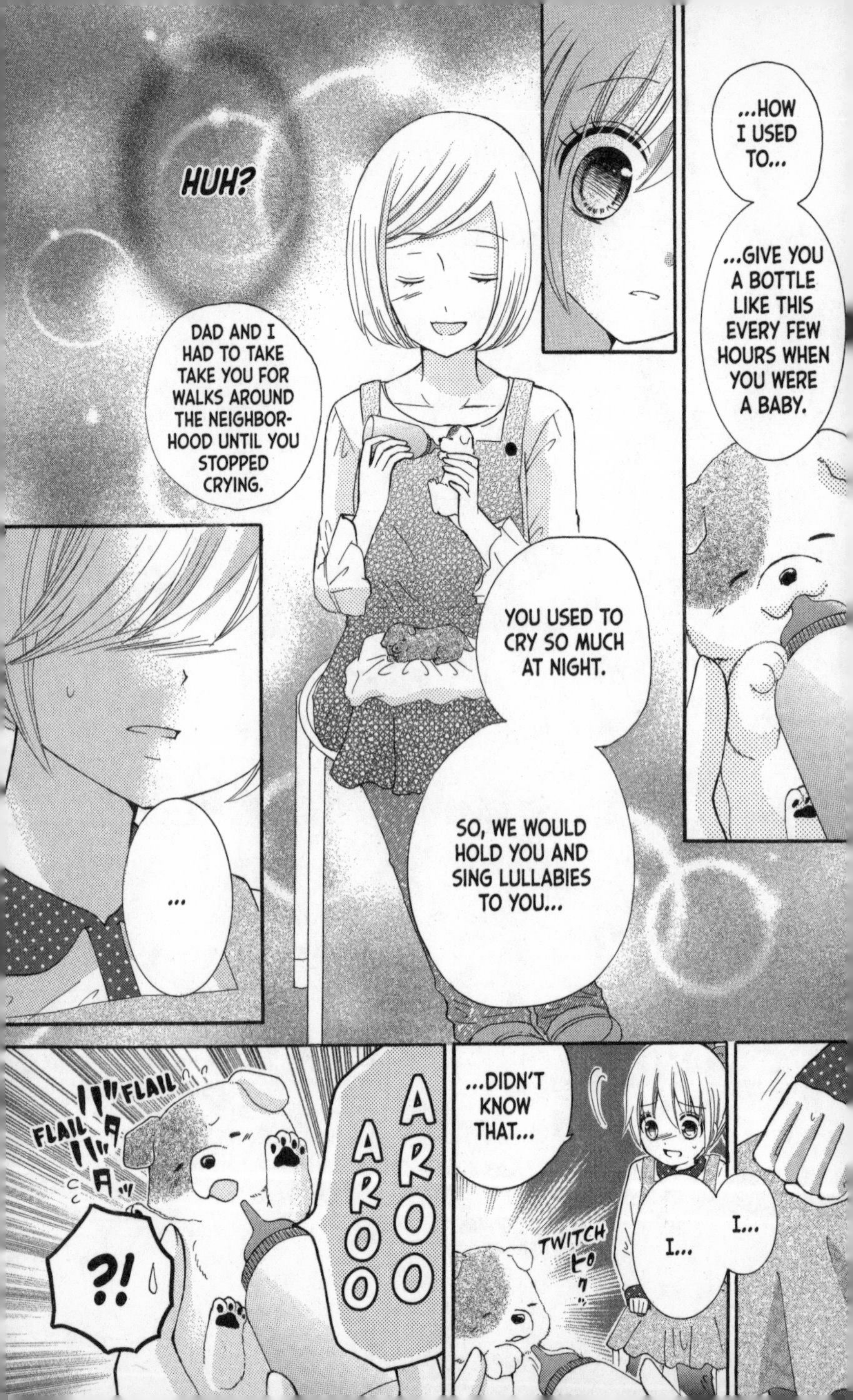
...HOW I USED TO...
...GIVE YOU A BOTTLE LIKE THIS EVERY FEW HOURS WHEN YOU WERE A BABY.
YOU USED TO CRY SO MUCH AT NIGHT.
SO, WE WOULD HOLD YOU AND SING LULLABIES TO YOU...
DAD AND I HAD TO TAKE TAKE YOU FOR WALKS AROUND THE NEIGHBOR-HOOD UNTIL YOU STOPPED CRYING.
HUH?
...
I...
I...
TWITCH
...DIDN'T KNOW THAT...
AROO
AROO
FLAIL
FLAIL
?!

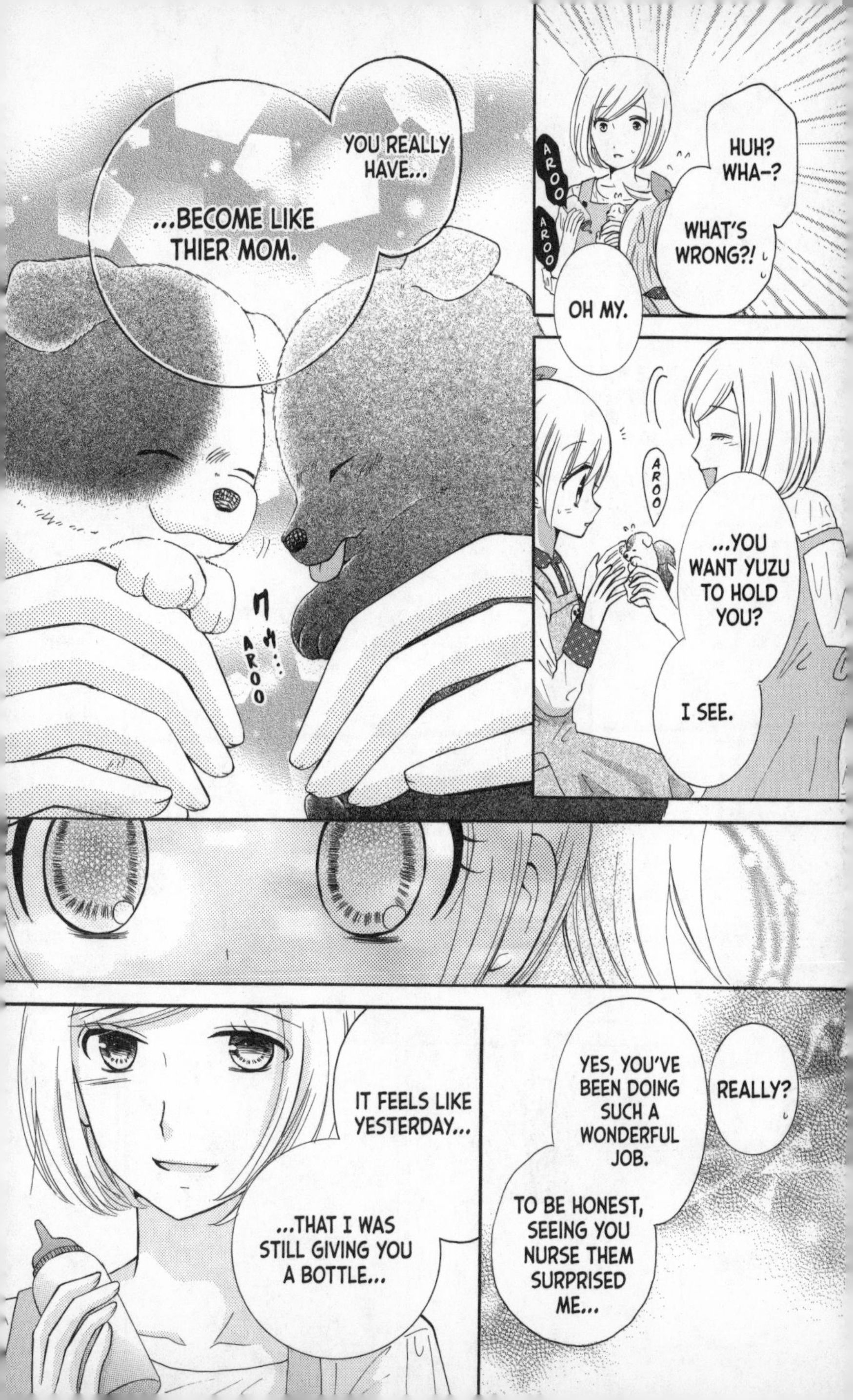

HUH? WHA-?
WHAT'S WRONG?!
AROO
AROO
OH MY.
AROO
...YOU WANT YUZU TO HOLD YOU?
I SEE.
YOU REALLY HAVE...
...BECOME LIKE THIER MOM.
AROO
REALLY?
YES, YOU'VE BEEN DOING SUCH A WONDERFUL JOB.
TO BE HONEST, SEEING YOU NURSE THEM SURPRISED ME...
IT FEELS LIKE YESTERDAY...
...THAT I WAS STILL GIVING YOU A BOTTLE...

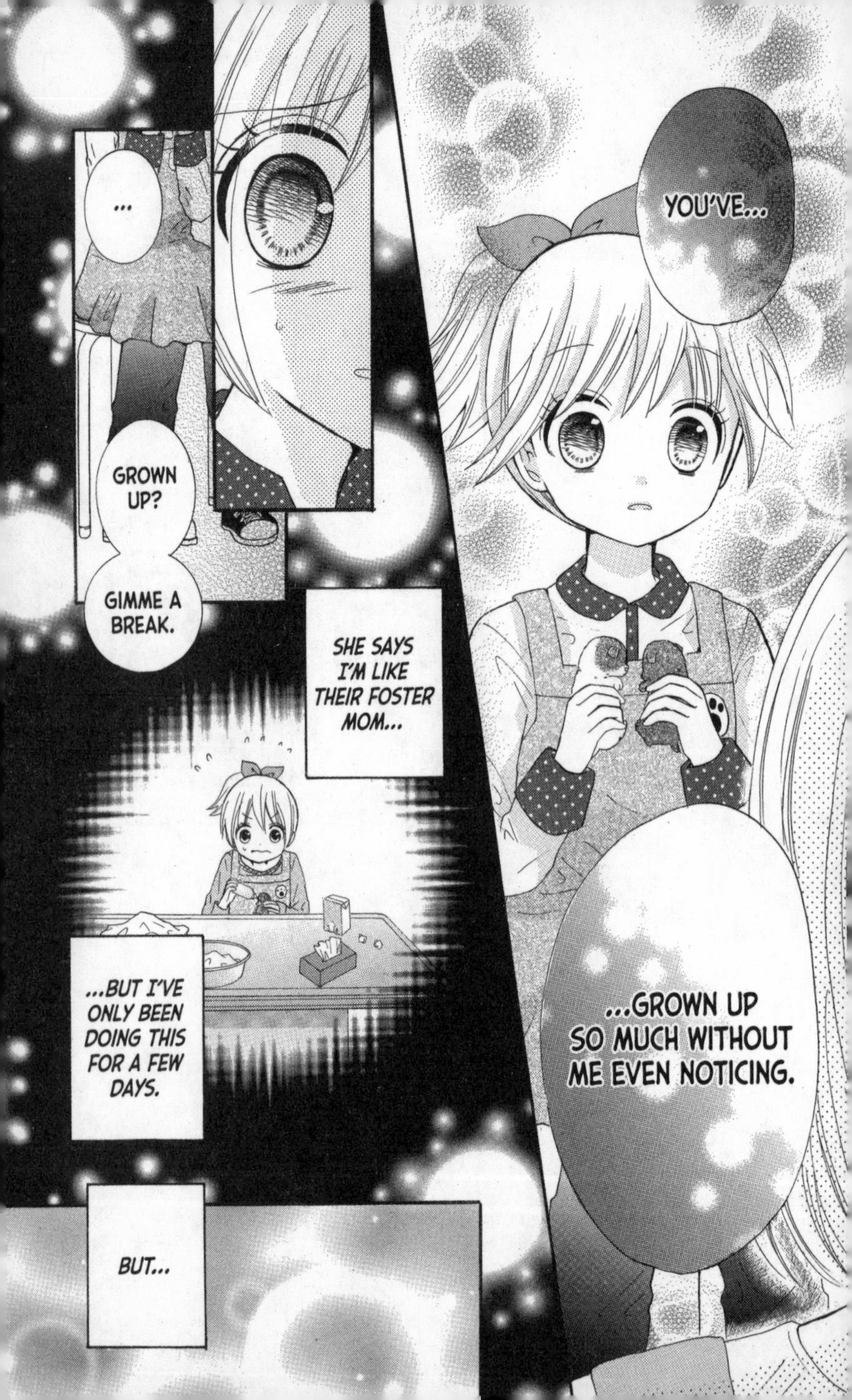
YOU'VE...
...GROWN UP SO MUCH WITHOUT ME EVEN NOTICING.
...
GROWN UP?
GIMME A BREAK.
SHE SAYS I'M LIKE THEIR FOSTER MOM...
...BUT I'VE ONLY BEEN DOING THIS FOR A FEW DAYS.
BUT...

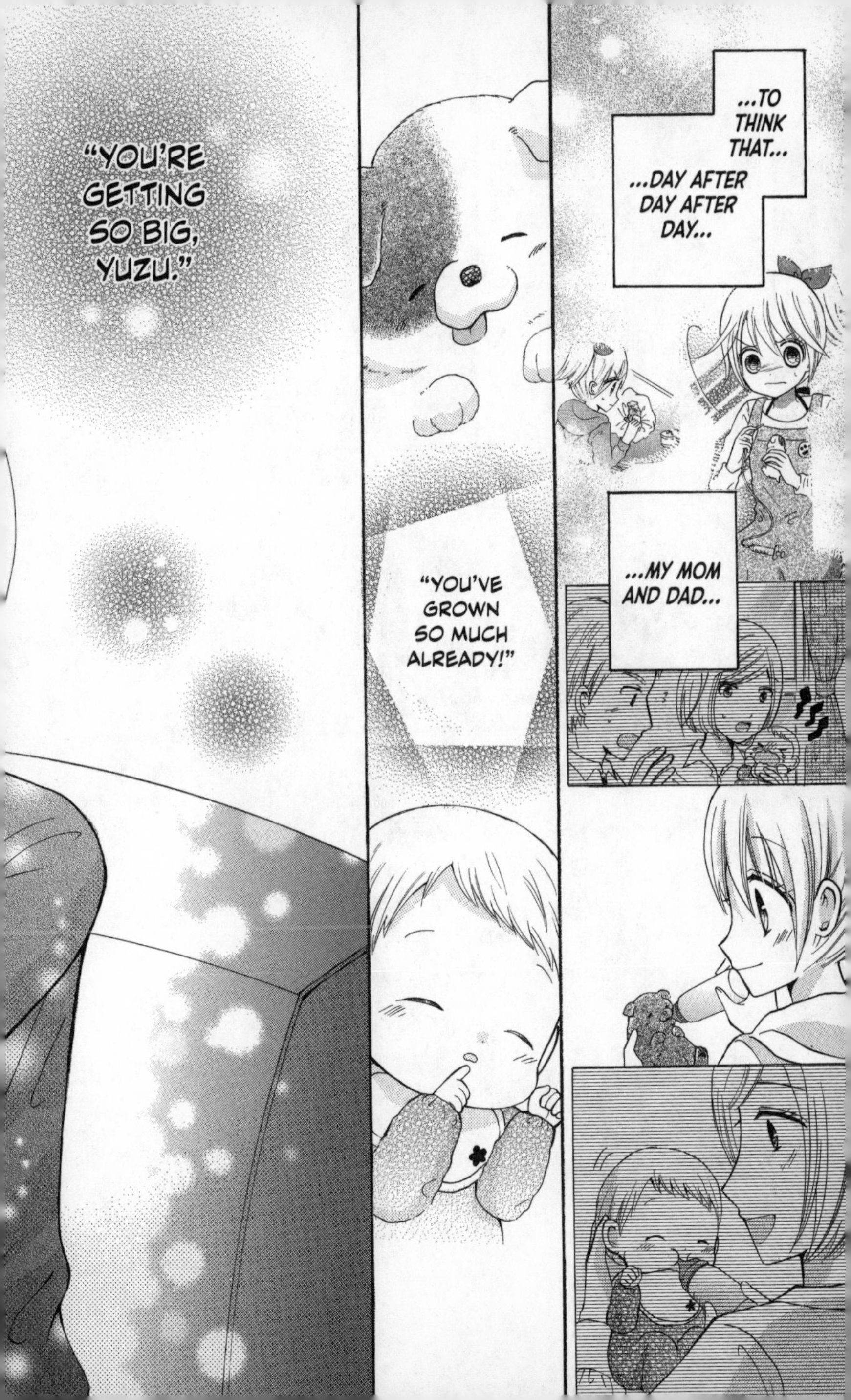
...TO THINK THAT...
...DAY AFTER DAY AFTER DAY...
...MY MOM AND DAD...
"YOU'VE GROWN SO MUCH ALREADY!"
"YOU'RE GETTING SO BIG, YUZU."

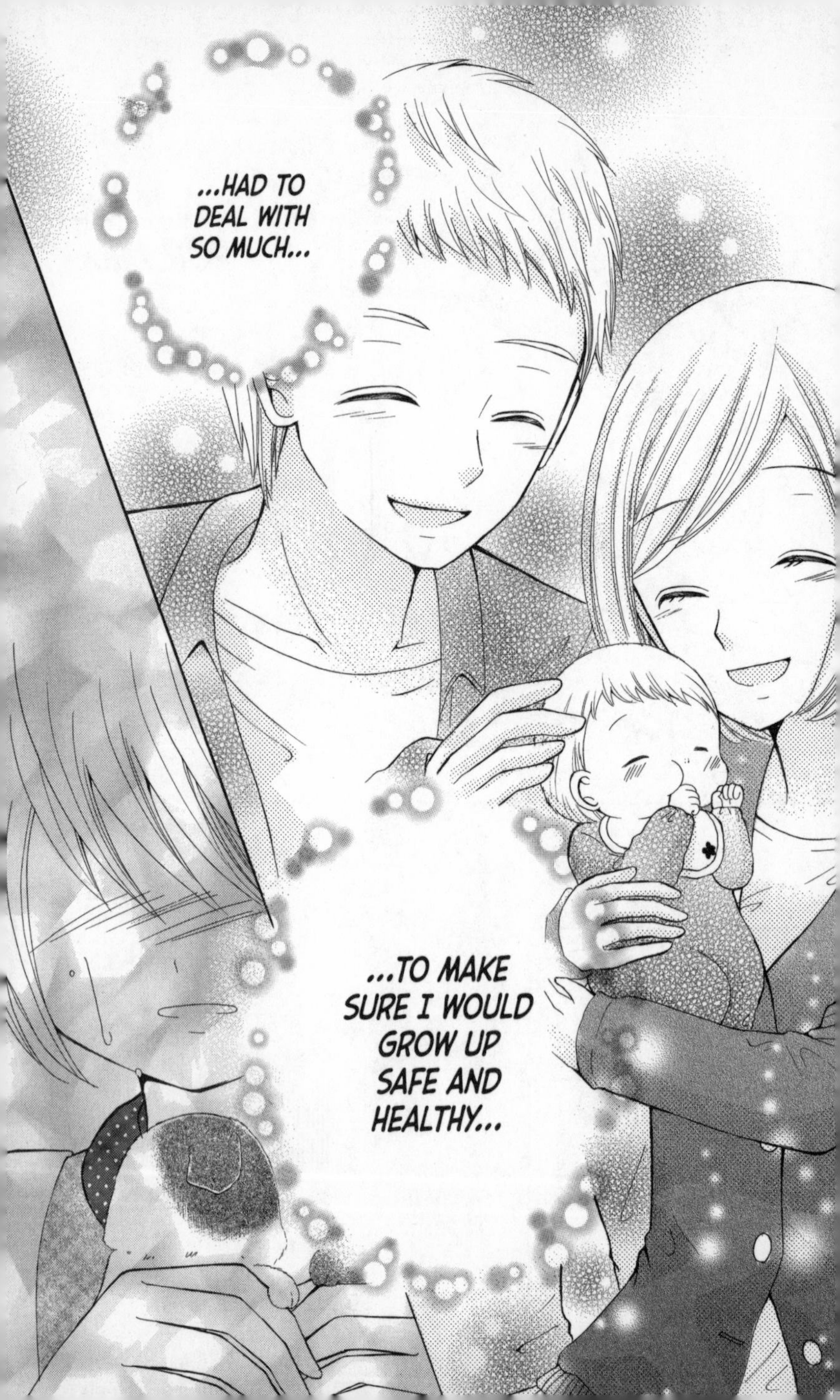
...HAD TO DEAL WITH SO MUCH...
...TO MAKE SURE I WOULD GROW UP SAFE AND HEALTHY...

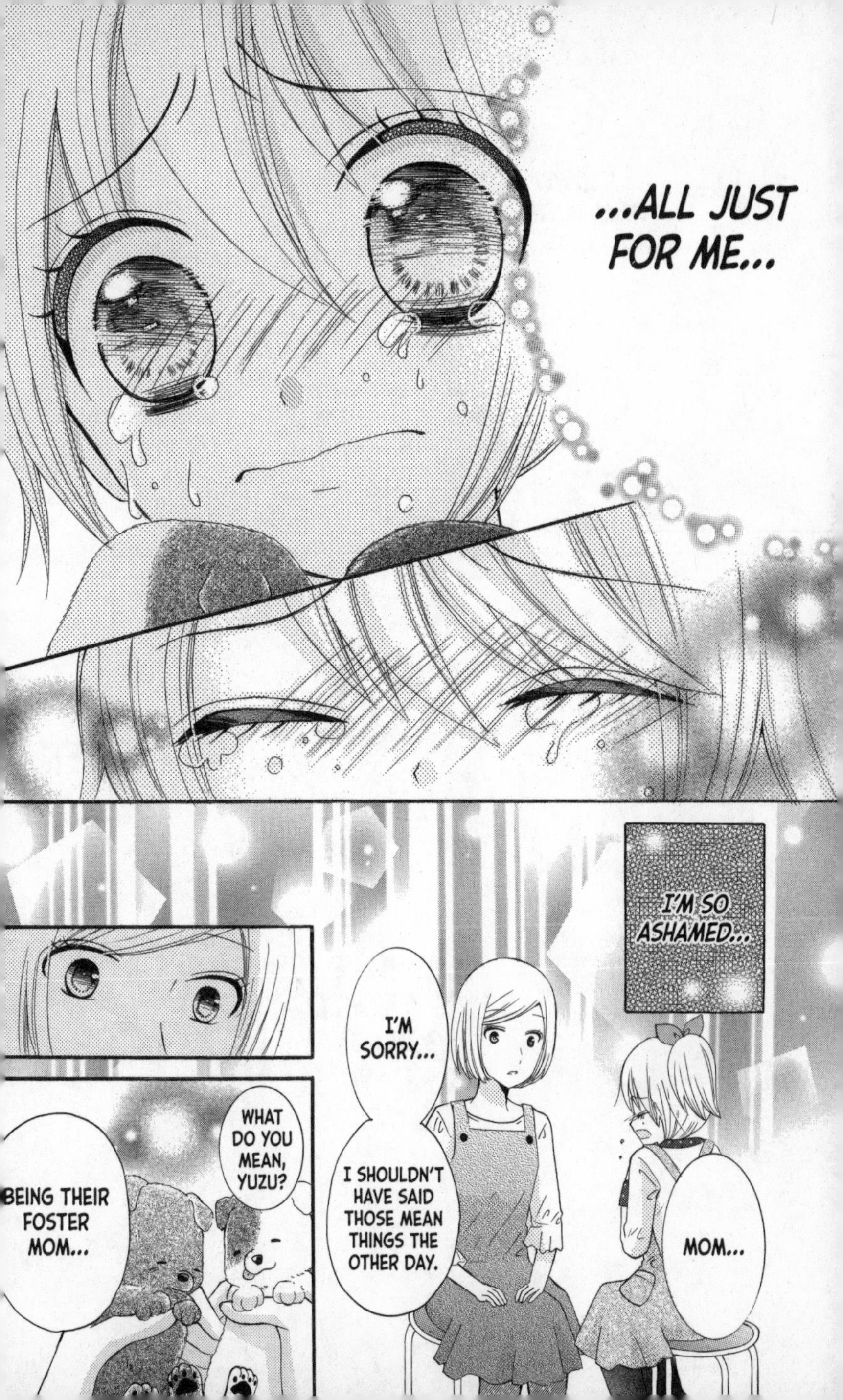
...ALL JUST FOR ME...
I'M SO ASHAMED...
MOM...
I'M SORRY...
I SHOULDN'T HAVE SAID THOSE MEAN THINGS THE OTHER DAY.
WHAT DO YOU MEAN, YUZU?
BEING THEIR FOSTER MOM...

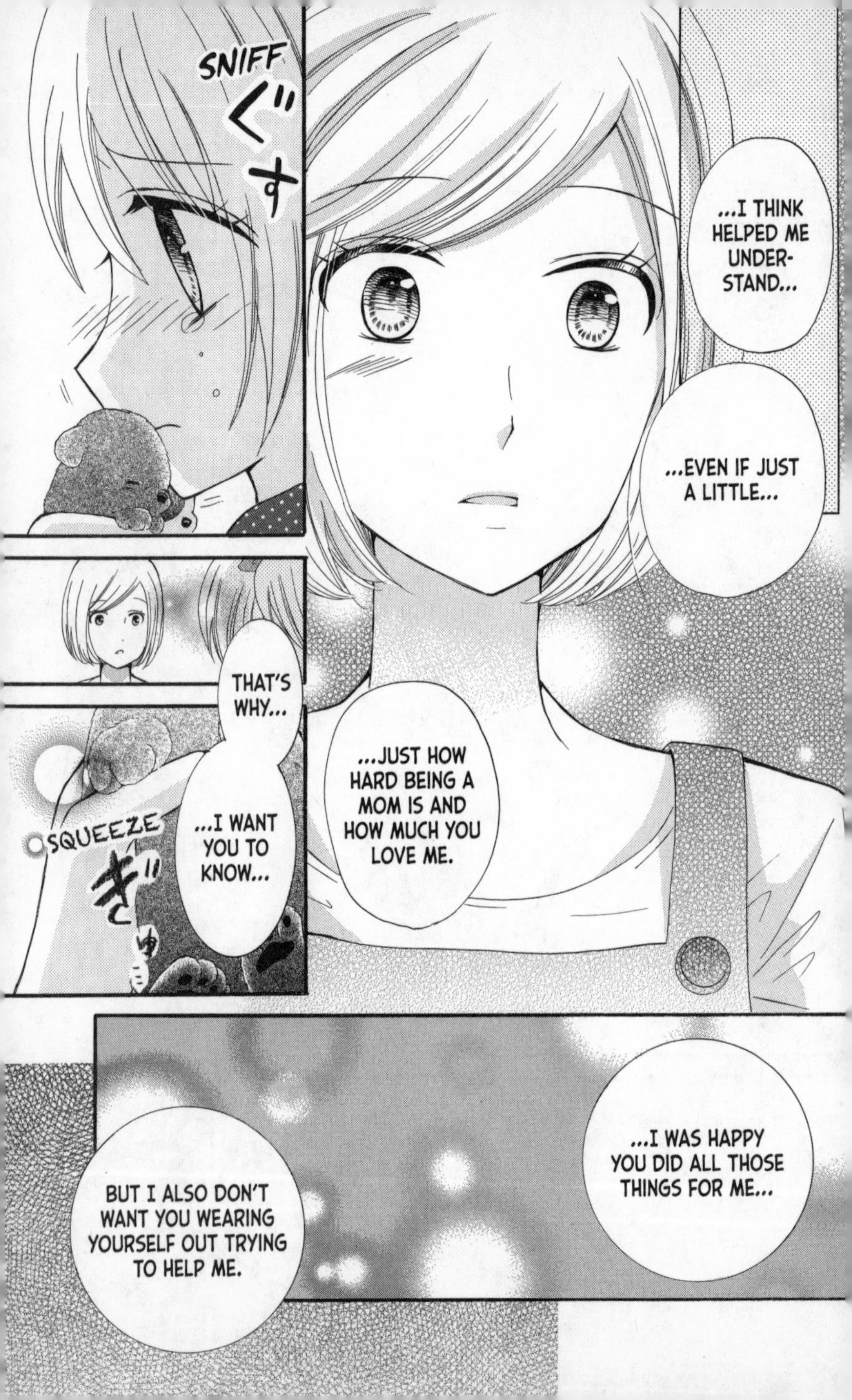
...I THINK HELPED ME UNDERSTAND...
...EVEN IF JUST A LITTLE...
...JUST HOW HARD BEING A MOM IS AND HOW MUCH YOU LOVE ME.
SNIFF
ぐす
THAT'S WHY...
...I WANT YOU TO KNOW...
SQUEEZE
ぎゅ
...I WAS HAPPY YOU DID ALL THOSE THINGS FOR ME...
BUT I ALSO DON'T WANT YOU WEARING YOURSELF OUT TRYING TO HELP ME.

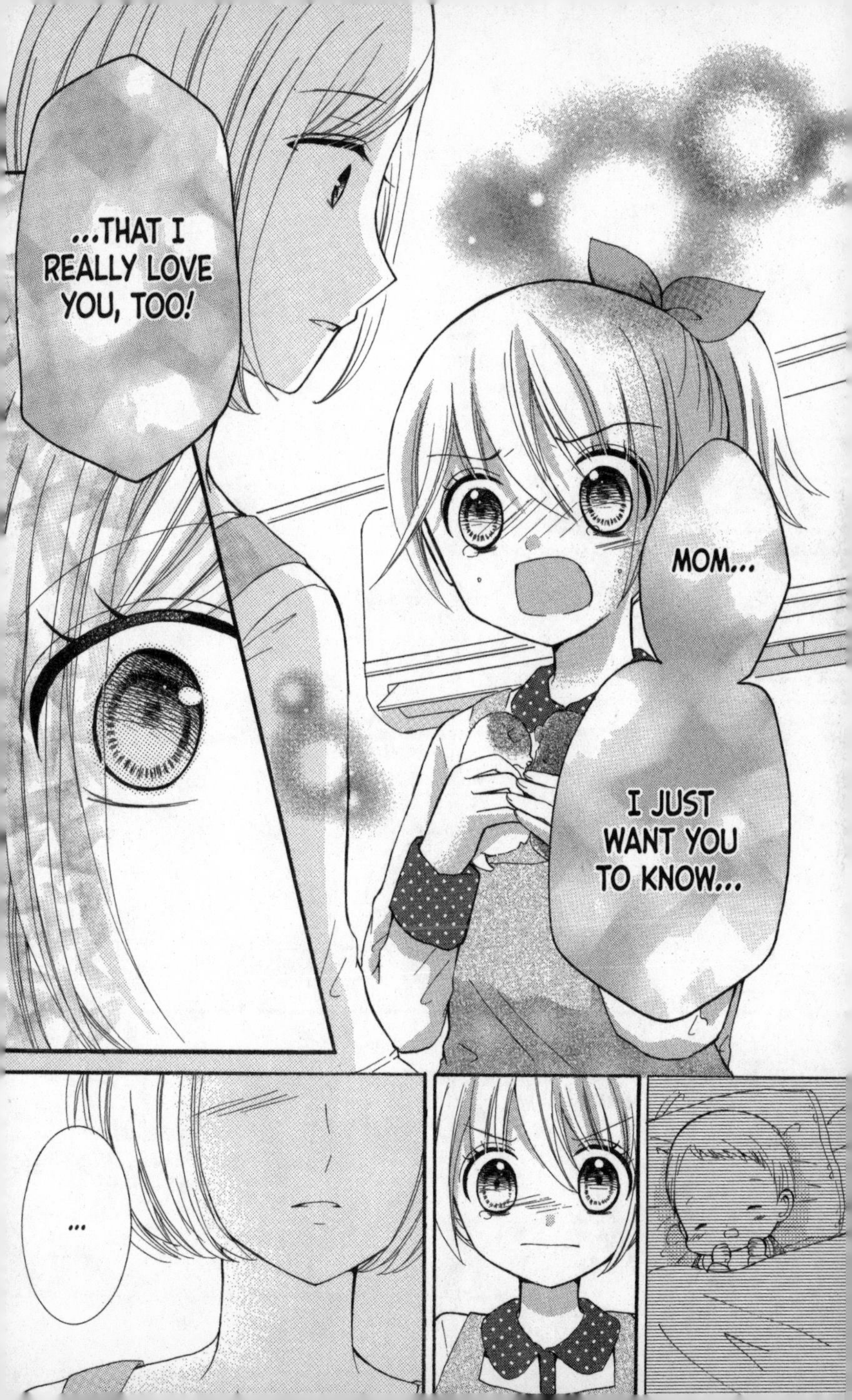
MOM...
I JUST WANT YOU TO KNOW...
...THAT I REALLY LOVE YOU, TOO!
...

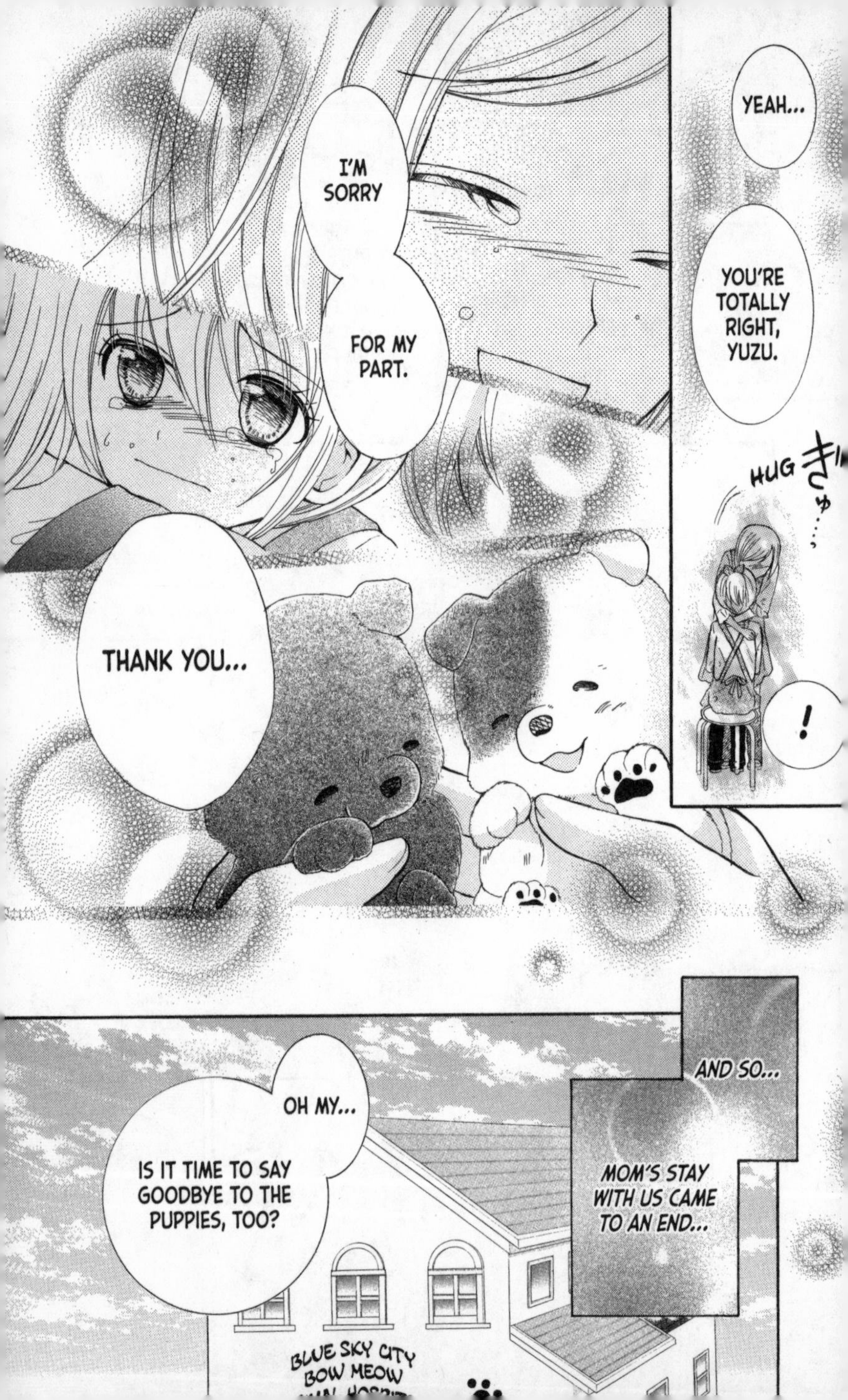
YEAH...
YOU'RE TOTALLY RIGHT, YUZU.
HUG ぎゅ…
!
I'M SORRY
FOR MY PART.
THANK YOU...
AND SO...
MOM'S STAY WITH US CAME TO AN END...
OH MY...
IS IT TIME TO SAY GOODBYE TO THE PUPPIES, TOO?
BLUE SKY CITY BOW MEOW

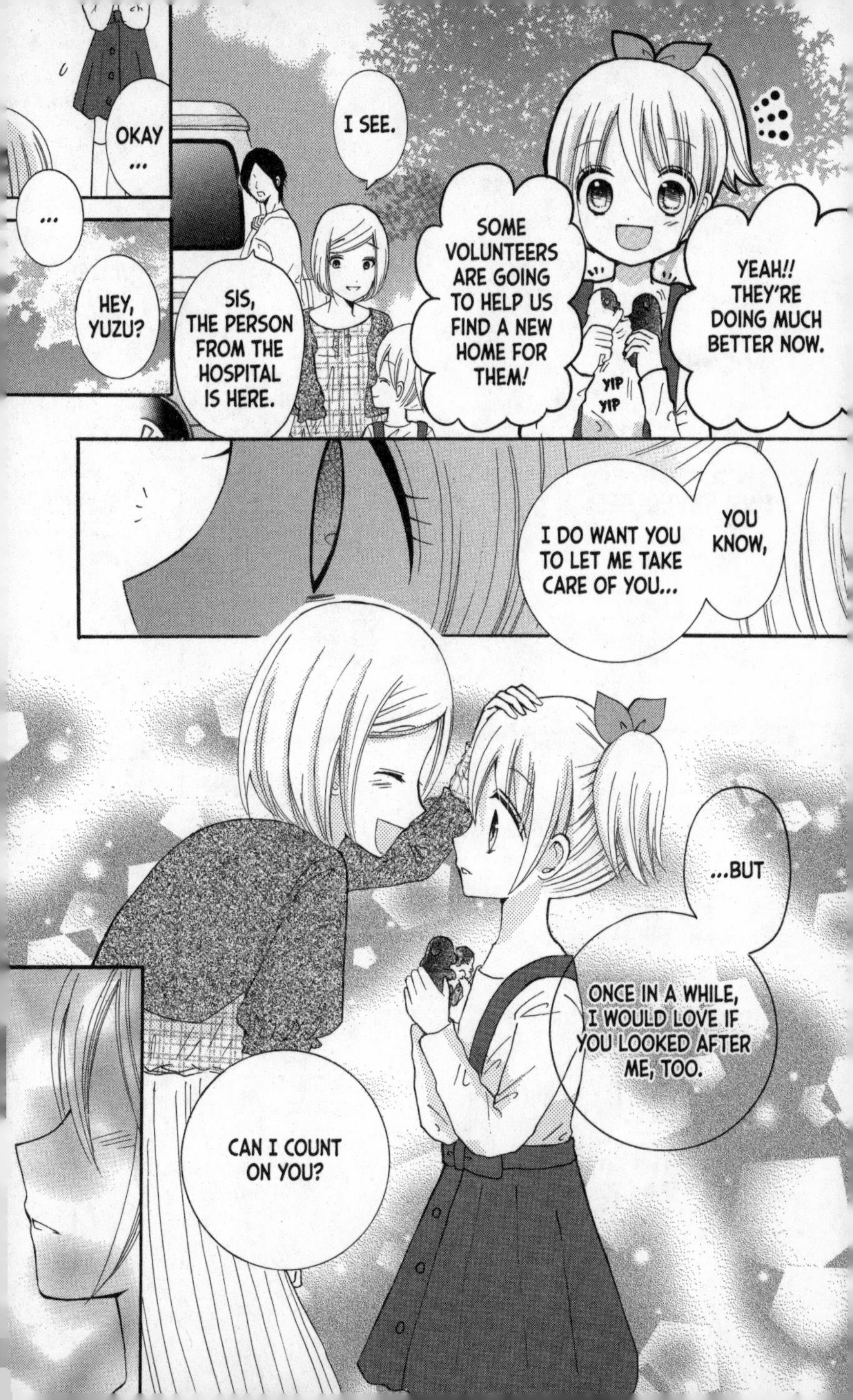
YEAH!! THEY'RE DOING MUCH BETTER NOW.
YIP YIP
SOME VOLUNTEERS ARE GOING TO HELP US FIND A NEW HOME FOR THEM!
I SEE.
SIS, THE PERSON FROM THE HOSPITAL IS HERE.
OKAY ...
...
HEY, YUZU?
YOU KNOW,
I DO WANT YOU TO LET ME TAKE CARE OF YOU...
...BUT
ONCE IN A WHILE, I WOULD LOVE IF YOU LOOKED AFTER ME, TOO.
CAN I COUNT ON YOU?

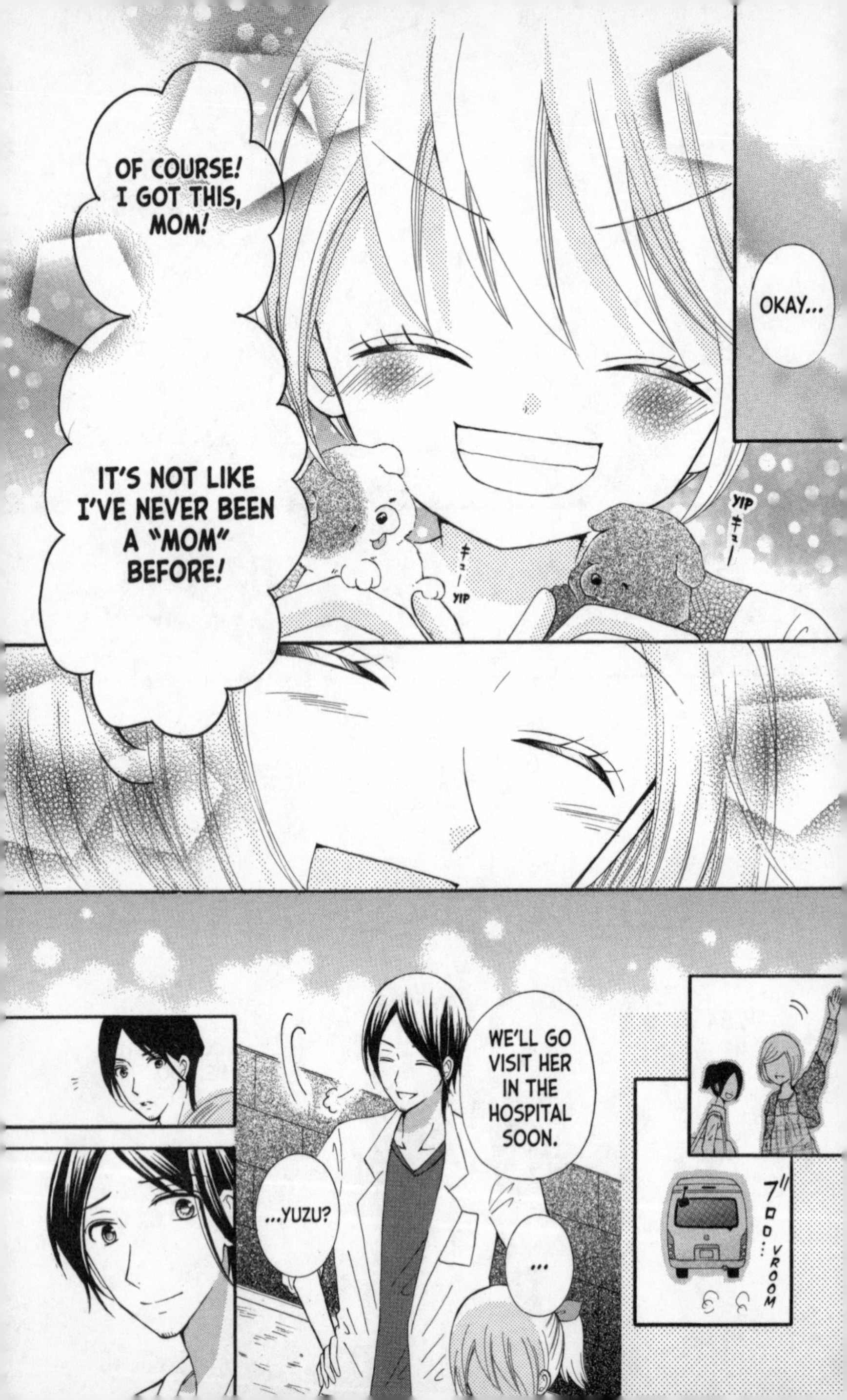
OKAY...
OF COURSE! I GOT THIS, MOM!
IT'S NOT LIKE I'VE NEVER BEEN A "MOM" BEFORE!
YIP
YIP
VROOM
WE'LL GO VISIT HER IN THE HOSPITAL SOON.
...
...YUZU?

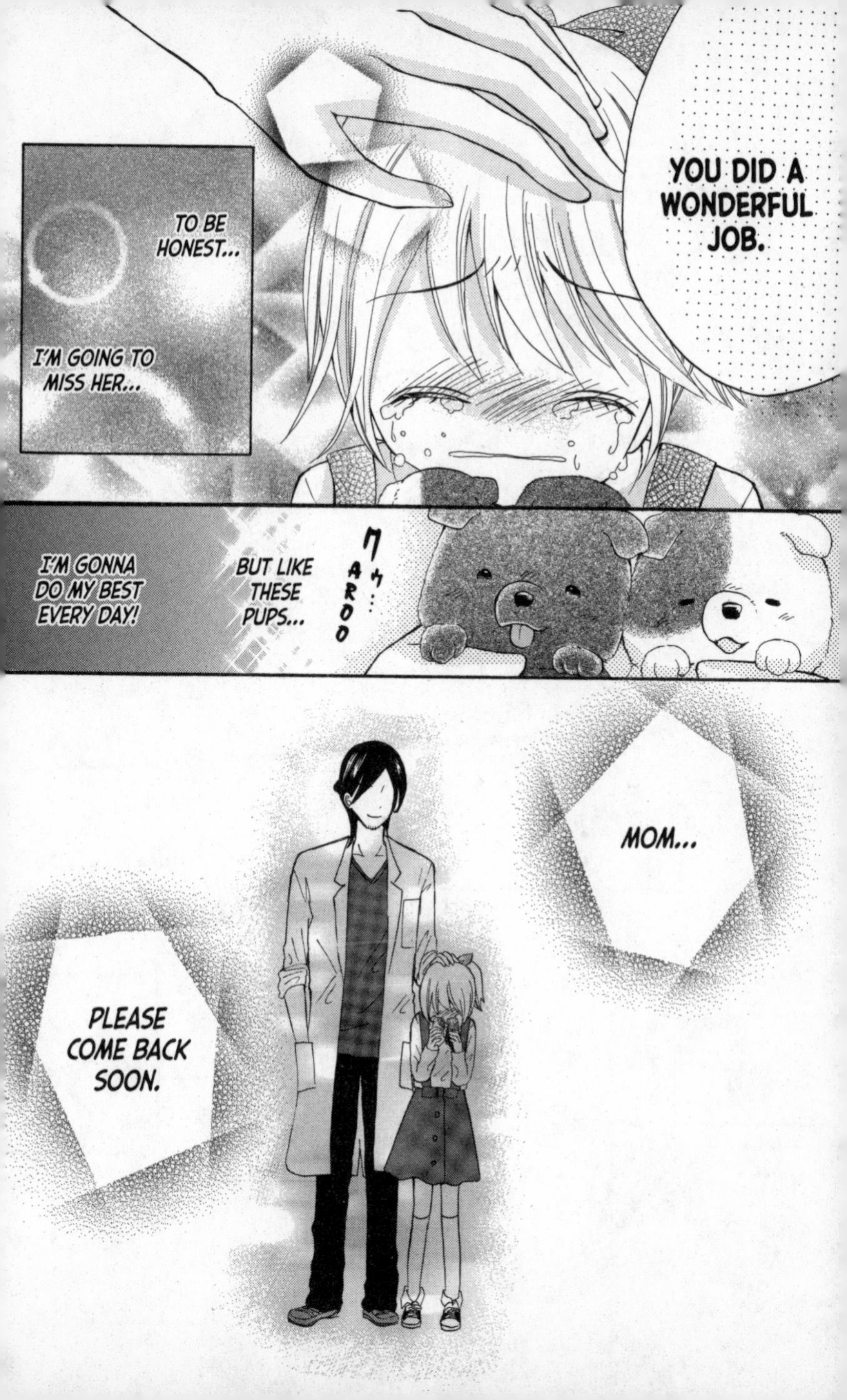
YOU DID A WONDERFUL JOB.
TO BE HONEST...
I'M GOING TO MISS HER...
AROO
BUT LIKE THESE PUPS...
I'M GONNA DO MY BEST EVERY DAY!
MOM...
PLEASE COME BACK SOON.

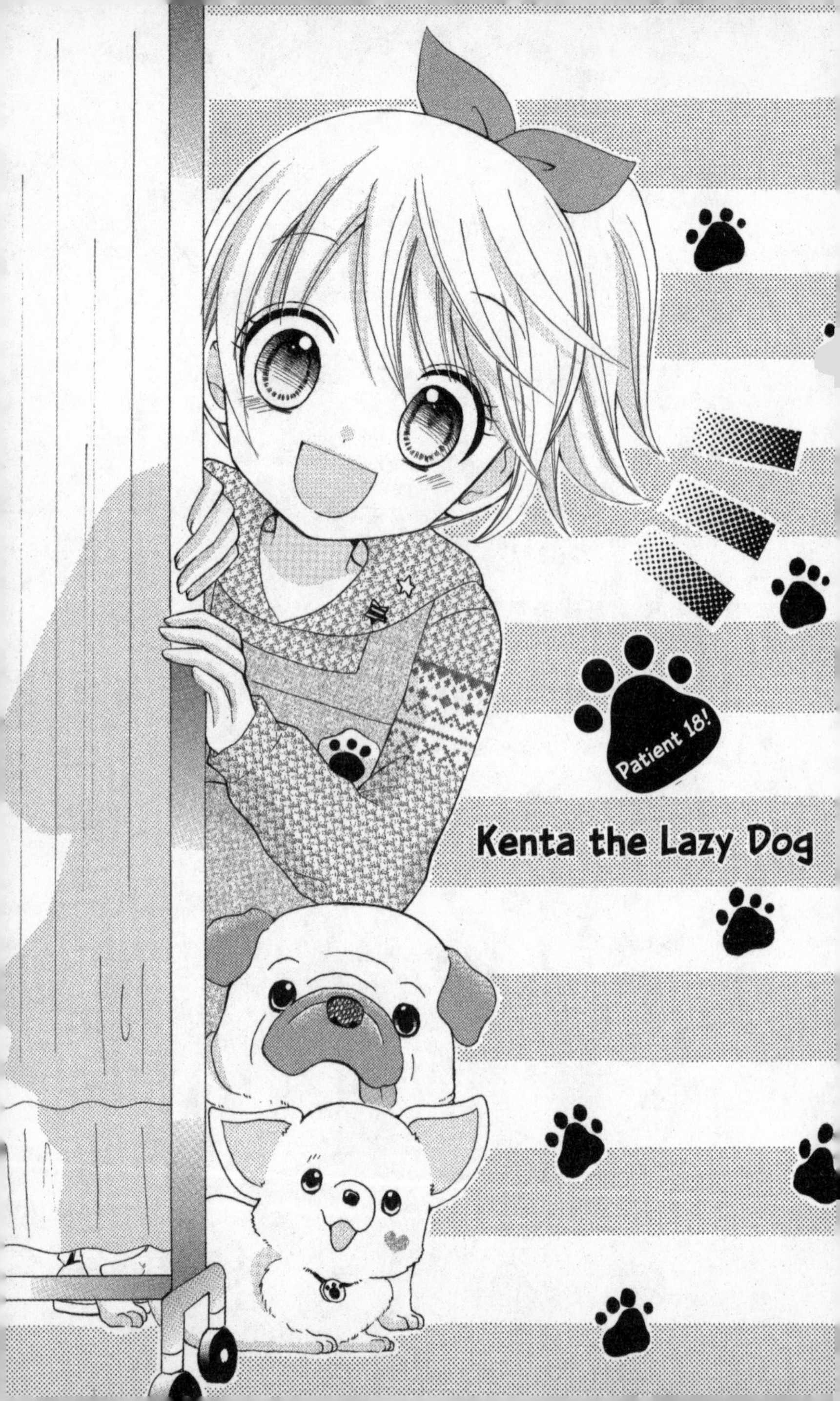
Patient 18!
Kenta the Lazy Dog

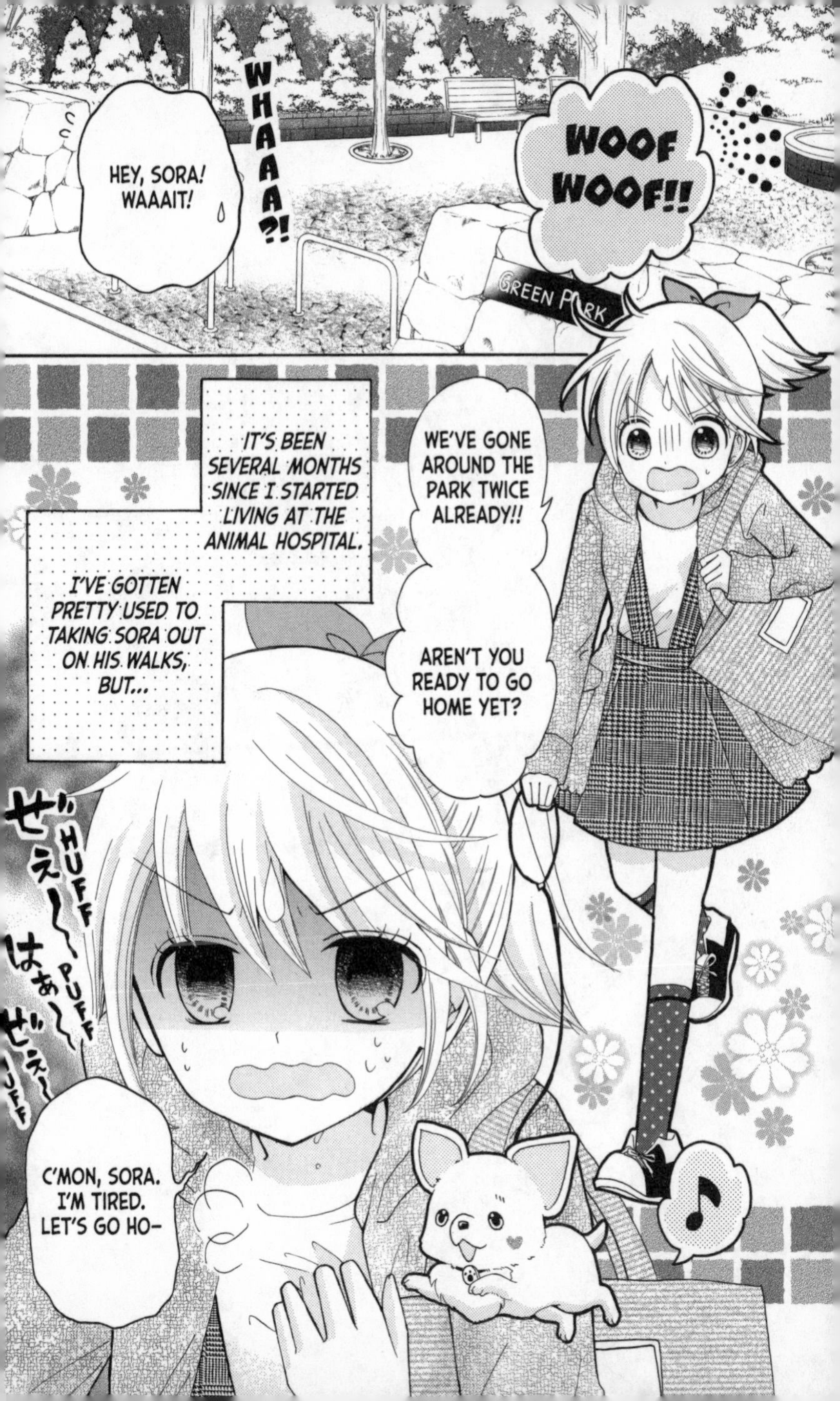
WOOF WOOF!!
GREEN PARK
WHAAAA?!
HEY, SORA! WAAAIT!
IT'S BEEN SEVERAL MONTHS SINCE I STARTED LIVING AT THE ANIMAL HOSPITAL.
I'VE GOTTEN PRETTY USED TO TAKING SORA OUT ON HIS WALKS, BUT...
WE'VE GONE AROUND THE PARK TWICE ALREADY!!
AREN'T YOU READY TO GO HOME YET?
ぜぇ～ HUFF
はぁ～ PUFF
ぜぇ～
C'MON, SORA. I'M TIRED. LET'S GO HO-

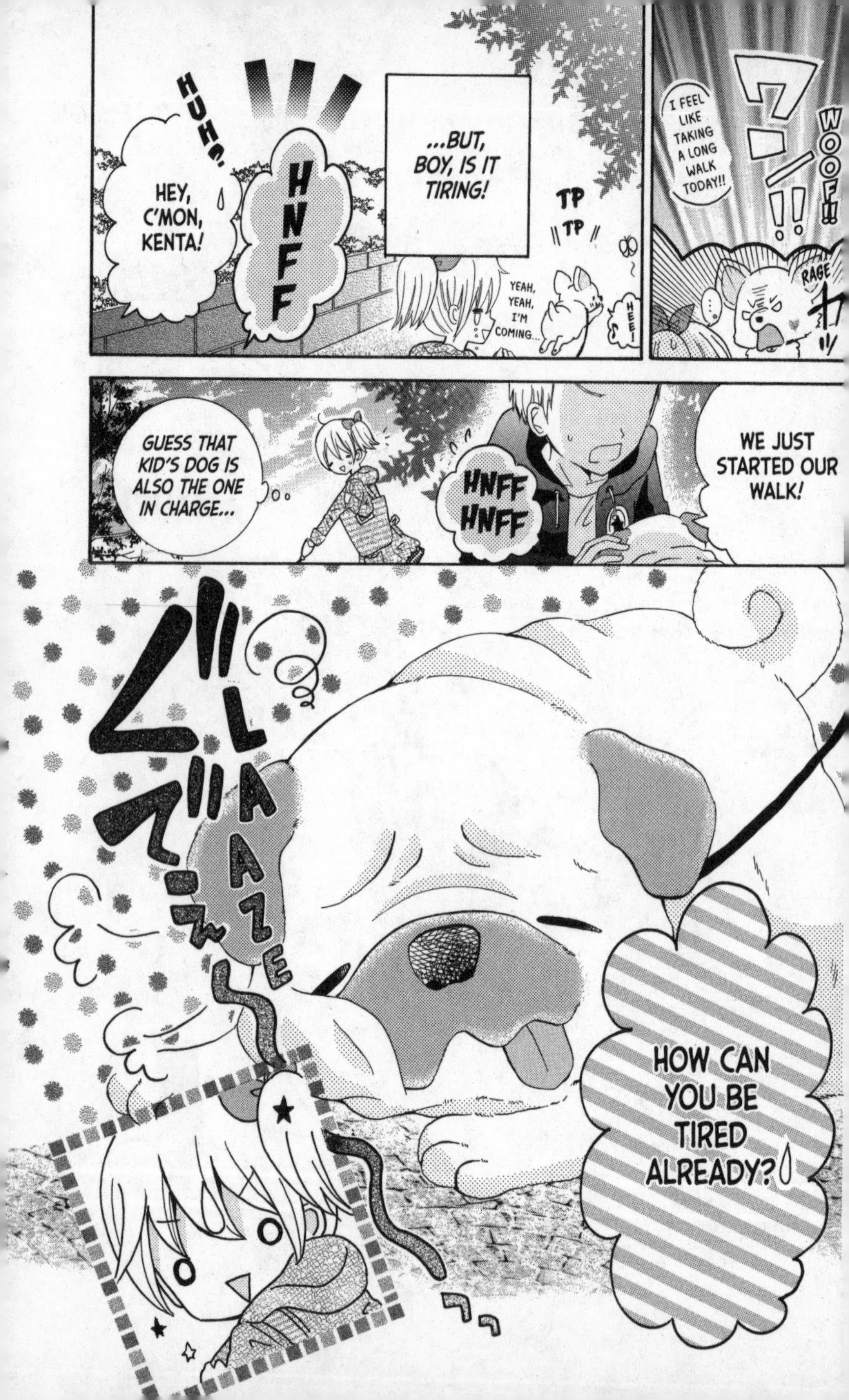
WOOF!!
I FEEL LIKE TAKING A LONG WALK TODAY!!
...
RAGE
...BUT, BOY, IS IT TIRING!
TP TP
YEAH, YEAH, I'M COMING...
HEE!
HNFF
HUH?
HEY, C'MON, KENTA!
WE JUST STARTED OUR WALK!
HNFF HNFF
GUESS THAT KID'S DOG IS ALSO THE ONE IN CHARGE...
HOW CAN YOU BE TIRED ALREADY?
LAZE

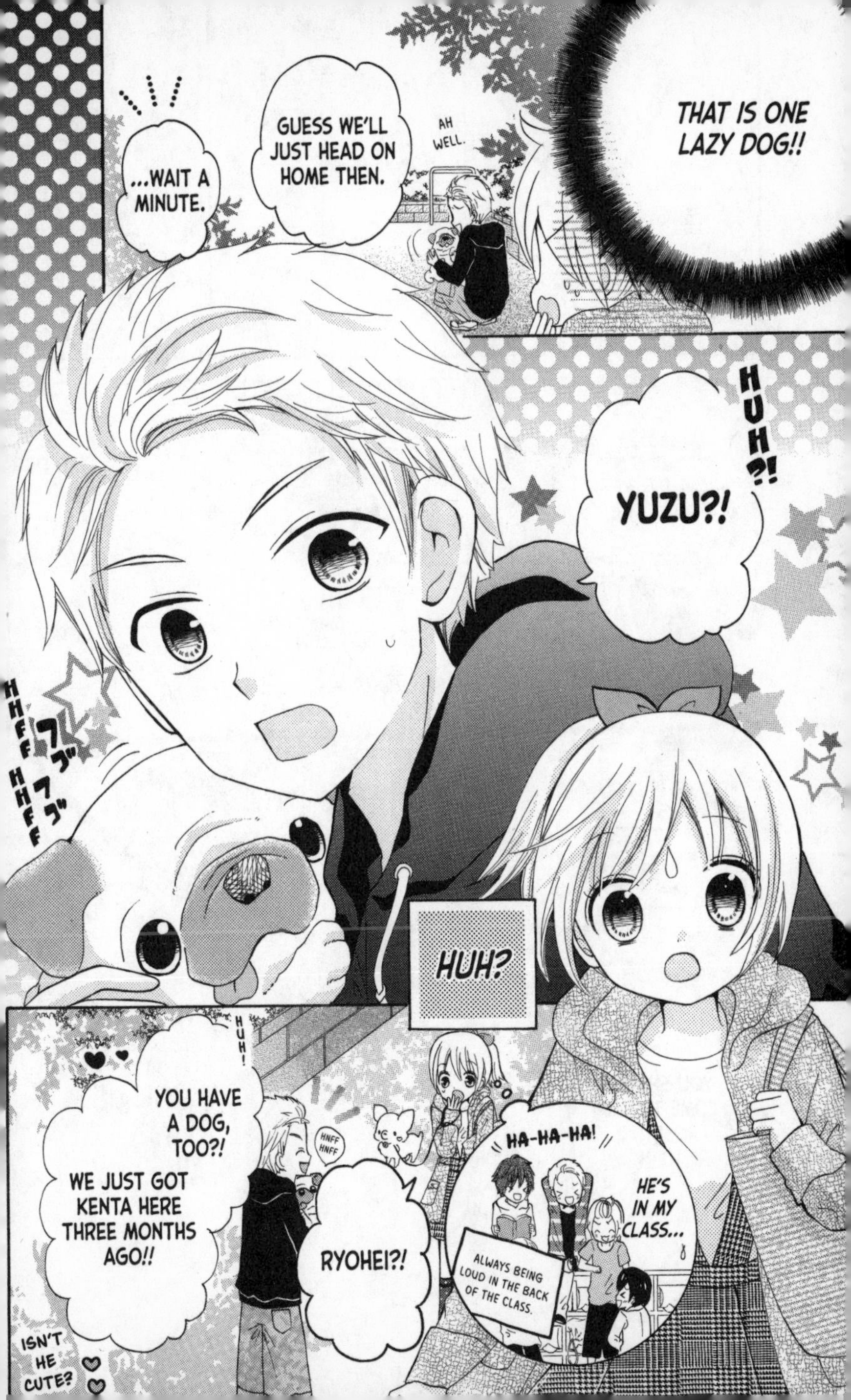
THAT IS ONE LAZY DOG!!
AH WELL.
GUESS WE'LL JUST HEAD ON HOME THEN.
...WAIT A MINUTE.
HUH?!
YUZU?!
HHFF HHFF
HUH?
HE'S IN MY CLASS...
ALWAYS BEING LOUD IN THE BACK OF THE CLASS.
HA-HA-HA!
RYOHEI?!
HNFF HNFF
HUH!
YOU HAVE A DOG, TOO?!
WE JUST GOT KENTA HERE THREE MONTHS AGO!!
ISN'T HE CUTE?

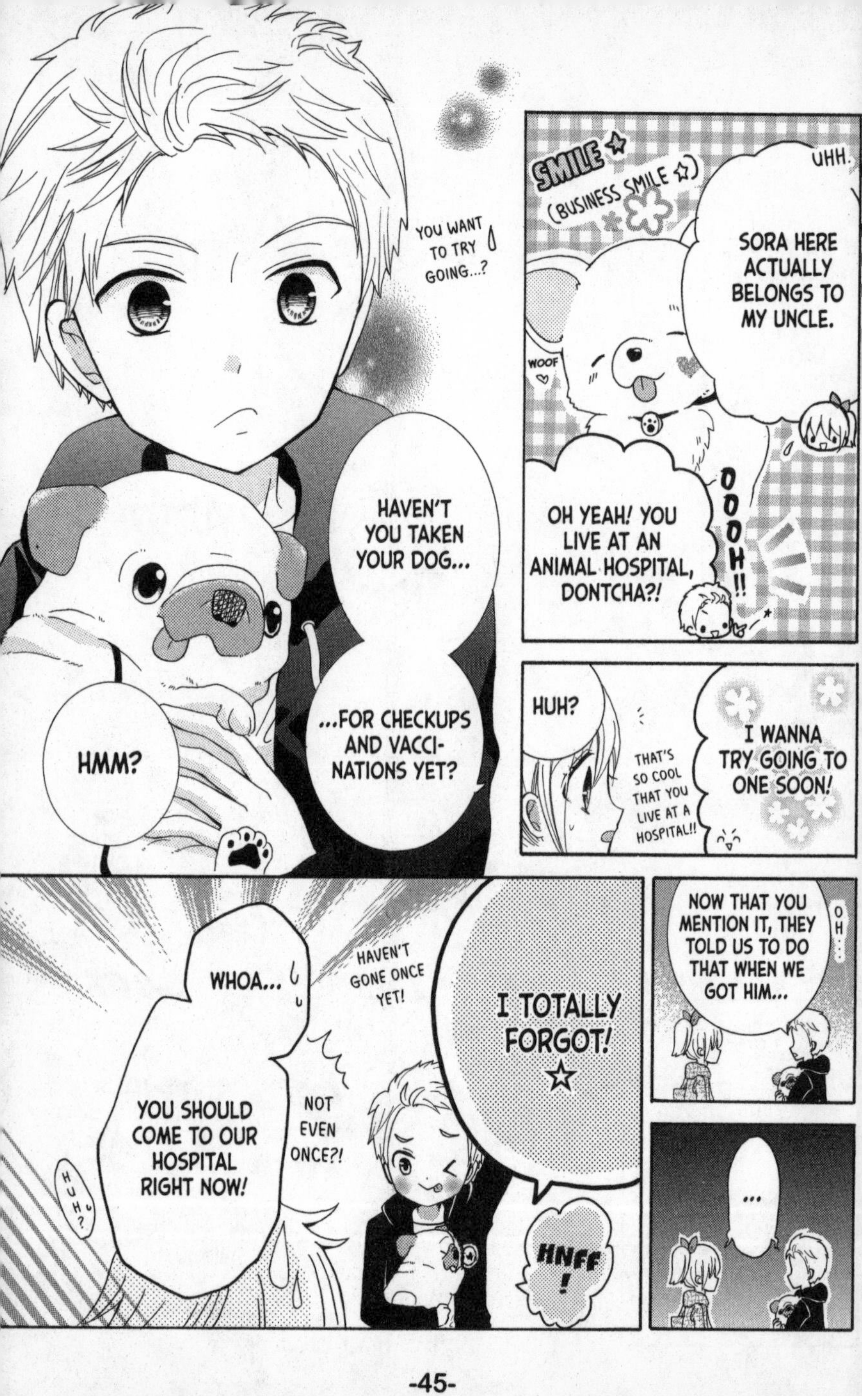
UHH.
SORA HERE ACTUALLY BELONGS TO MY UNCLE.
SMILE ☆
(BUSINESS SMILE ☆)
WOOF
OOOOH!!
OH YEAH! YOU LIVE AT AN ANIMAL HOSPITAL, DONTCHA?!
I WANNA TRY GOING TO ONE SOON!
THAT'S SO COOL THAT YOU LIVE AT A HOSPITAL!!
HUH?
YOU WANT TO TRY GOING...?
HAVEN'T YOU TAKEN YOUR DOG...
...FOR CHECKUPS AND VACCI-NATIONS YET?
HMM?
OH...
NOW THAT YOU MENTION IT, THEY TOLD US TO DO THAT WHEN WE GOT HIM...
...
I TOTALLY FORGOT! ☆
HNFF!
HAVEN'T GONE ONCE YET!
NOT EVEN ONCE?!
WHOA...
YOU SHOULD COME TO OUR HOSPITAL RIGHT NOW!
HUH?

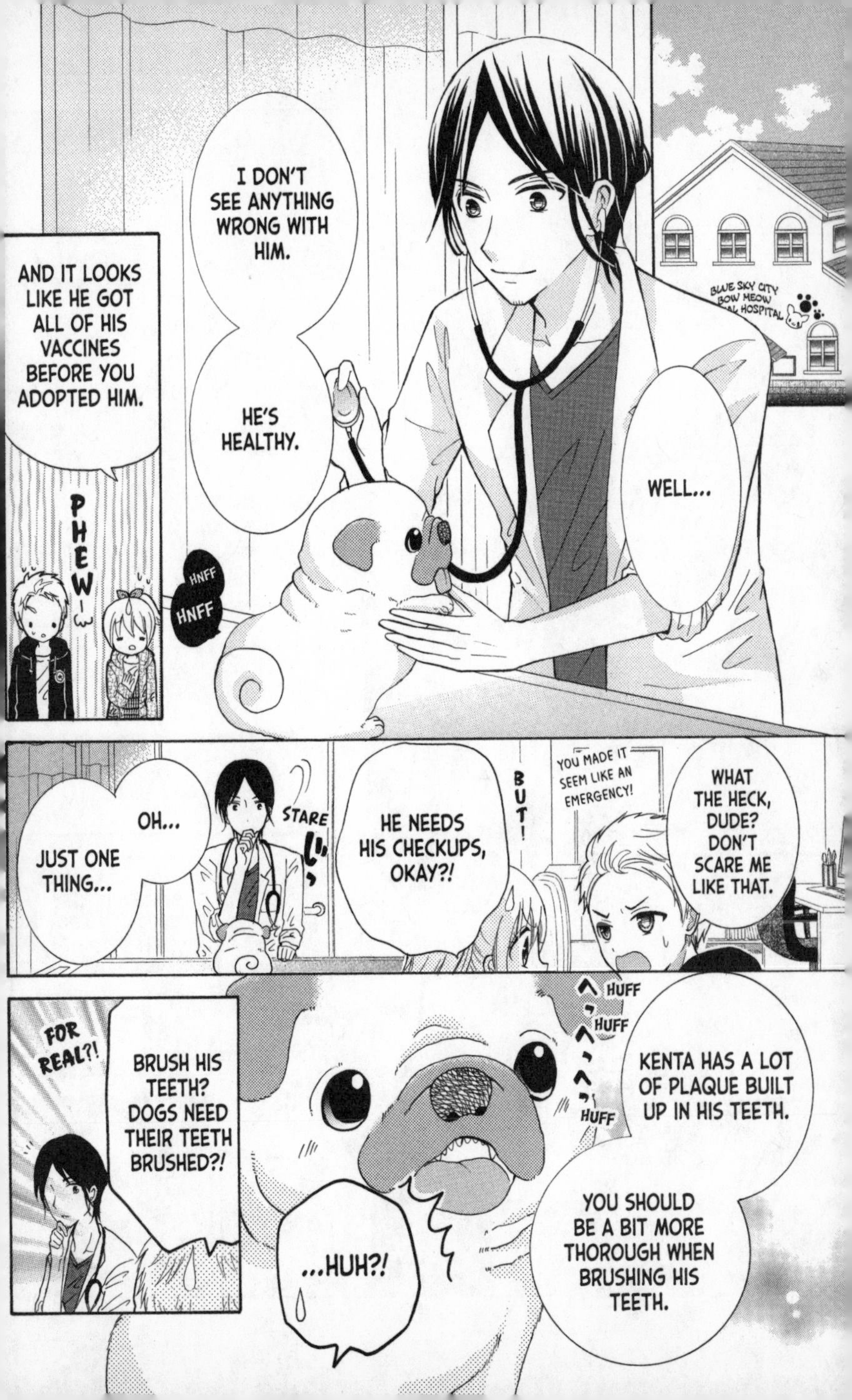
BLUE SKY CITY BOW MEOW
HOSPITAL
WELL...
I DON'T SEE ANYTHING WRONG WITH HIM.
HE'S HEALTHY.
HNFF
HNFF
AND IT LOOKS LIKE HE GOT ALL OF HIS VACCINES BEFORE YOU ADOPTED HIM.
PHEW
WHAT THE HECK, DUDE? DON'T SCARE ME LIKE THAT.
YOU MADE IT SEEM LIKE AN EMERGENCY!
BUT!
HE NEEDS HIS CHECKUPS, OKAY?!
STARE
OH...
JUST ONE THING...
KENTA HAS A LOT OF PLAQUE BUILT UP IN HIS TEETH.
YOU SHOULD BE A BIT MORE THOROUGH WHEN BRUSHING HIS TEETH.
HUFF
HUFF
HUFF
...HUH?!
BRUSH HIS TEETH? DOGS NEED THEIR TEETH BRUSHED?!
FOR REAL?!

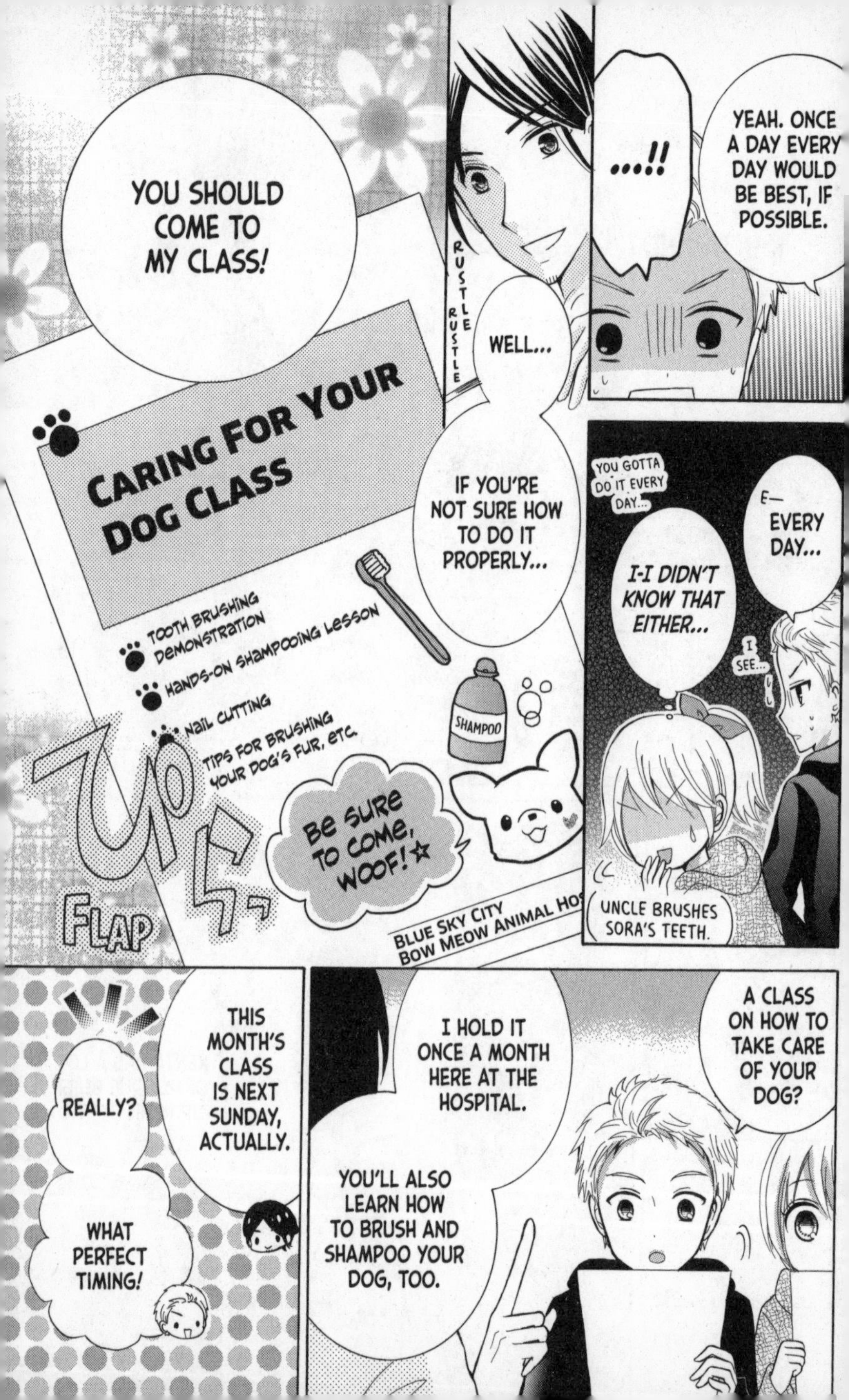
YEAH. ONCE A DAY EVERY DAY WOULD BE BEST, IF POSSIBLE.
...!!
E— EVERY DAY...
YOU GOTTA DO IT EVERY DAY...
I-I DIDN'T KNOW THAT EITHER...
I SEE...
UNCLE BRUSHES SORA'S TEETH.
RUSTLE RUSTLE
WELL...
IF YOU'RE NOT SURE HOW TO DO IT PROPERLY...
YOU SHOULD COME TO MY CLASS!
CARING FOR YOUR DOG CLASS
TOOTH BRUSHING DEMONSTRATION
HANDS-ON SHAMPOOING LESSON
NAIL CUTTING
TIPS FOR BRUSHING YOUR DOG'S FUR, ETC.
SHAMPOO
Be sure to come, woof! ☆
BLUE SKY CITY BOW MEOW ANIMAL HOS
FLAP
A CLASS ON HOW TO TAKE CARE OF YOUR DOG?
I HOLD IT ONCE A MONTH HERE AT THE HOSPITAL.
YOU'LL ALSO LEARN HOW TO BRUSH AND SHAMPOO YOUR DOG, TOO.
THIS MONTH'S CLASS IS NEXT SUNDAY, ACTUALLY.
REALLY?
WHAT PERFECT TIMING!

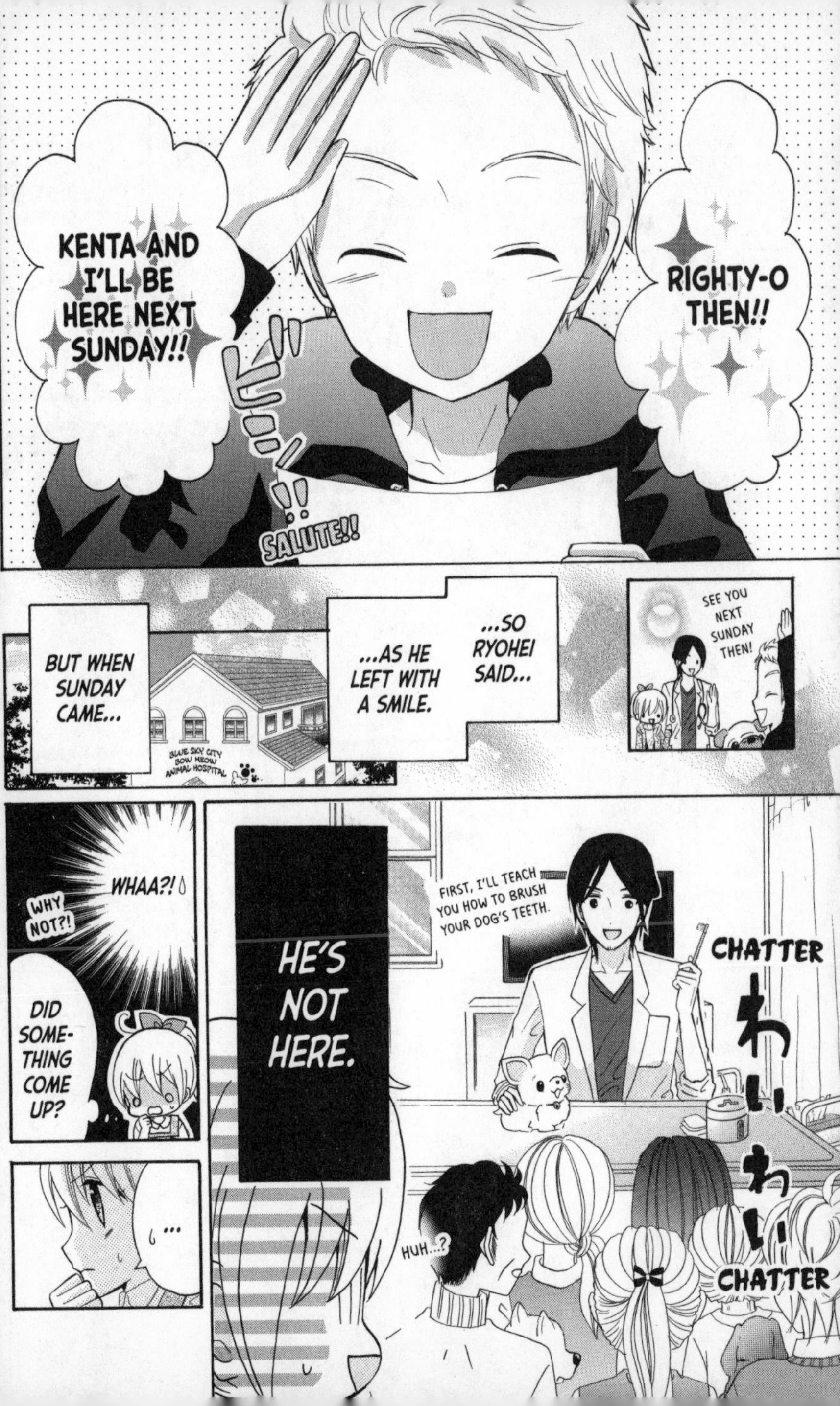
RIGHTY-O THEN!!
KENTA AND I'LL BE HERE NEXT SUNDAY!!
SALUTE!!
SEE YOU NEXT SUNDAY THEN!
...SO RYOHEI SAID...
...AS HE LEFT WITH A SMILE.
BUT WHEN SUNDAY CAME...
BLUE SKY CITY BOW MEOW ANIMAL HOSPITAL
FIRST, I'LL TEACH YOU HOW TO BRUSH YOUR DOG'S TEETH.
CHATTER
CHATTER
HUH...?
HE'S NOT HERE.
WHAA?!
WHY NOT?!
DID SOME-THING COME UP?
...

COLORED ILLUSTRATIONS

WHILE THERE ARE A LOT OF PEOPLE WHO DRAW THEIR MANGA DIGITALLY NOW, I STILL DO ALL MY WORK BY HAND, BE IT BLACK AND WHITE OR COLOR ILLUSTRATIONS. I KEEP THINKING I NEED TO LEARN HOW TO DRAW DIGITALLY, BUT I'M... REALLY BAD...WITH COMPUTERS...

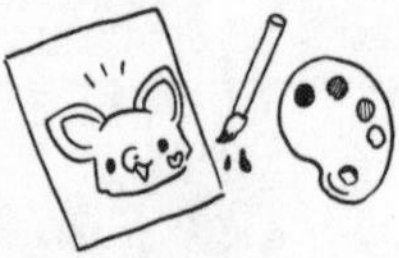

I'M DELIGHTED TO HEAR THAT THERE ARE SO MANY READERS WHO LIKE MY COLOR ILLUSTRATIONS, NONETHELESS! ✧✧

THE TOOLS I USE REGULARLY ARE COLORED INK, COPIC MARKERS, AND ONCE IN A WHILE COLORED PENCILS OR PASTELS. I ALSO USE WATER-COLOR PAINTS. SOME DAY, I HOPE I'LL BE AS GOOD AS I AM WITH A COMPUTER AS I AM WORKING BY HAND.

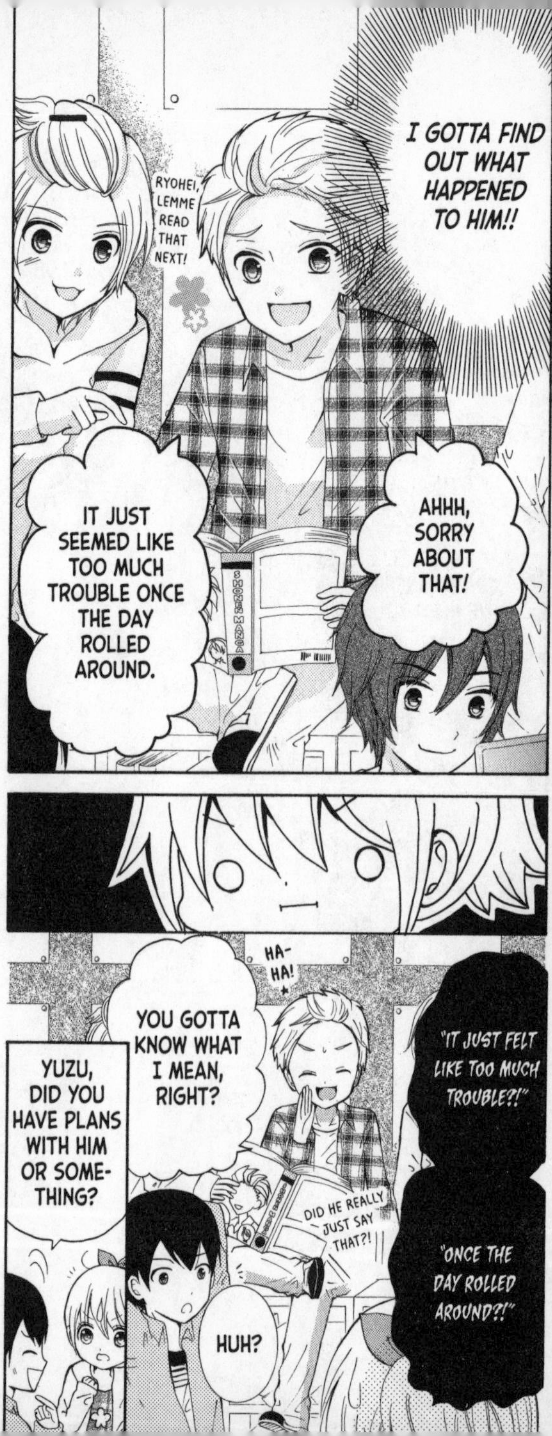
I GOTTA FIND OUT WHAT HAPPENED TO HIM!!
RYOHEI, LEMME READ THAT NEXT!
AHHH, SORRY ABOUT THAT!
IT JUST SEEMED LIKE TOO MUCH TROUBLE ONCE THE DAY ROLLED AROUND.
"IT JUST FELT LIKE TOO MUCH TROUBLE?!"
"ONCE THE DAY ROLLED AROUND?!"
HA-HA!
YOU GOTTA KNOW WHAT I MEAN, RIGHT?
DID HE REALLY JUST SAY THAT?!
YUZU, DID YOU HAVE PLANS WITH HIM OR SOME-THING?
HUH?

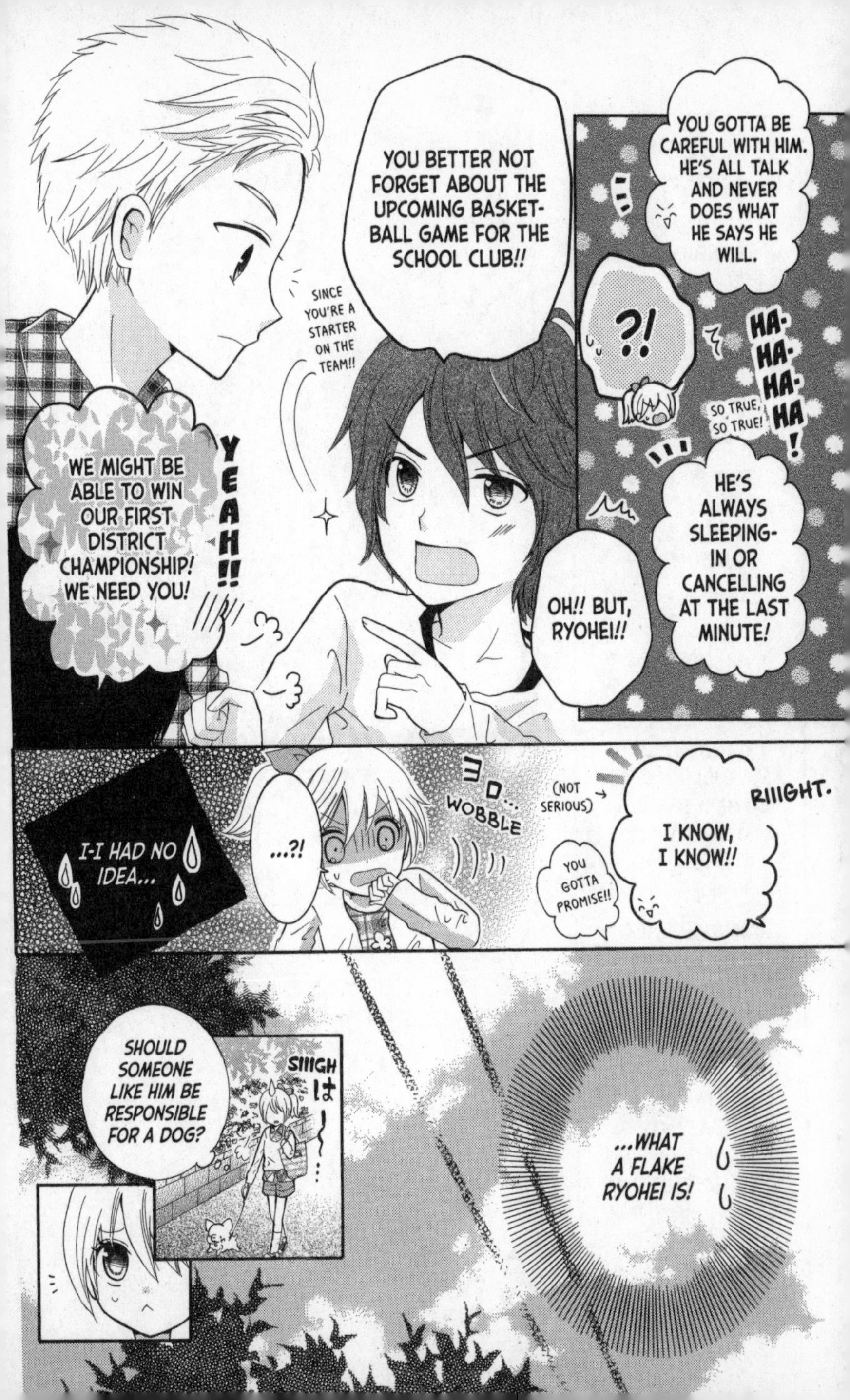

YOU BETTER NOT FORGET ABOUT THE UPCOMING BASKET-BALL GAME FOR THE SCHOOL CLUB!!
SINCE YOU'RE A STARTER ON THE TEAM!!
WE MIGHT BE ABLE TO WIN OUR FIRST DISTRICT CHAMPIONSHIP! WE NEED YOU!
YEAH!!
OH!! BUT, RYOHEI!!
YOU GOTTA BE CAREFUL WITH HIM. HE'S ALL TALK AND NEVER DOES WHAT HE SAYS HE WILL.
?!
HA-HA-HA-HA!
SO TRUE, SO TRUE!
HE'S ALWAYS SLEEPING-IN OR CANCELLING AT THE LAST MINUTE!
RIIIGHT.
(NOT SERIOUS) →
I KNOW, I KNOW!!
YOU GOTTA PROMISE!!
ヨロ… WOBBLE
...?!
I-I HAD NO IDEA...
...WHAT A FLAKE RYOHEI IS!
SIIIGH
はー…
SHOULD SOMEONE LIKE HIM BE RESPONSIBLE FOR A DOG?

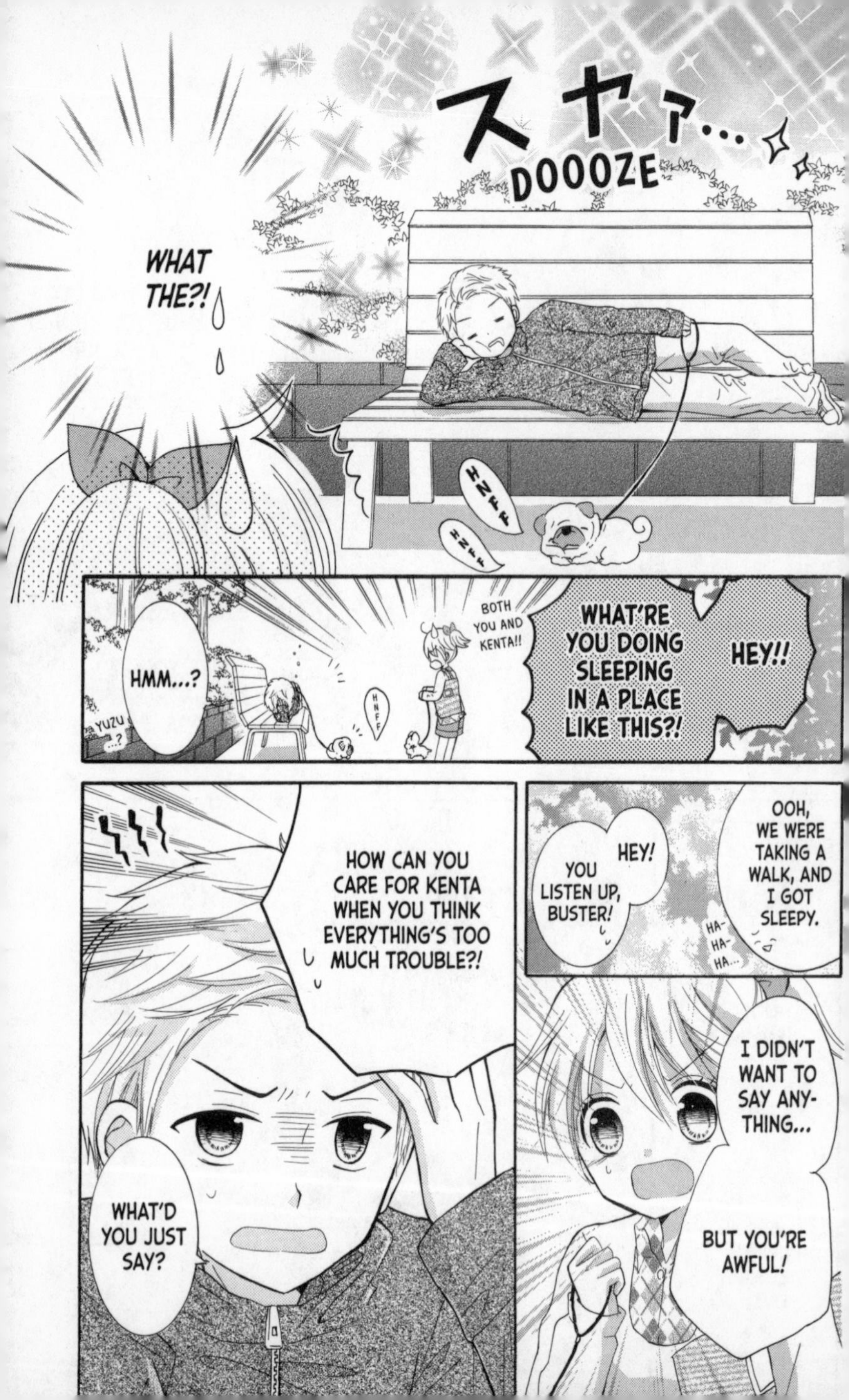

スヤァ…
DOOOZE
HNFF
HNFF
WHAT THE?!
HEY!!
WHAT'RE YOU DOING SLEEPING IN A PLACE LIKE THIS?!
BOTH YOU AND KENTA!!
HNFF
HMM...?
YUZU ...?
OOH, WE WERE TAKING A WALK, AND I GOT SLEEPY.
HA-HA-HA...
HEY!
YOU LISTEN UP, BUSTER!
I DIDN'T WANT TO SAY ANYTHING...
BUT YOU'RE AWFUL!
HOW CAN YOU CARE FOR KENTA WHEN YOU THINK EVERYTHING'S TOO MUCH TROUBLE?!
WHAT'D YOU JUST SAY?

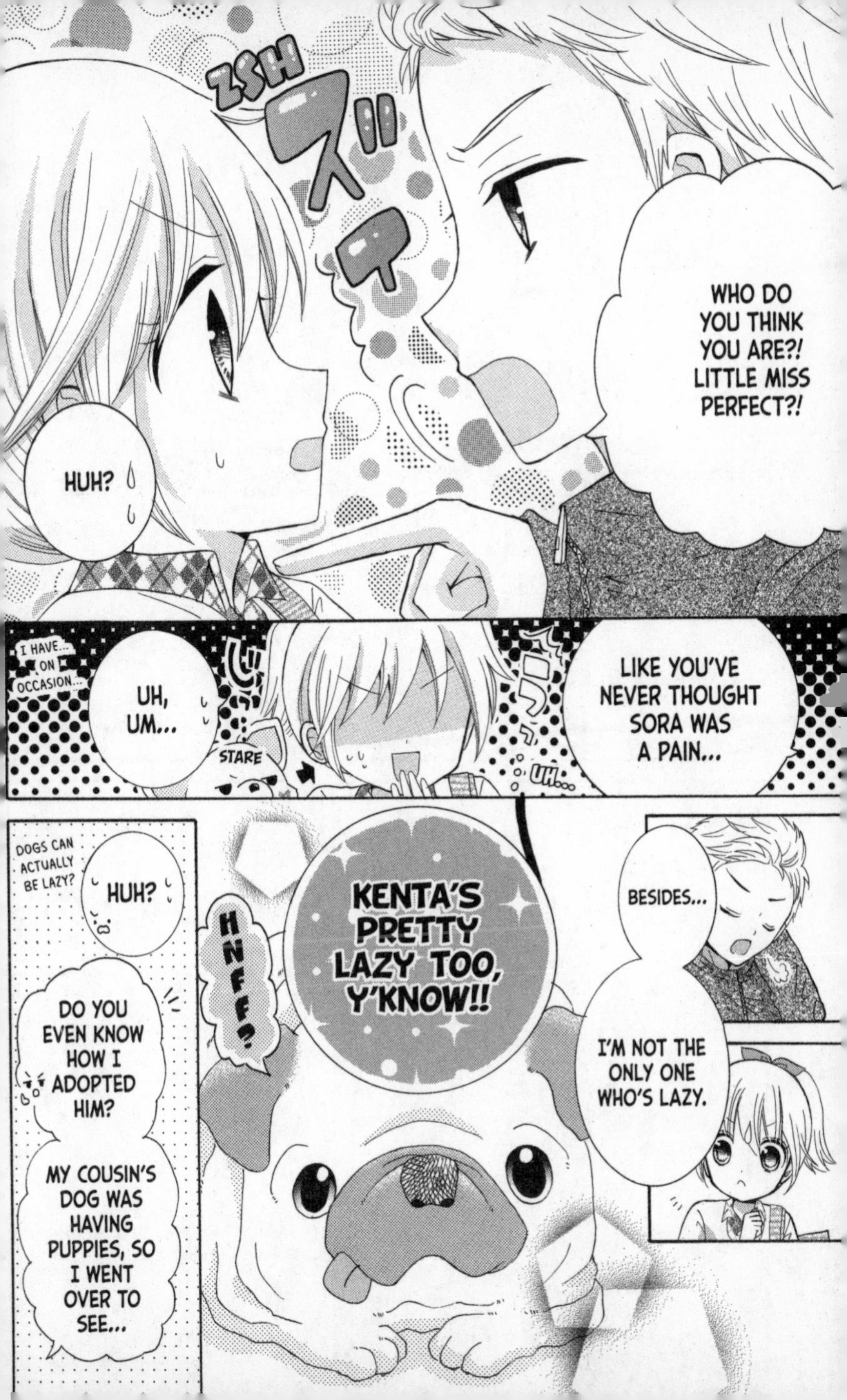
ZSH
WHO DO YOU THINK YOU ARE?! LITTLE MISS PERFECT?!
HUH?
LIKE YOU'VE NEVER THOUGHT SORA WAS A PAIN...
UH...
STARE
UH, UM...
I HAVE... ON OCCASION...
BESIDES...
I'M NOT THE ONLY ONE WHO'S LAZY.
KENTA'S PRETTY LAZY TOO, Y'KNOW!!
HNFF?
HUH?
DOGS CAN ACTUALLY BE LAZY?
DO YOU EVEN KNOW HOW I ADOPTED HIM?
MY COUSIN'S DOG WAS HAVING PUPPIES, SO I WENT OVER TO SEE...

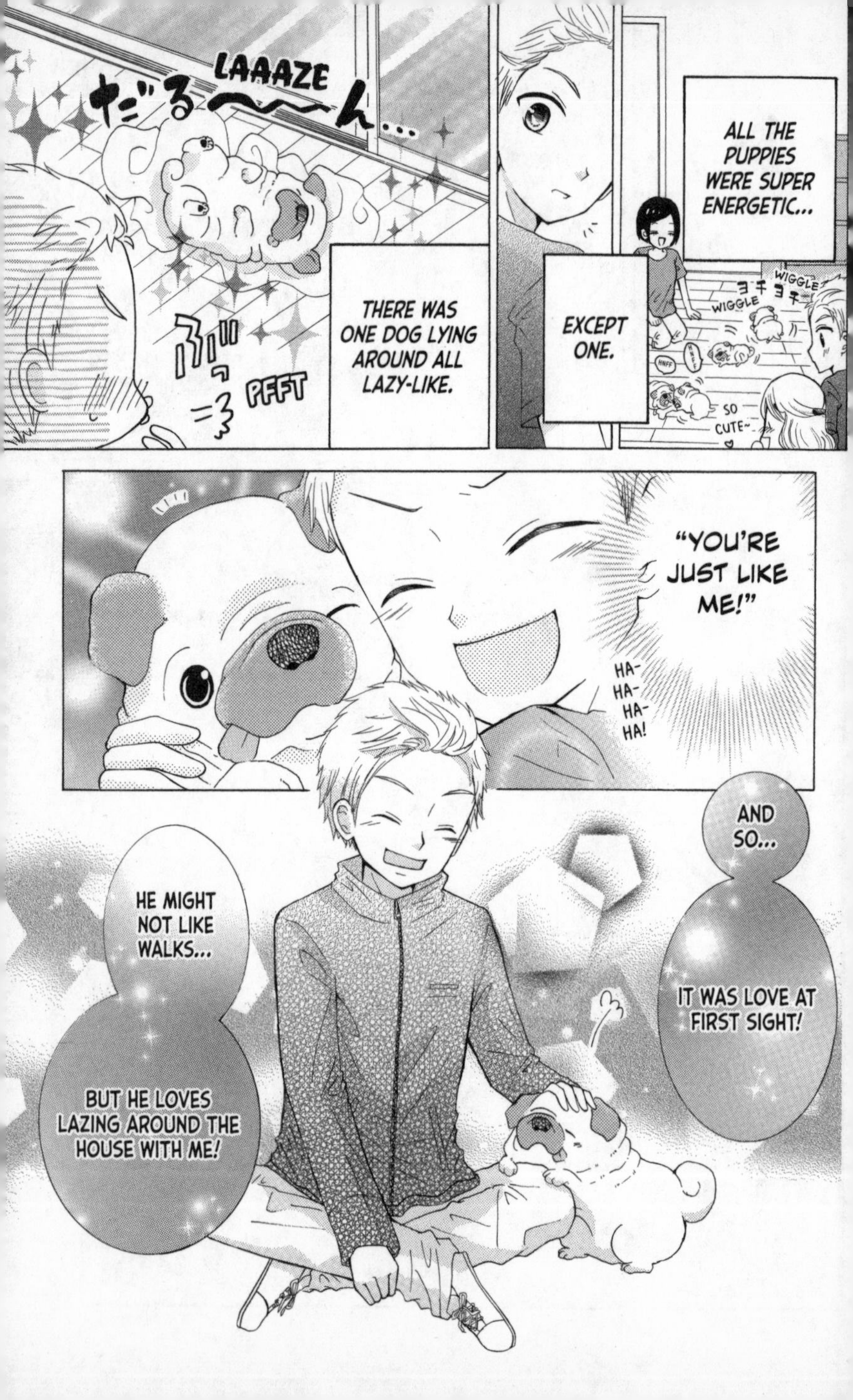
ALL THE PUPPIES WERE SUPER ENERGETIC...
WIGGLE
WIGGLE
HNFF
SO CUTE~
EXCEPT ONE.
LAAAZE
THERE WAS ONE DOG LYING AROUND ALL LAZY-LIKE.
PFFT
"YOU'RE JUST LIKE ME!"
HA-HA-HA-HA!
AND SO...
IT WAS LOVE AT FIRST SIGHT!
HE MIGHT NOT LIKE WALKS...
BUT HE LOVES LAZING AROUND THE HOUSE WITH ME!

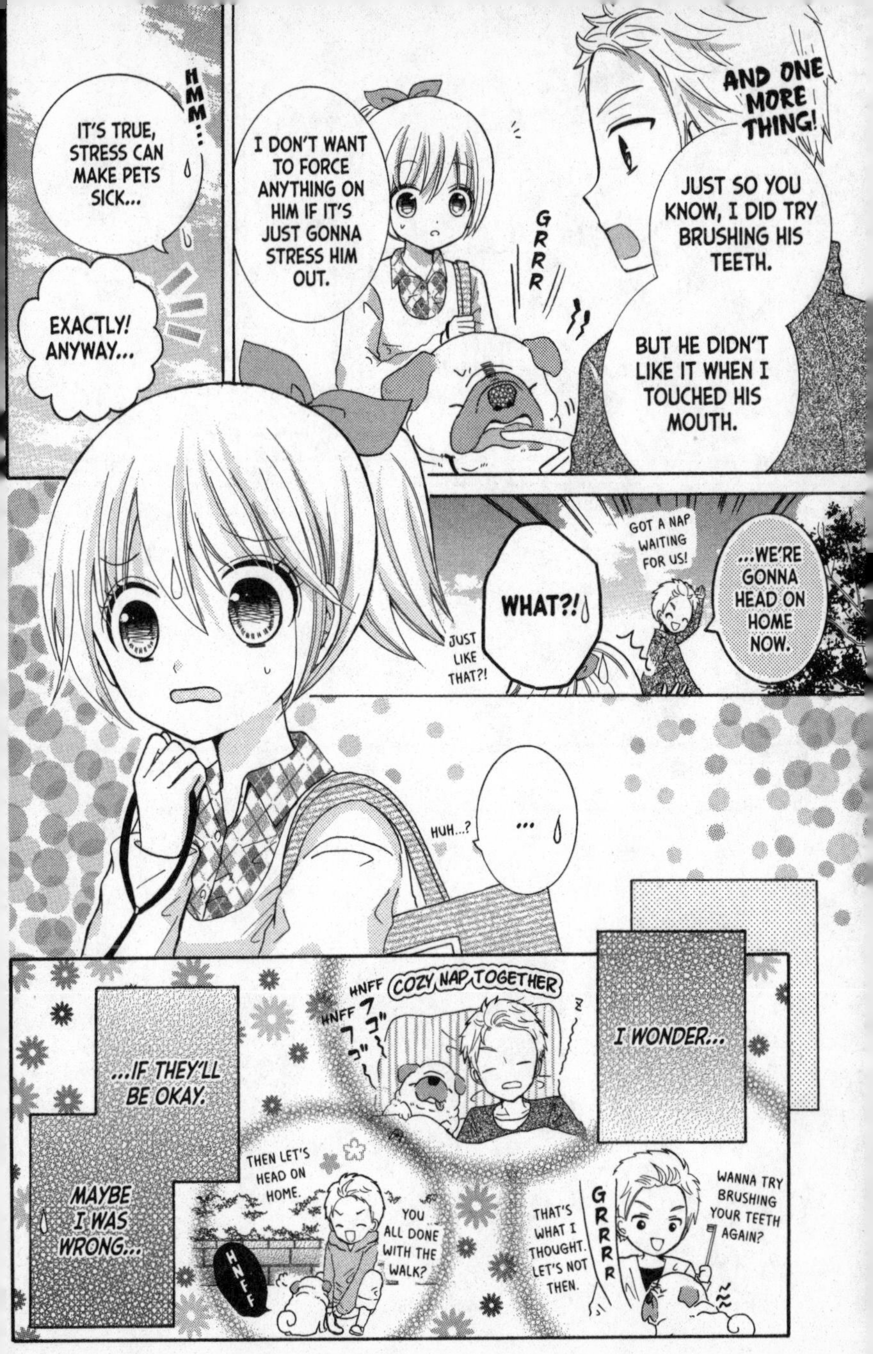
AND ONE MORE THING!
JUST SO YOU KNOW, I DID TRY BRUSHING HIS TEETH.
BUT HE DIDN'T LIKE IT WHEN I TOUCHED HIS MOUTH.
GRRR
I DON'T WANT TO FORCE ANYTHING ON HIM IF IT'S JUST GONNA STRESS HIM OUT.
HMM...
IT'S TRUE, STRESS CAN MAKE PETS SICK...
EXACTLY! ANYWAY...
...WE'RE GONNA HEAD ON HOME NOW.
GOT A NAP WAITING FOR US!
WHAT?!
JUST LIKE THAT?!
...
HUH...?
I WONDER...
WANNA TRY BRUSHING YOUR TEETH AGAIN?
GRRR
THAT'S WHAT I THOUGHT. LET'S NOT THEN.
COZY NAP TOGETHER
HNFF
HNFF
YOU ALL DONE WITH THE WALK?
HNFF
THEN LET'S HEAD ON HOME.
...IF THEY'LL BE OKAY.
MAYBE I WAS WRONG...

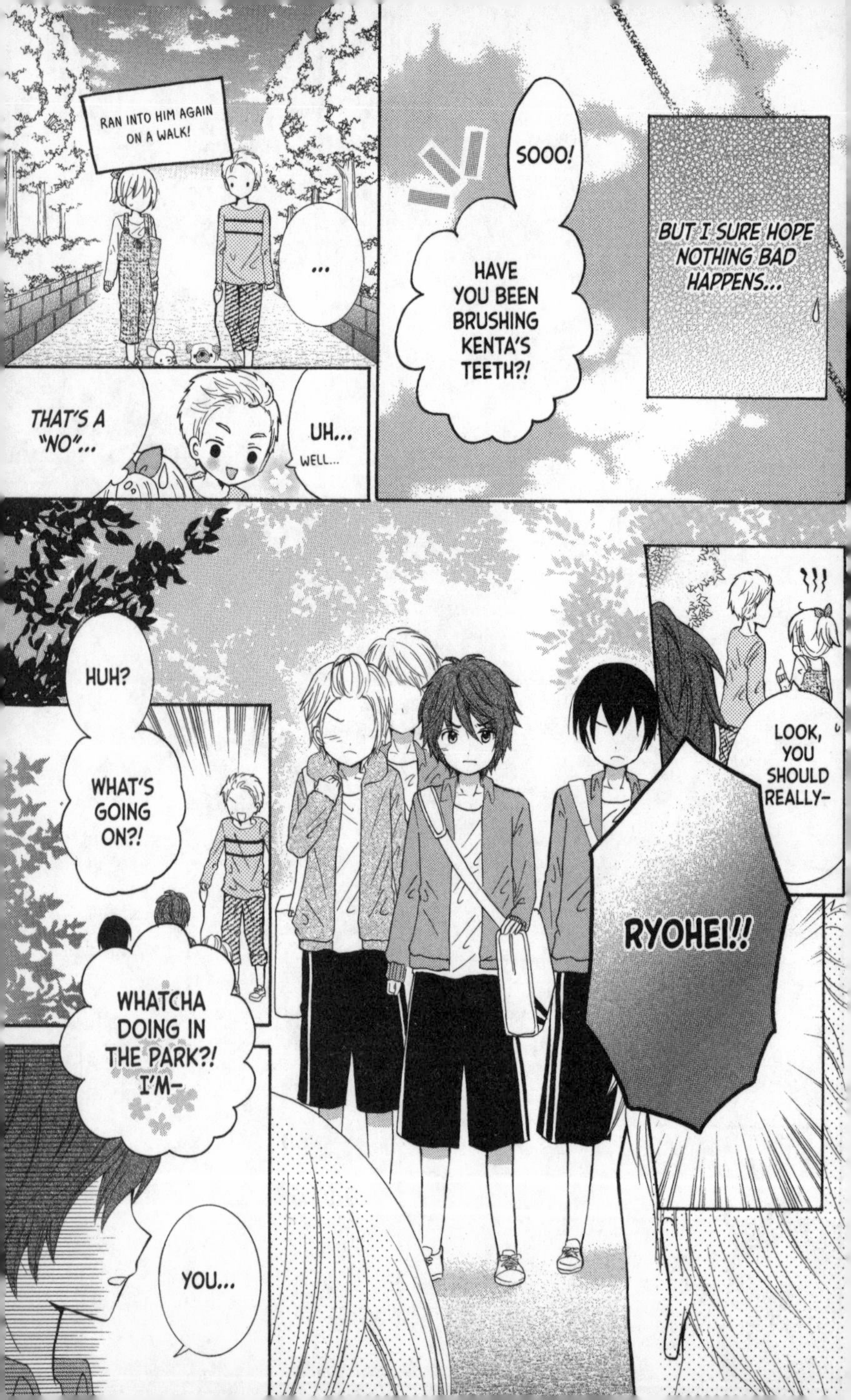

BUT I SURE HOPE NOTHING BAD HAPPENS...
SOOO!
HAVE YOU BEEN BRUSHING KENTA'S TEETH?!
RAN INTO HIM AGAIN ON A WALK!
...
UH... WELL...
THAT'S A "NO"...
LOOK, YOU SHOULD REALLY—
RYOHEI!!
HUH?
WHAT'S GOING ON?!
WHATCHA DOING IN THE PARK?! I'M—
YOU...

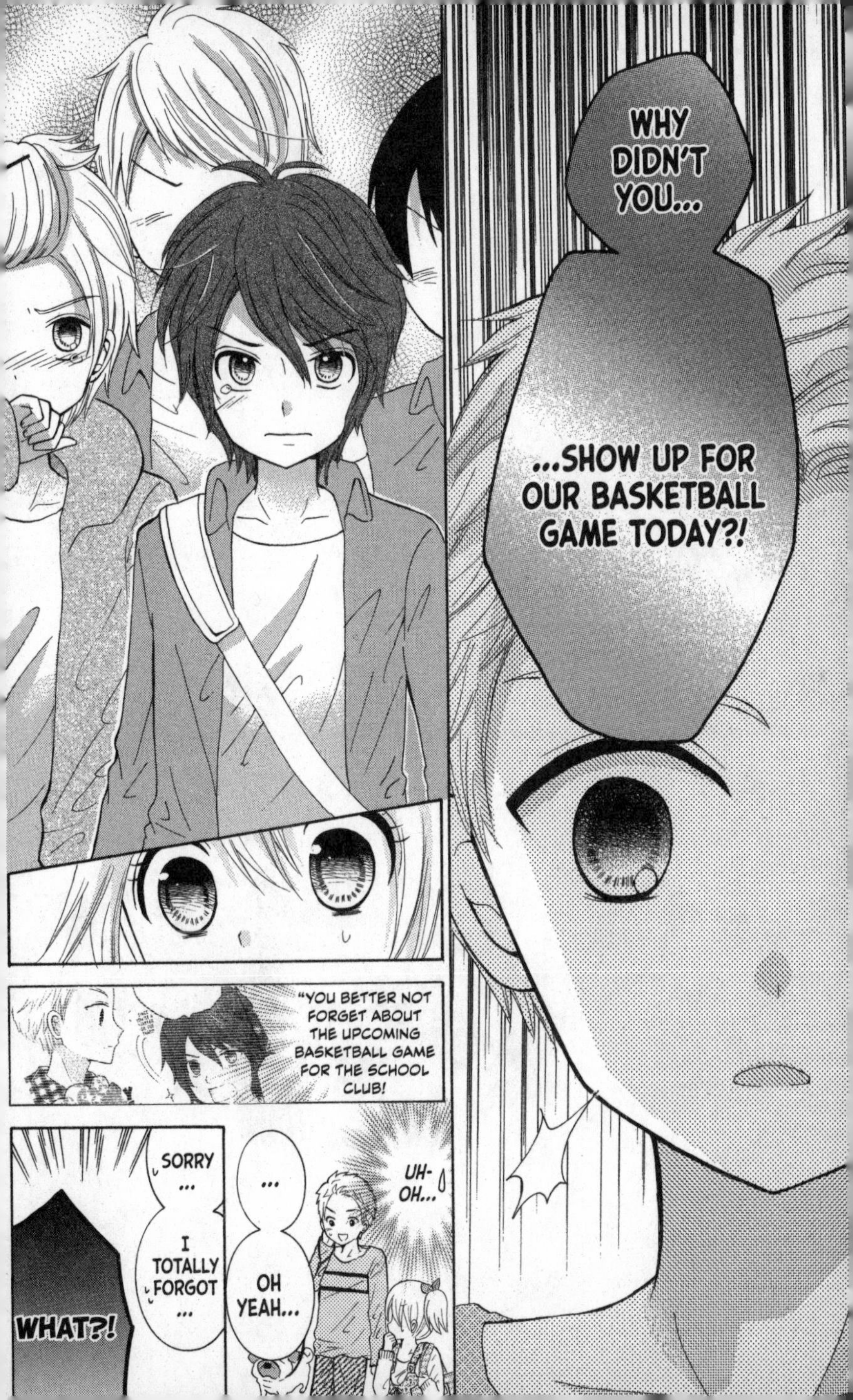
WHY DIDN'T YOU...
...SHOW UP FOR OUR BASKETBALL GAME TODAY?!
"YOU BETTER NOT FORGET ABOUT THE UPCOMING BASKETBALL GAME FOR THE SCHOOL CLUB!
UH-OH...
...
OH YEAH...
SORRY...
I TOTALLY FORGOT...
WHAT?!

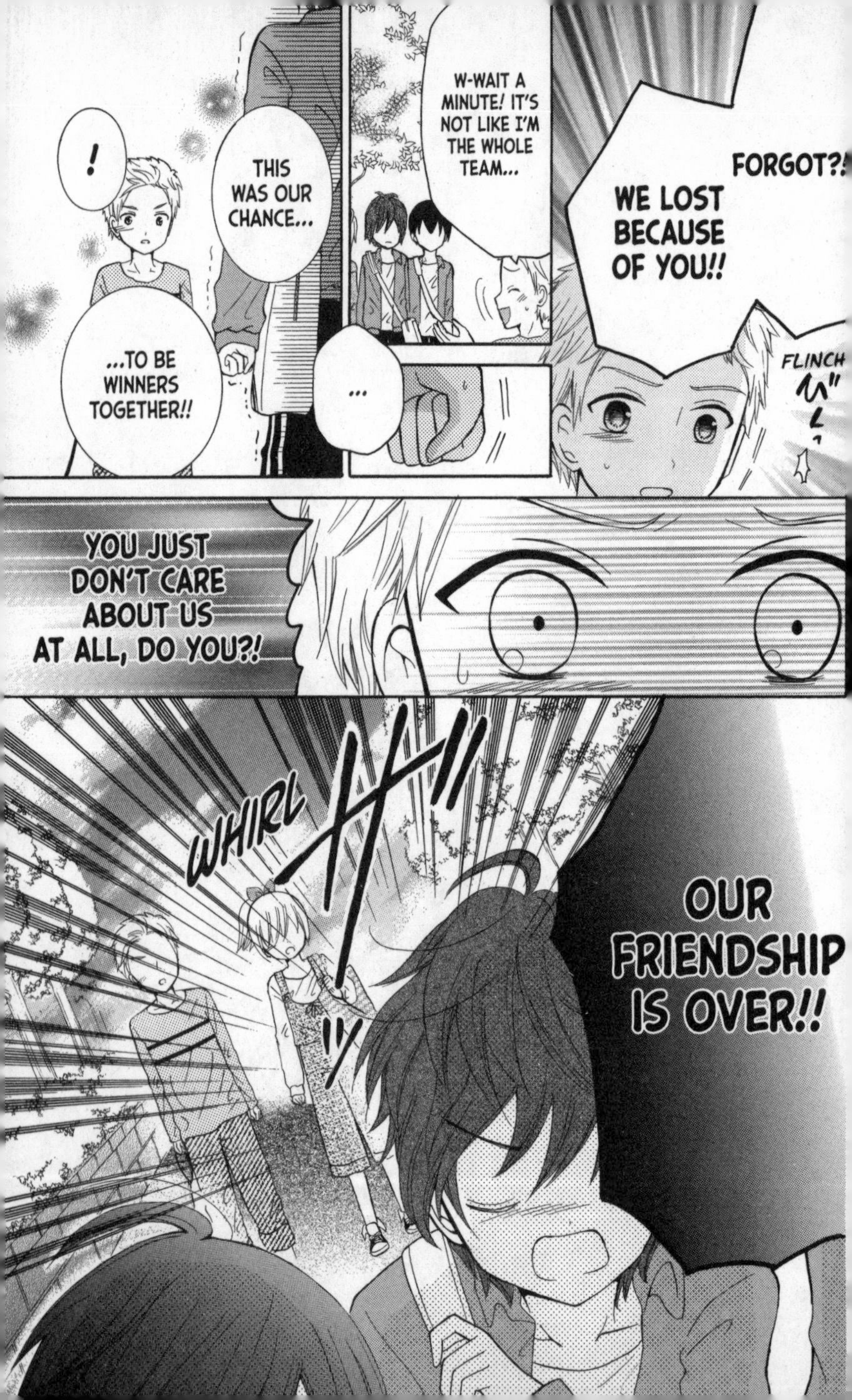
FORGOT?!
WE LOST BECAUSE OF YOU!!
FLINCH
W-WAIT A MINUTE! IT'S NOT LIKE I'M THE WHOLE TEAM...
...
THIS WAS OUR CHANCE...
!
...TO BE WINNERS TOGETHER!!
YOU JUST DON'T CARE ABOUT US AT ALL, DO YOU?!
OUR FRIENDSHIP IS OVER!!
WHIRL

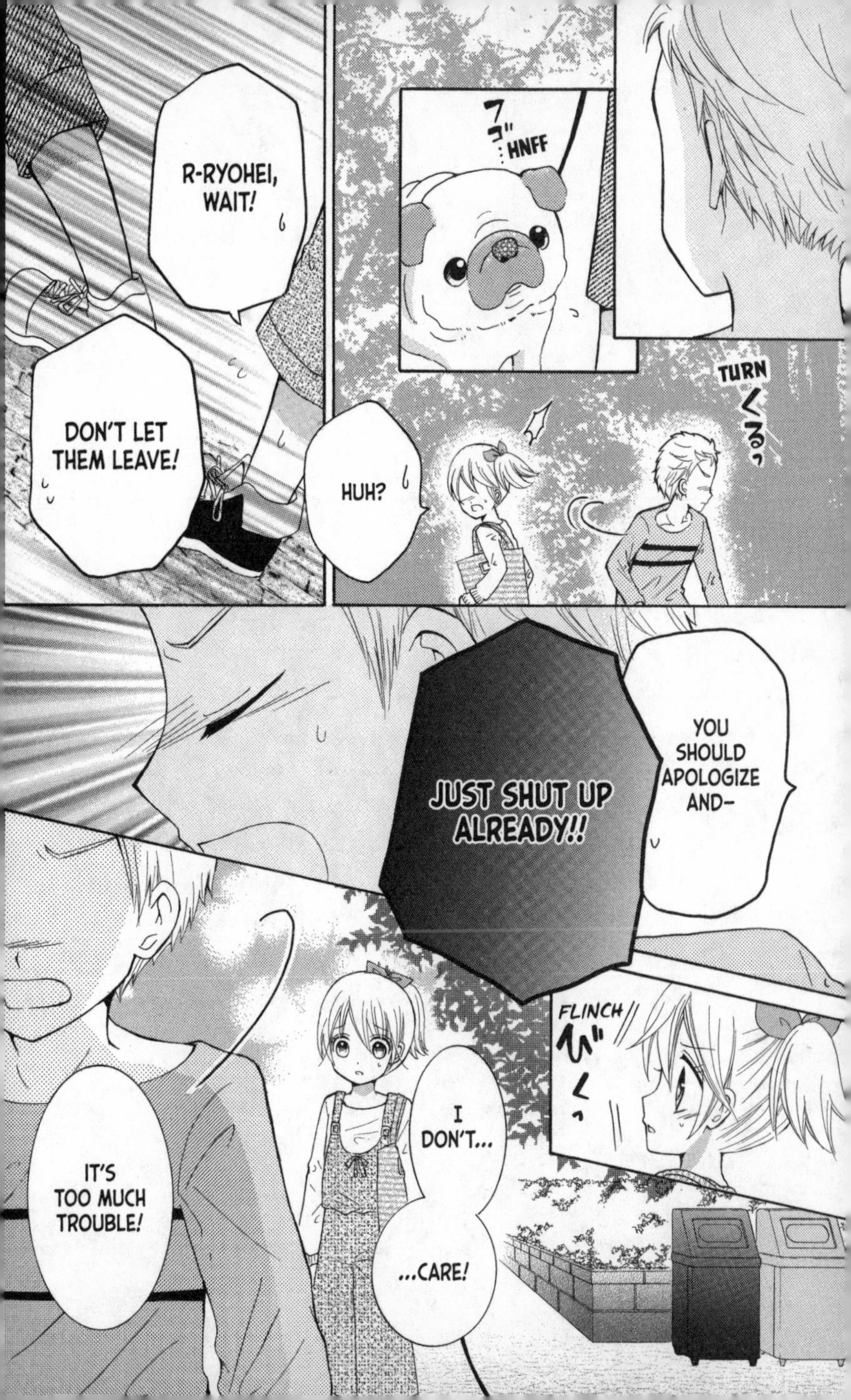
フゴ…
HNFF
TURN
くるっ
HUH?
R-RYOHEI, WAIT!
DON'T LET THEM LEAVE!
YOU SHOULD APOLOGIZE AND–
JUST SHUT UP ALREADY!!
FLINCH
びくっ
I DON'T...
...CARE!
IT'S TOO MUCH TROUBLE!

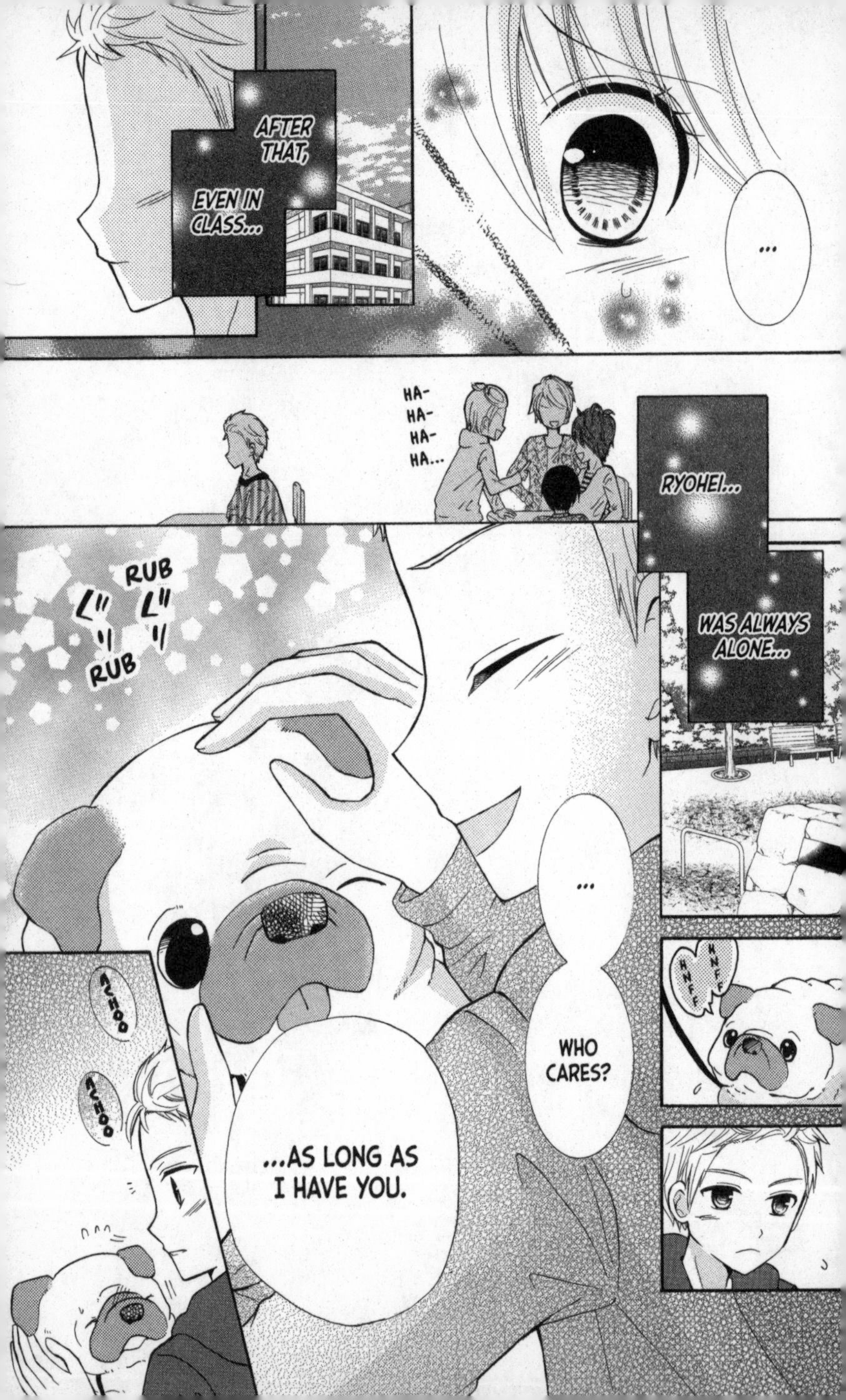
...
AFTER THAT,
EVEN IN CLASS...
RYOHEI...
HA-HA-HA-HA...
WAS ALWAYS ALONE...
HNFF HNFF
RUB RUB
...
WHO CARES?
...AS LONG AS I HAVE YOU.
ACHOO
ACHOO

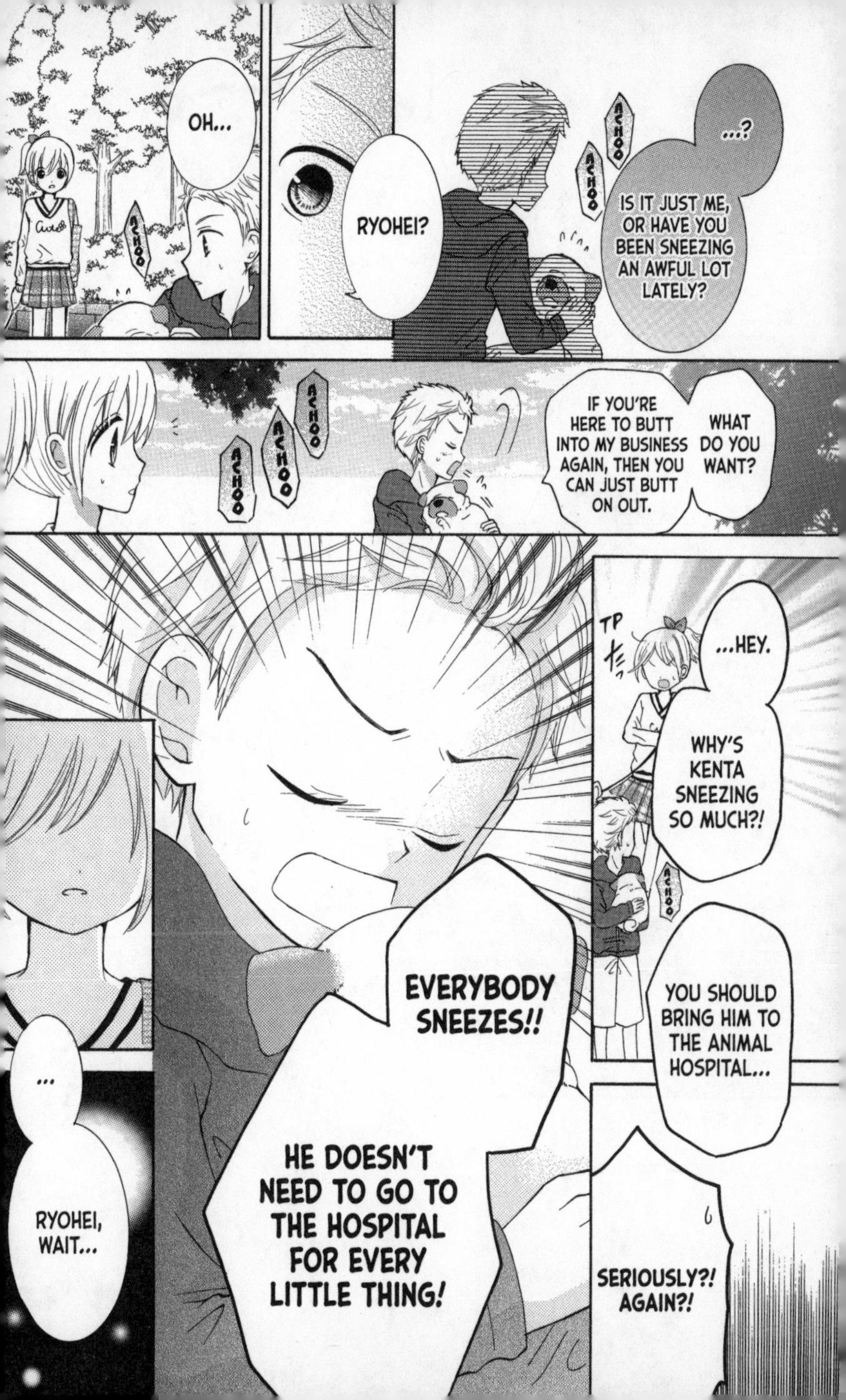
...?
ACHOO
ACHOO
IS IT JUST ME, OR HAVE YOU BEEN SNEEZING AN AWFUL LOT LATELY?
RYOHEI?
OH...
ACHOO
WHAT DO YOU WANT?
IF YOU'RE HERE TO BUTT INTO MY BUSINESS AGAIN, THEN YOU CAN JUST BUTT ON OUT.
ACHOO
ACHOO
ACHOO
TP
...HEY.
WHY'S KENTA SNEEZING SO MUCH?!
ACHOO
YOU SHOULD BRING HIM TO THE ANIMAL HOSPITAL...
SERIOUSLY?! AGAIN?!
EVERYBODY SNEEZES!!
HE DOESN'T NEED TO GO TO THE HOSPITAL FOR EVERY LITTLE THING!
...
RYOHEI, WAIT...

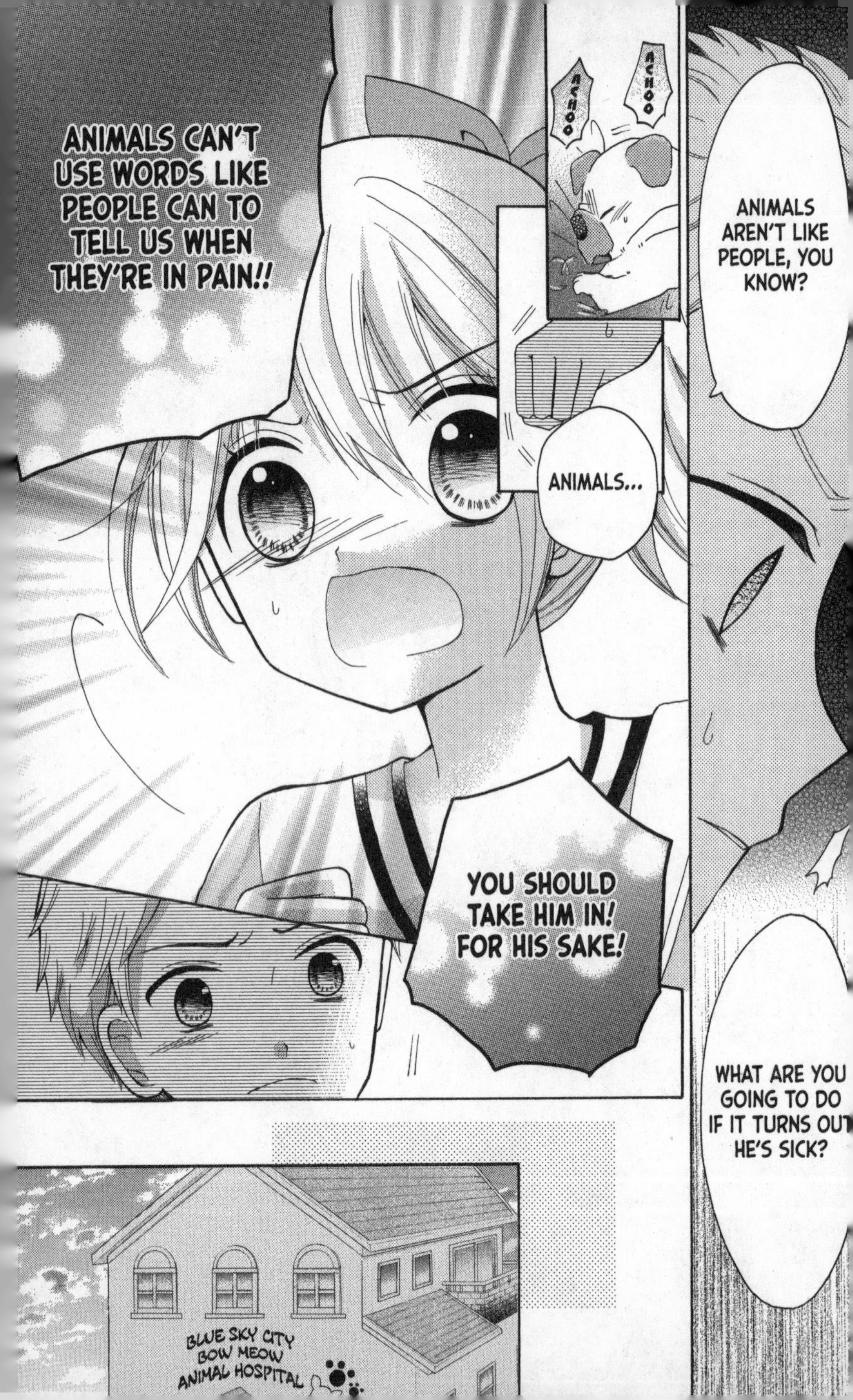
ANIMALS AREN'T LIKE PEOPLE, YOU KNOW?
WHAT ARE YOU GOING TO DO IF IT TURNS OUT HE'S SICK?
ACHOO
ACHOO
ANIMALS...
ANIMALS CAN'T USE WORDS LIKE PEOPLE CAN TO TELL US WHEN THEY'RE IN PAIN!!
YOU SHOULD TAKE HIM IN! FOR HIS SAKE!
BLUE SKY CITY BOW MEOW ANIMAL HOSPITAL

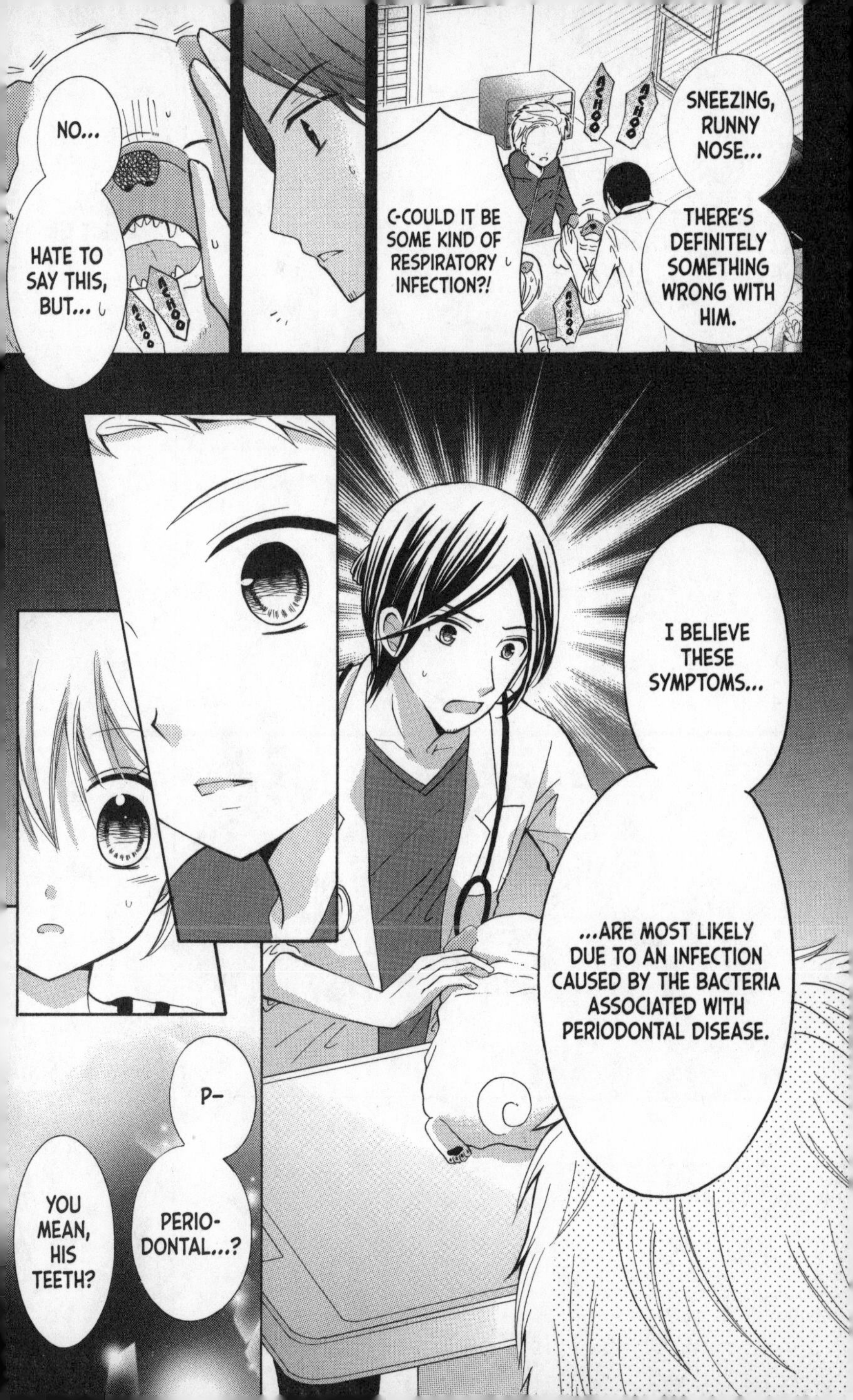
SNEEZING, RUNNY NOSE...
ACHOO
ACHOO
ACHOO
THERE'S DEFINITELY SOMETHING WRONG WITH HIM.
C-COULD IT BE SOME KIND OF RESPIRATORY INFECTION?!
NO...
HATE TO SAY THIS, BUT...
ACHOO
ACHOO
I BELIEVE THESE SYMPTOMS...
...ARE MOST LIKELY DUE TO AN INFECTION CAUSED BY THE BACTERIA ASSOCIATED WITH PERIODONTAL DISEASE.
P-
PERIO-DONTAL...?
YOU MEAN, HIS TEETH?

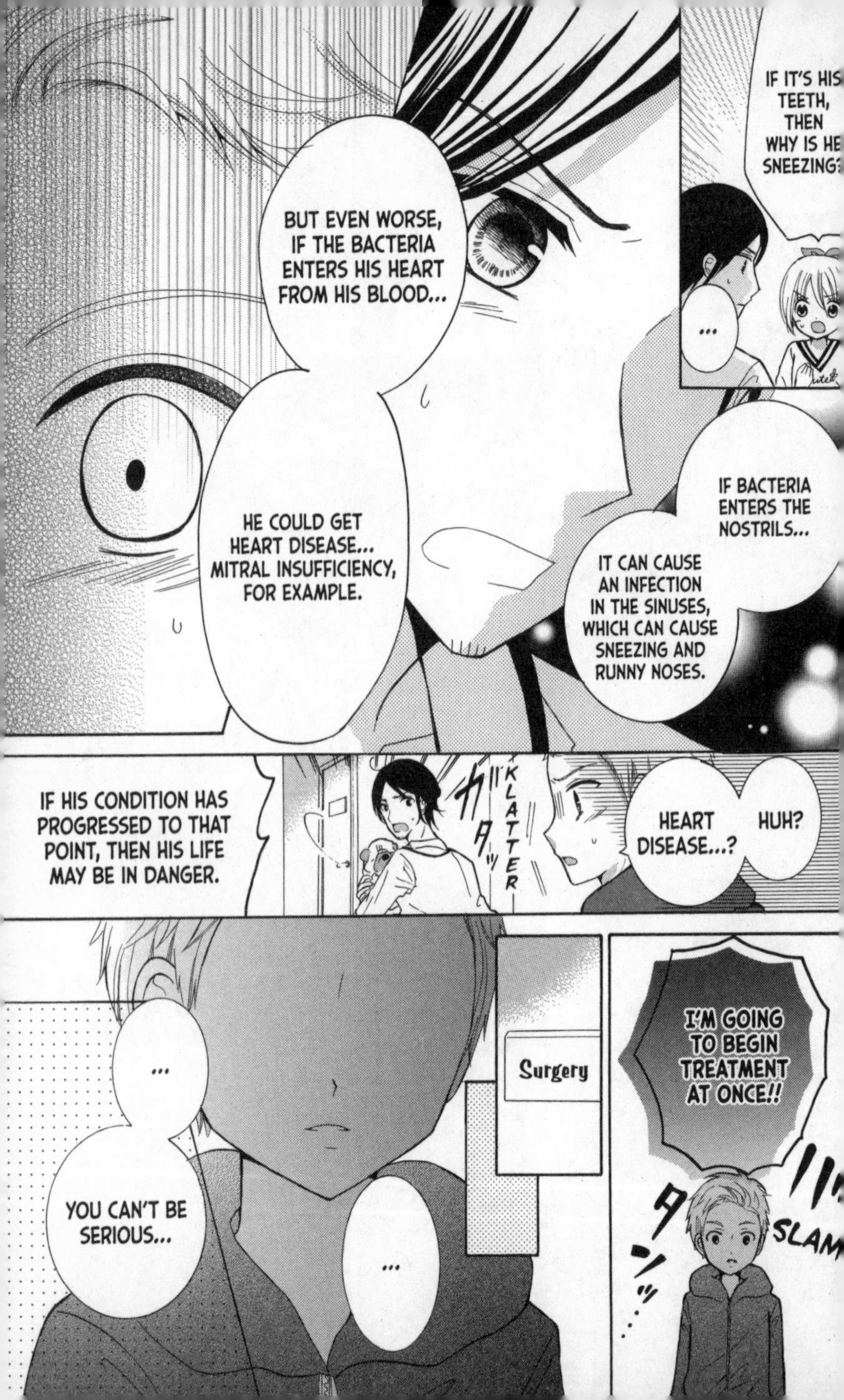
IF IT'S HIS TEETH, THEN WHY IS HE SNEEZING?
...
IF BACTERIA ENTERS THE NOSTRILS...
IT CAN CAUSE AN INFECTION IN THE SINUSES, WHICH CAN CAUSE SNEEZING AND RUNNY NOSES.
BUT EVEN WORSE, IF THE BACTERIA ENTERS HIS HEART FROM HIS BLOOD...
HE COULD GET HEART DISEASE... MITRAL INSUFFICIENCY, FOR EXAMPLE.
HUH?
HEART DISEASE...?
KLATTER
IF HIS CONDITION HAS PROGRESSED TO THAT POINT, THEN HIS LIFE MAY BE IN DANGER.
I'M GOING TO BEGIN TREATMENT AT ONCE!!
SLAM
Surgery
...
YOU CAN'T BE SERIOUS...
...

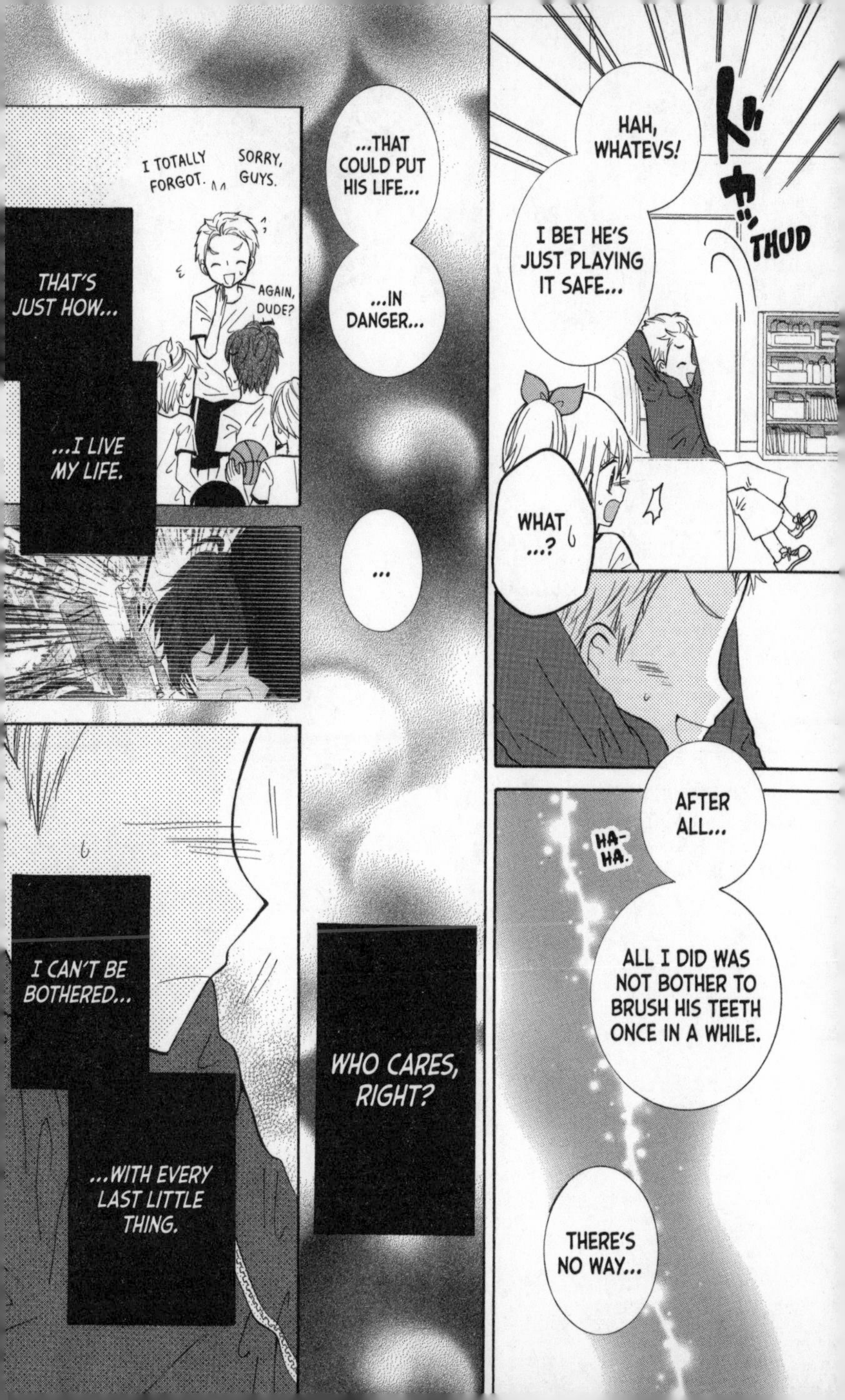
HAH, WHATEVS!
I BET HE'S JUST PLAYING IT SAFE...
THUD
WHAT ...?
AFTER ALL...
HA-HA.
ALL I DID WAS NOT BOTHER TO BRUSH HIS TEETH ONCE IN A WHILE.
THERE'S NO WAY...
...THAT COULD PUT HIS LIFE...
...IN DANGER...
SORRY, GUYS.
I TOTALLY FORGOT.
AGAIN, DUDE?
THAT'S JUST HOW...
...I LIVE MY LIFE.
...
WHO CARES, RIGHT?
I CAN'T BE BOTHERED...
...WITH EVERY LAST LITTLE THING.

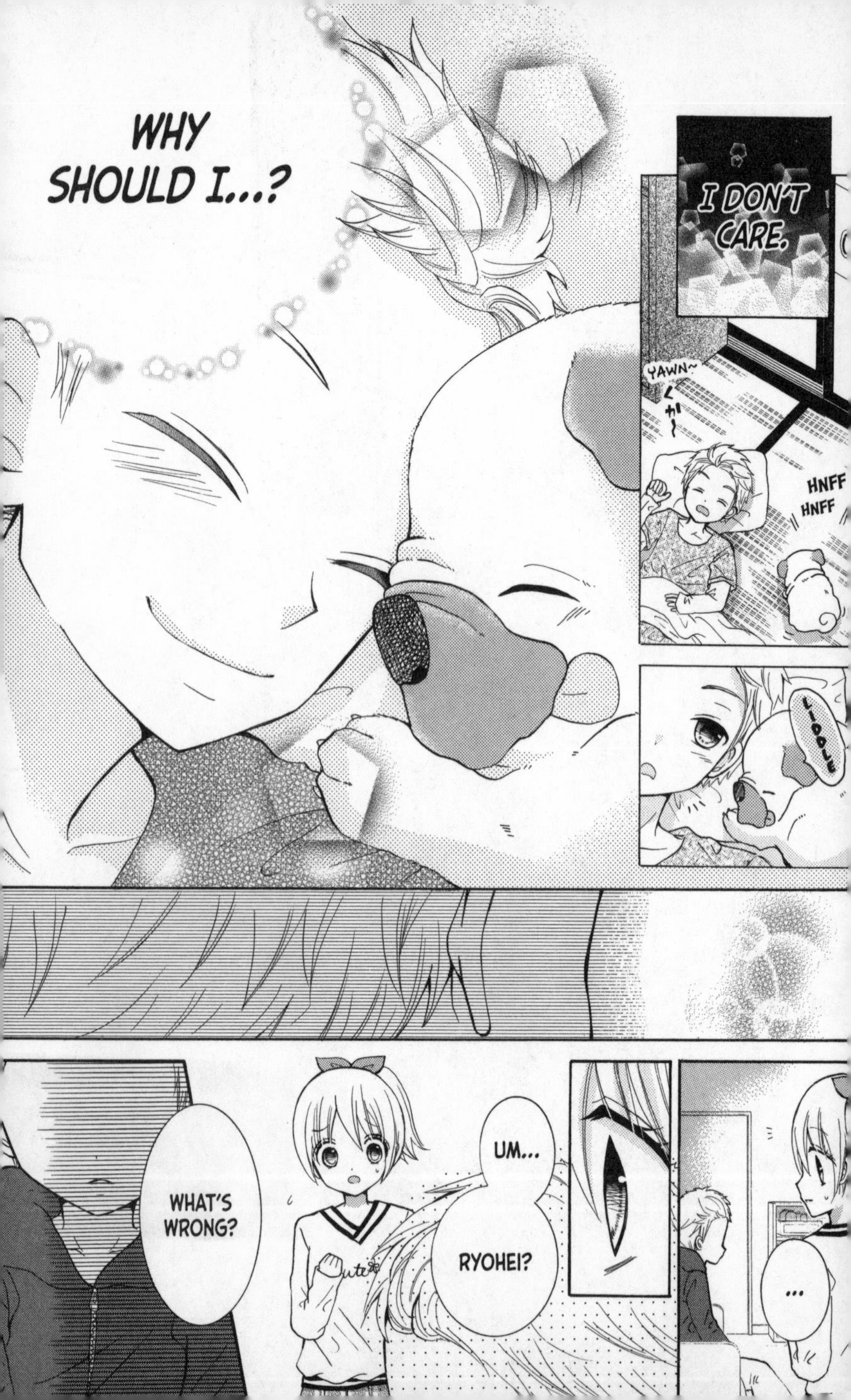
I DON'T CARE.
YAWN~
くか~
HNFF HNFF
LIDDLE
WHY SHOULD I...?
...
UM...
RYOHEI?
WHAT'S WRONG?

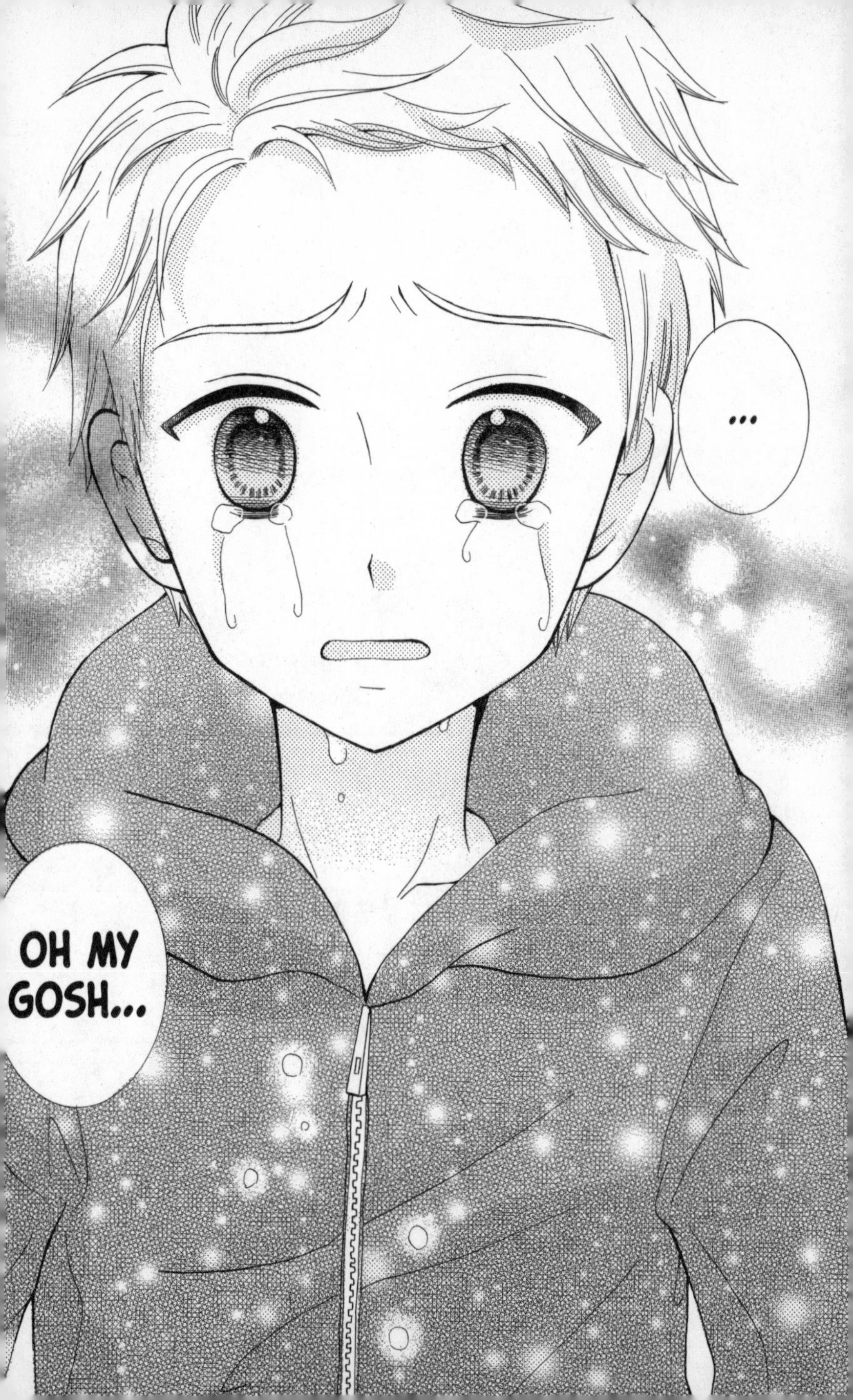
...
OH MY GOSH...

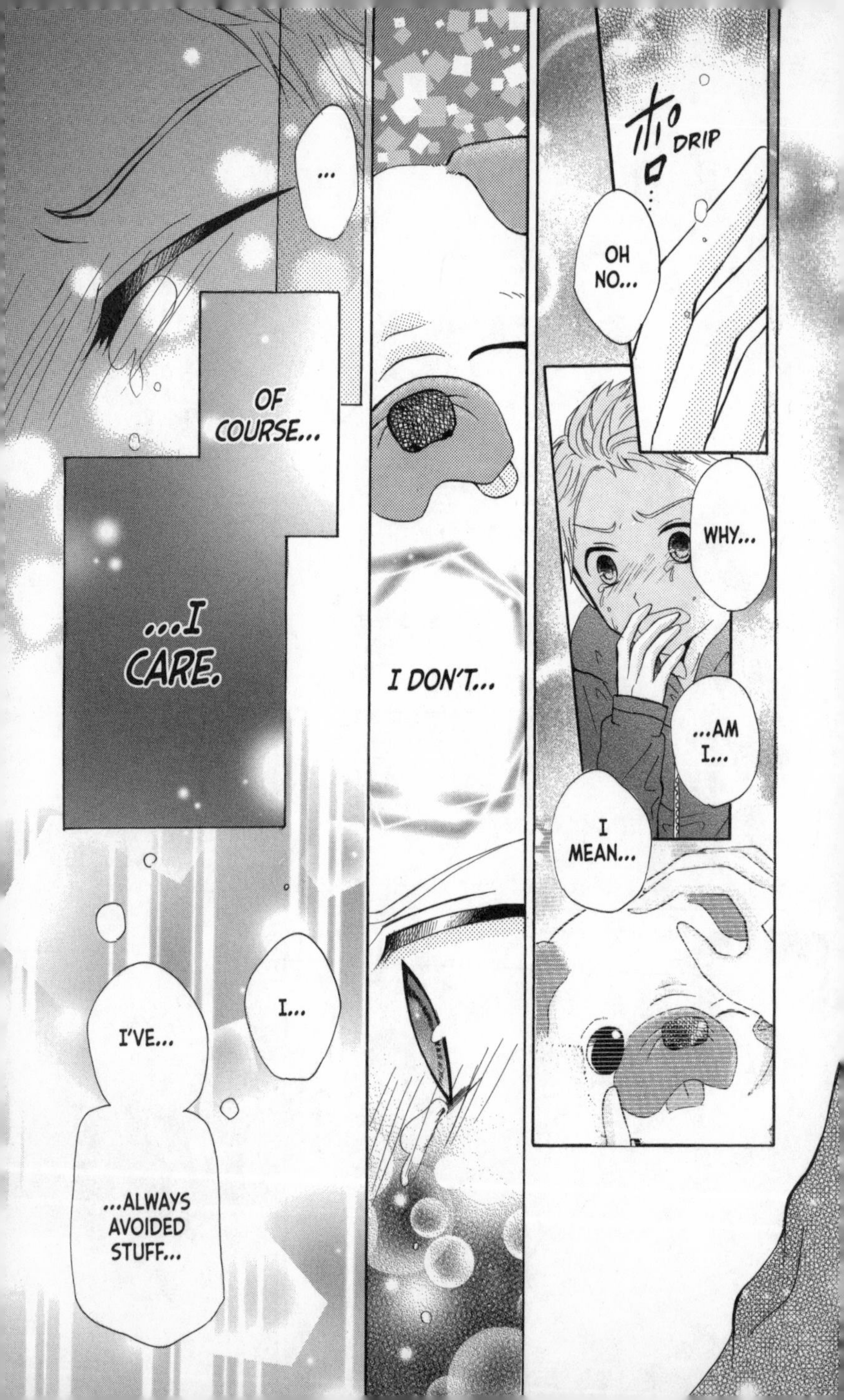
DRIP
OH NO...
WHY...
...AM I...
I MEAN...
I DON'T...
...
OF COURSE...
...I CARE.
I...
I'VE...
...ALWAYS AVOIDED STUFF...

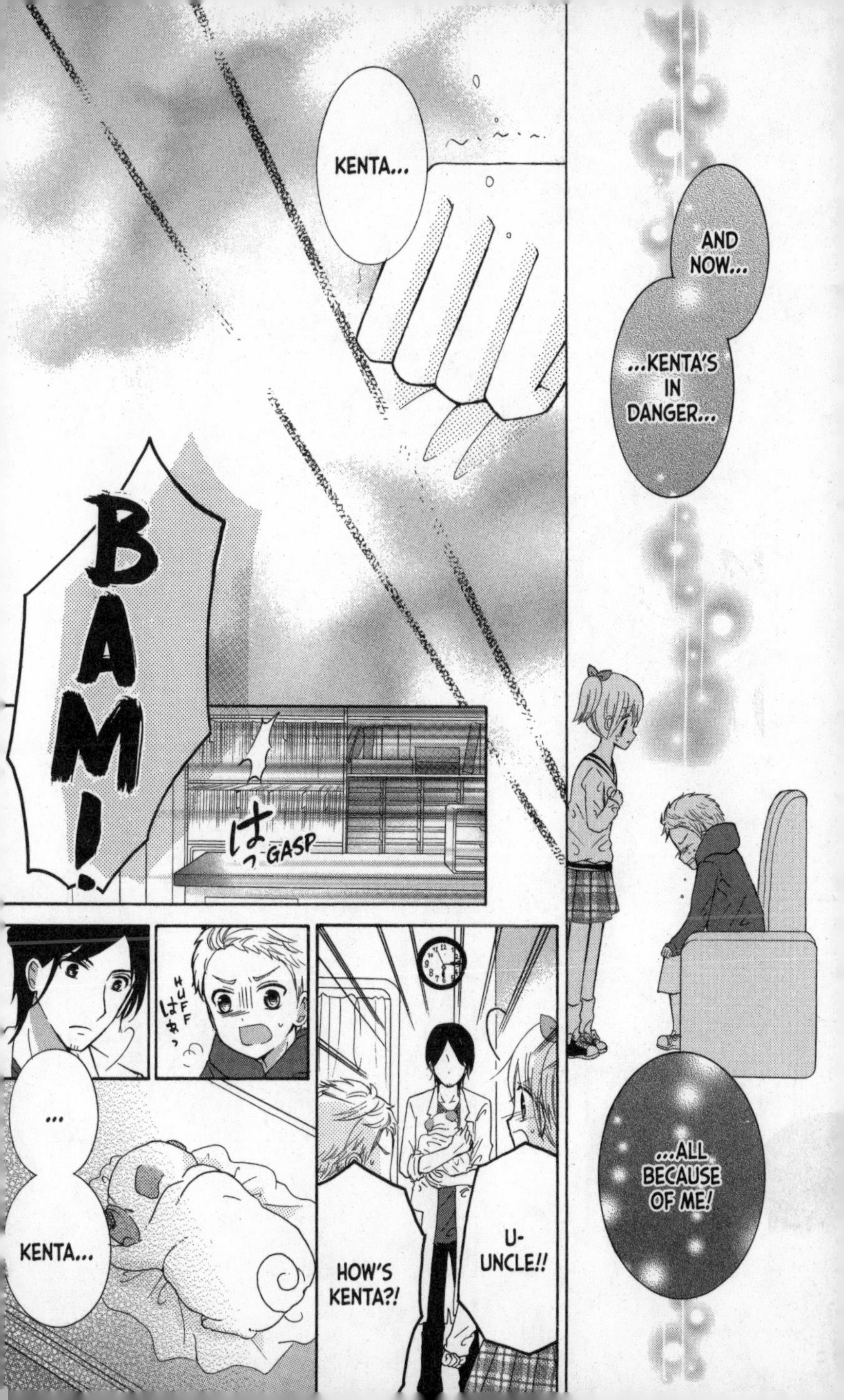
AND NOW...
...KENTA'S IN DANGER...
...ALL BECAUSE OF ME!
KENTA...
BAM!
はっ GASP
U- UNCLE!!
HOW'S KENTA?!
はぁっ HUFF
...
KENTA...

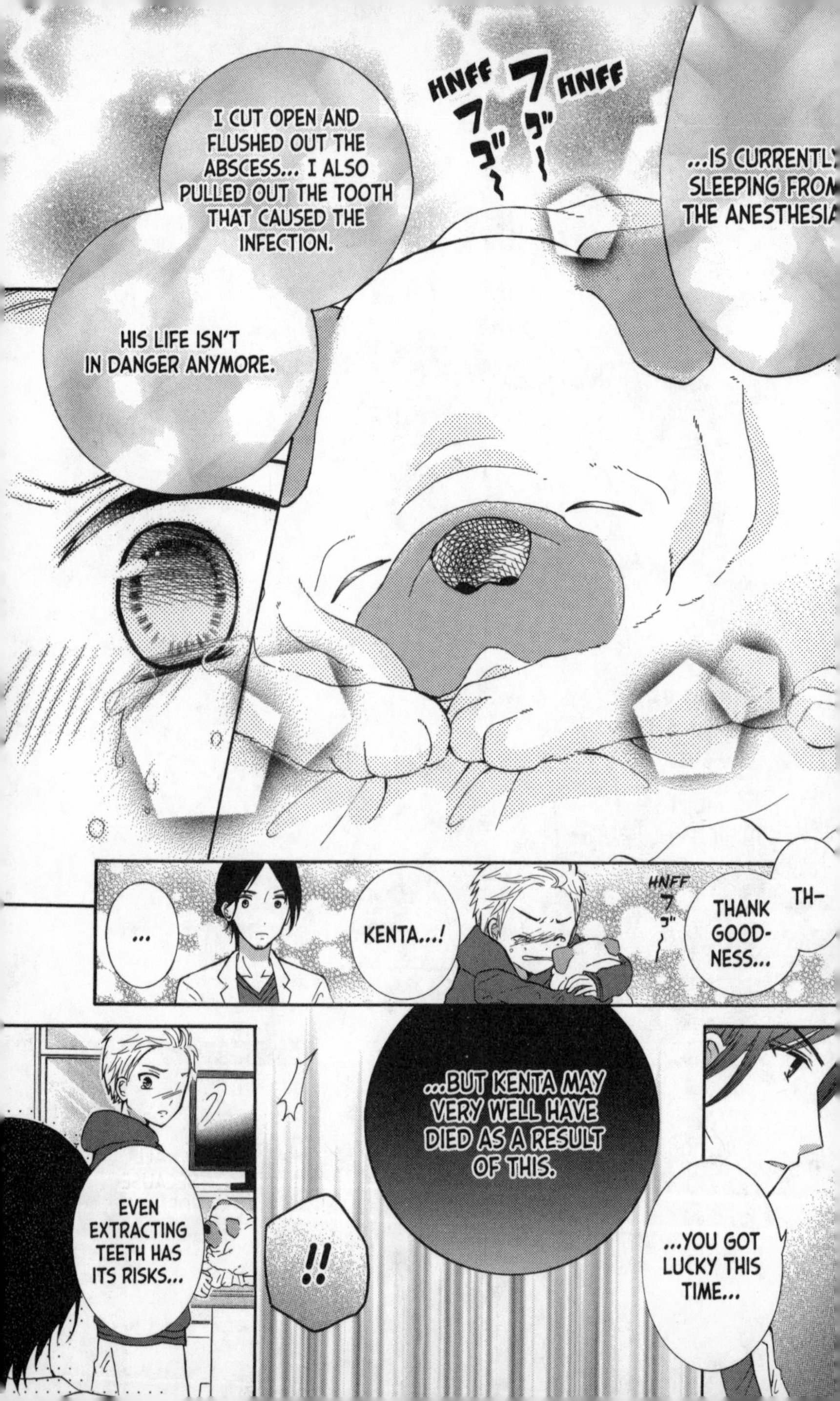
...IS CURRENTL SLEEPING FROM THE ANESTHESIA
HNFF
HNFF
I CUT OPEN AND FLUSHED OUT THE ABSCESS... I ALSO PULLED OUT THE TOOTH THAT CAUSED THE INFECTION.
HIS LIFE ISN'T IN DANGER ANYMORE.
TH-
THANK GOODNESS...
HNFF
KENTA...!
...
...YOU GOT LUCKY THIS TIME...
EVEN EXTRACTING TEETH HAS ITS RISKS...
...BUT KENTA MAY VERY WELL HAVE DIED AS A RESULT OF THIS.
!!

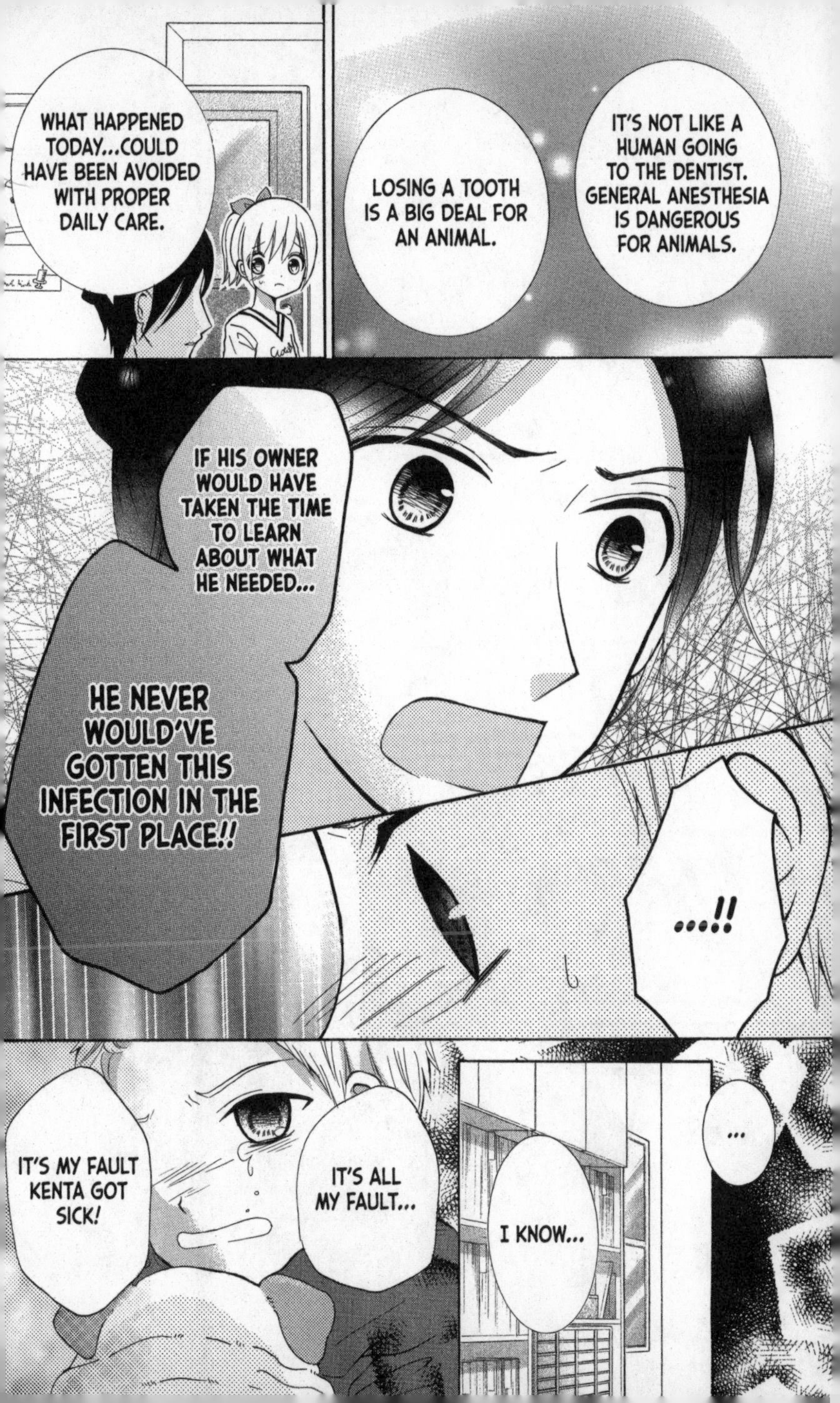
IT'S NOT LIKE A HUMAN GOING TO THE DENTIST. GENERAL ANESTHESIA IS DANGEROUS FOR ANIMALS.
LOSING A TOOTH IS A BIG DEAL FOR AN ANIMAL.
WHAT HAPPENED TODAY...COULD HAVE BEEN AVOIDED WITH PROPER DAILY CARE.
IF HIS OWNER WOULD HAVE TAKEN THE TIME TO LEARN ABOUT WHAT HE NEEDED...
HE NEVER WOULD'VE GOTTEN THIS INFECTION IN THE FIRST PLACE!!
...!!
...
I KNOW...
IT'S ALL MY FAULT...
IT'S MY FAULT KENTA GOT SICK!

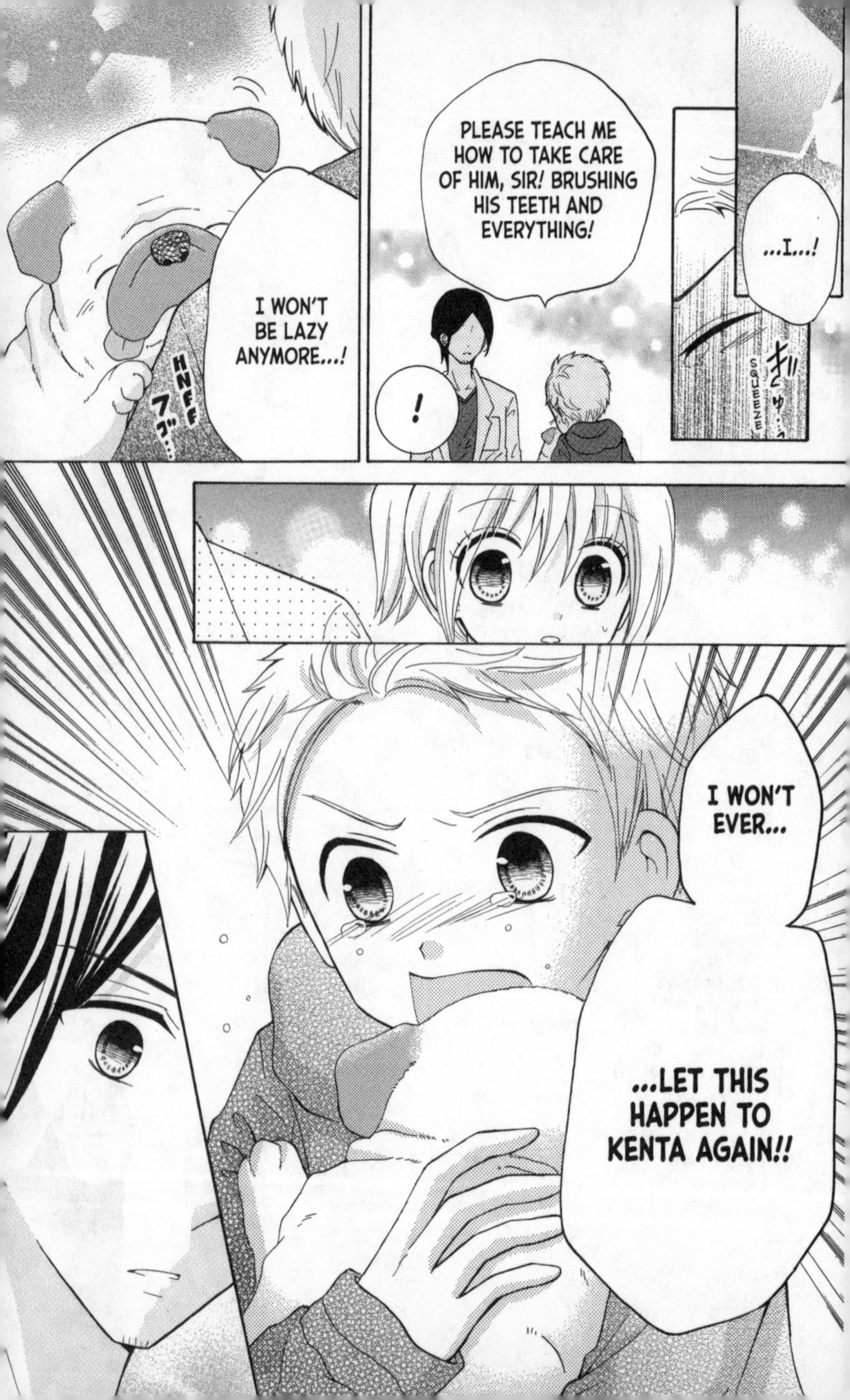
...I...!
SQUEEZE
ぎゅ…っ
PLEASE TEACH ME HOW TO TAKE CARE OF HIM, SIR! BRUSHING HIS TEETH AND EVERYTHING!
!
I WON'T BE LAZY ANYMORE...!
HNFF
フゴ…
I WON'T EVER...
...LET THIS HAPPEN TO KENTA AGAIN!!

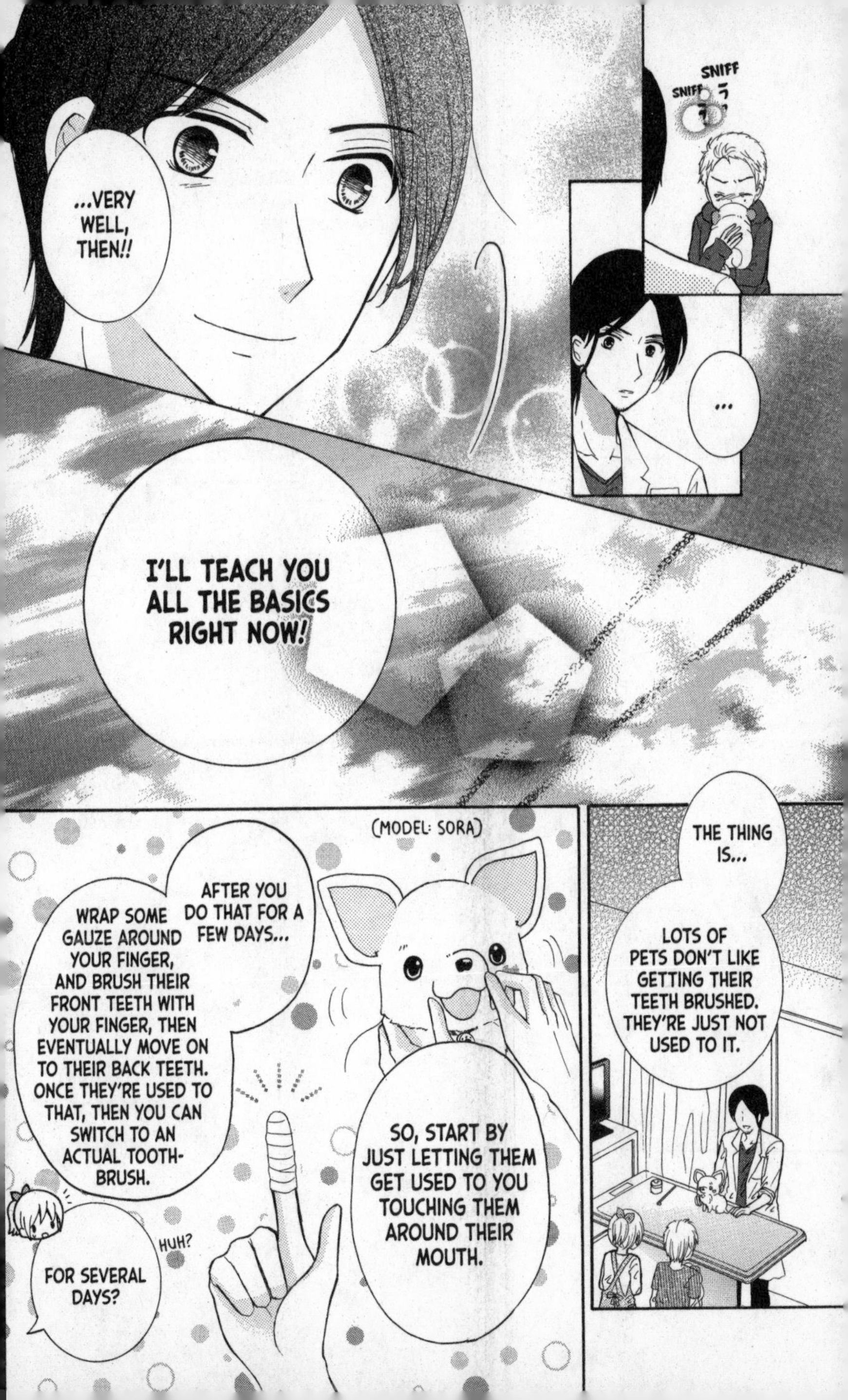
SNIFF
SNIFF
...
...VERY WELL, THEN!!
I'LL TEACH YOU ALL THE BASICS RIGHT NOW!
THE THING IS...
LOTS OF PETS DON'T LIKE GETTING THEIR TEETH BRUSHED. THEY'RE JUST NOT USED TO IT.
(MODEL: SORA)
SO, START BY JUST LETTING THEM GET USED TO YOU TOUCHING THEM AROUND THEIR MOUTH.
AFTER YOU DO THAT FOR A FEW DAYS...
WRAP SOME GAUZE AROUND YOUR FINGER, AND BRUSH THEIR FRONT TEETH WITH YOUR FINGER, THEN EVENTUALLY MOVE ON TO THEIR BACK TEETH. ONCE THEY'RE USED TO THAT, THEN YOU CAN SWITCH TO AN ACTUAL TOOTH-BRUSH.
HUH?
FOR SEVERAL DAYS?

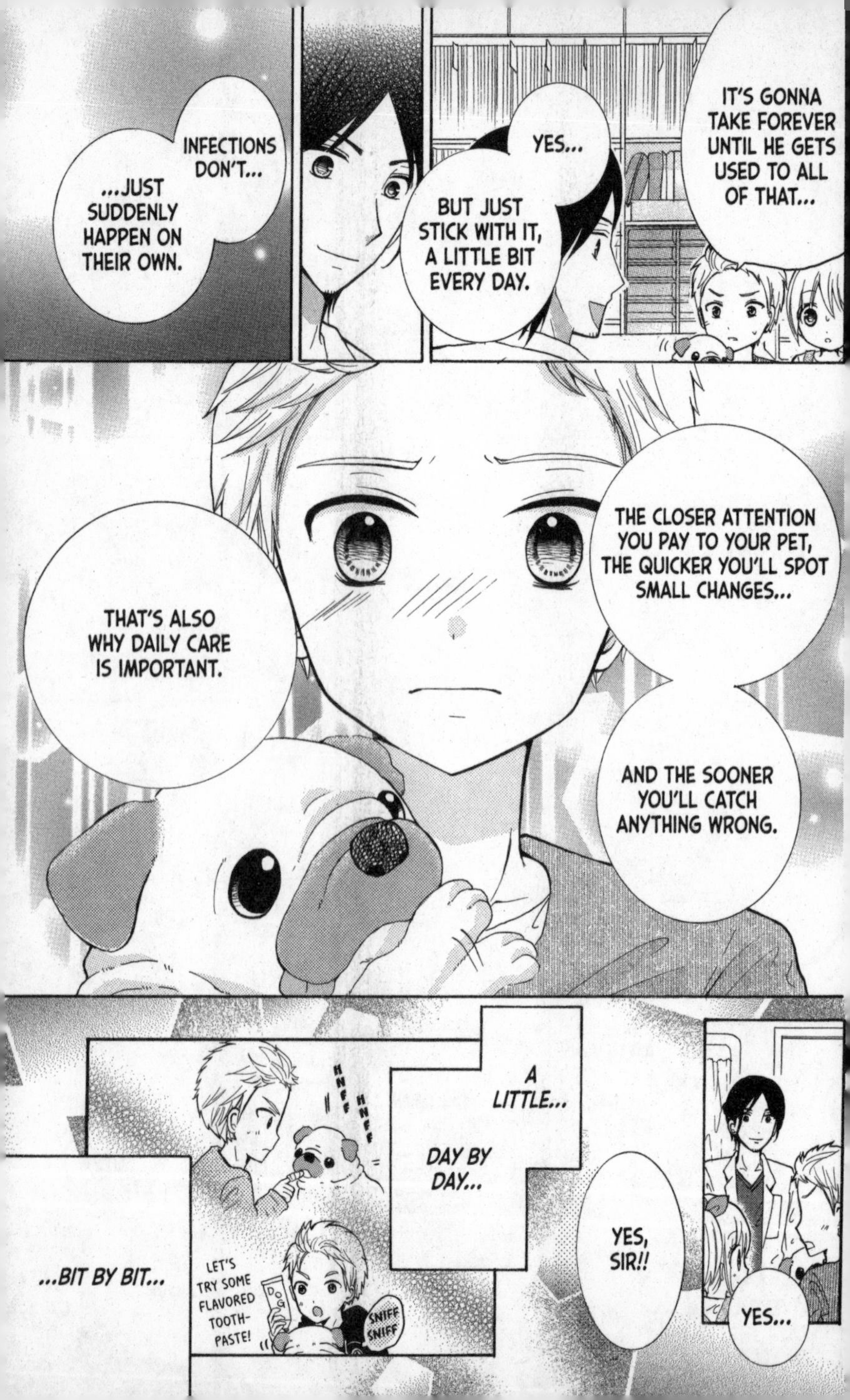
IT'S GONNA TAKE FOREVER UNTIL HE GETS USED TO ALL OF THAT...
YES...
BUT JUST STICK WITH IT, A LITTLE BIT EVERY DAY.
INFECTIONS DON'T...
...JUST SUDDENLY HAPPEN ON THEIR OWN.
THE CLOSER ATTENTION YOU PAY TO YOUR PET, THE QUICKER YOU'LL SPOT SMALL CHANGES...
AND THE SOONER YOU'LL CATCH ANYTHING WRONG.
THAT'S ALSO WHY DAILY CARE IS IMPORTANT.
YES, SIR!!
YES...
A LITTLE...
DAY BY DAY...
HNFF HNFF
...BIT BY BIT...
LET'S TRY SOME FLAVORED TOOTH-PASTE!
DOG
SNIFF SNIFF

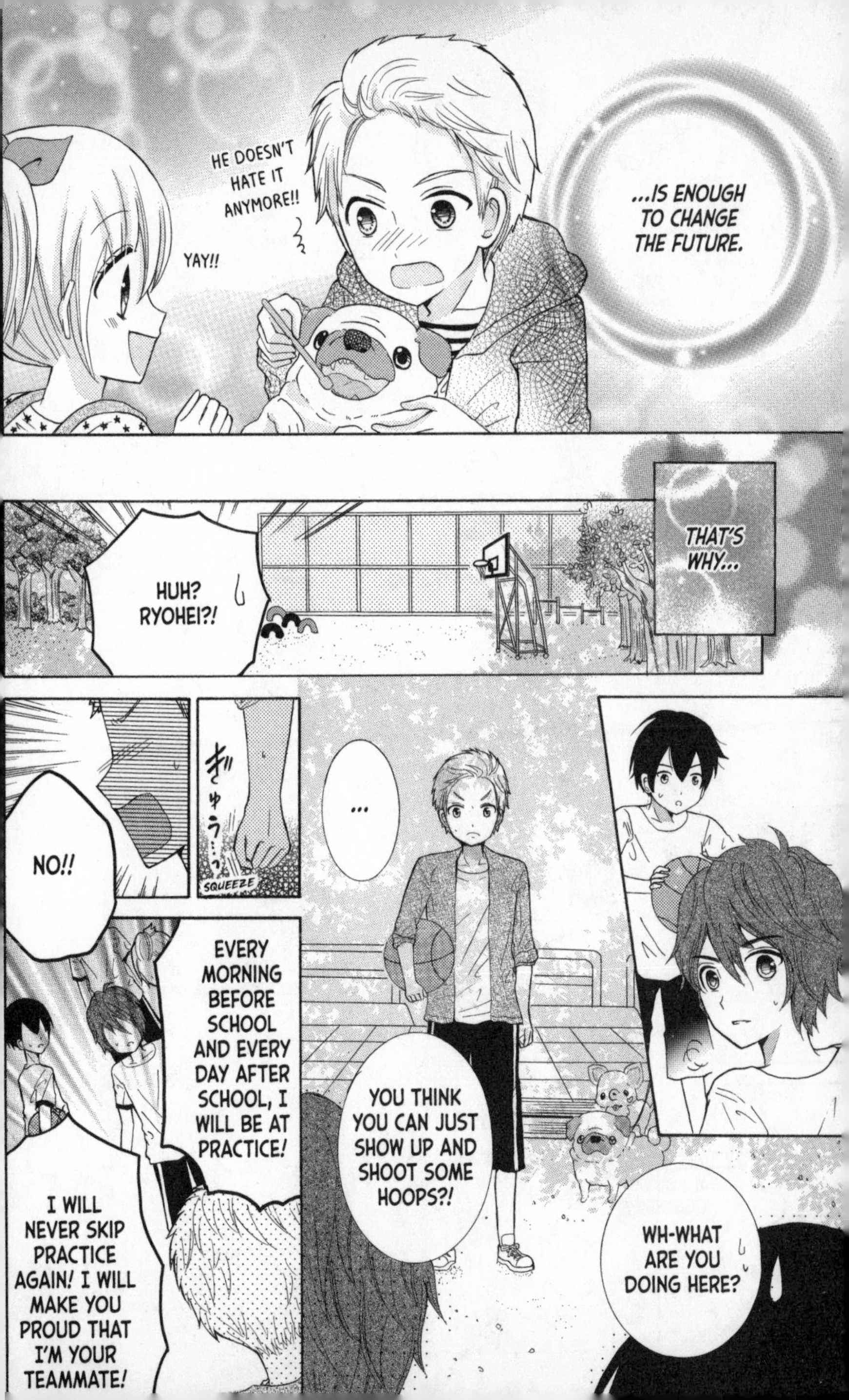

...IS ENOUGH TO CHANGE THE FUTURE.
HE DOESN'T HATE IT ANYMORE!!
YAY!!
THAT'S WHY...
HUH? RYOHEI?!
WH-WHAT ARE YOU DOING HERE?
...
YOU THINK YOU CAN JUST SHOW UP AND SHOOT SOME HOOPS?!
ぎゅう…っ
SQUEEZE
NO!!
EVERY MORNING BEFORE SCHOOL AND EVERY DAY AFTER SCHOOL, I WILL BE AT PRACTICE!
I WILL NEVER SKIP PRACTICE AGAIN! I WILL MAKE YOU PROUD THAT I'M YOUR TEAMMATE!

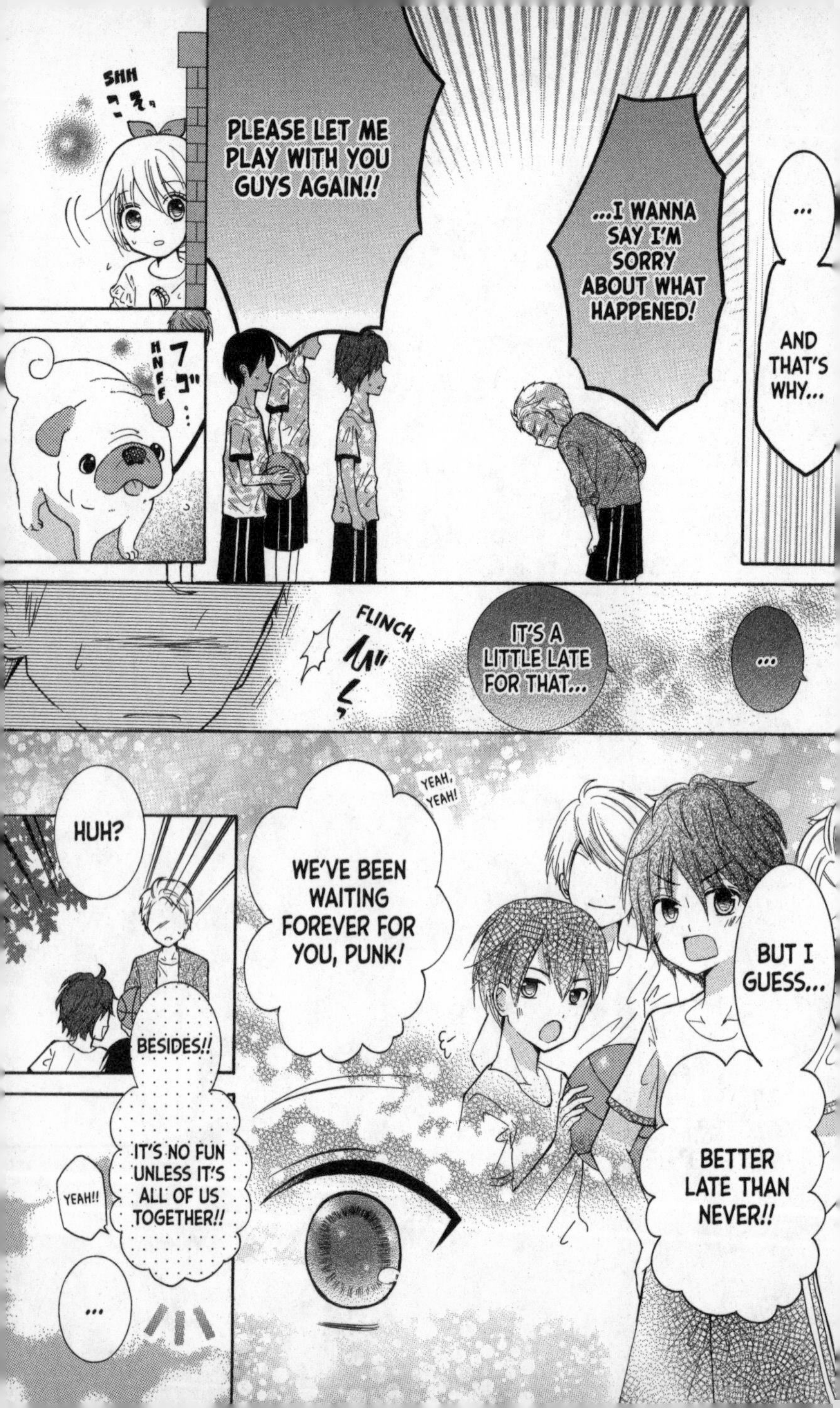
...
AND THAT'S WHY...
...I WANNA SAY I'M SORRY ABOUT WHAT HAPPENED!
PLEASE LET ME PLAY WITH YOU GUYS AGAIN!!
SHH
HNFF
...
IT'S A LITTLE LATE FOR THAT...
FLINCH
BUT I GUESS...
BETTER LATE THAN NEVER!!
YEAH, YEAH!
WE'VE BEEN WAITING FOREVER FOR YOU, PUNK!
HUH?
BESIDES!!
IT'S NO FUN UNLESS IT'S ALL OF US TOGETHER!!
YEAH!!
...

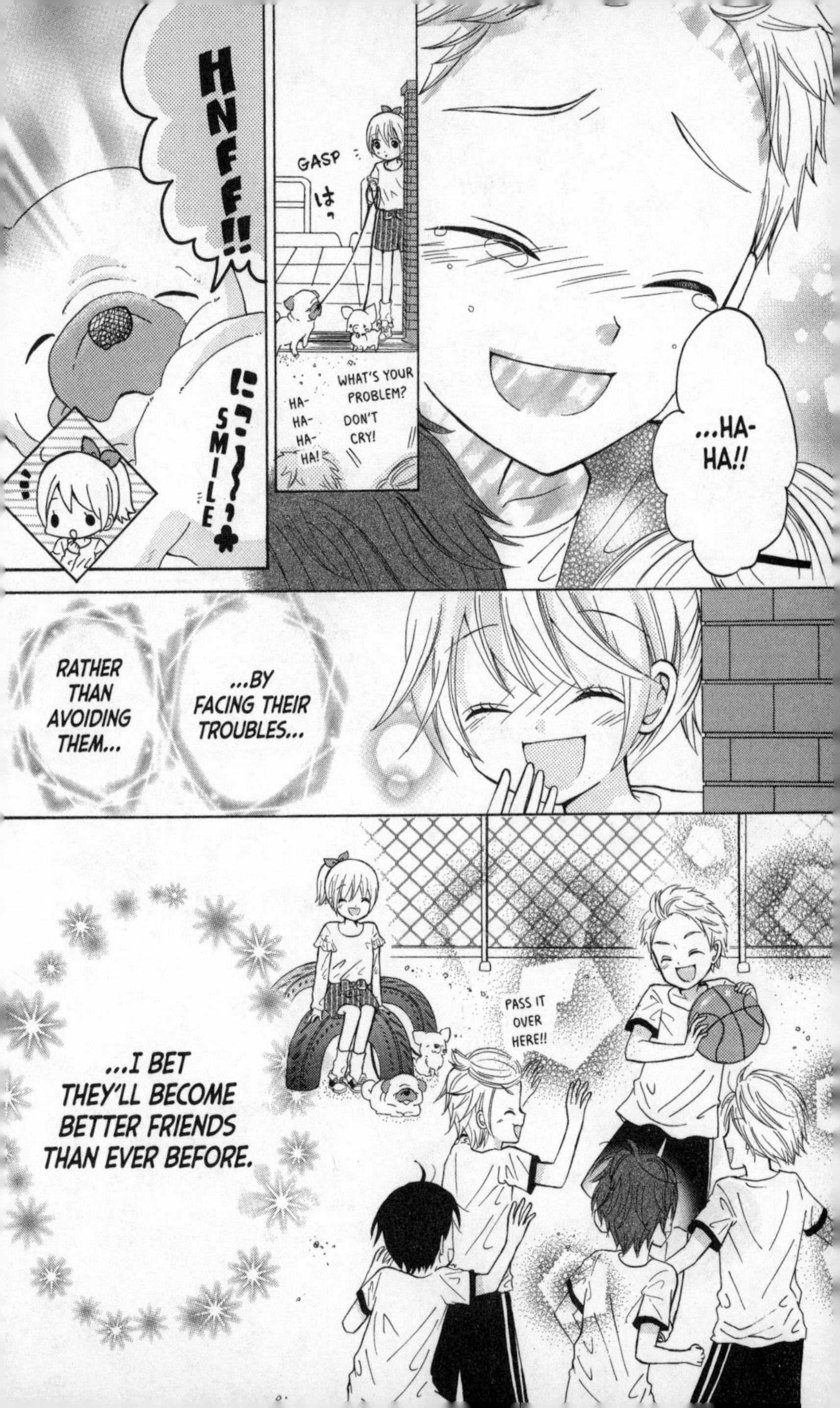
...HA-HA!!
GASP
は
WHAT'S YOUR PROBLEM? DON'T CRY!
HA-HA-HA-HA!
HNFF!!
にこ~
SMILE
...BY FACING THEIR TROUBLES...
RATHER THAN AVOIDING THEM...
PASS IT OVER HERE!!
...I BET THEY'LL BECOME BETTER FRIENDS THAN EVER BEFORE.

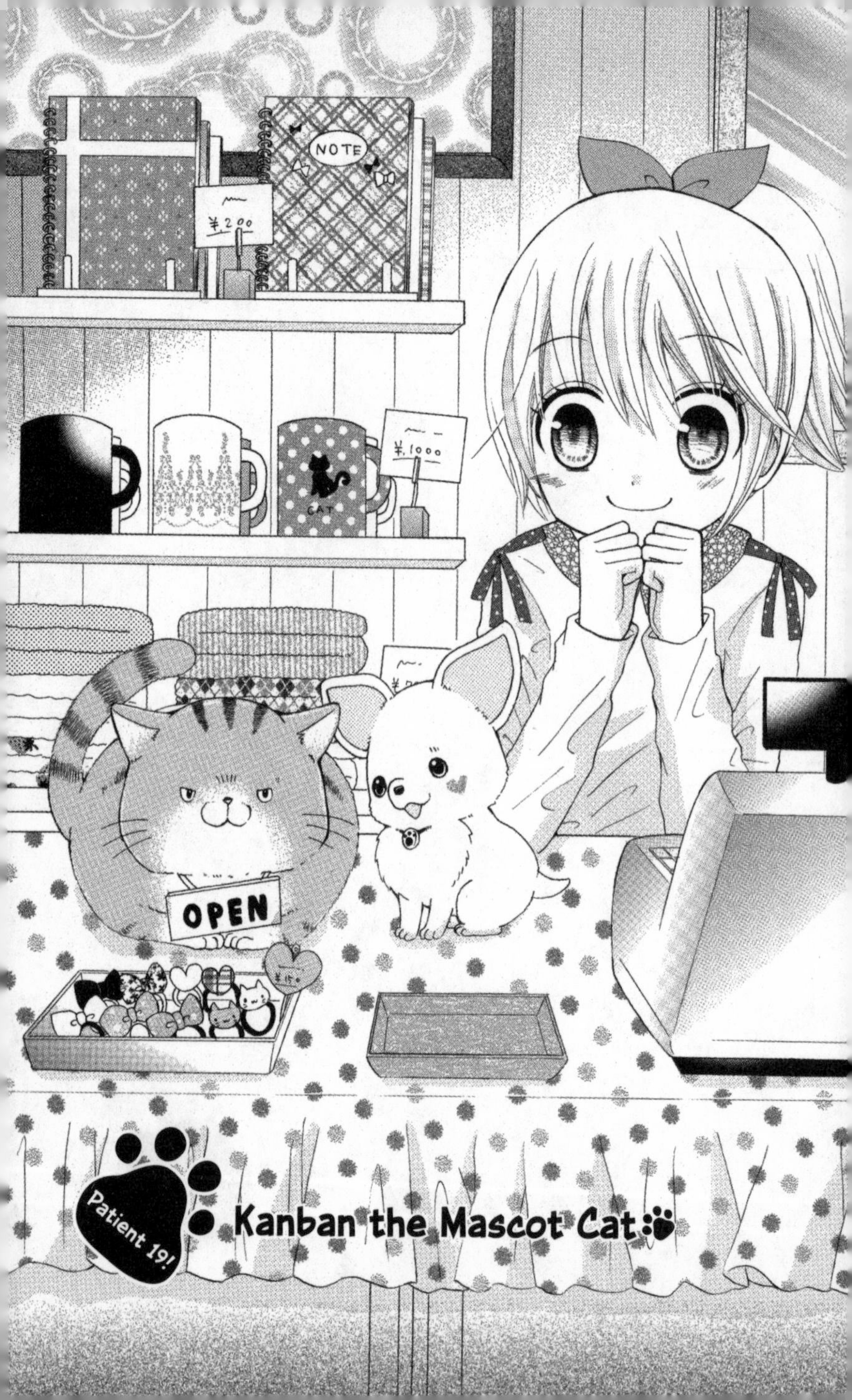
NOTE
¥200
¥1000
CAT
OPEN
Patient 19!
Kanban the Mascot Cat

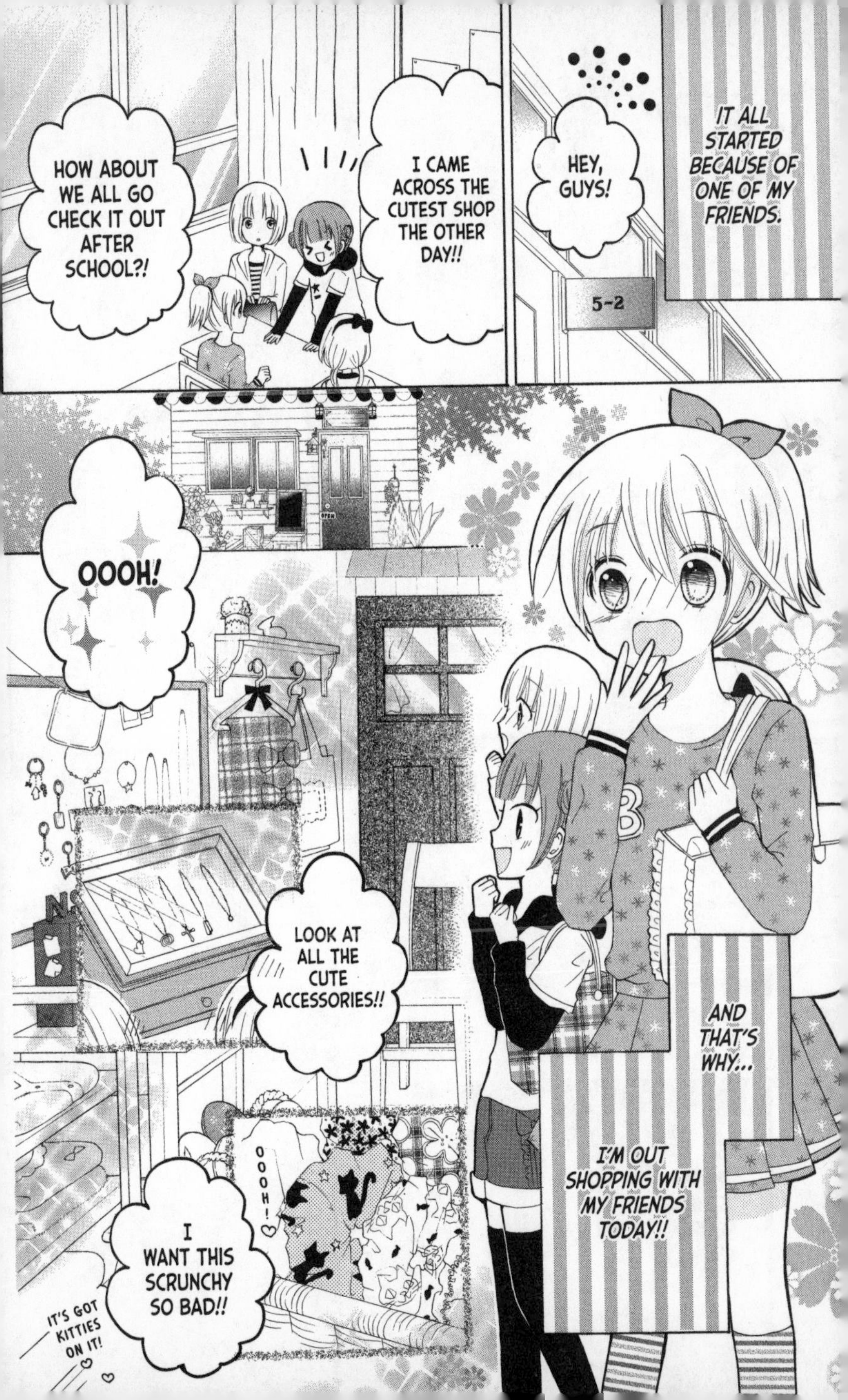
IT ALL STARTED BECAUSE OF ONE OF MY FRIENDS.
HEY, GUYS!
5-2
I CAME ACROSS THE CUTEST SHOP THE OTHER DAY!!
HOW ABOUT WE ALL GO CHECK IT OUT AFTER SCHOOL?!
AND THAT'S WHY...
I'M OUT SHOPPING WITH MY FRIENDS TODAY!!
OPEN
OOOH!
LOOK AT ALL THE CUTE ACCESSORIES!!
OOOH!
I WANT THIS SCRUNCHY SO BAD!!
IT'S GOT KITTIES ON IT!

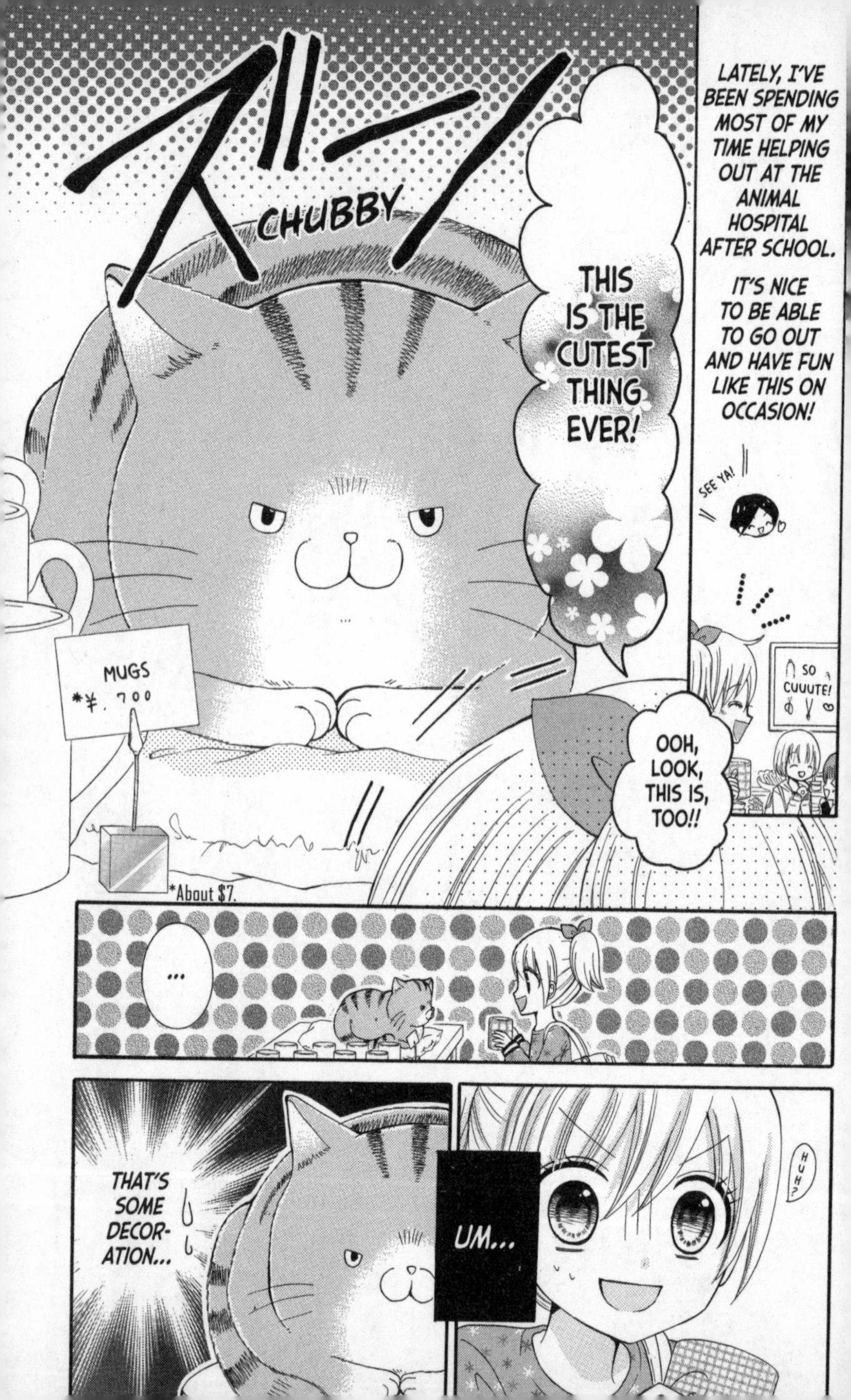

LATELY, I'VE BEEN SPENDING MOST OF MY TIME HELPING OUT AT THE ANIMAL HOSPITAL AFTER SCHOOL.
IT'S NICE TO BE ABLE TO GO OUT AND HAVE FUN LIKE THIS ON OCCASION!
SEE YA!
SO CUUUTE!
CHUBBY
THIS IS THE CUTEST THING EVER!
OOH, LOOK, THIS IS, TOO!!
MUGS
*¥. 700
*About $7.
...
UM...
HUH?
THAT'S SOME DECORATION...

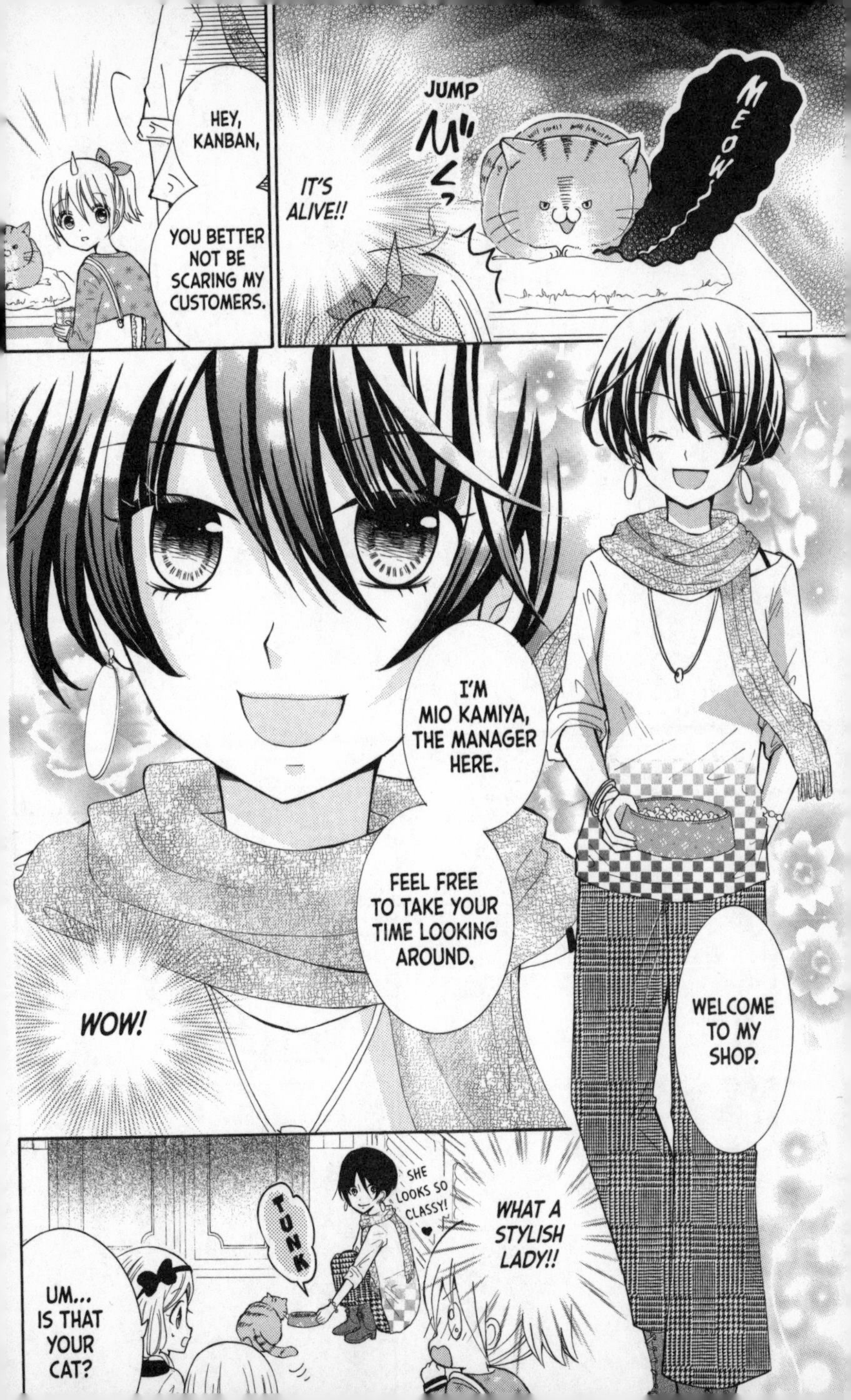
MEOW
JUMP
IT'S ALIVE!!
HEY, KANBAN,
YOU BETTER NOT BE SCARING MY CUSTOMERS.
WELCOME TO MY SHOP.
I'M MIO KAMIYA, THE MANAGER HERE.
FEEL FREE TO TAKE YOUR TIME LOOKING AROUND.
WOW!
WHAT A STYLISH LADY!!
SHE LOOKS SO CLASSY!
TUNK
UM... IS THAT YOUR CAT?

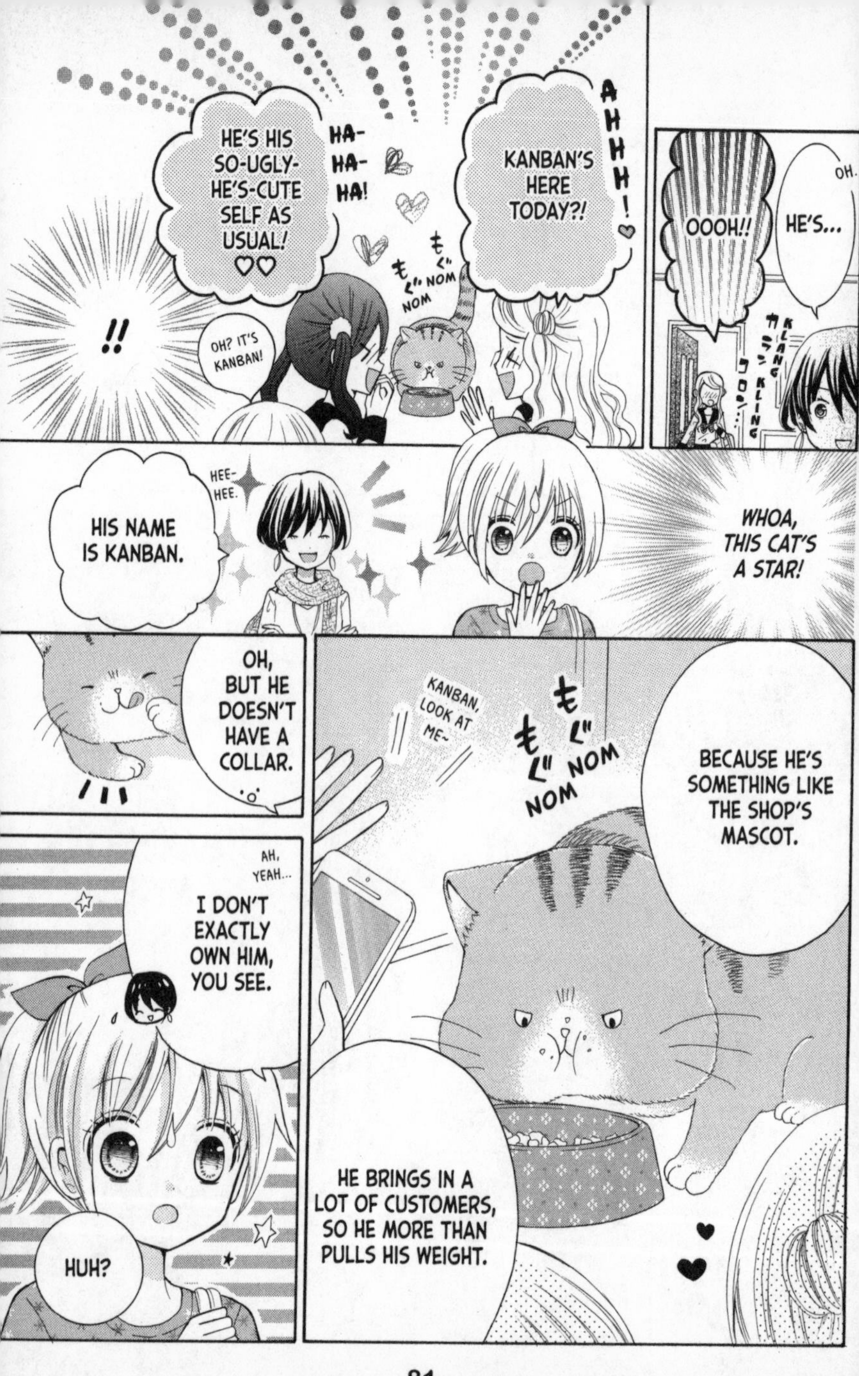
OH. HE'S...
OOOH!!
KLING KLANG KLING
AHHHH!
KANBAN'S HERE TODAY?!
HA-HA-HA!
HE'S HIS SO-UGLY-HE'S-CUTE SELF AS USUAL! ♡♡
NOM NOM
OH? IT'S KANBAN!
!!
WHOA, THIS CAT'S A STAR!
HEE-HEE.
HIS NAME IS KANBAN.
BECAUSE HE'S SOMETHING LIKE THE SHOP'S MASCOT.
NOM NOM
KANBAN, LOOK AT ME~
HE BRINGS IN A LOT OF CUSTOMERS, SO HE MORE THAN PULLS HIS WEIGHT.
OH, BUT HE DOESN'T HAVE A COLLAR.
AH, YEAH...
I DON'T EXACTLY OWN HIM, YOU SEE.
HUH?

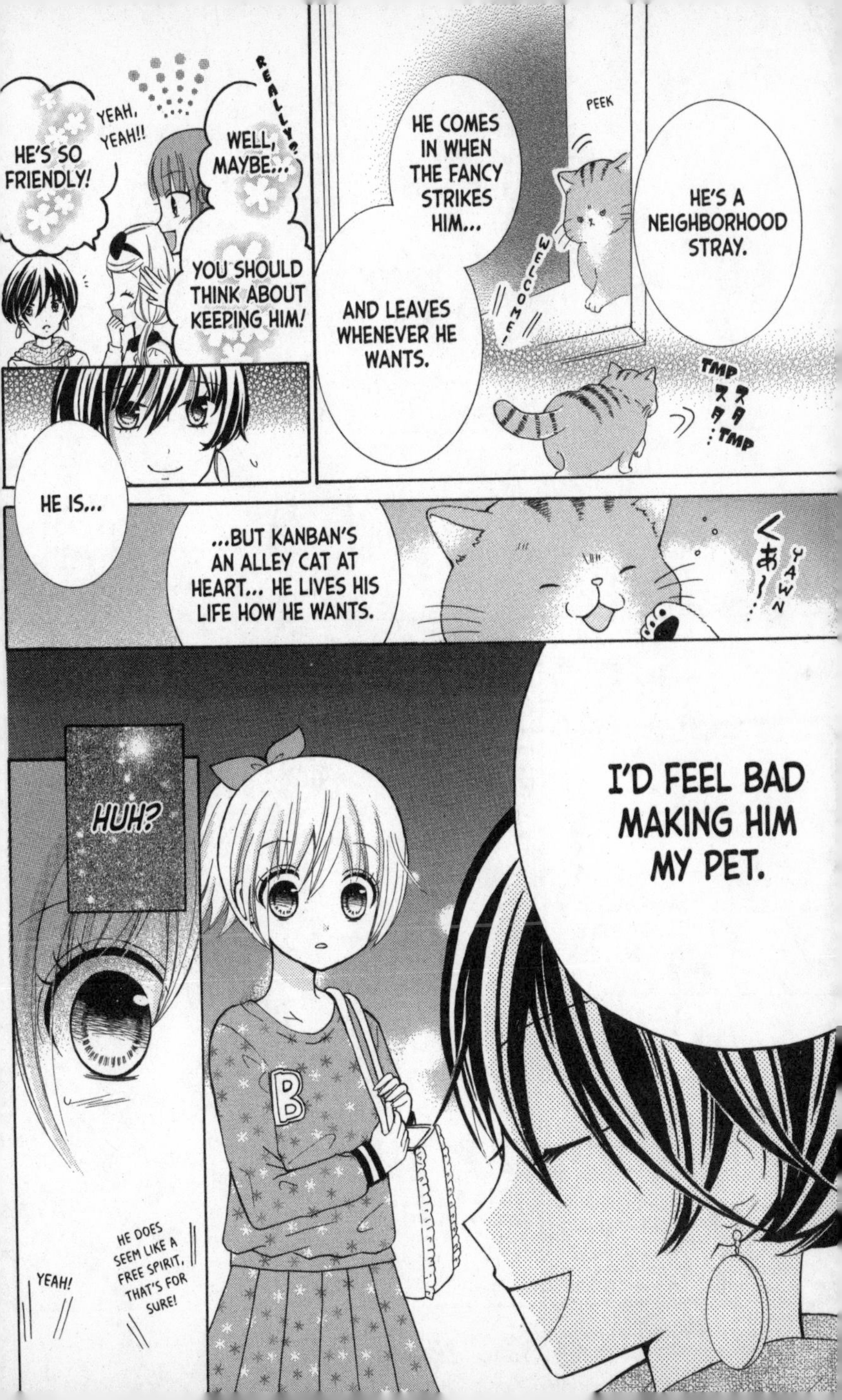
PEEK
HE'S A NEIGHBORHOOD STRAY.
WELCOME!
HE COMES IN WHEN THE FANCY STRIKES HIM...
AND LEAVES WHENEVER HE WANTS.
TMP スタ スタ TMP
REALLY?
WELL, MAYBE...
YEAH, YEAH!!
HE'S SO FRIENDLY!
YOU SHOULD THINK ABOUT KEEPING HIM!
HE IS...
...BUT KANBAN'S AN ALLEY CAT AT HEART... HE LIVES HIS LIFE HOW HE WANTS.
くあ~ YAWN...
I'D FEEL BAD MAKING HIM MY PET.
HUH?
HE DOES SEEM LIKE A FREE SPIRIT, THAT'S FOR SURE!
YEAH!

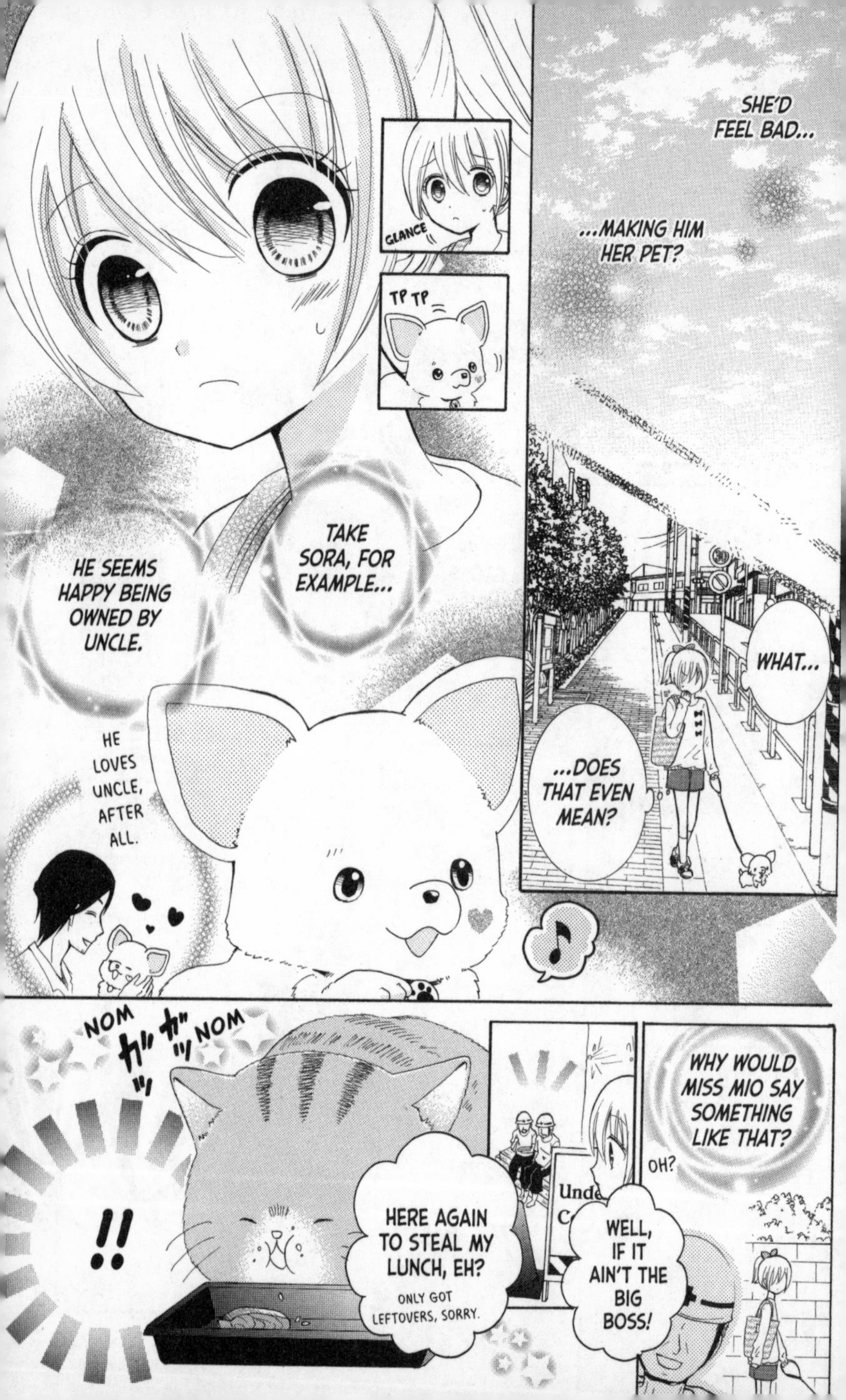
SHE'D FEEL BAD...
...MAKING HIM HER PET?
WHAT...
...DOES THAT EVEN MEAN?
GLANCE
TP TP
TAKE SORA, FOR EXAMPLE...
HE SEEMS HAPPY BEING OWNED BY UNCLE.
HE LOVES UNCLE, AFTER ALL.
WHY WOULD MISS MIO SAY SOMETHING LIKE THAT?
OH?
WELL, IF IT AIN'T THE BIG BOSS!
HERE AGAIN TO STEAL MY LUNCH, EH?
ONLY GOT LEFTOVERS, SORRY.
NOM ガツガツ NOM
!!

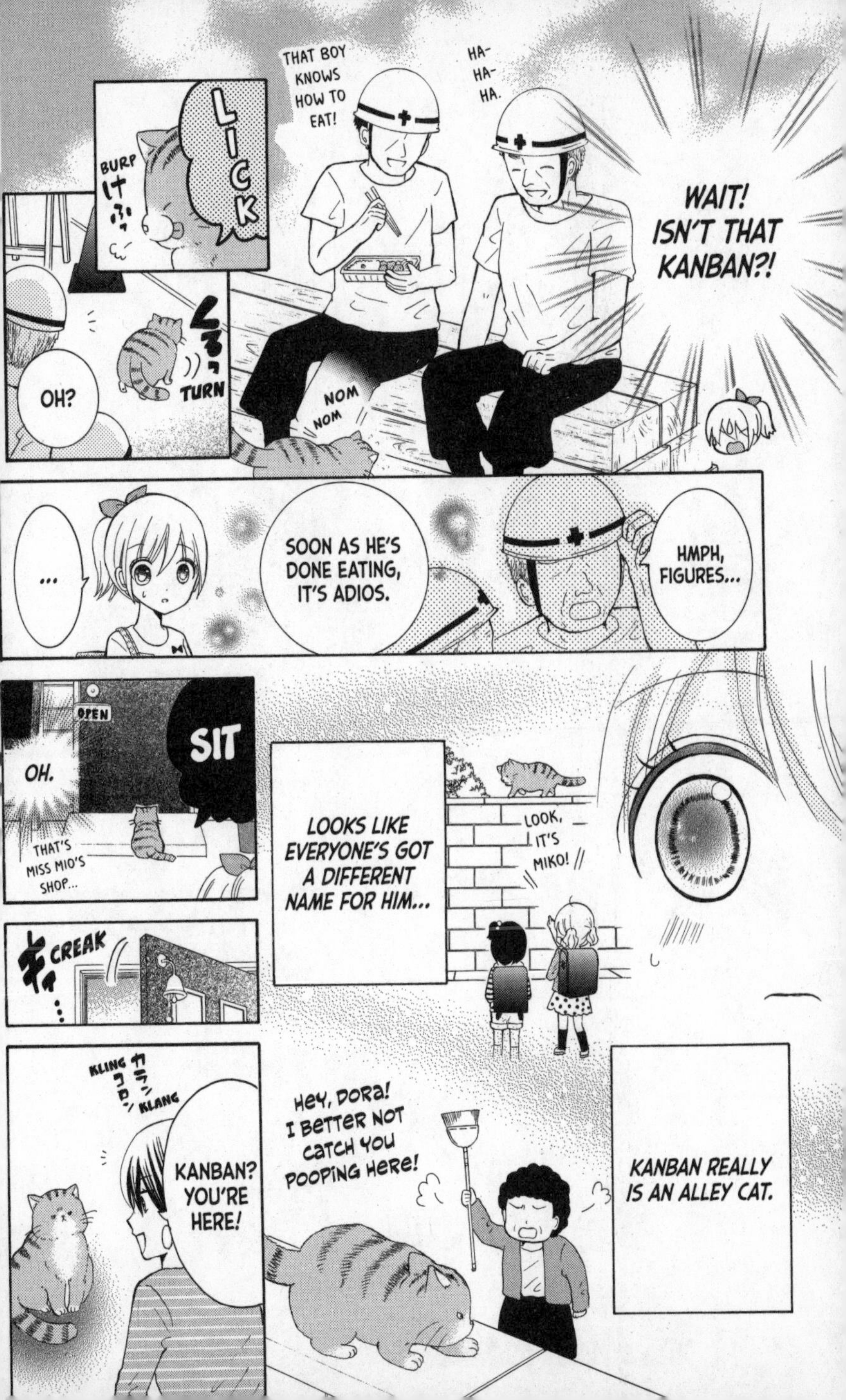
WAIT! ISN'T THAT KANBAN?!
HA-HA-HA.
THAT BOY KNOWS HOW TO EAT!
NOM NOM
LICK
BURP
OH?
TURN
HMPH, FIGURES...
SOON AS HE'S DONE EATING, IT'S ADIOS.
...
LOOK, IT'S MIKO!
LOOKS LIKE EVERYONE'S GOT A DIFFERENT NAME FOR HIM...
SIT
OPEN
OH.
THAT'S MISS MIO'S SHOP...
CREAK
KANBAN REALLY IS AN ALLEY CAT.
Hey, DORA! I BETTER NOT CATCH YOU POOPING HERE!
KANBAN? YOU'RE HERE!
KLING KLANG

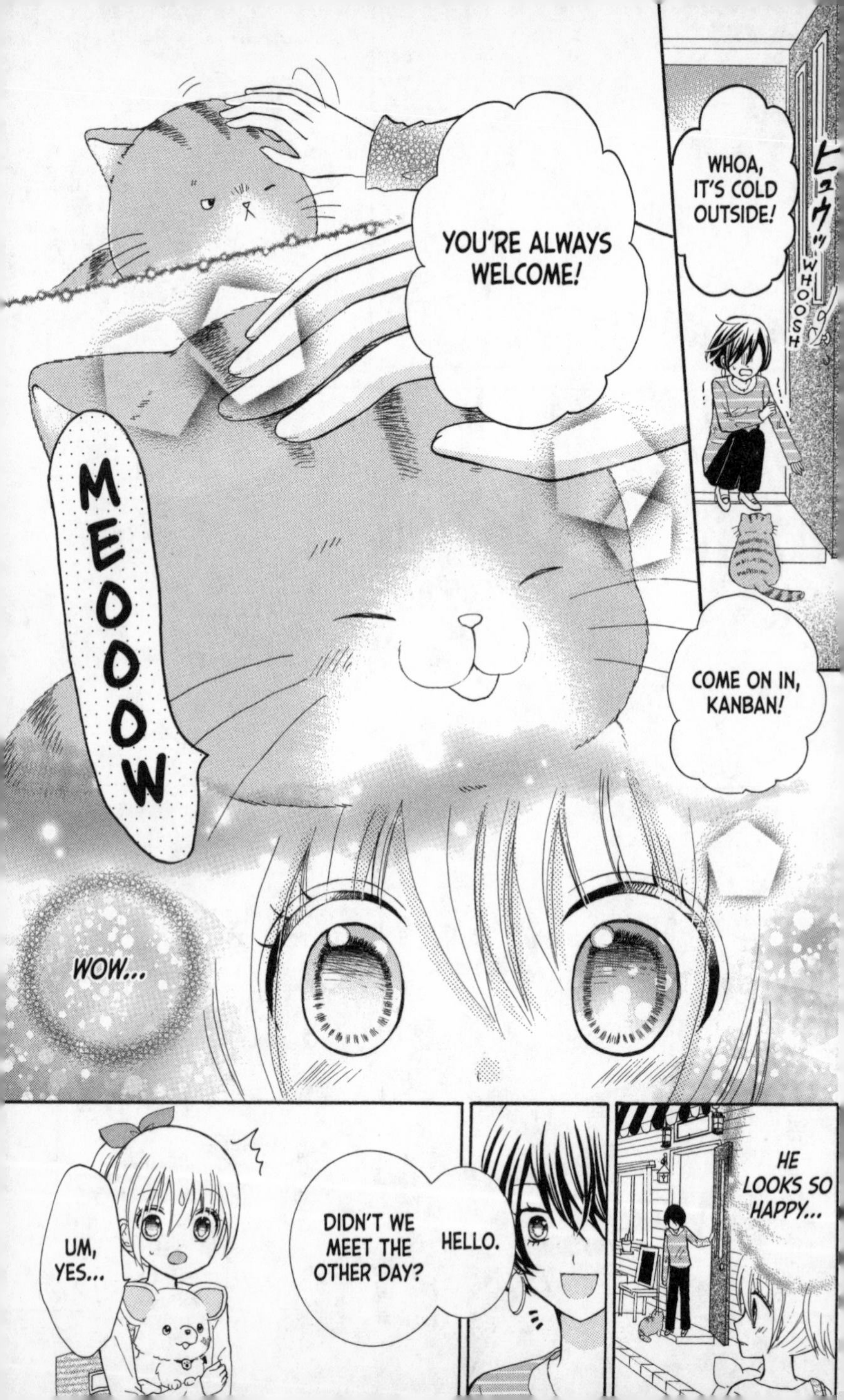
ヒュウッ
WHOOSH
WHOA, IT'S COLD OUTSIDE!
COME ON IN, KANBAN!
YOU'RE ALWAYS WELCOME!
MEOOOW
WOW...
HE LOOKS SO HAPPY...
HELLO.
DIDN'T WE MEET THE OTHER DAY?
UM, YES...

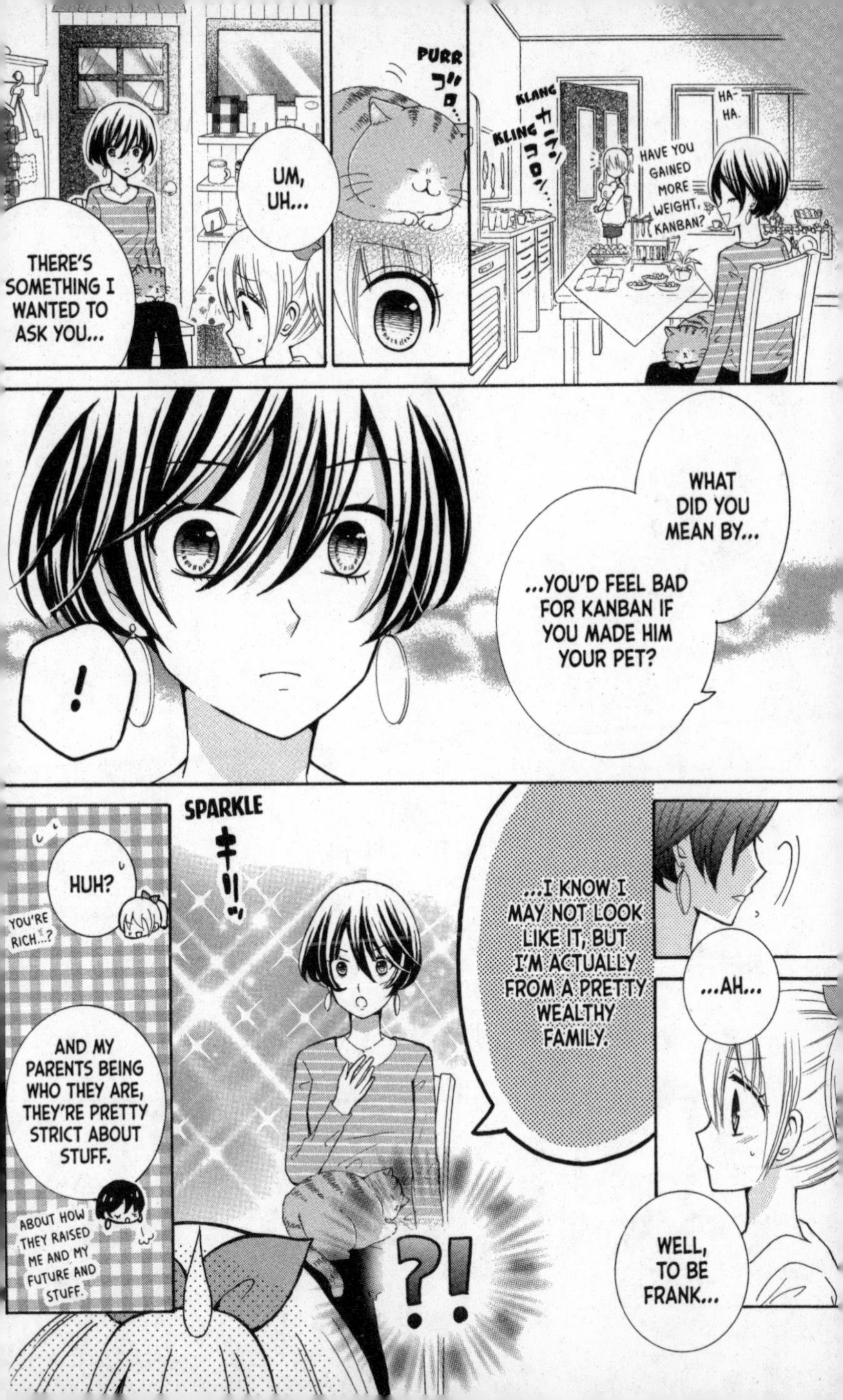
HA-HA.
HAVE YOU GAINED MORE WEIGHT, KANBAN?
KLANG
カラン
KLING
コロン...
PURR
ゴロ...
UM, UH...
THERE'S SOMETHING I WANTED TO ASK YOU...
WHAT DID YOU MEAN BY...
...YOU'D FEEL BAD FOR KANBAN IF YOU MADE HIM YOUR PET?
!
...AH...
WELL, TO BE FRANK...
...I KNOW I MAY NOT LOOK LIKE IT, BUT I'M ACTUALLY FROM A PRETTY WEALTHY FAMILY.
SPARKLE
キリッ
?!
HUH?
YOU'RE RICH...?
AND MY PARENTS BEING WHO THEY ARE, THEY'RE PRETTY STRICT ABOUT STUFF.
ABOUT HOW THEY RAISED ME AND MY FUTURE AND STUFF.

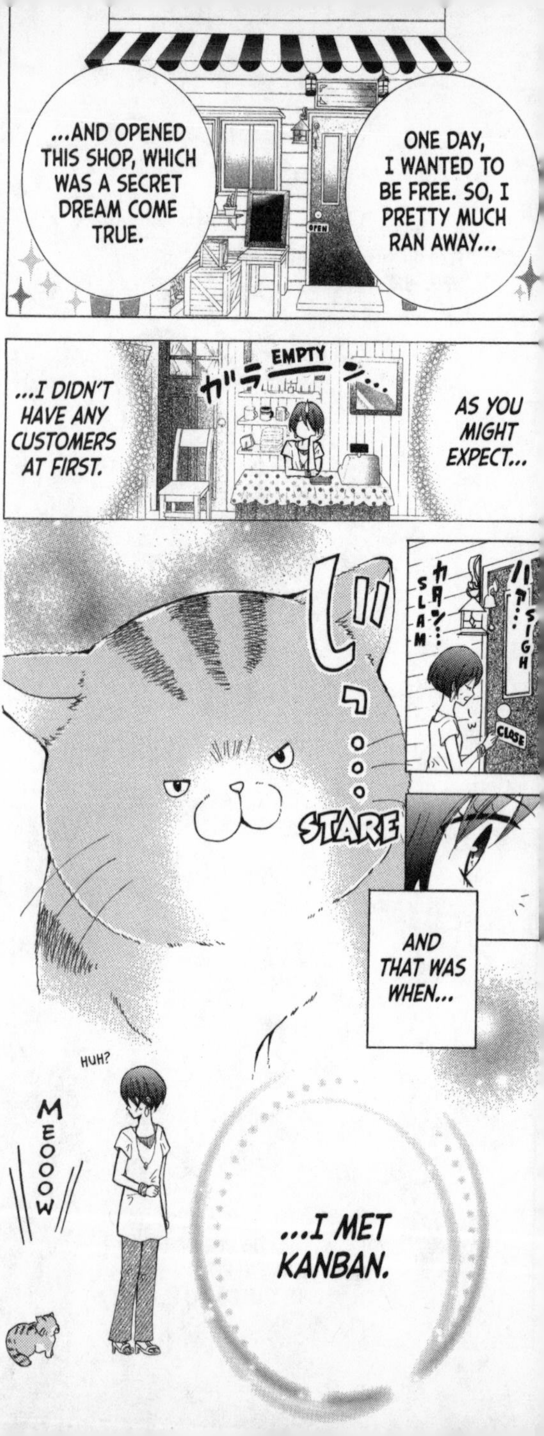
ONE DAY, I WANTED TO BE FREE. SO, I PRETTY MUCH RAN AWAY...
...AND OPENED THIS SHOP, WHICH WAS A SECRET DREAM COME TRUE.
OPEN
AS YOU MIGHT EXPECT...
EMPTY
...I DIDN'T HAVE ANY CUSTOMERS AT FIRST.
SIGH
SLAM
CLOSE
STARE
AND THAT WAS WHEN...
HUH?
MEOOOW
...I MET KANBAN.

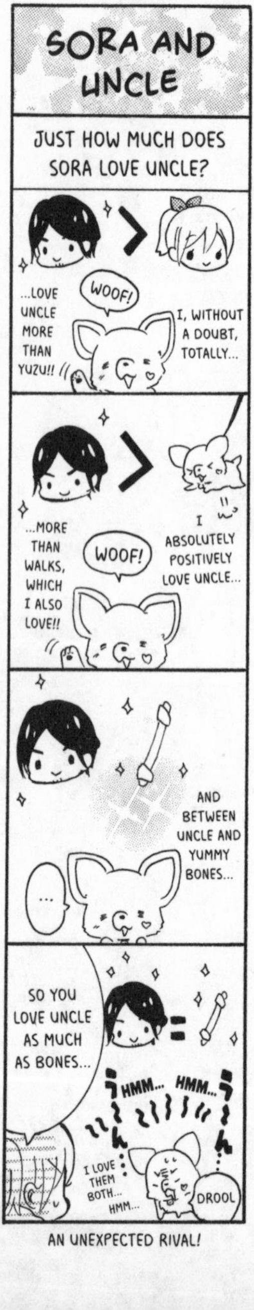
SORA AND UNCLE
JUST HOW MUCH DOES SORA LOVE UNCLE?
I, WITHOUT A DOUBT, TOTALLY...
WOOF!
...LOVE UNCLE MORE THAN YUZU!!
I ABSOLUTELY POSITIVELY LOVE UNCLE...
WOOF!
...MORE THAN WALKS, WHICH I ALSO LOVE!!
AND BETWEEN UNCLE AND YUMMY BONES...
...
SO YOU LOVE UNCLE AS MUCH AS BONES...
HMM... HMM...
I LOVE THEM BOTH... HMM...
DROOL
AN UNEXPECTED RIVAL!

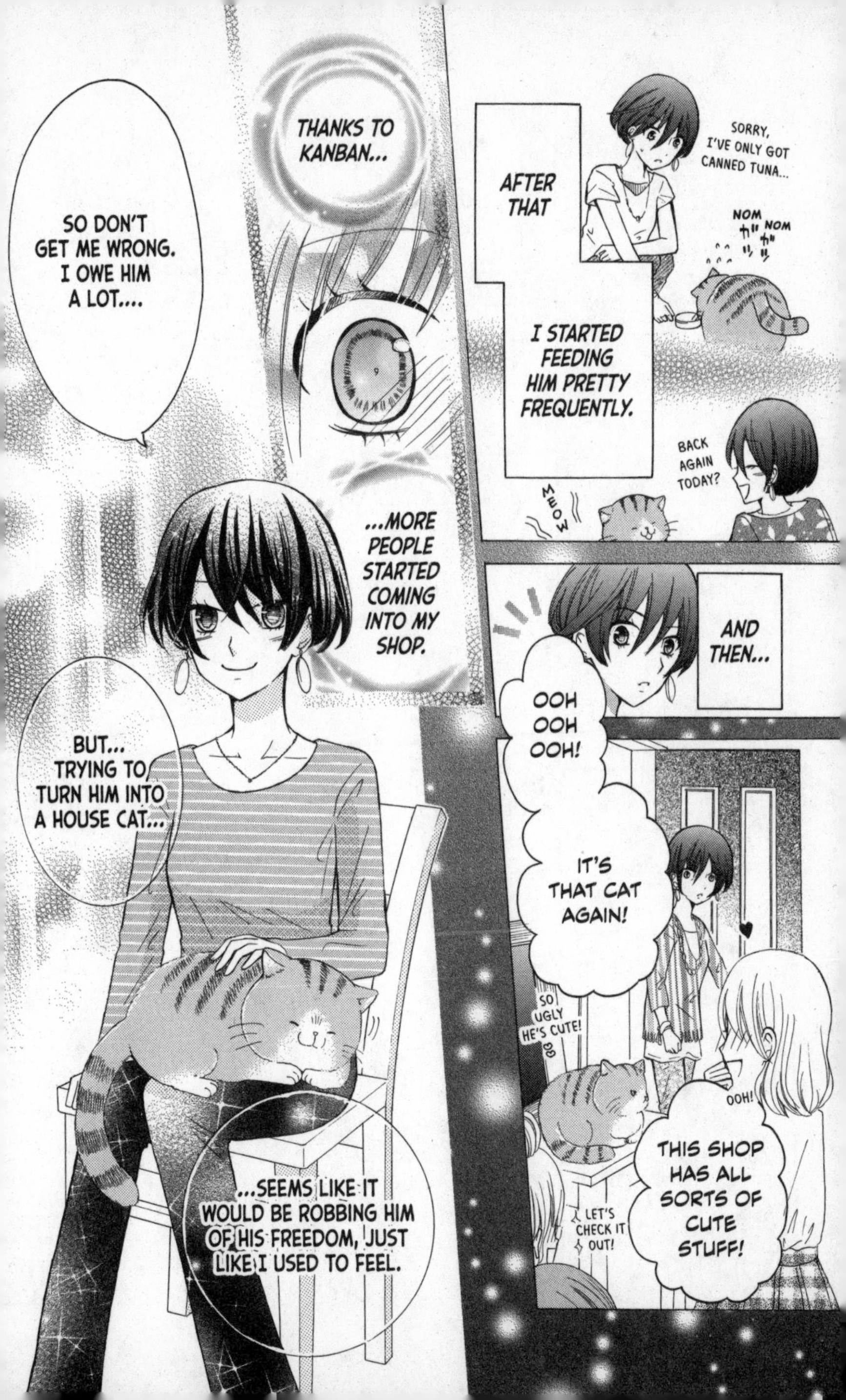
AFTER THAT
SORRY, I'VE ONLY GOT CANNED TUNA...
NOM NOM
I STARTED FEEDING HIM PRETTY FREQUENTLY.
BACK AGAIN TODAY?
MEOW
AND THEN...
OOH OOH OOH!
IT'S THAT CAT AGAIN!
SO UGLY HE'S CUTE!
OOH!
THIS SHOP HAS ALL SORTS OF CUTE STUFF!
LET'S CHECK IT OUT!
THANKS TO KANBAN...
...MORE PEOPLE STARTED COMING INTO MY SHOP.
SO DON'T GET ME WRONG. I OWE HIM A LOT....
BUT... TRYING TO TURN HIM INTO A HOUSE CAT...
...SEEMS LIKE IT WOULD BE ROBBING HIM OF HIS FREEDOM, JUST LIKE I USED TO FEEL.

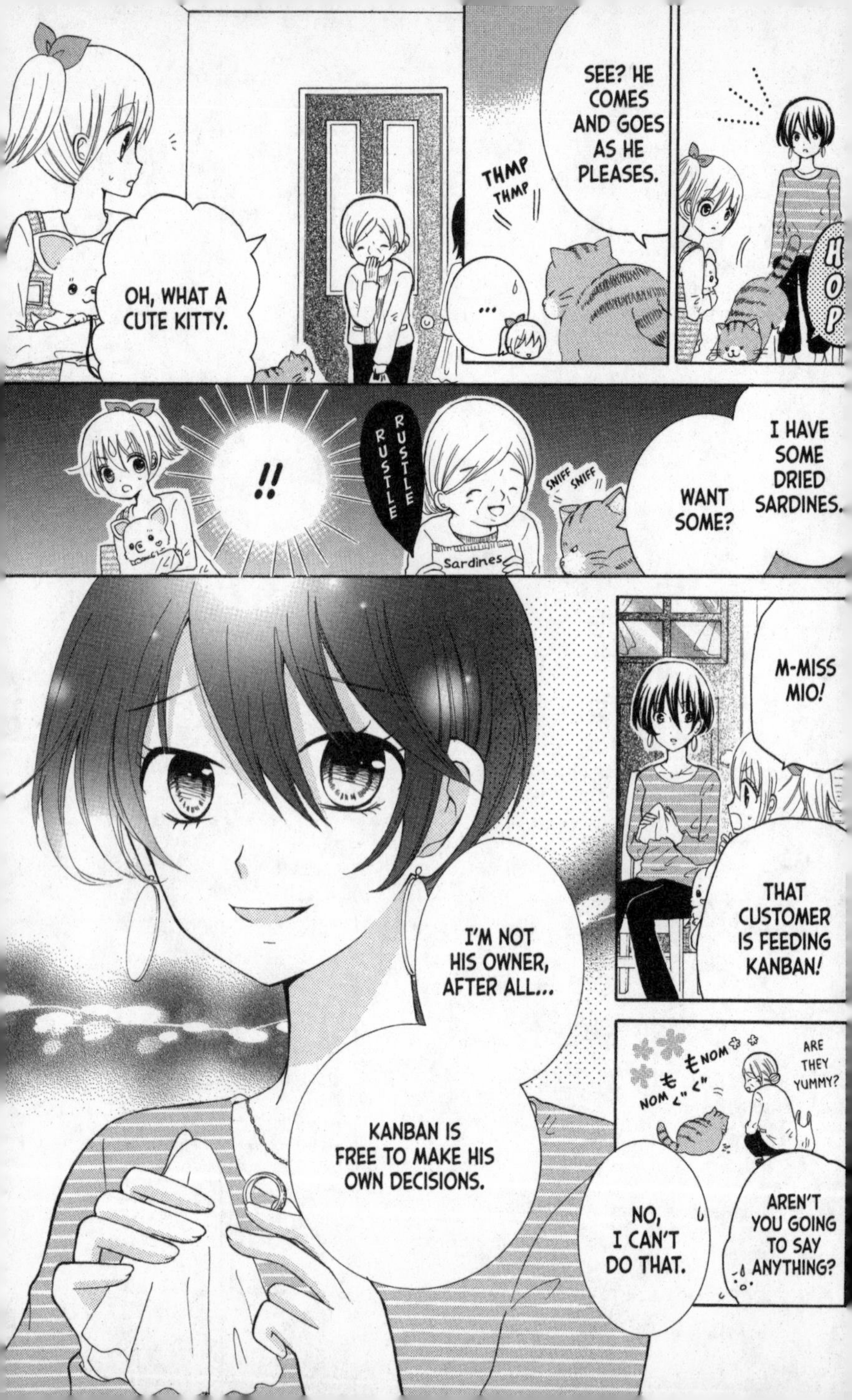
HOP
SEE? HE COMES AND GOES AS HE PLEASES.
THMP THMP
...
OH, WHAT A CUTE KITTY.
I HAVE SOME DRIED SARDINES.
WANT SOME?
SNIFF SNIFF
Sardines
RUSTLE RUSTLE
!!
M-MISS MIO!
THAT CUSTOMER IS FEEDING KANBAN!
ARE THEY YUMMY?
NOM NOM
AREN'T YOU GOING TO SAY ANYTHING?
NO, I CAN'T DO THAT.
I'M NOT HIS OWNER, AFTER ALL...
KANBAN IS FREE TO MAKE HIS OWN DECISIONS.

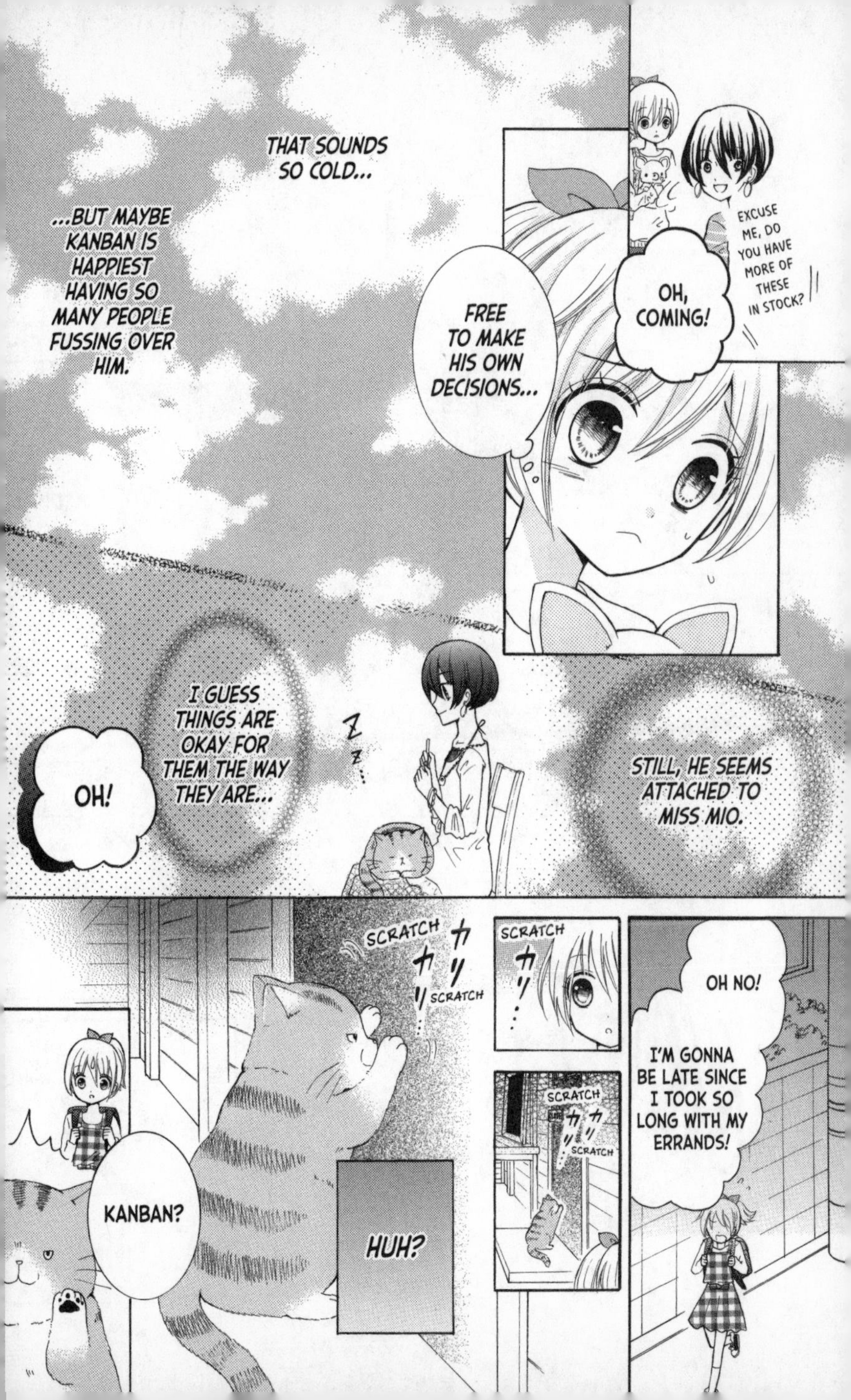
EXCUSE ME, DO YOU HAVE MORE OF THESE IN STOCK?
OH, COMING!
FREE TO MAKE HIS OWN DECISIONS...
THAT SOUNDS SO COLD...
...BUT MAYBE KANBAN IS HAPPIEST HAVING SO MANY PEOPLE FUSSING OVER HIM.
STILL, HE SEEMS ATTACHED TO MISS MIO.
I GUESS THINGS ARE OKAY FOR THEM THE WAY THEY ARE...
OH!
OH NO!
I'M GONNA BE LATE SINCE I TOOK SO LONG WITH MY ERRANDS!
SCRATCH
カリ...
SCRATCH
カリ
カリ
SCRATCH
SCRATCH
カリ
カリ...
SCRATCH
HUH?
KANBAN?

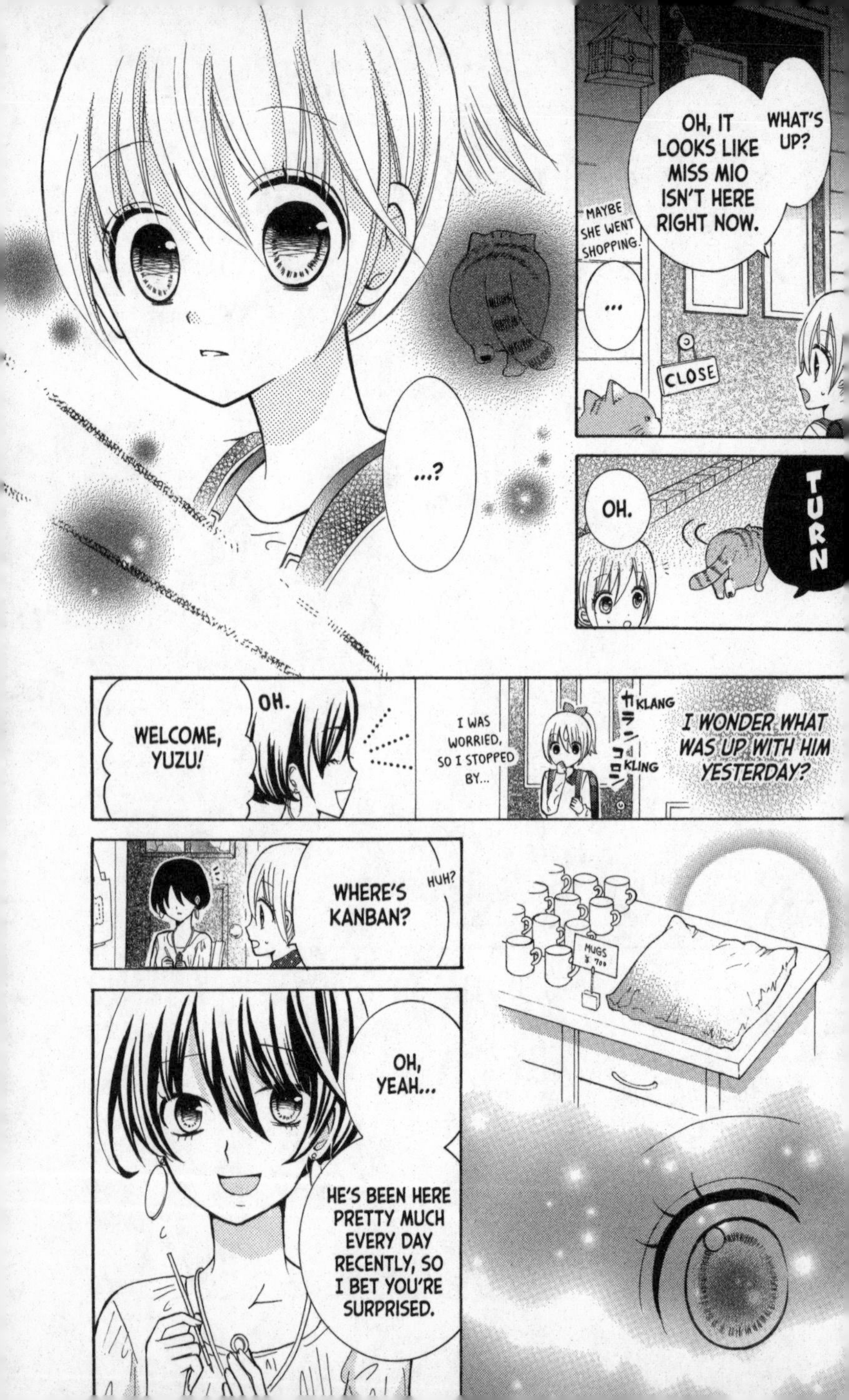
WHAT'S UP?
OH, IT LOOKS LIKE MISS MIO ISN'T HERE RIGHT NOW.
MAYBE SHE WENT SHOPPING.
...
CLOSE
TURN
OH.
...?
I WONDER WHAT WAS UP WITH HIM YESTERDAY?
KLANG
KLING
I WAS WORRIED, SO I STOPPED BY...
OH.
WELCOME, YUZU!
MUGS
HUH?
WHERE'S KANBAN?
OH, YEAH...
HE'S BEEN HERE PRETTY MUCH EVERY DAY RECENTLY, SO I BET YOU'RE SURPRISED.

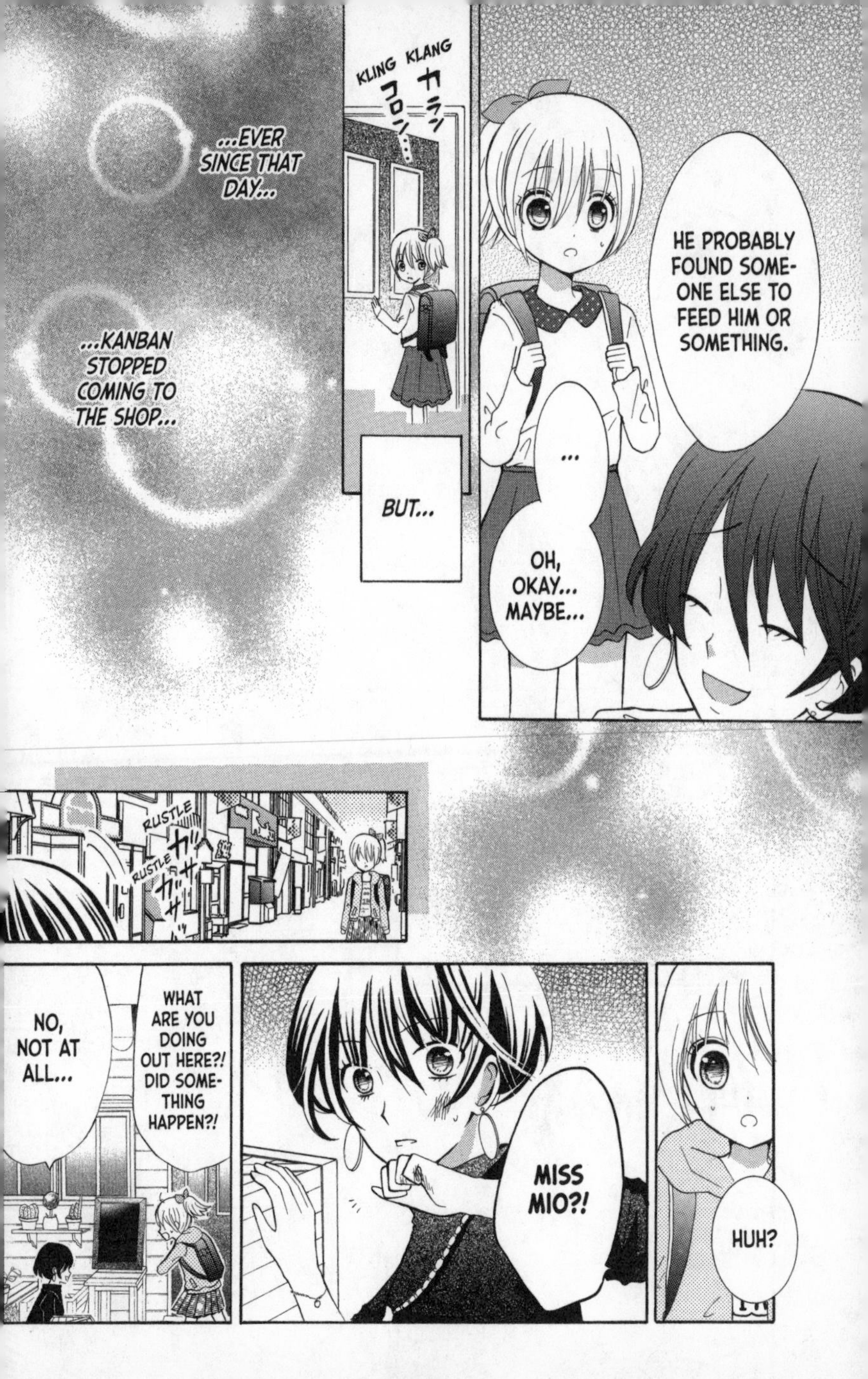
HE PROBABLY FOUND SOME-ONE ELSE TO FEED HIM OR SOMETHING.
...
OH, OKAY... MAYBE...
KLING KLANG
BUT...
...EVER SINCE THAT DAY...
...KANBAN STOPPED COMING TO THE SHOP...
RUSTLE
RUSTLE
HUH?
MISS MIO?!
WHAT ARE YOU DOING OUT HERE?! DID SOME-THING HAPPEN?!
NO, NOT AT ALL...

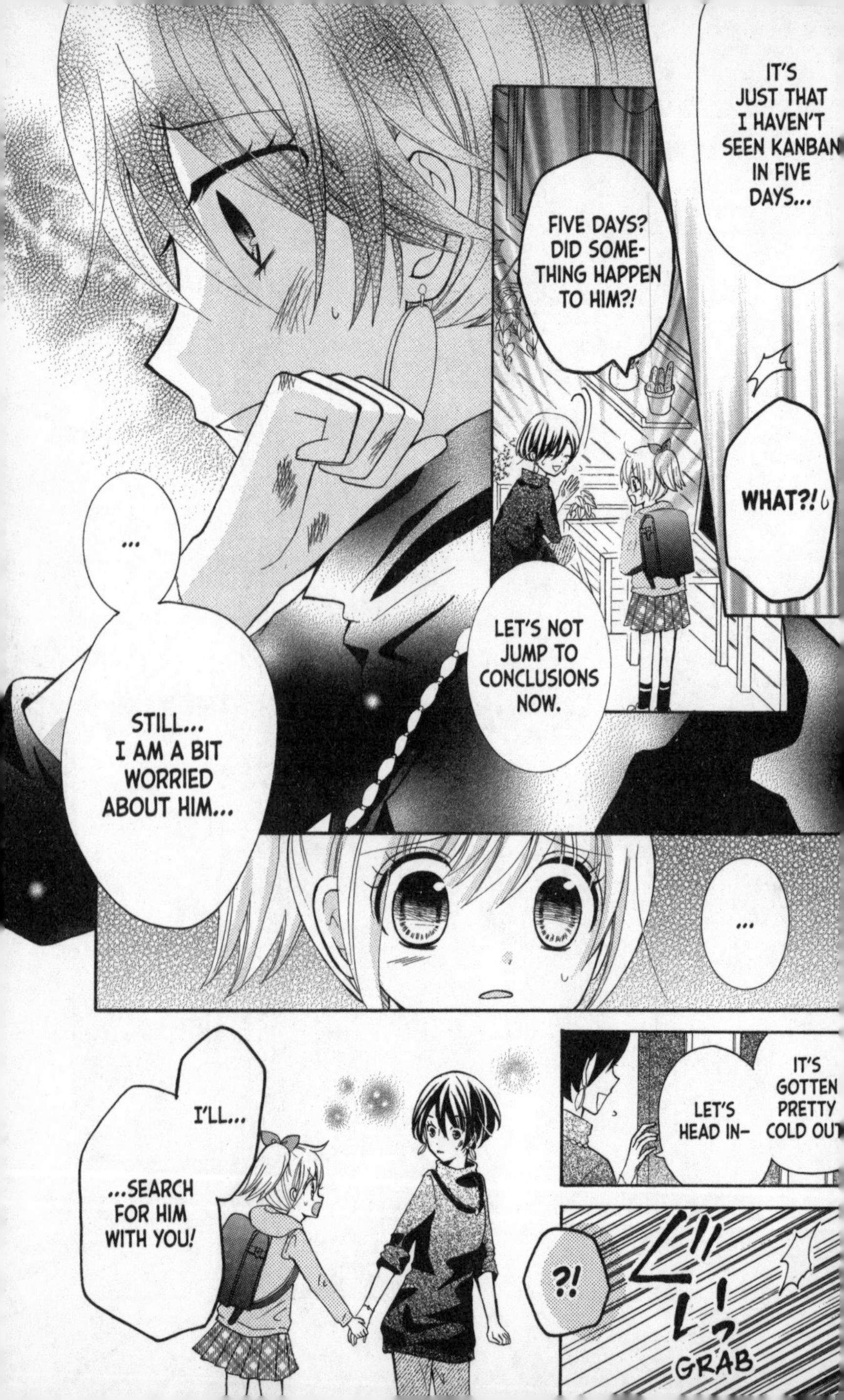
IT'S JUST THAT I HAVEN'T SEEN KANBAN IN FIVE DAYS...
WHAT?!
FIVE DAYS? DID SOME-THING HAPPEN TO HIM?!
LET'S NOT JUMP TO CONCLUSIONS NOW.
...
STILL... I AM A BIT WORRIED ABOUT HIM...
...
IT'S GOTTEN PRETTY COLD OUT
LET'S HEAD IN-
?!
GRAB
I'LL...
...SEARCH FOR HIM WITH YOU!

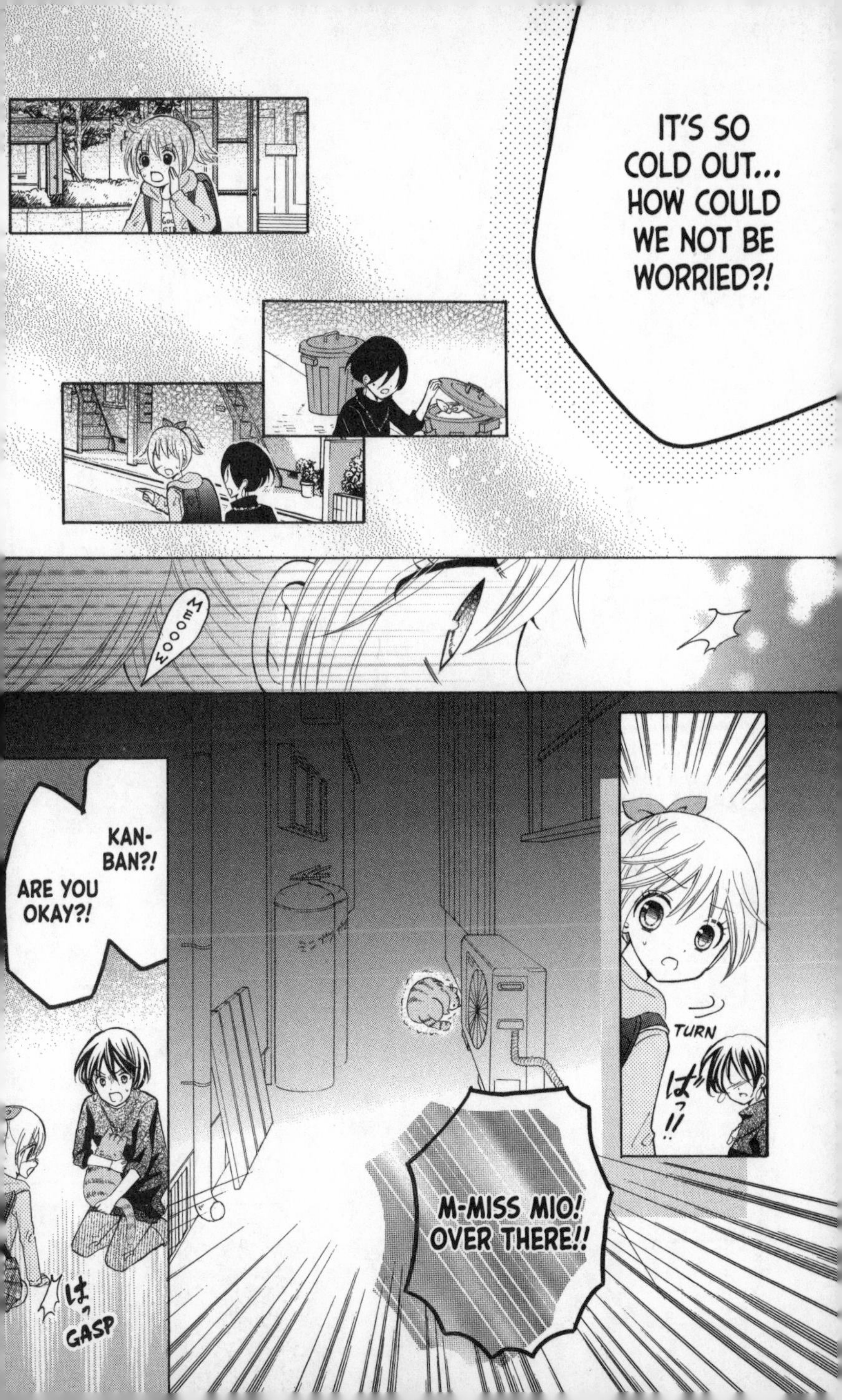
IT'S SO COLD OUT... HOW COULD WE NOT BE WORRIED?!
MEOOOW
TURN
ばっ!!
M-MISS MIO! OVER THERE!!
KAN-BAN?!
ARE YOU OKAY?!
はっ
GASP

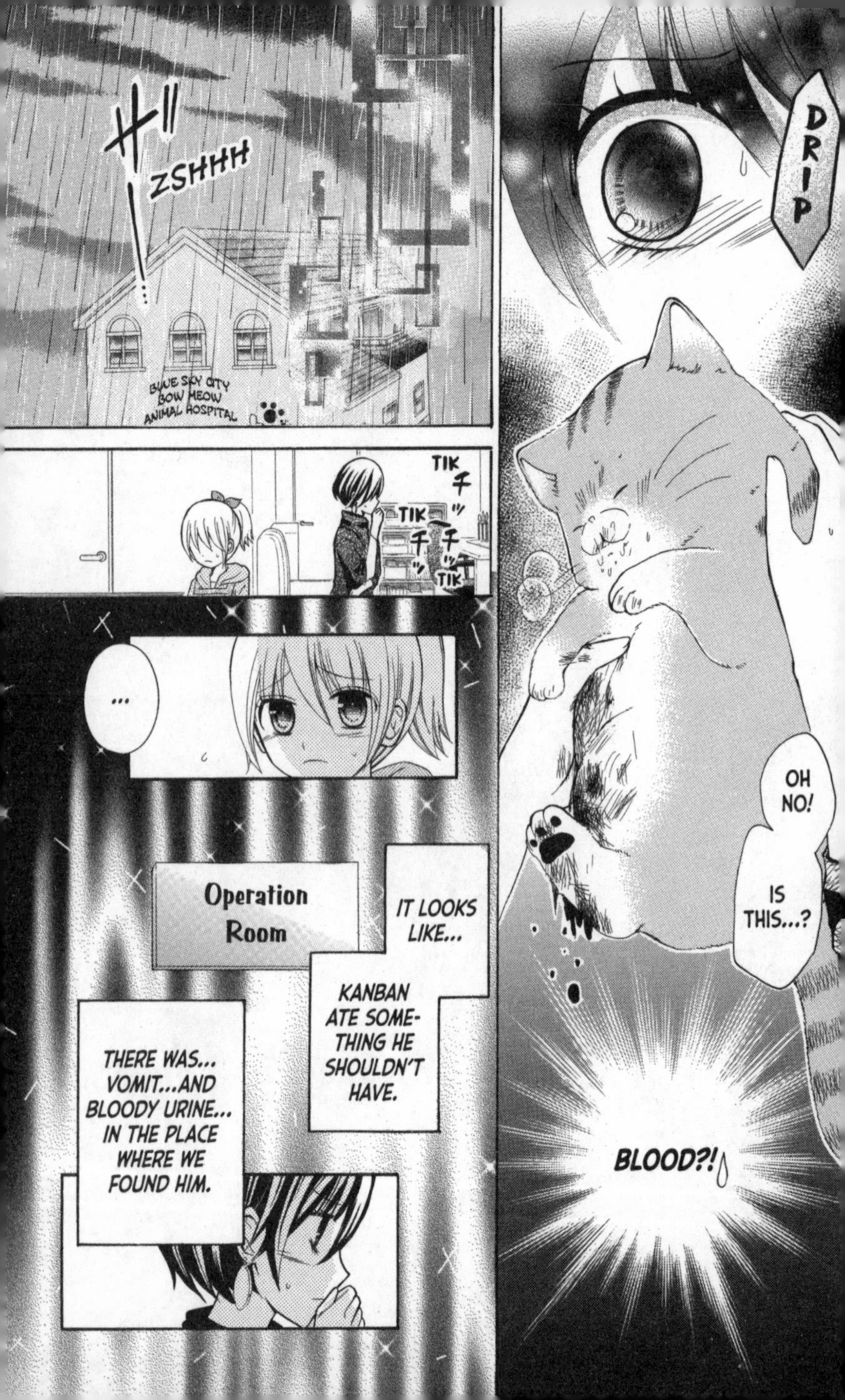
DRIP
OH NO!
IS THIS...?
BLOOD?!
ZSHHH
BLUE SKY CITY BOW MEOW ANIMAL HOSPITAL
TIK
TIK
TIK
...
Operation Room
IT LOOKS LIKE...
KANBAN ATE SOME-THING HE SHOULDN'T HAVE.
THERE WAS... VOMIT...AND BLOODY URINE... IN THE PLACE WHERE WE FOUND HIM.

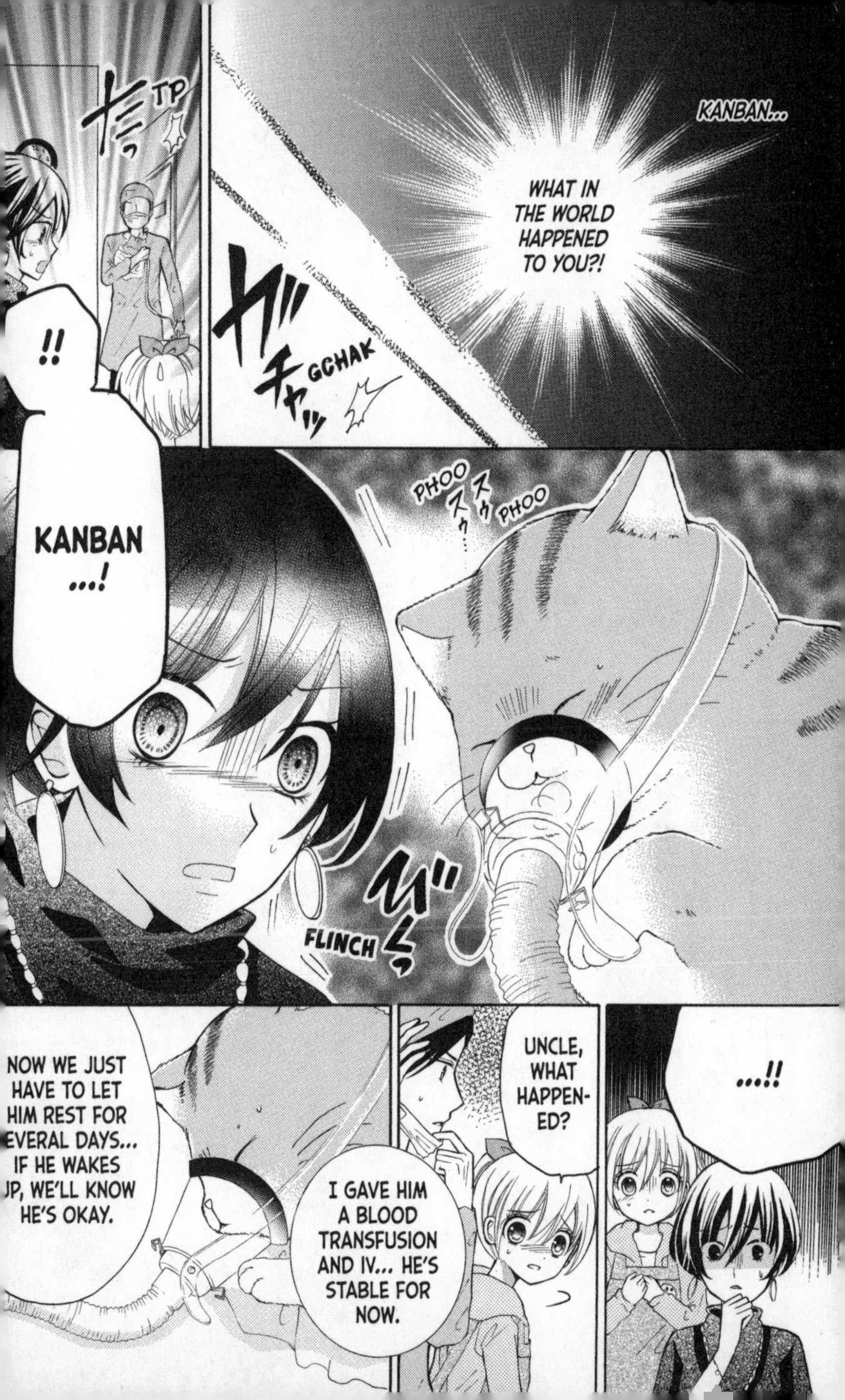
KANBAN...
WHAT IN THE WORLD HAPPENED TO YOU?!
GCHAK
TP
!!
KANBAN ...!
PHOO PHOO
FLINCH
...!!
UNCLE, WHAT HAPPEN-ED?
I GAVE HIM A BLOOD TRANSFUSION AND IV... HE'S STABLE FOR NOW.
NOW WE JUST HAVE TO LET HIM REST FOR EVERAL DAYS... IF HE WAKES JP, WE'LL KNOW HE'S OKAY.

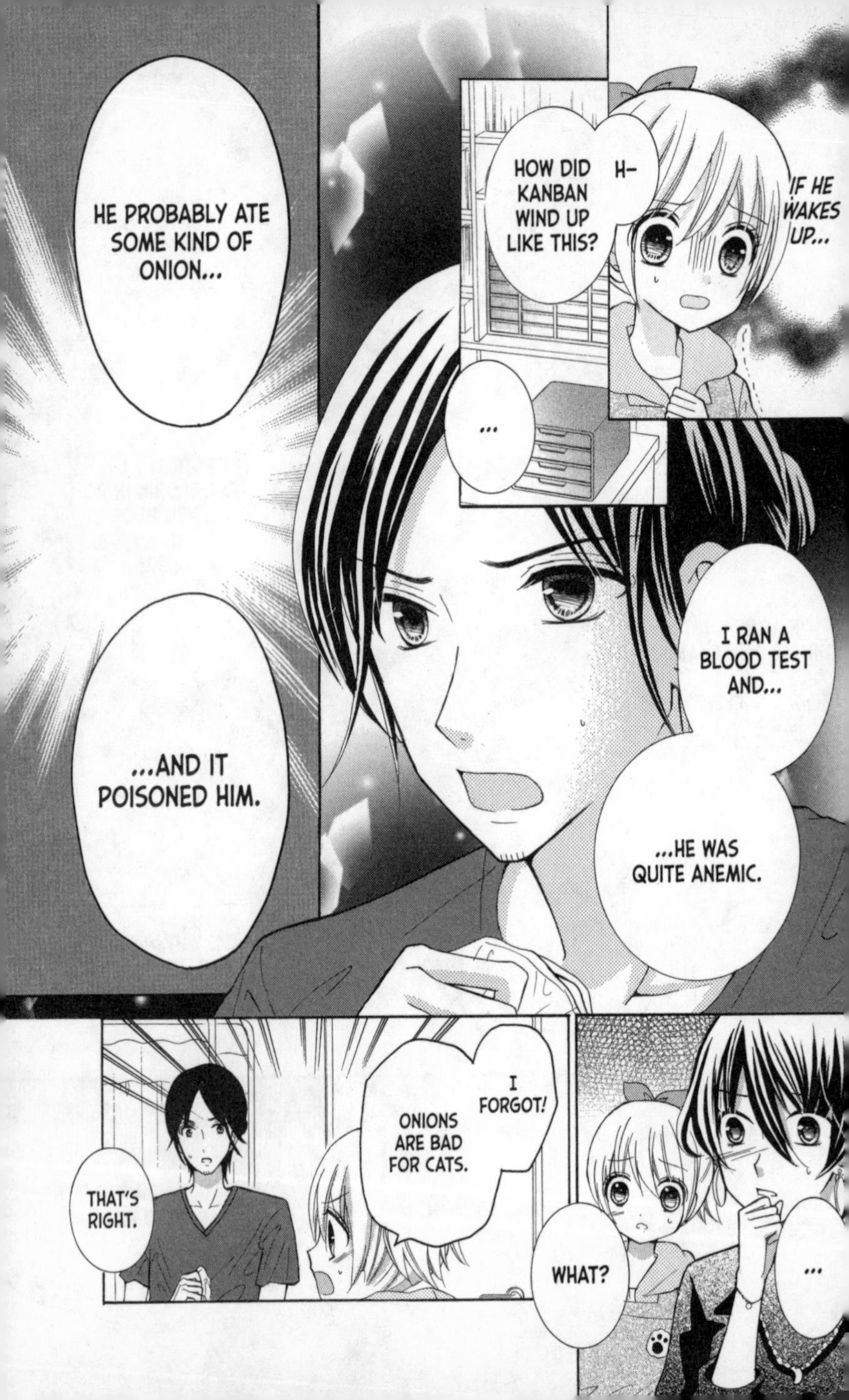

IF HE WAKES UP...
H– HOW DID KANBAN WIND UP LIKE THIS?
...
I RAN A BLOOD TEST AND...
...HE WAS QUITE ANEMIC.
HE PROBABLY ATE SOME KIND OF ONION...
...AND IT POISONED HIM.
...
WHAT?
I FORGOT! ONIONS ARE BAD FOR CATS.
THAT'S RIGHT.

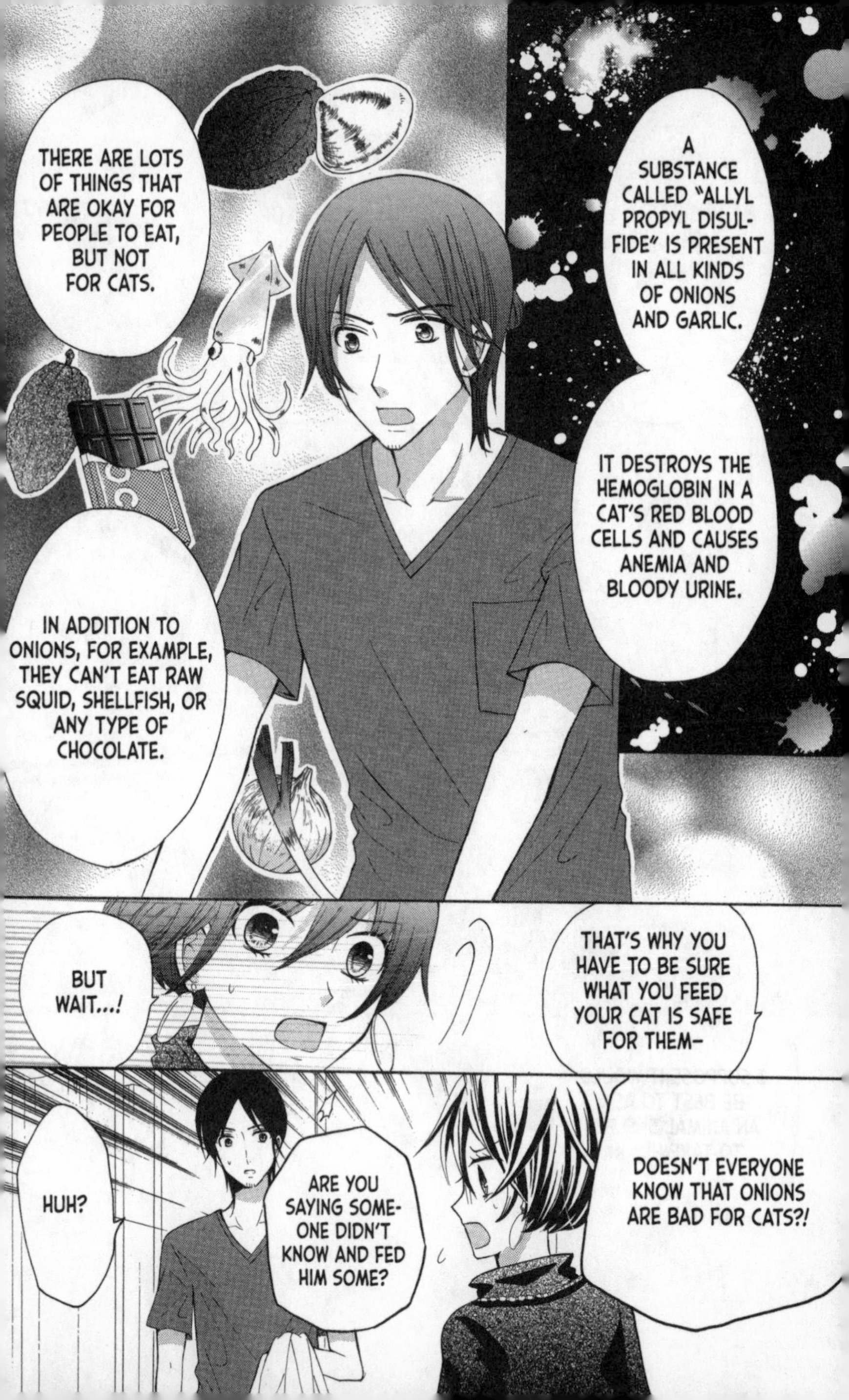

A SUBSTANCE CALLED "ALLYL PROPYL DISULFIDE" IS PRESENT IN ALL KINDS OF ONIONS AND GARLIC.
IT DESTROYS THE HEMOGLOBIN IN A CAT'S RED BLOOD CELLS AND CAUSES ANEMIA AND BLOODY URINE.
THERE ARE LOTS OF THINGS THAT ARE OKAY FOR PEOPLE TO EAT, BUT NOT FOR CATS.
IN ADDITION TO ONIONS, FOR EXAMPLE, THEY CAN'T EAT RAW SQUID, SHELLFISH, OR ANY TYPE OF CHOCOLATE.
THAT'S WHY YOU HAVE TO BE SURE WHAT YOU FEED YOUR CAT IS SAFE FOR THEM—
BUT WAIT...!
DOESN'T EVERYONE KNOW THAT ONIONS ARE BAD FOR CATS?!
ARE YOU SAYING SOME-ONE DIDN'T KNOW AND FED HIM SOME?
HUH?

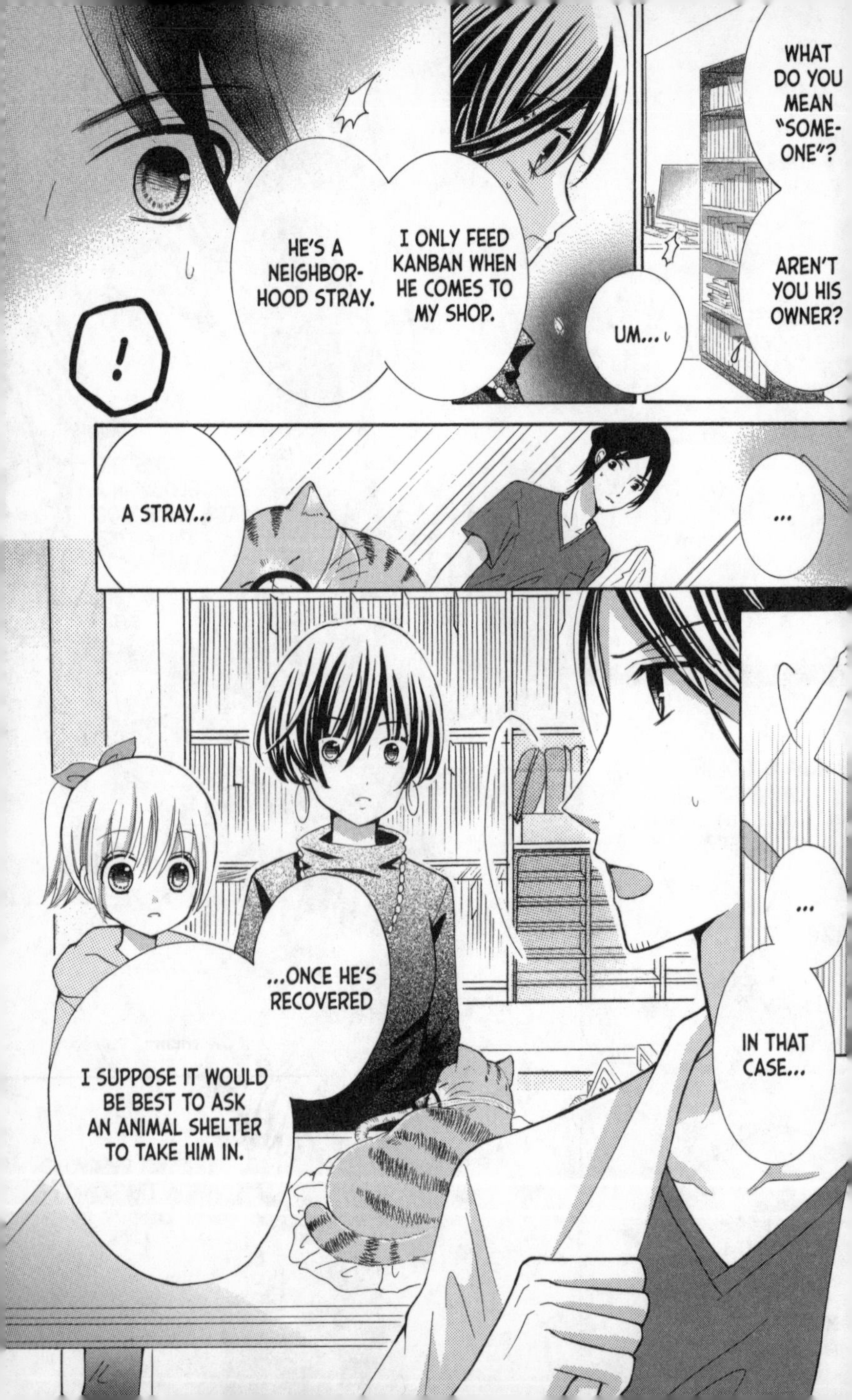
WHAT DO YOU MEAN "SOME-ONE"?
AREN'T YOU HIS OWNER?
UM...
I ONLY FEED KANBAN WHEN HE COMES TO MY SHOP.
HE'S A NEIGHBOR-HOOD STRAY.
!
...
A STRAY...
...
IN THAT CASE...
...ONCE HE'S RECOVERED
I SUPPOSE IT WOULD BE BEST TO ASK AN ANIMAL SHELTER TO TAKE HIM IN.

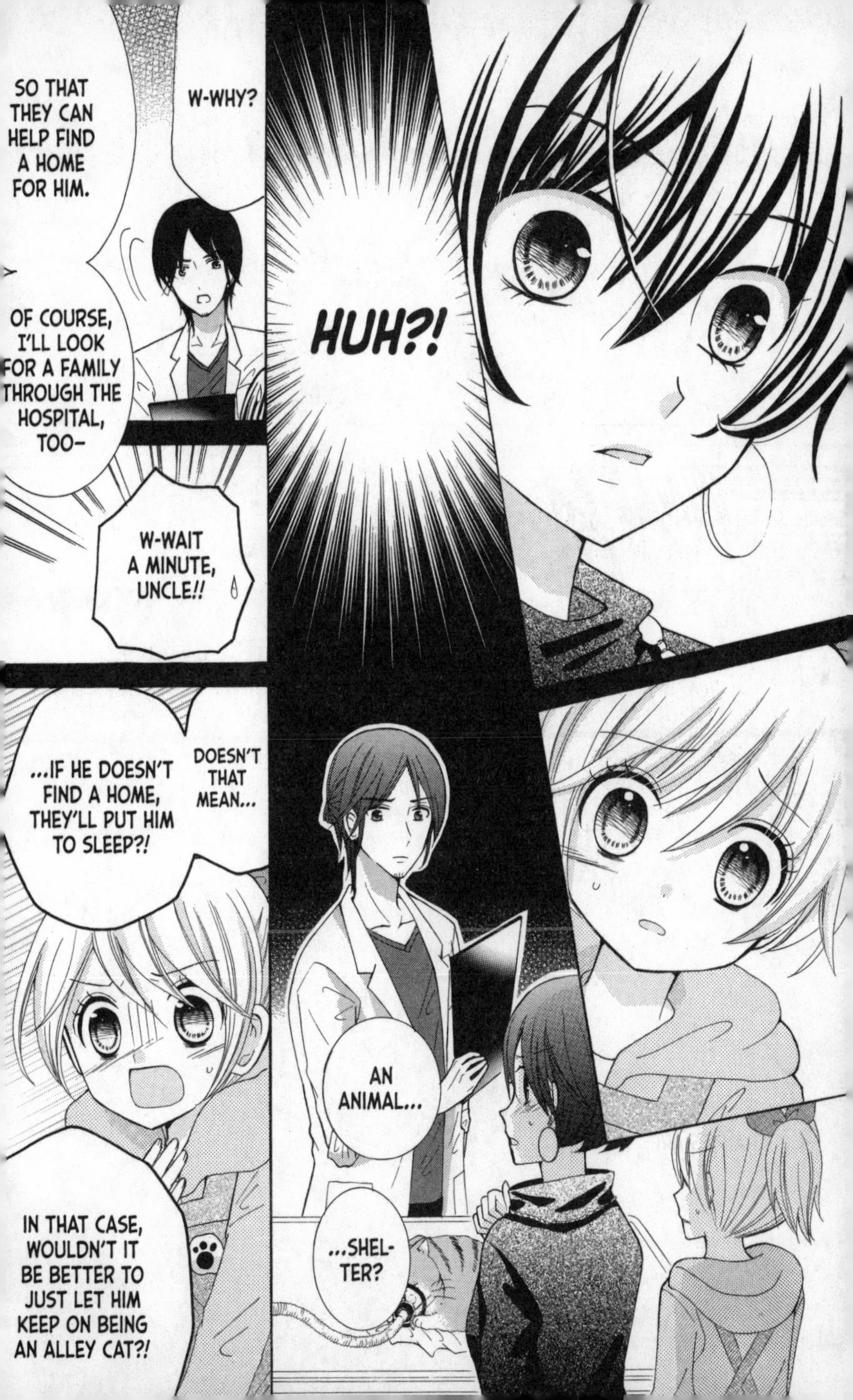
HUH?!
W-WHY?
SO THAT THEY CAN HELP FIND A HOME FOR HIM.
OF COURSE, I'LL LOOK FOR A FAMILY THROUGH THE HOSPITAL, TOO–
W-WAIT A MINUTE, UNCLE!!
AN ANIMAL...
...SHEL-TER?
DOESN'T THAT MEAN...
...IF HE DOESN'T FIND A HOME, THEY'LL PUT HIM TO SLEEP?!
IN THAT CASE, WOULDN'T IT BE BETTER TO JUST LET HIM KEEP ON BEING AN ALLEY CAT?!

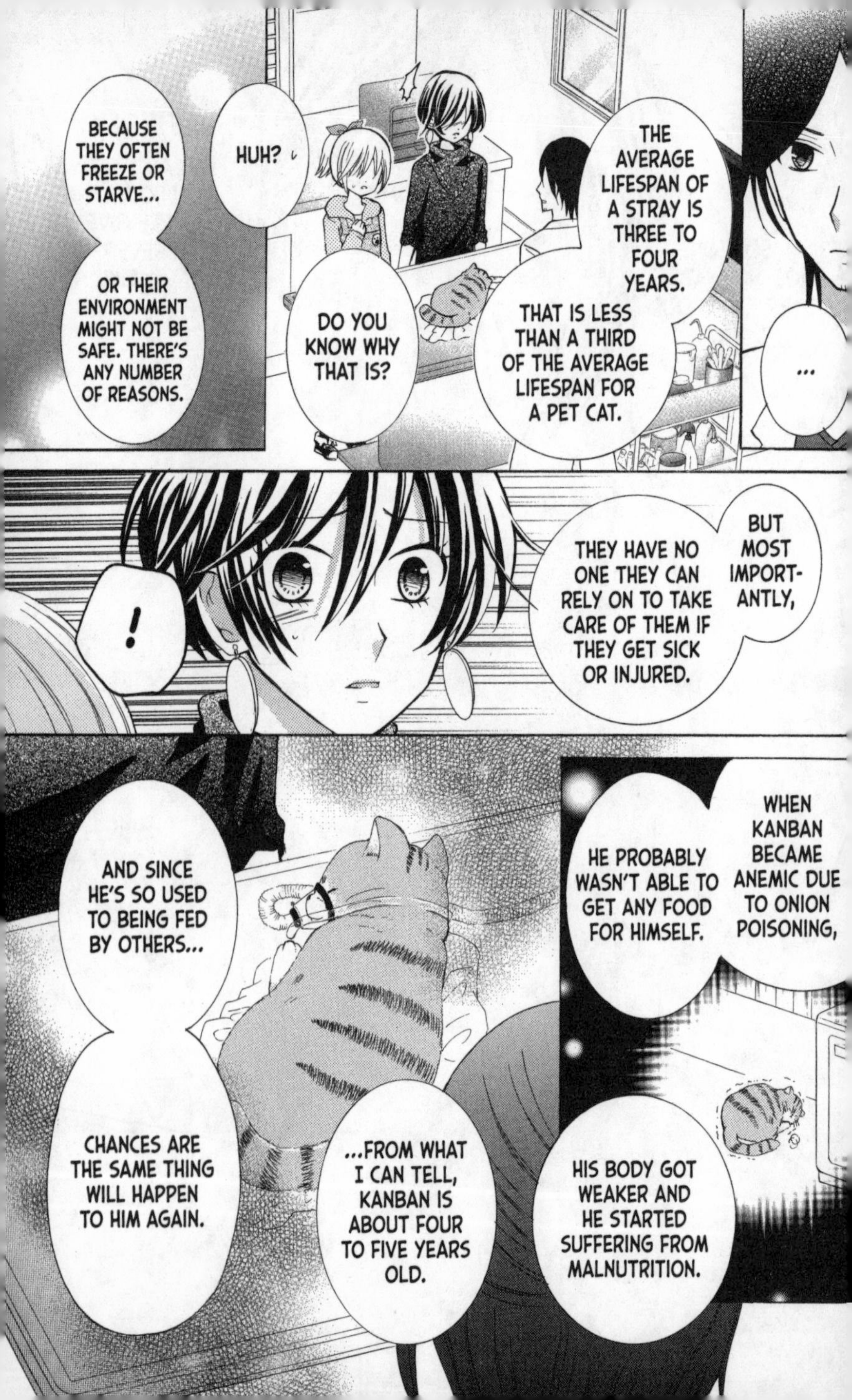
...
THE AVERAGE LIFESPAN OF A STRAY IS THREE TO FOUR YEARS.
THAT IS LESS THAN A THIRD OF THE AVERAGE LIFESPAN FOR A PET CAT.
HUH?
DO YOU KNOW WHY THAT IS?
BECAUSE THEY OFTEN FREEZE OR STARVE...
OR THEIR ENVIRONMENT MIGHT NOT BE SAFE. THERE'S ANY NUMBER OF REASONS.
BUT MOST IMPORTANTLY,
THEY HAVE NO ONE THEY CAN RELY ON TO TAKE CARE OF THEM IF THEY GET SICK OR INJURED.
!
WHEN KANBAN BECAME ANEMIC DUE TO ONION POISONING,
HE PROBABLY WASN'T ABLE TO GET ANY FOOD FOR HIMSELF.
HIS BODY GOT WEAKER AND HE STARTED SUFFERING FROM MALNUTRITION.
...FROM WHAT I CAN TELL, KANBAN IS ABOUT FOUR TO FIVE YEARS OLD.
AND SINCE HE'S SO USED TO BEING FED BY OTHERS...
CHANCES ARE THE SAME THING WILL HAPPEN TO HIM AGAIN.

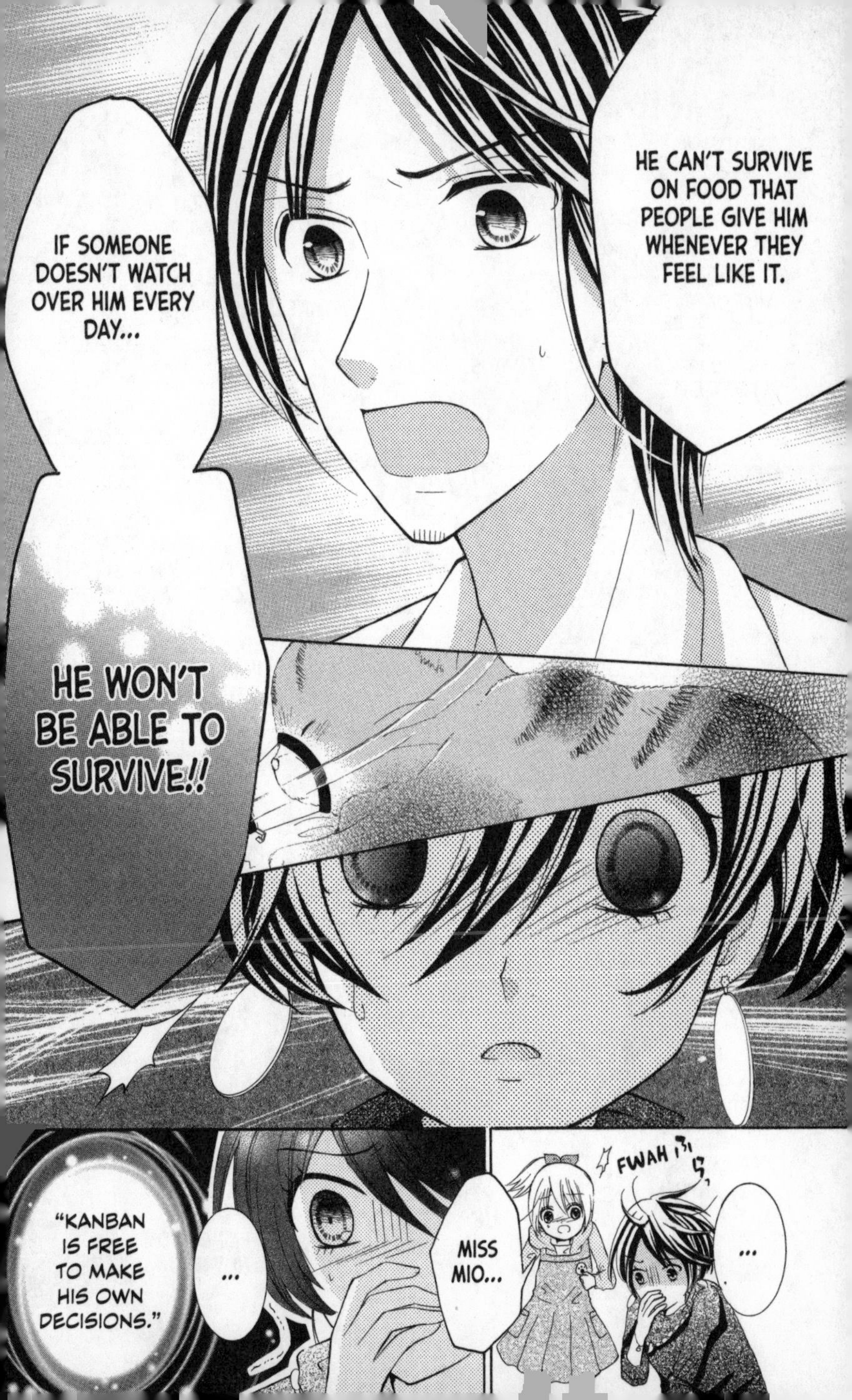
HE CAN'T SURVIVE ON FOOD THAT PEOPLE GIVE HIM WHENEVER THEY FEEL LIKE IT.
IF SOMEONE DOESN'T WATCH OVER HIM EVERY DAY...
HE WON'T BE ABLE TO SURVIVE!!
FWAH
...
MISS MIO...
...
"KANBAN IS FREE TO MAKE HIS OWN DECISIONS."

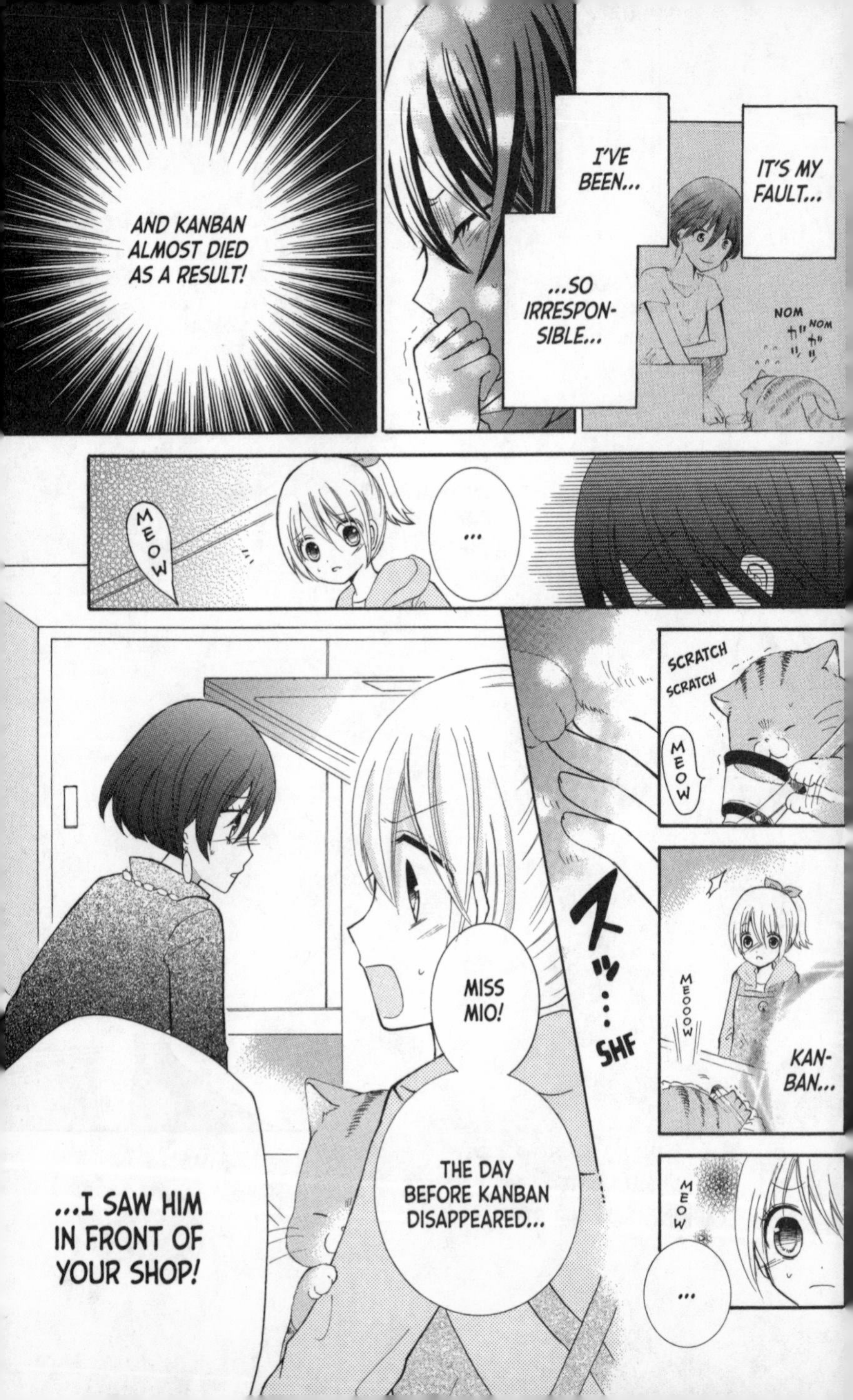
IT'S MY FAULT...
NOM NOM
I'VE BEEN...
...SO IRRESPONSIBLE...
AND KANBAN ALMOST DIED AS A RESULT!
...
MEOW
SCRATCH SCRATCH
MEOW
KAN-BAN...
MEOOOW
MEOW
...
スッ... SHF
MISS MIO!
THE DAY BEFORE KANBAN DISAPPEARED...
...I SAW HIM IN FRONT OF YOUR SHOP!

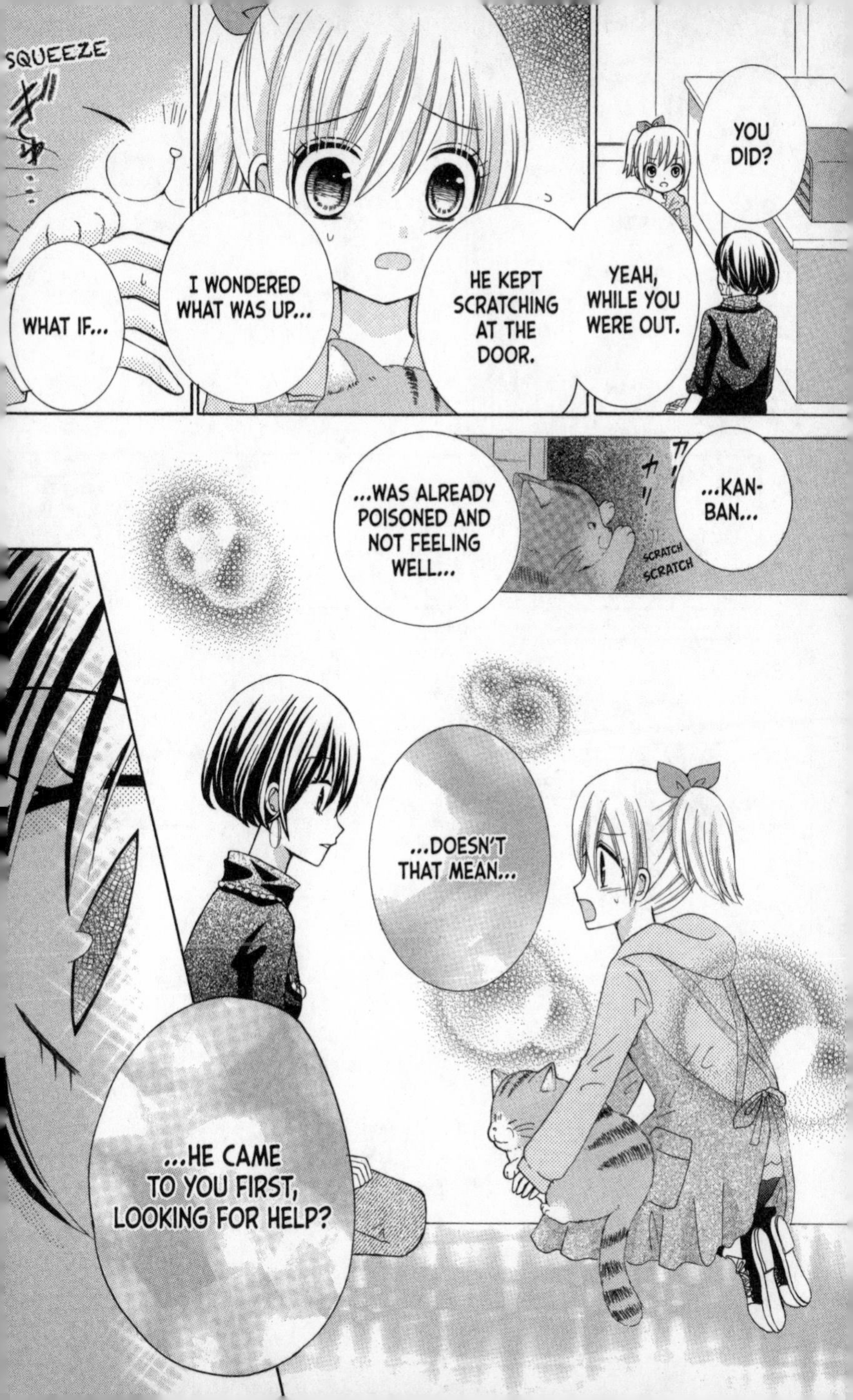
YOU DID?
YEAH, WHILE YOU WERE OUT.
HE KEPT SCRATCHING AT THE DOOR.
I WONDERED WHAT WAS UP...
SQUEEZE
WHAT IF...
...KAN-BAN...
SCRATCH SCRATCH
...WAS ALREADY POISONED AND NOT FEELING WELL...
...DOESN'T THAT MEAN...
...HE CAME TO YOU FIRST, LOOKING FOR HELP?

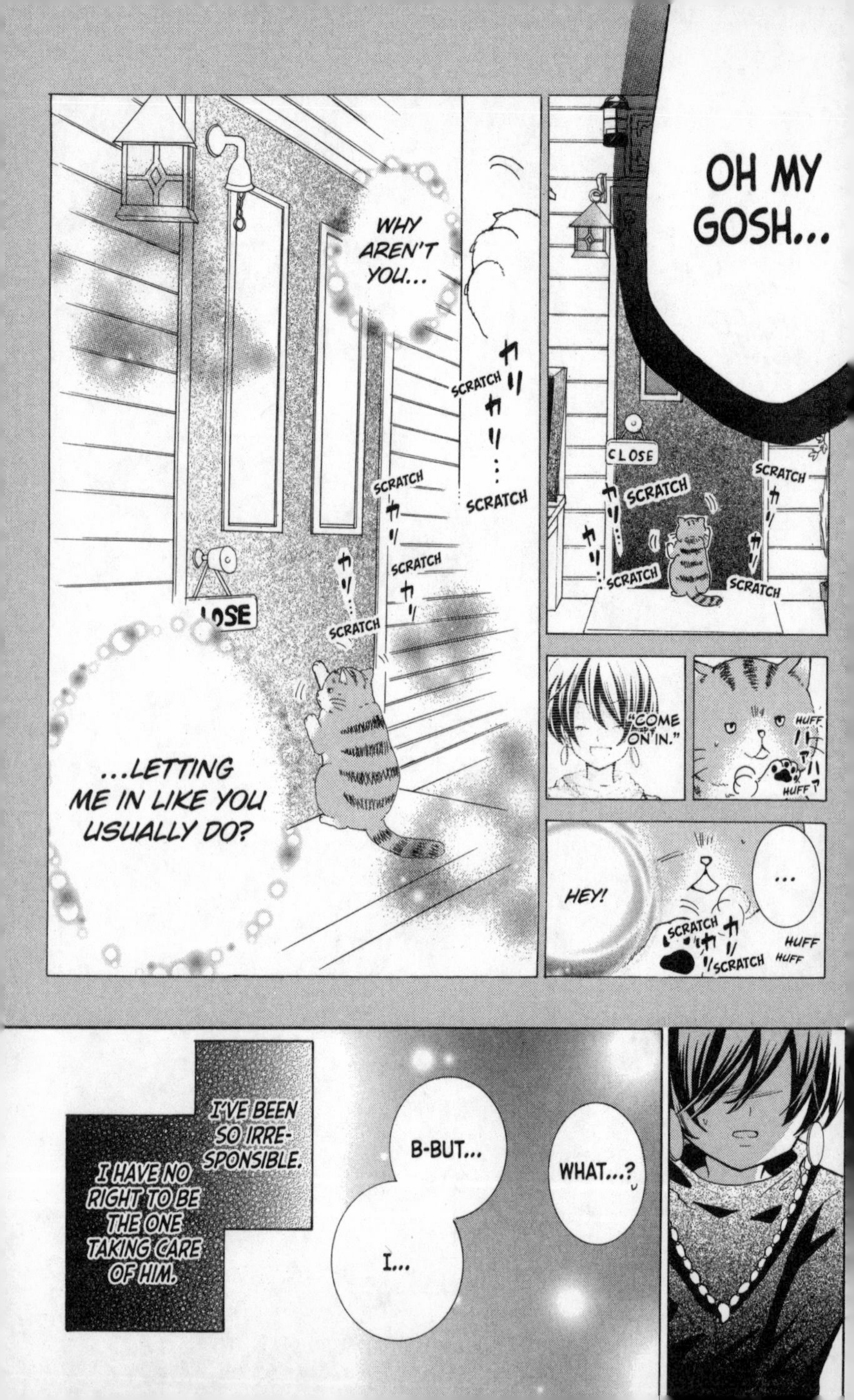
OH MY GOSH...
CLOSE
SCRATCH
SCRATCH
SCRATCH
SCRATCH
SCRATCH
HUFF
HUFF
"COME ON IN."
...
HEY!
SCRATCH
SCRATCH
HUFF
HUFF
WHY AREN'T YOU...
SCRATCH
SCRATCH
SCRATCH
SCRATCH
SCRATCH
LOSE
...LETTING ME IN LIKE YOU USUALLY DO?
WHAT...?
B-BUT...
I...
I'VE BEEN SO IRRE-SPONSIBLE.
I HAVE NO RIGHT TO BE THE ONE TAKING CARE OF HIM.

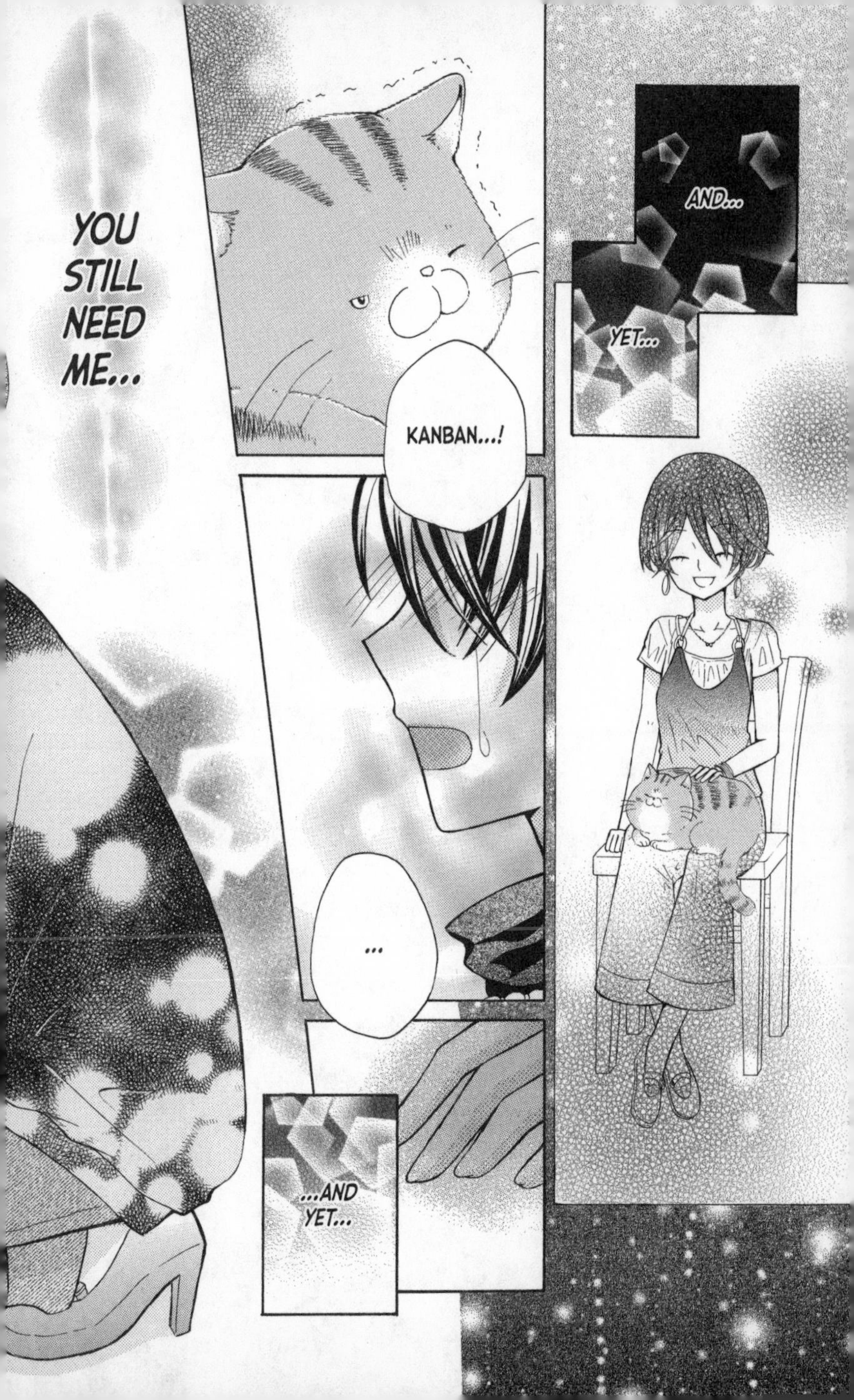
AND...
YET...
KANBAN...!
...
...AND YET...
YOU STILL NEED ME...

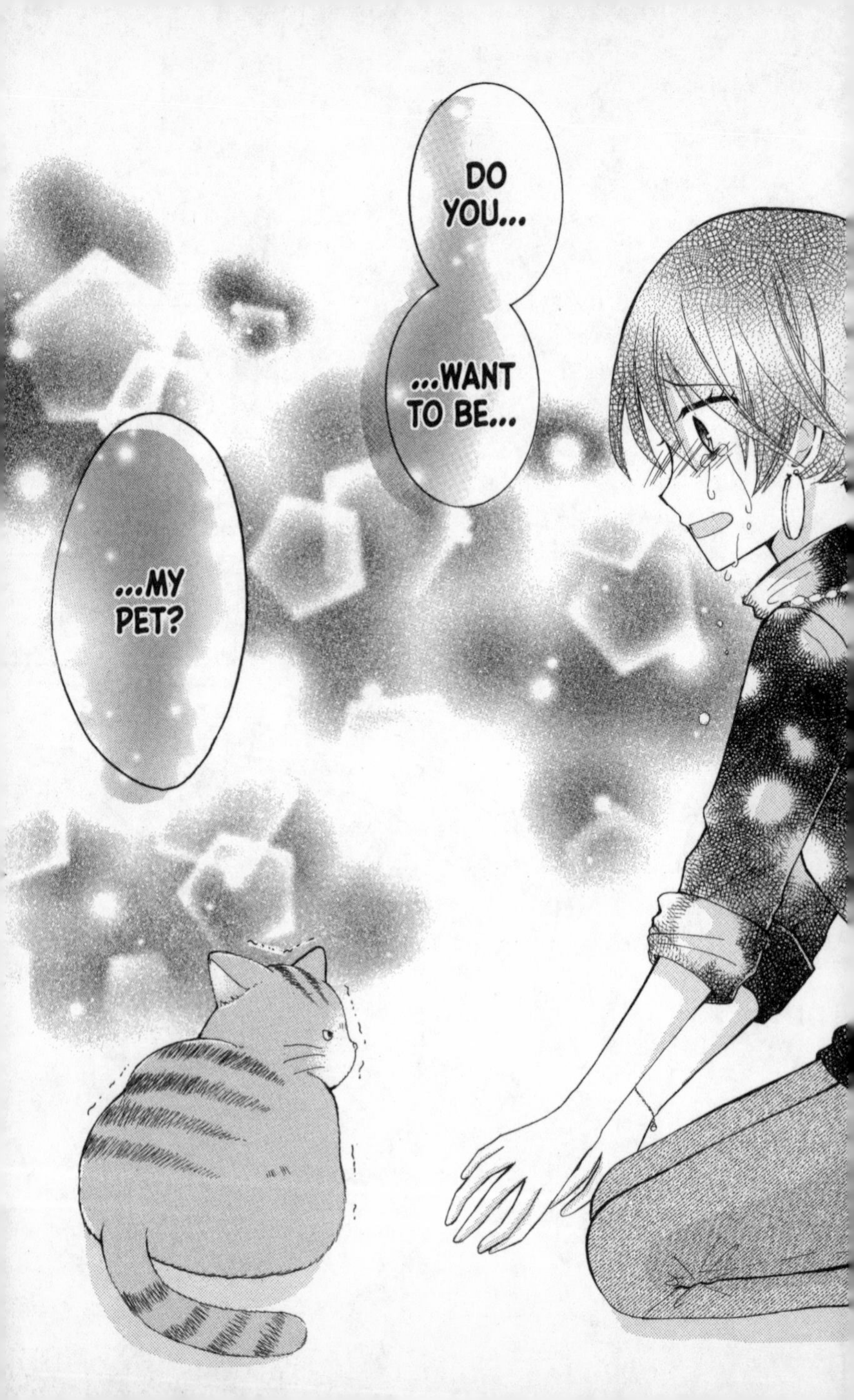
DO YOU...
...WANT TO BE...
...MY PET?

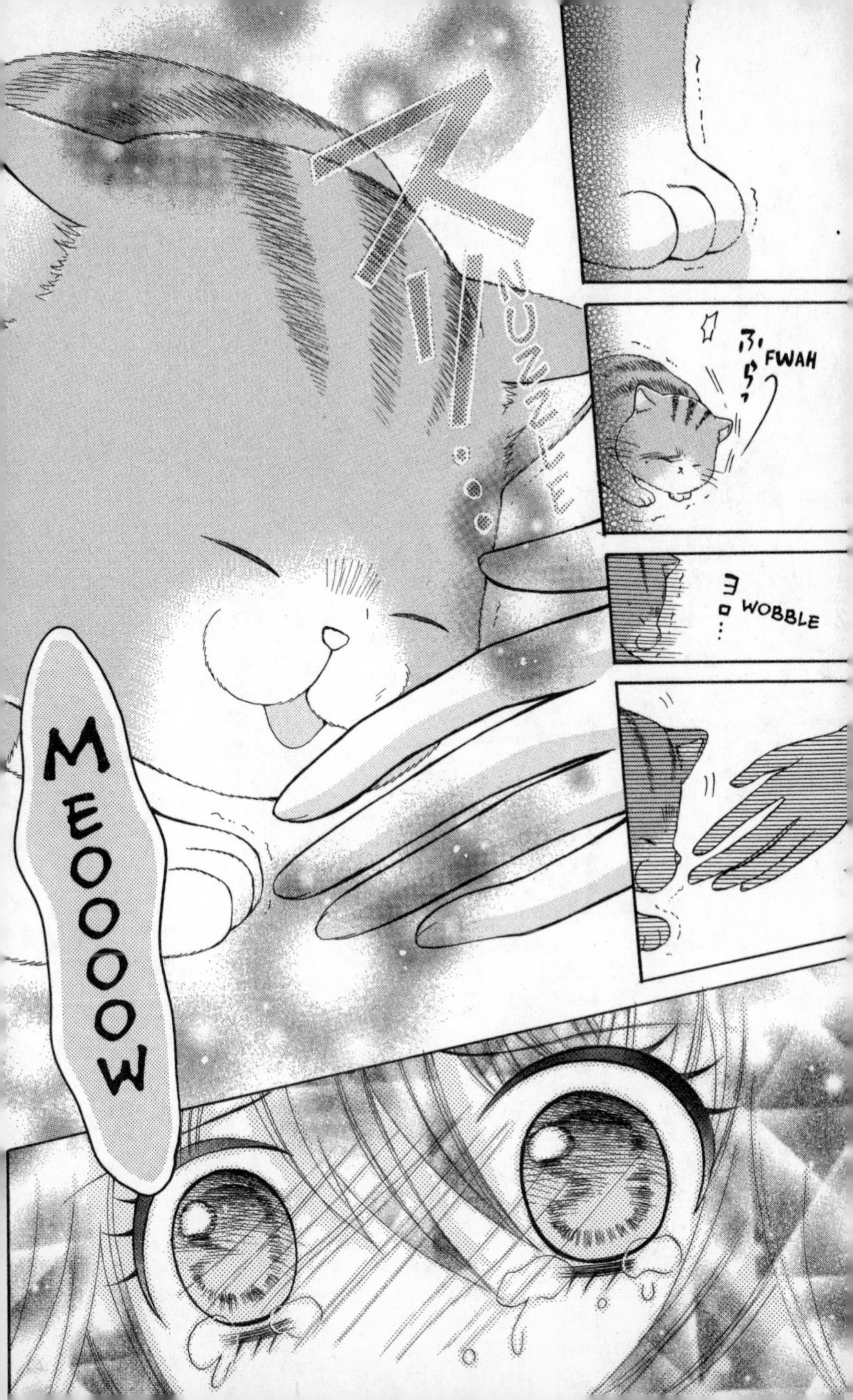
ふら FWAH
ヨロ… WOBBLE
NUZZLE...
MEOOOOW

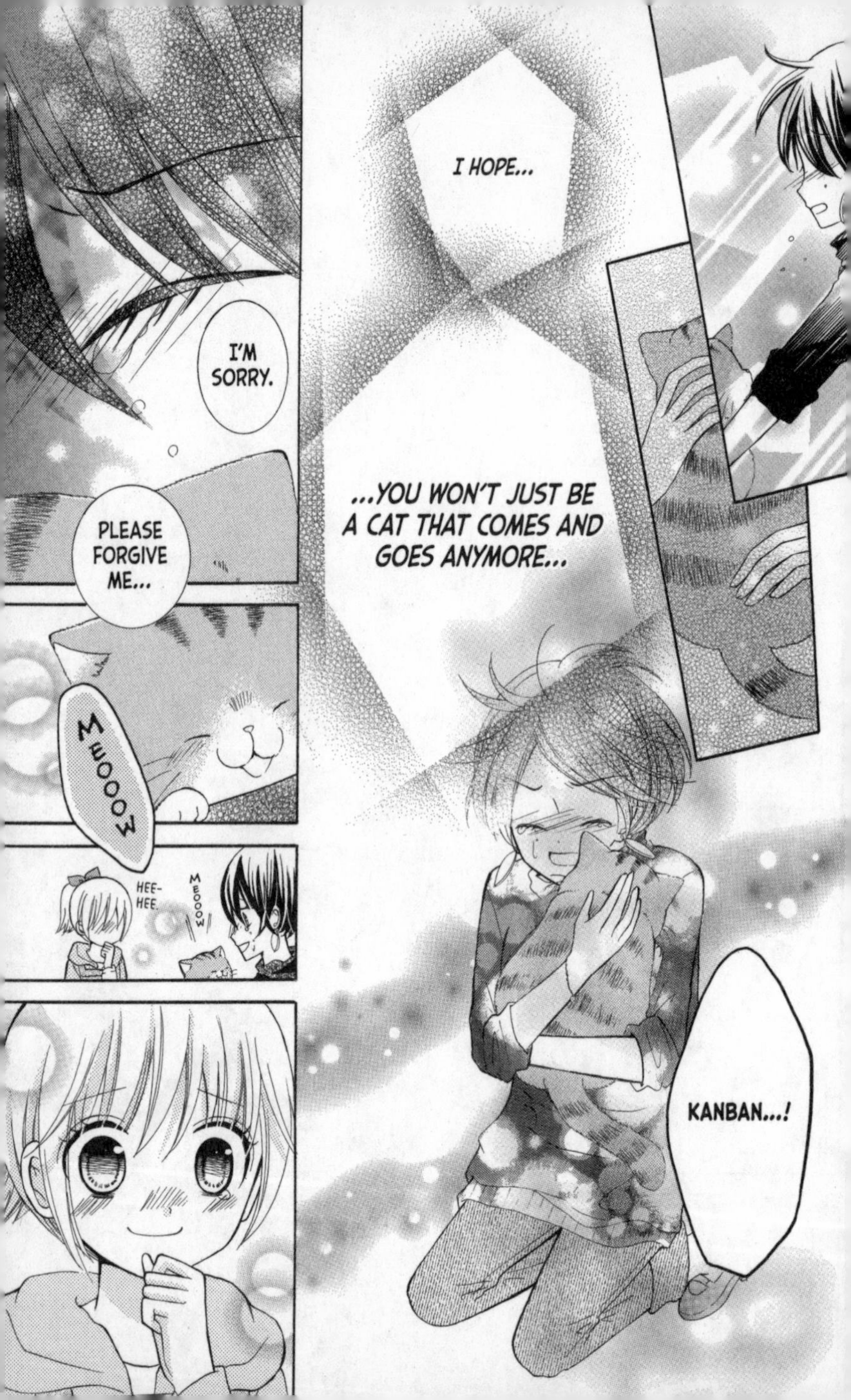
I HOPE...
...YOU WON'T JUST BE A CAT THAT COMES AND GOES ANYMORE...
KANBAN...!
I'M SORRY.
PLEASE FORGIVE ME...
MEOOOW
MEOOOW
HEE-HEE.

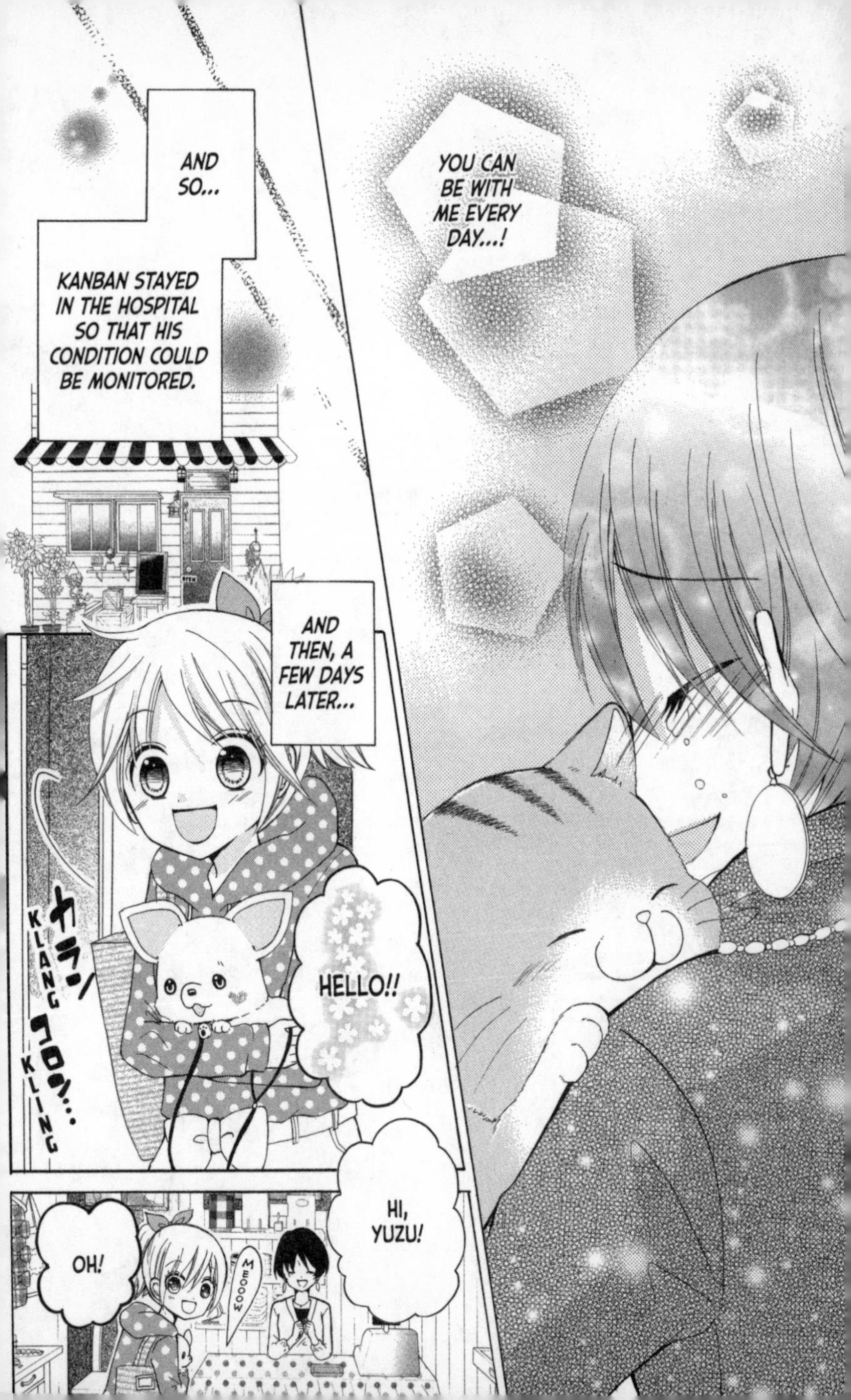
YOU CAN BE WITH ME EVERY DAY...!
AND SO...
KANBAN STAYED IN THE HOSPITAL SO THAT HIS CONDITION COULD BE MONITORED.
AND THEN, A FEW DAYS LATER...
HELLO!!
KLANG
KLING
HI, YUZU!
MEOOOW
OH!

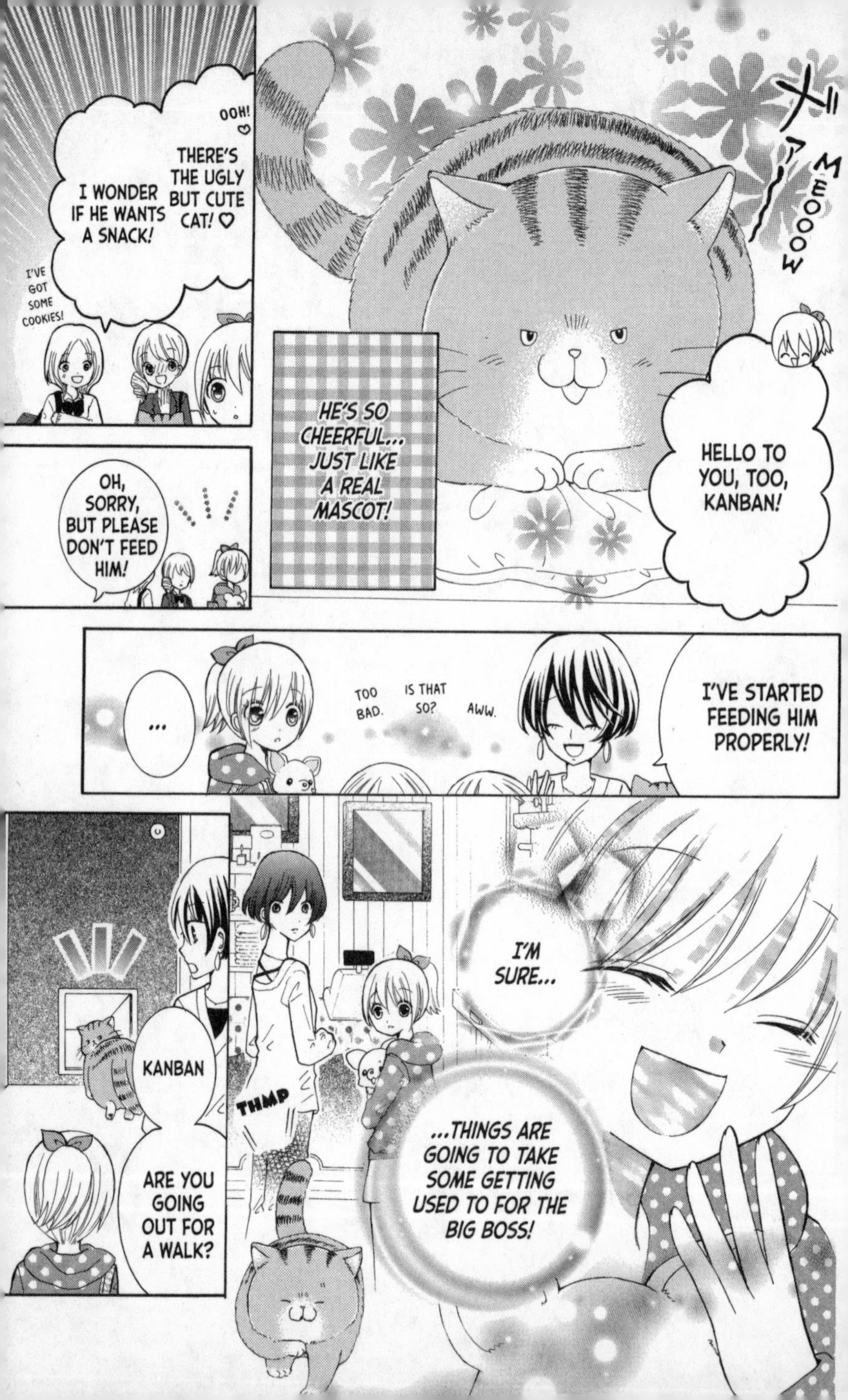
MEOOOOW
HELLO TO YOU, TOO, KANBAN!
HE'S SO CHEERFUL... JUST LIKE A REAL MASCOT!
OOH! ♡
THERE'S THE UGLY BUT CUTE CAT! ♡
I WONDER IF HE WANTS A SNACK!
I'VE GOT SOME COOKIES!
OH, SORRY, BUT PLEASE DON'T FEED HIM!
I'VE STARTED FEEDING HIM PROPERLY!
AWW.
IS THAT SO?
TOO BAD.
...
I'M SURE...
...THINGS ARE GOING TO TAKE SOME GETTING USED TO FOR THE BIG BOSS!
THMP
KANBAN
ARE YOU GOING OUT FOR A WALK?

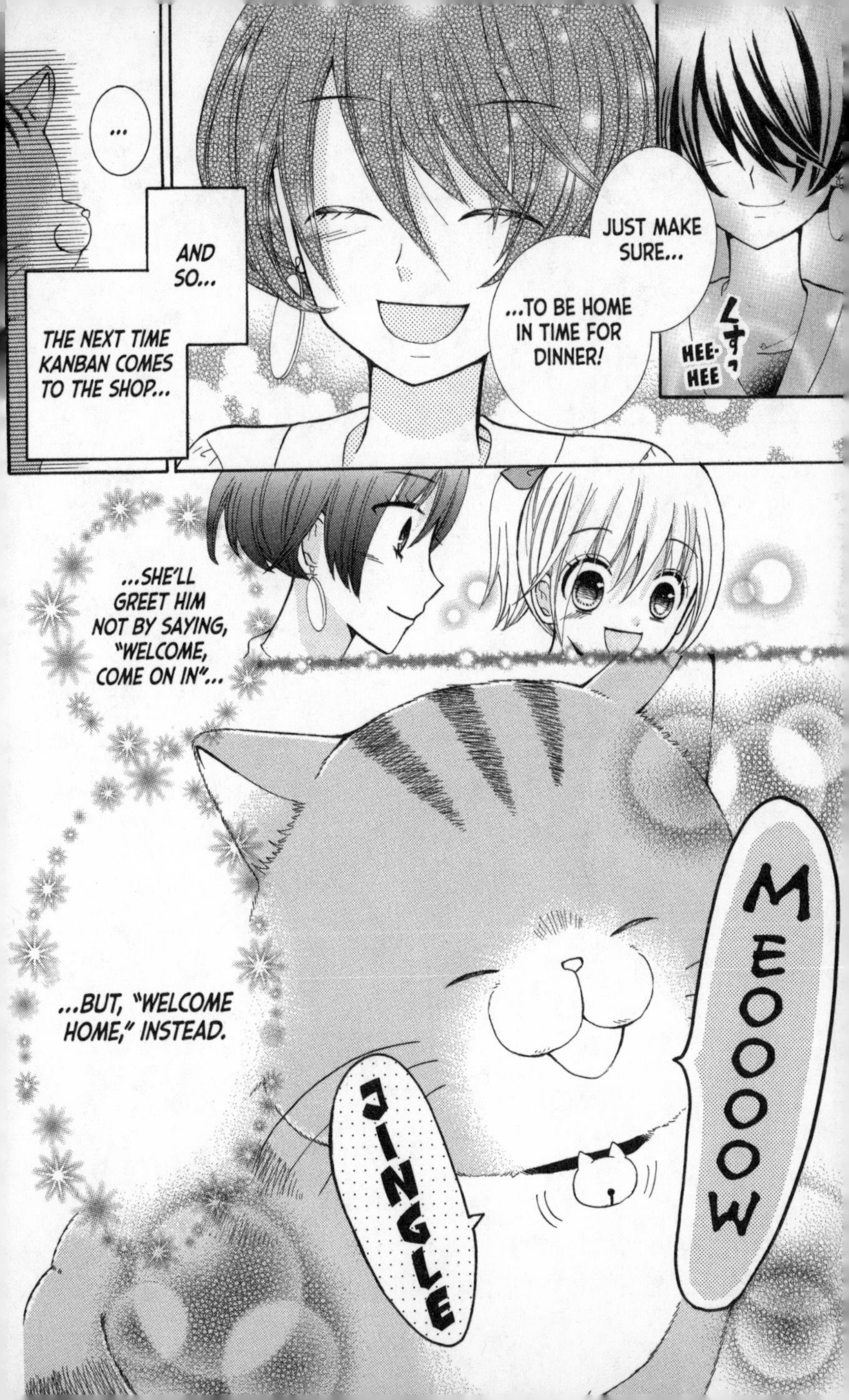
JUST MAKE SURE...
HEE-HEE
...TO BE HOME IN TIME FOR DINNER!
AND SO...
THE NEXT TIME KANBAN COMES TO THE SHOP...
...
...SHE'LL GREET HIM NOT BY SAYING, "WELCOME, COME ON IN"...
...BUT, "WELCOME HOME," INSTEAD.
MEOOOOOW
JINGLE

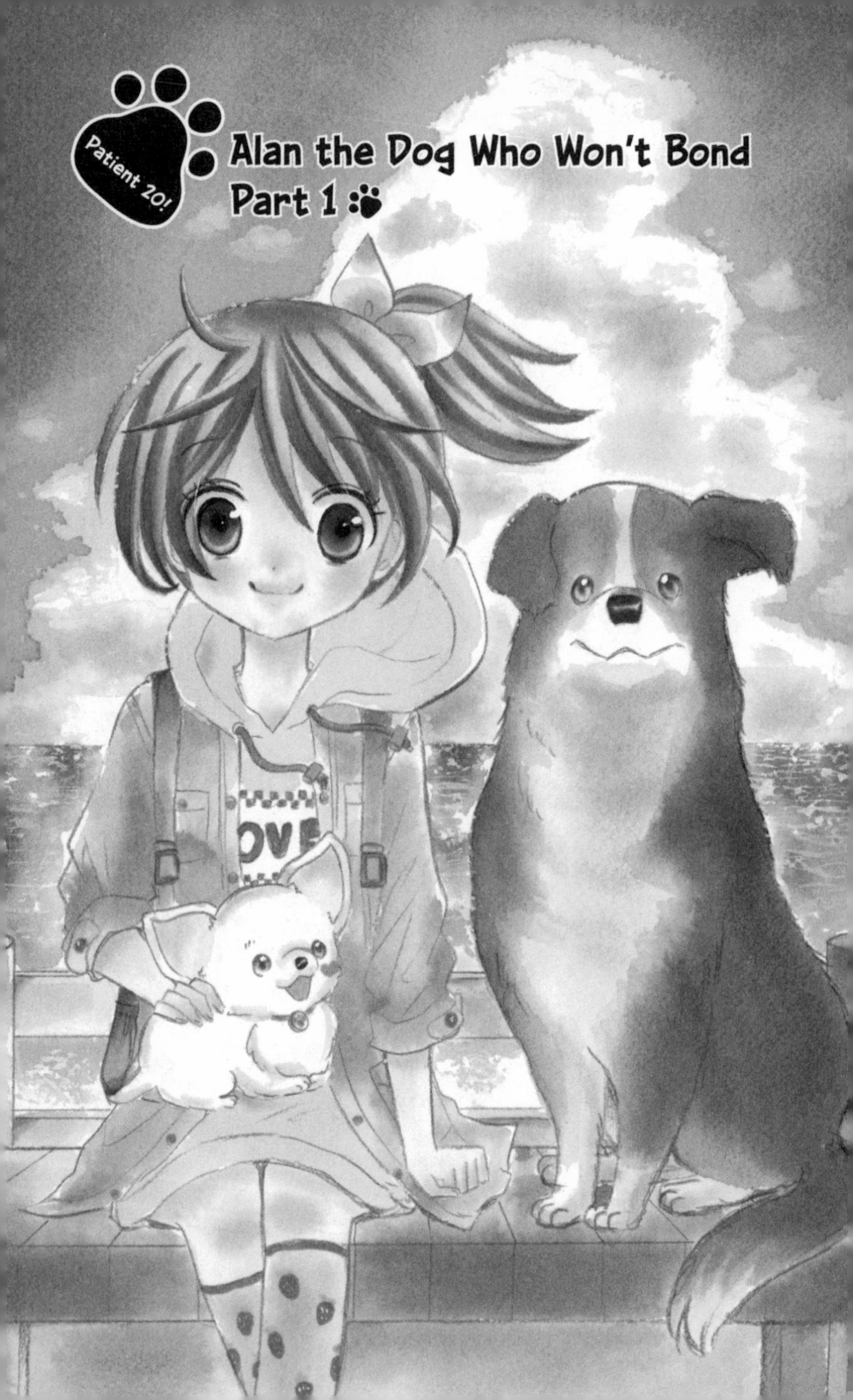
Patient 20!
Alan the Dog Who Won't Bond
Part 1

YUZU THE PET VET

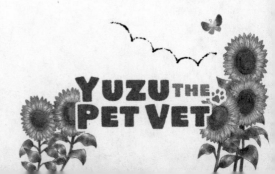

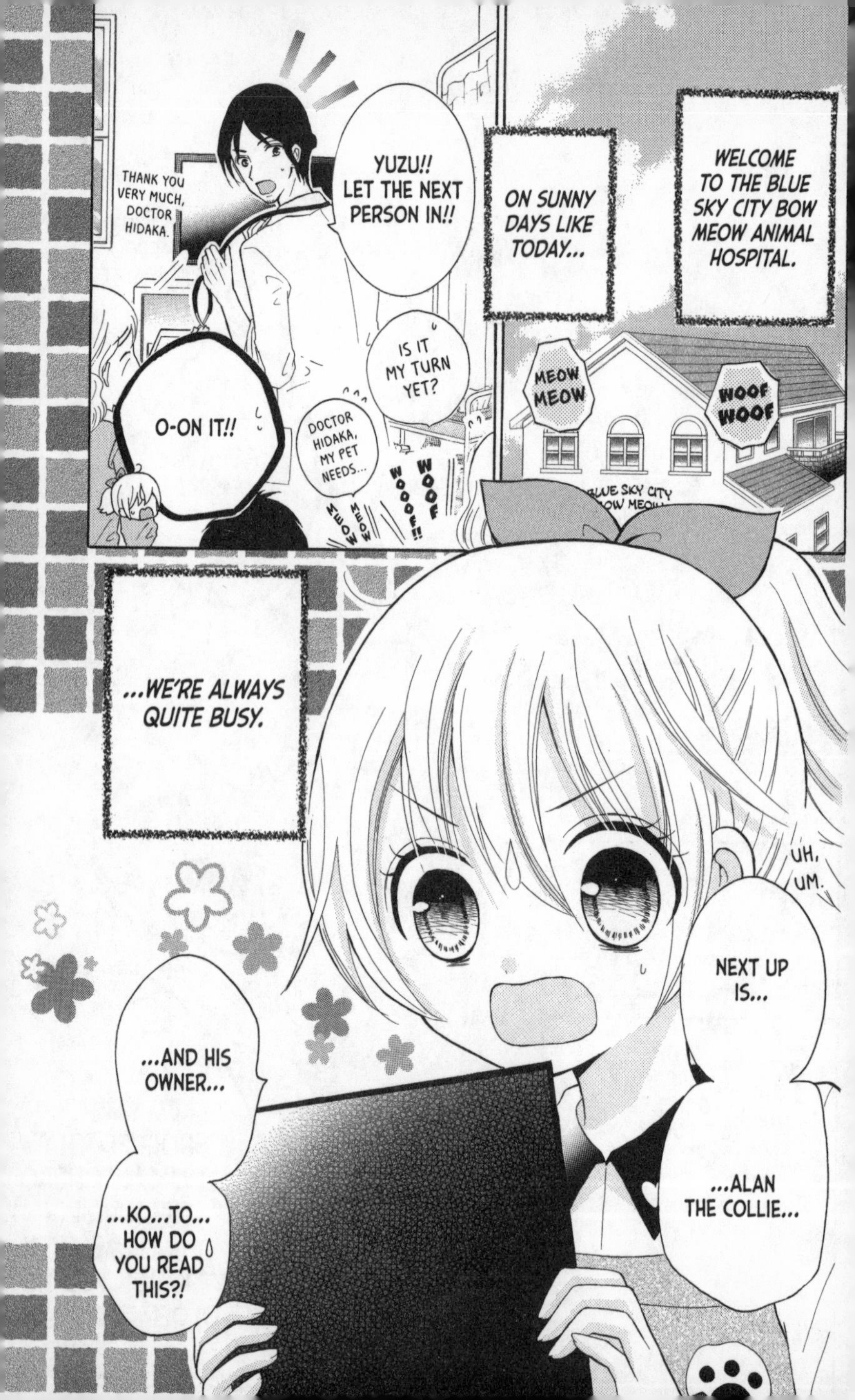
WELCOME TO THE BLUE SKY CITY BOW MEOW ANIMAL HOSPITAL.
ON SUNNY DAYS LIKE TODAY...
WOOF WOOF
MEOW MEOW
BLUE SKY CITY
YUZU!! LET THE NEXT PERSON IN!!
THANK YOU VERY MUCH, DOCTOR HIDAKA.
IS IT MY TURN YET?
DOCTOR HIDAKA, MY PET NEEDS...
WOOF
WOOOOF!!
MEOW
MEOW
O-ON IT!!
...WE'RE ALWAYS QUITE BUSY.
UH, UM.
NEXT UP IS...
...ALAN THE COLLIE...
...AND HIS OWNER...
...KO...TO... HOW DO YOU READ THIS?!

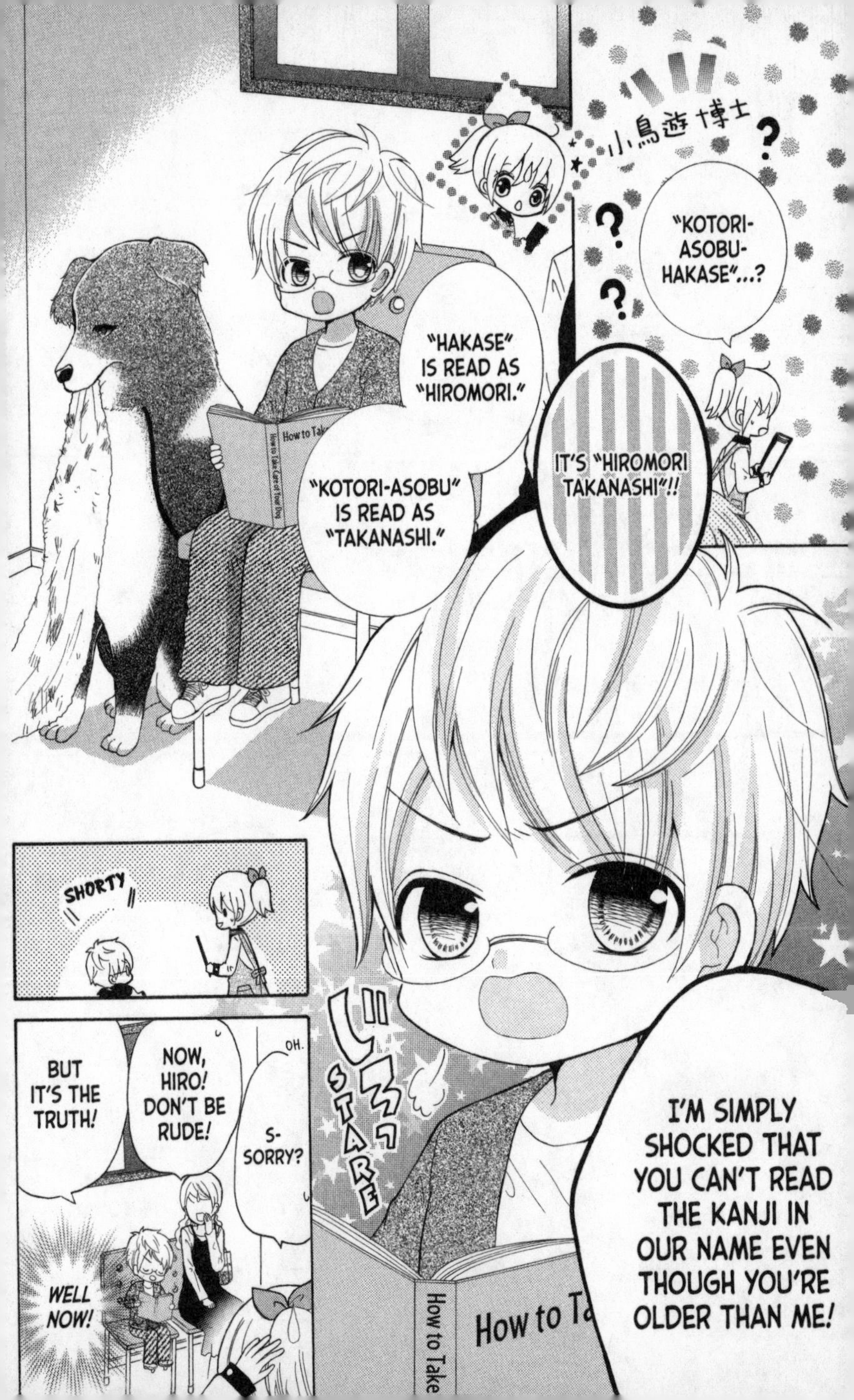
小鳥遊博士
"KOTORI-ASOBU-HAKASE"...?
IT'S "HIROMORI TAKANASHI"!!
"HAKASE" IS READ AS "HIROMORI."
"KOTORI-ASOBU" IS READ AS "TAKANASHI."
How to Take Care of Your Dog
STARE
I'M SIMPLY SHOCKED THAT YOU CAN'T READ THE KANJI IN OUR NAME EVEN THOUGH YOU'RE OLDER THAN ME!
How to Take
SHORTY
OH.
S-SORRY?
NOW, HIRO! DON'T BE RUDE!
BUT IT'S THE TRUTH!
WELL NOW!

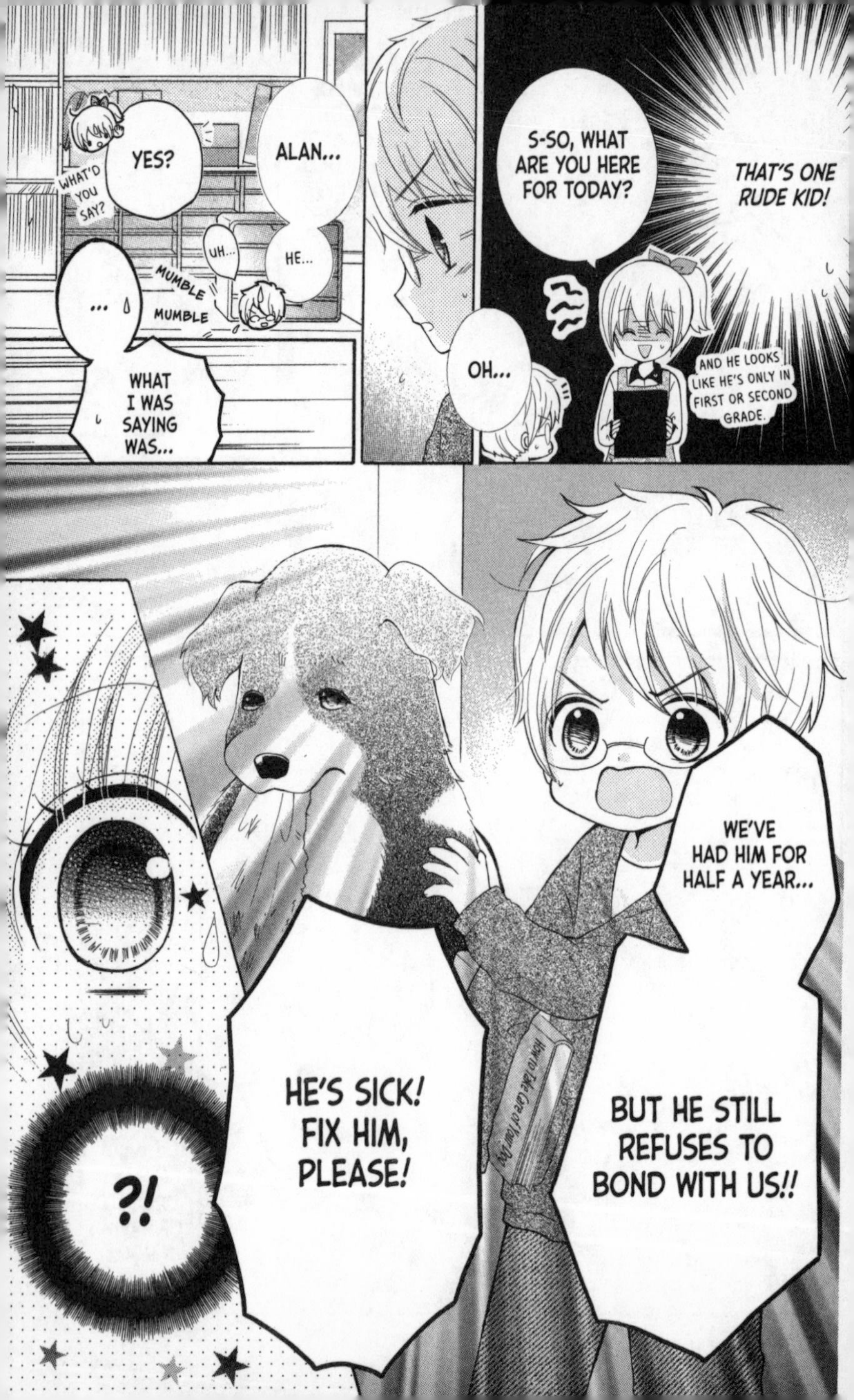
THAT'S ONE RUDE KID!
S-SO, WHAT ARE YOU HERE FOR TODAY?
AND HE LOOKS LIKE HE'S ONLY IN FIRST OR SECOND GRADE.
ALAN...
HE...
OH...
YES?
WHAT'D YOU SAY?
UH...
MUMBLE
MUMBLE
...
WHAT I WAS SAYING WAS...
WE'VE HAD HIM FOR HALF A YEAR...
BUT HE STILL REFUSES TO BOND WITH US!!
HE'S SICK! FIX HIM, PLEASE!
?!

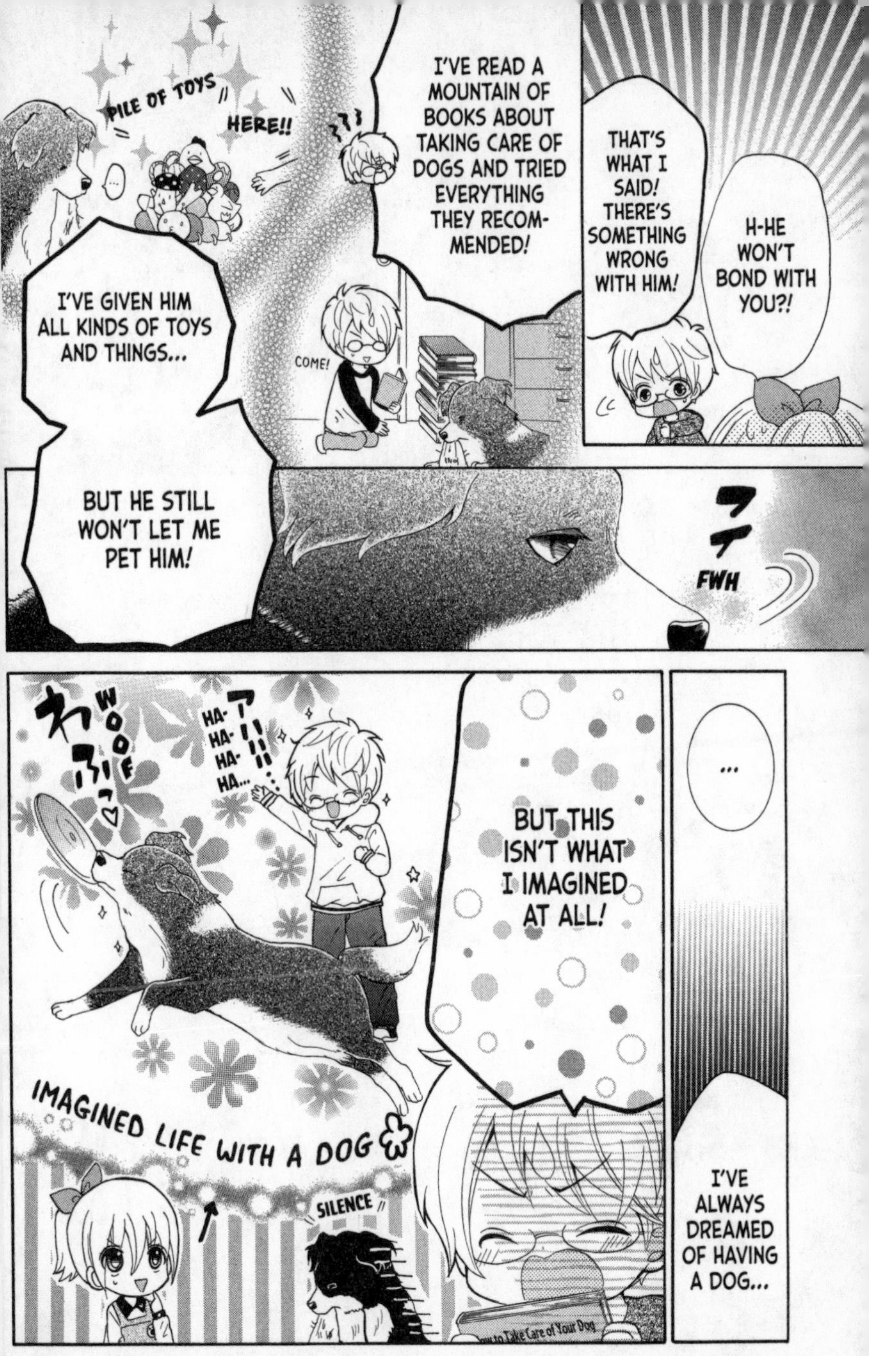
H-HE WON'T BOND WITH YOU?!
THAT'S WHAT I SAID! THERE'S SOMETHING WRONG WITH HIM!
I'VE READ A MOUNTAIN OF BOOKS ABOUT TAKING CARE OF DOGS AND TRIED EVERYTHING THEY RECOM-MENDED!
COME!
PILE OF TOYS
HERE!!
...
I'VE GIVEN HIM ALL KINDS OF TOYS AND THINGS...
BUT HE STILL WON'T LET ME PET HIM!
FWH
...
I'VE ALWAYS DREAMED OF HAVING A DOG...
BUT THIS ISN'T WHAT I IMAGINED AT ALL!
HA- HA- HA- HA...
WOOF
IMAGINED LIFE WITH A DOG
SILENCE

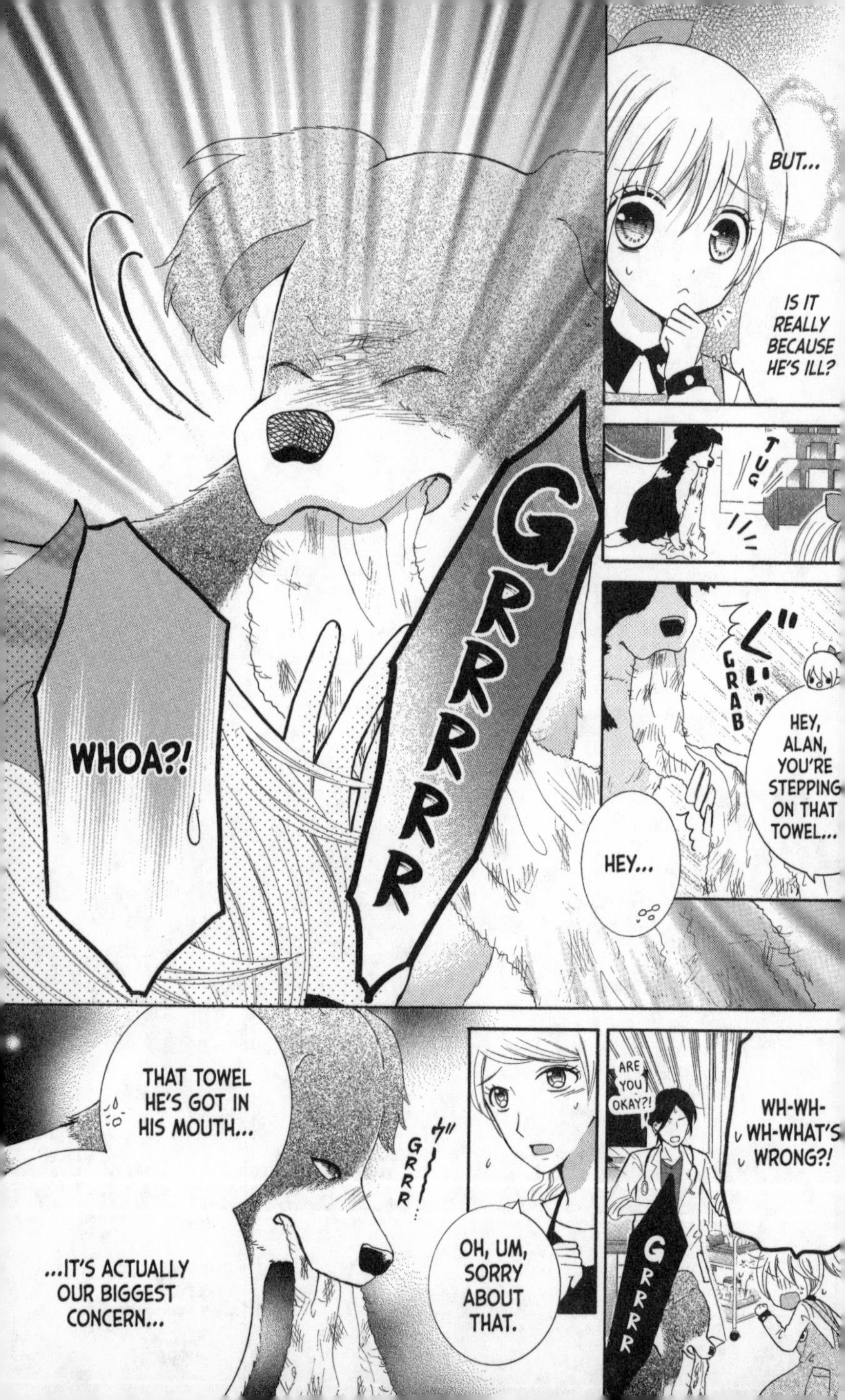
BUT...
IS IT REALLY BECAUSE HE'S ILL?
TUG
GRAB
HEY, ALAN, YOU'RE STEPPING ON THAT TOWEL...
HEY...
GRRRRRR
WHOA?!
WH-WH-WH-WHAT'S WRONG?!
ARE YOU OKAY?!
GRRRR
OH, UM, SORRY ABOUT THAT.
THAT TOWEL HE'S GOT IN HIS MOUTH...
GRRR
...IT'S ACTUALLY OUR BIGGEST CONCERN...

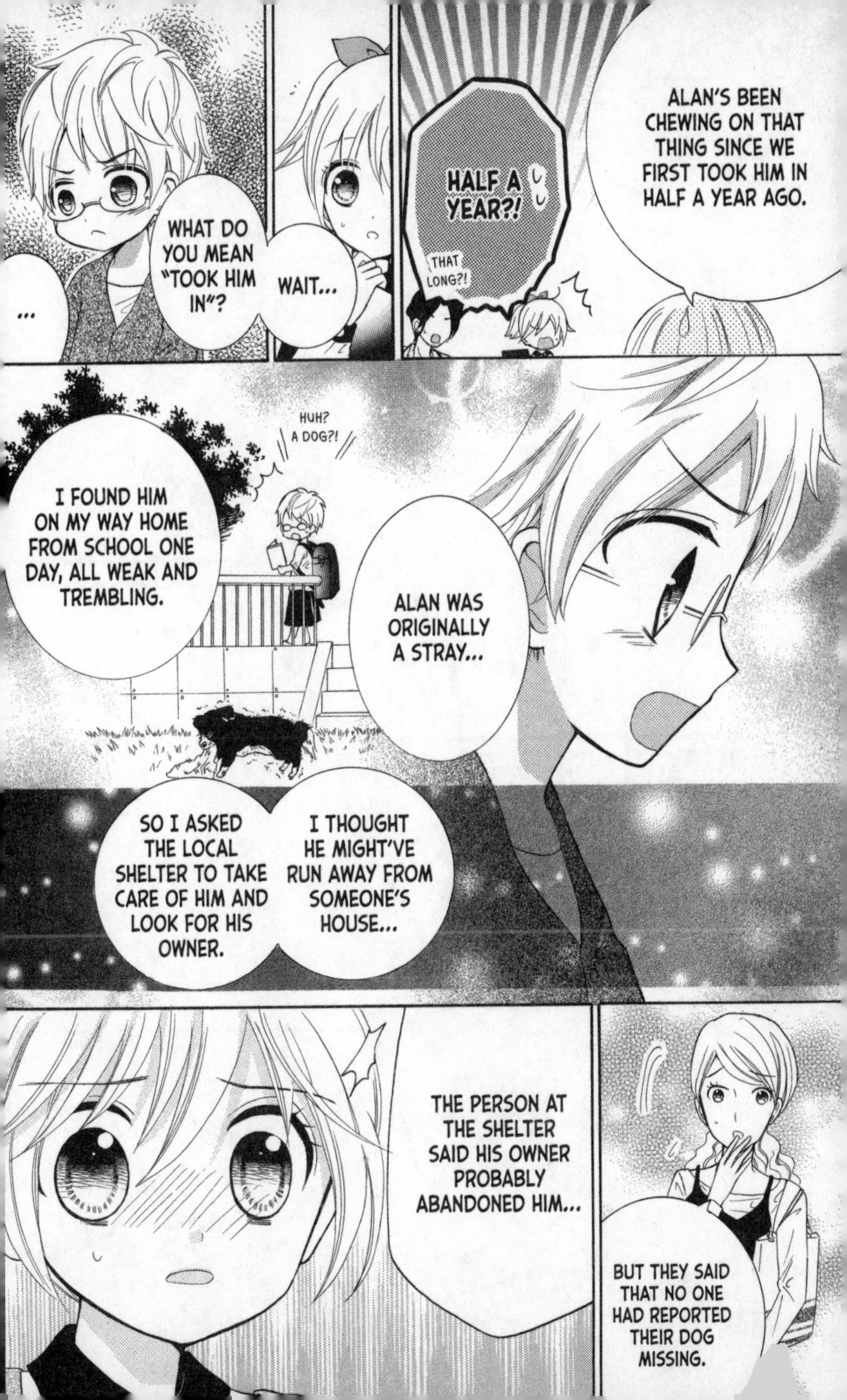
ALAN'S BEEN CHEWING ON THAT THING SINCE WE FIRST TOOK HIM IN HALF A YEAR AGO.
HALF A YEAR?!
THAT LONG?!
WAIT...
WHAT DO YOU MEAN "TOOK HIM IN"?
...
ALAN WAS ORIGINALLY A STRAY...
HUH? A DOG?!
I FOUND HIM ON MY WAY HOME FROM SCHOOL ONE DAY, ALL WEAK AND TREMBLING.
I THOUGHT HE MIGHT'VE RUN AWAY FROM SOMEONE'S HOUSE...
SO I ASKED THE LOCAL SHELTER TO TAKE CARE OF HIM AND LOOK FOR HIS OWNER.
BUT THEY SAID THAT NO ONE HAD REPORTED THEIR DOG MISSING.
THE PERSON AT THE SHELTER SAID HIS OWNER PROBABLY ABANDONED HIM...

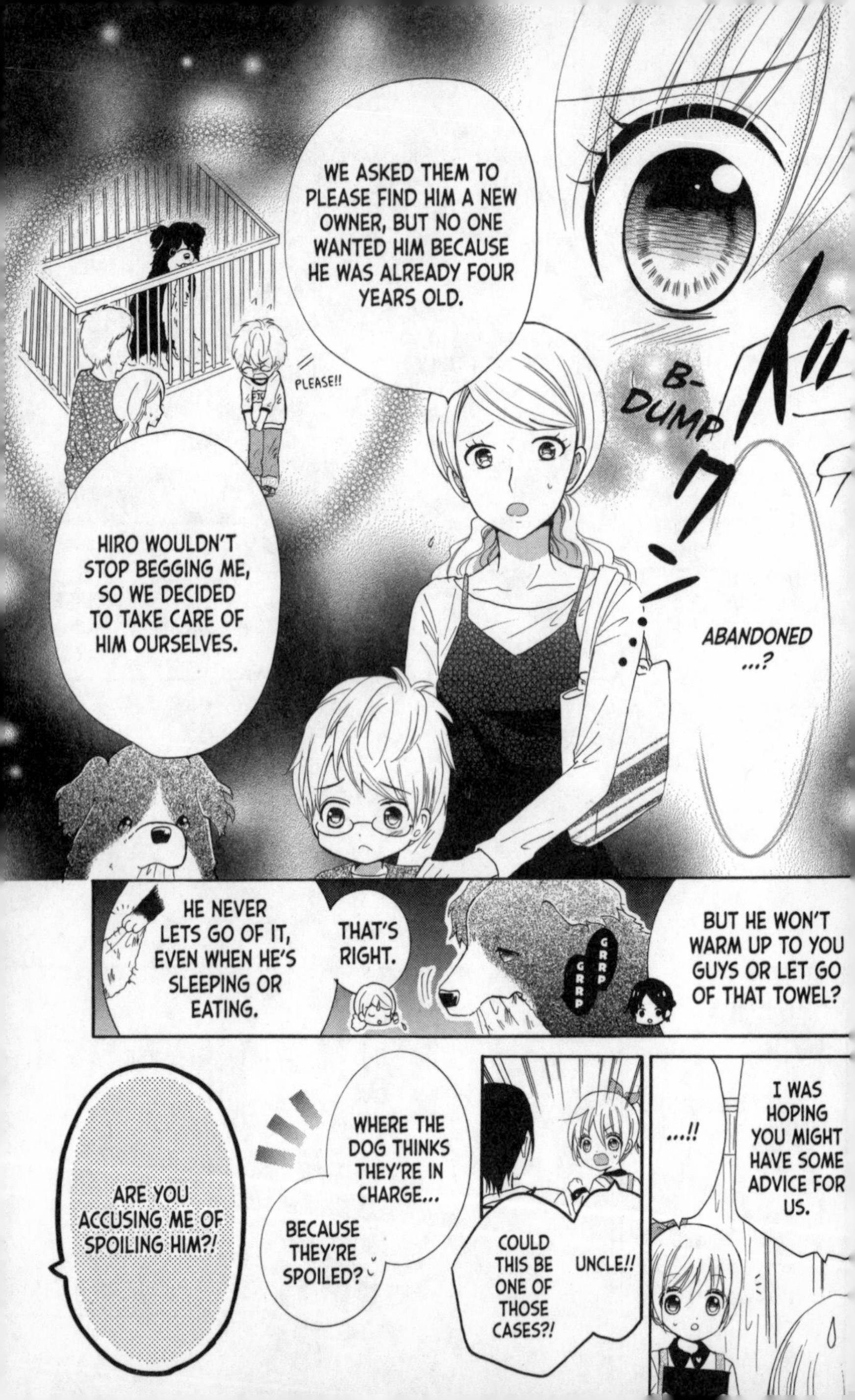
B-DUMP
ABANDONED ...?
WE ASKED THEM TO PLEASE FIND HIM A NEW OWNER, BUT NO ONE WANTED HIM BECAUSE HE WAS ALREADY FOUR YEARS OLD.
PLEASE!!
HIRO WOULDN'T STOP BEGGING ME, SO WE DECIDED TO TAKE CARE OF HIM OURSELVES.
BUT HE WON'T WARM UP TO YOU GUYS OR LET GO OF THAT TOWEL?
GRRP
GRRP
THAT'S RIGHT.
HE NEVER LETS GO OF IT, EVEN WHEN HE'S SLEEPING OR EATING.
I WAS HOPING YOU MIGHT HAVE SOME ADVICE FOR US.
...!!
COULD THIS BE ONE OF THOSE CASES?!
UNCLE!!
WHERE THE DOG THINKS THEY'RE IN CHARGE...
BECAUSE THEY'RE SPOILED?
ARE YOU ACCUSING ME OF SPOILING HIM?!

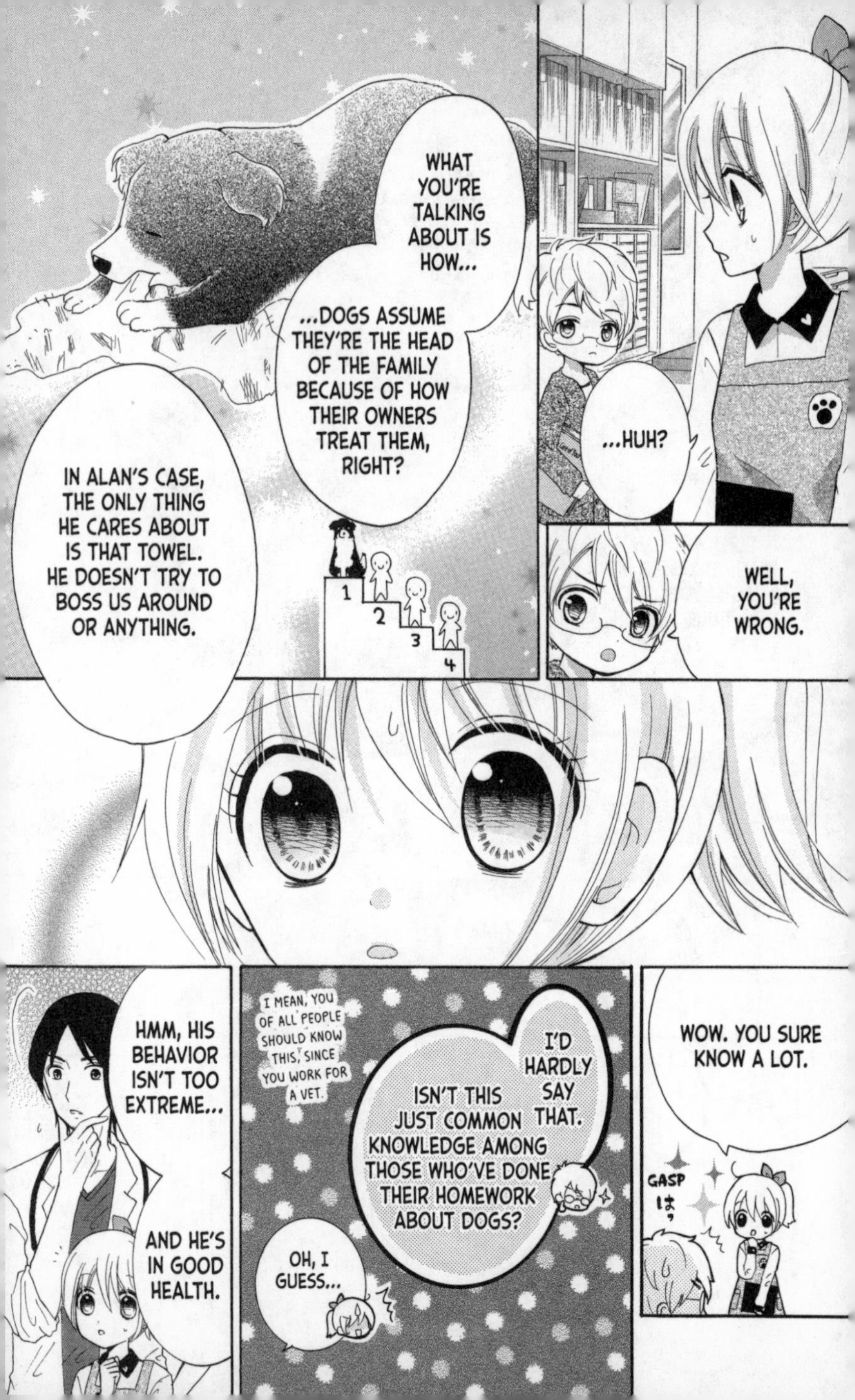
...HUH?
WELL, YOU'RE WRONG.
WHAT YOU'RE TALKING ABOUT IS HOW...
...DOGS ASSUME THEY'RE THE HEAD OF THE FAMILY BECAUSE OF HOW THEIR OWNERS TREAT THEM, RIGHT?
1
2
3
4
IN ALAN'S CASE, THE ONLY THING HE CARES ABOUT IS THAT TOWEL. HE DOESN'T TRY TO BOSS US AROUND OR ANYTHING.
WOW. YOU SURE KNOW A LOT.
GASP
は
I'D HARDLY SAY THAT.
ISN'T THIS JUST COMMON KNOWLEDGE AMONG THOSE WHO'VE DONE THEIR HOMEWORK ABOUT DOGS?
I MEAN, YOU OF ALL PEOPLE SHOULD KNOW THIS, SINCE YOU WORK FOR A VET.
OH, I GUESS...
HMM, HIS BEHAVIOR ISN'T TOO EXTREME...
AND HE'S IN GOOD HEALTH.

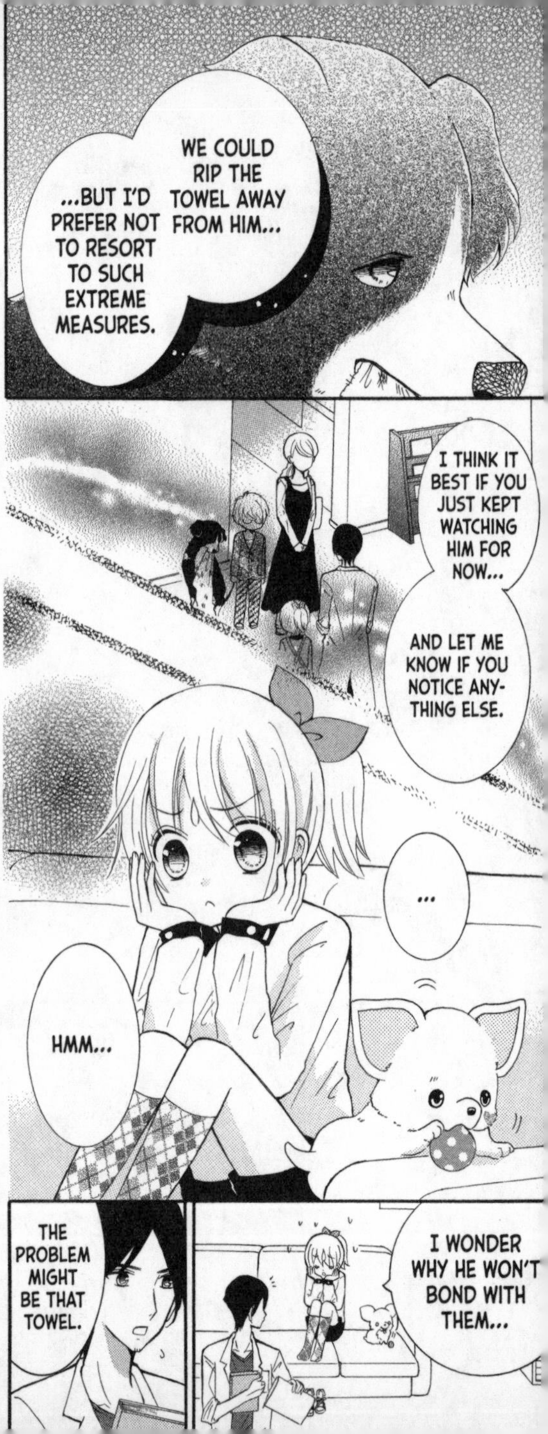
WE COULD RIP THE TOWEL AWAY FROM HIM...
...BUT I'D PREFER NOT TO RESORT TO SUCH EXTREME MEASURES.
I THINK IT BEST IF YOU JUST KEPT WATCHING HIM FOR NOW...
AND LET ME KNOW IF YOU NOTICE ANYTHING ELSE.
...
HMM...
I WONDER WHY HE WON'T BOND WITH THEM...
THE PROBLEM MIGHT BE THAT TOWEL.

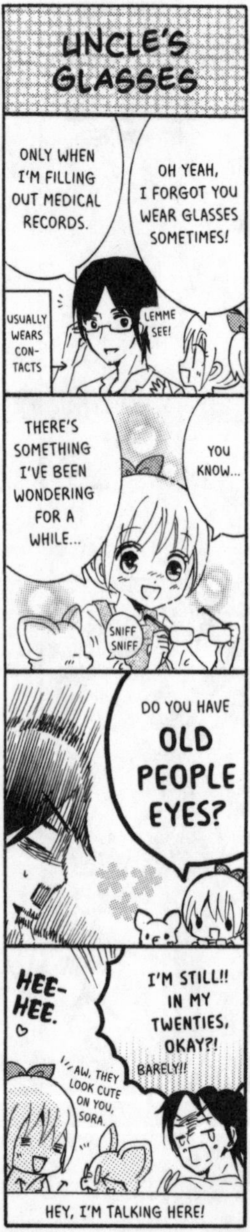
UNCLE'S GLASSES
OH YEAH, I FORGOT YOU WEAR GLASSES SOMETIMES!
ONLY WHEN I'M FILLING OUT MEDICAL RECORDS.
LEMME SEE!
USUALLY WEARS CONTACTS
YOU KNOW...
THERE'S SOMETHING I'VE BEEN WONDERING FOR A WHILE...
SNIFF SNIFF
DO YOU HAVE OLD PEOPLE EYES?
I'M STILL!! IN MY TWENTIES, OKAY?!
BARELY!!
HEE-HEE.
AW, THEY LOOK CUTE ON YOU, SORA.
HEY, I'M TALKING HERE!

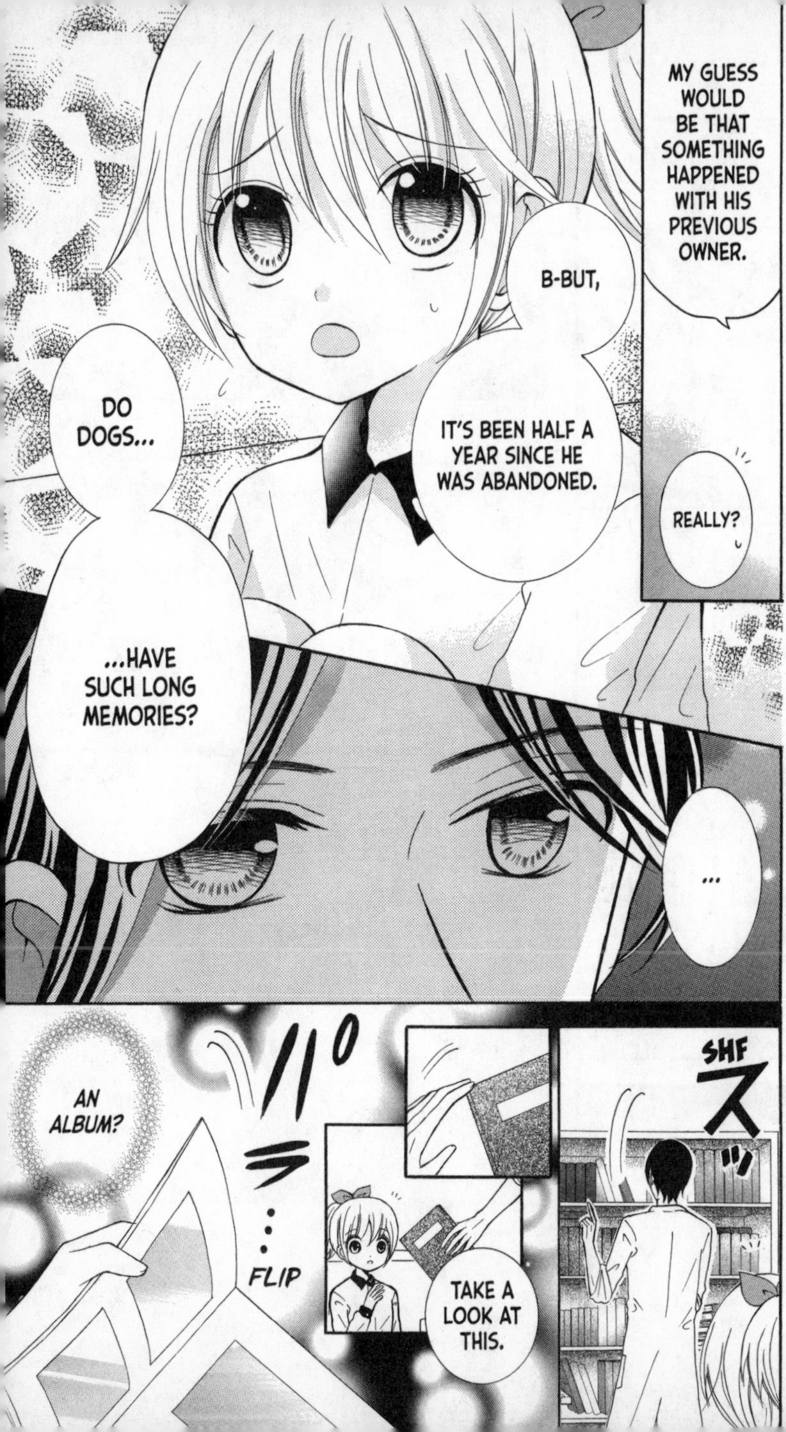
MY GUESS WOULD BE THAT SOMETHING HAPPENED WITH HIS PREVIOUS OWNER.
REALLY?
B-BUT,
IT'S BEEN HALF A YEAR SINCE HE WAS ABANDONED.
DO DOGS...
...HAVE SUCH LONG MEMORIES?
...
SHF
TAKE A LOOK AT THIS.
...
FLIP
AN ALBUM?

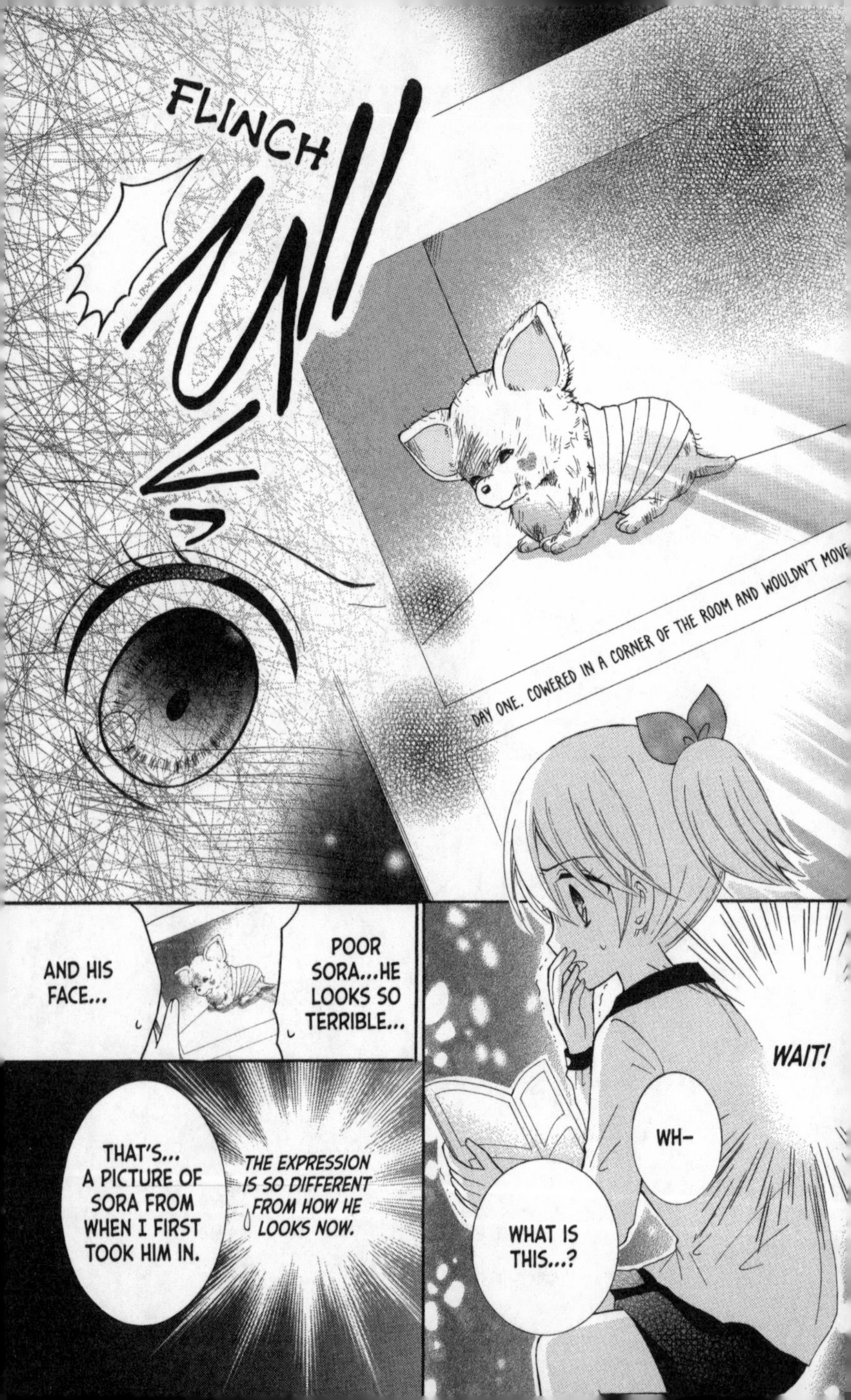
DAY ONE. COWERED IN A CORNER OF THE ROOM AND WOULDN'T MOVE
FLINCH
WAIT!
WH-
WHAT IS THIS...?
POOR SORA...HE LOOKS SO TERRIBLE...
AND HIS FACE...
THAT'S... A PICTURE OF SORA FROM WHEN I FIRST TOOK HIM IN.
THE EXPRESSION IS SO DIFFERENT FROM HOW HE LOOKS NOW.

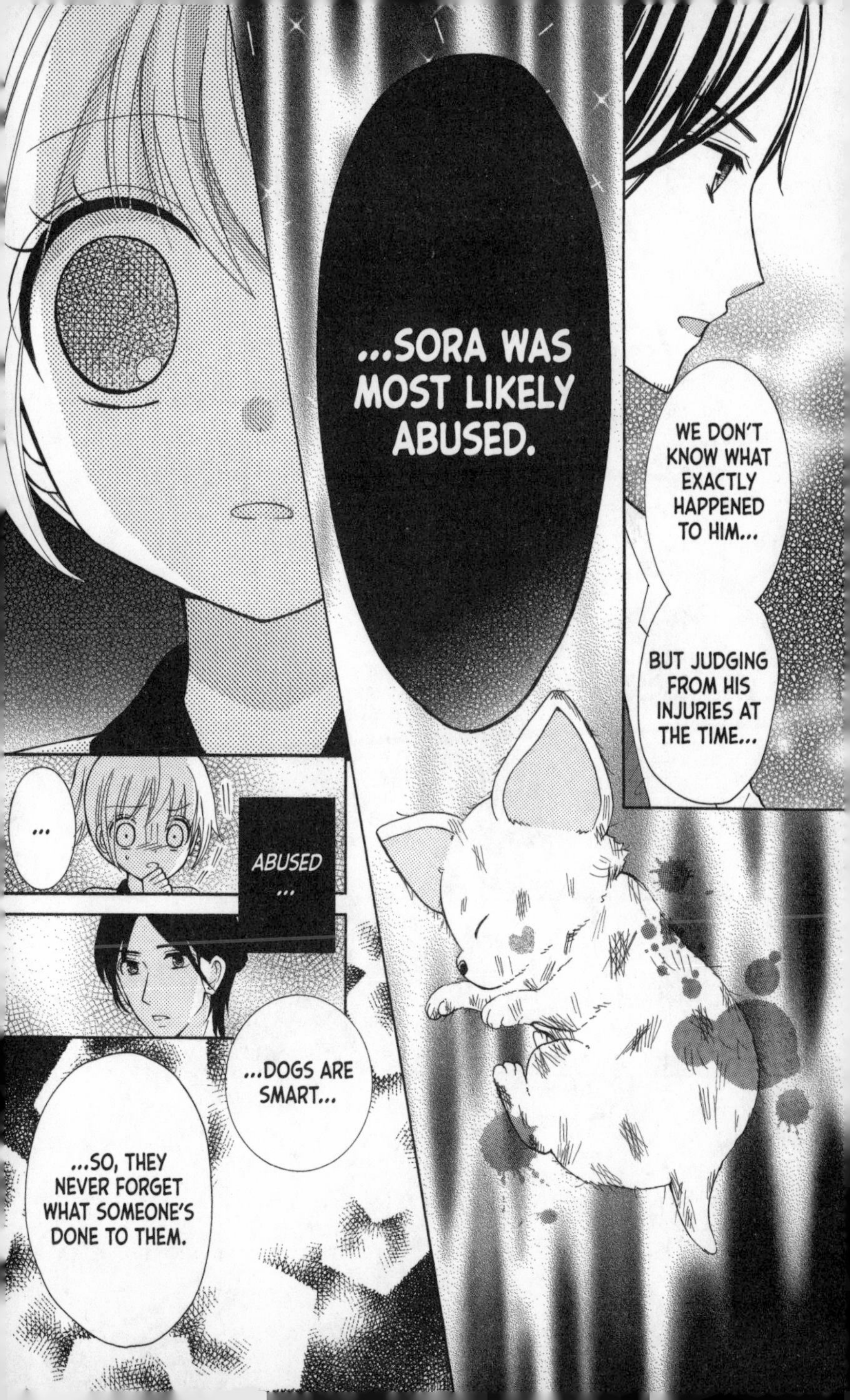
WE DON'T KNOW WHAT EXACTLY HAPPENED TO HIM...
BUT JUDGING FROM HIS INJURIES AT THE TIME...
...SORA WAS MOST LIKELY ABUSED.
ABUSED...
...
...DOGS ARE SMART...
...SO, THEY NEVER FORGET WHAT SOMEONE'S DONE TO THEM.

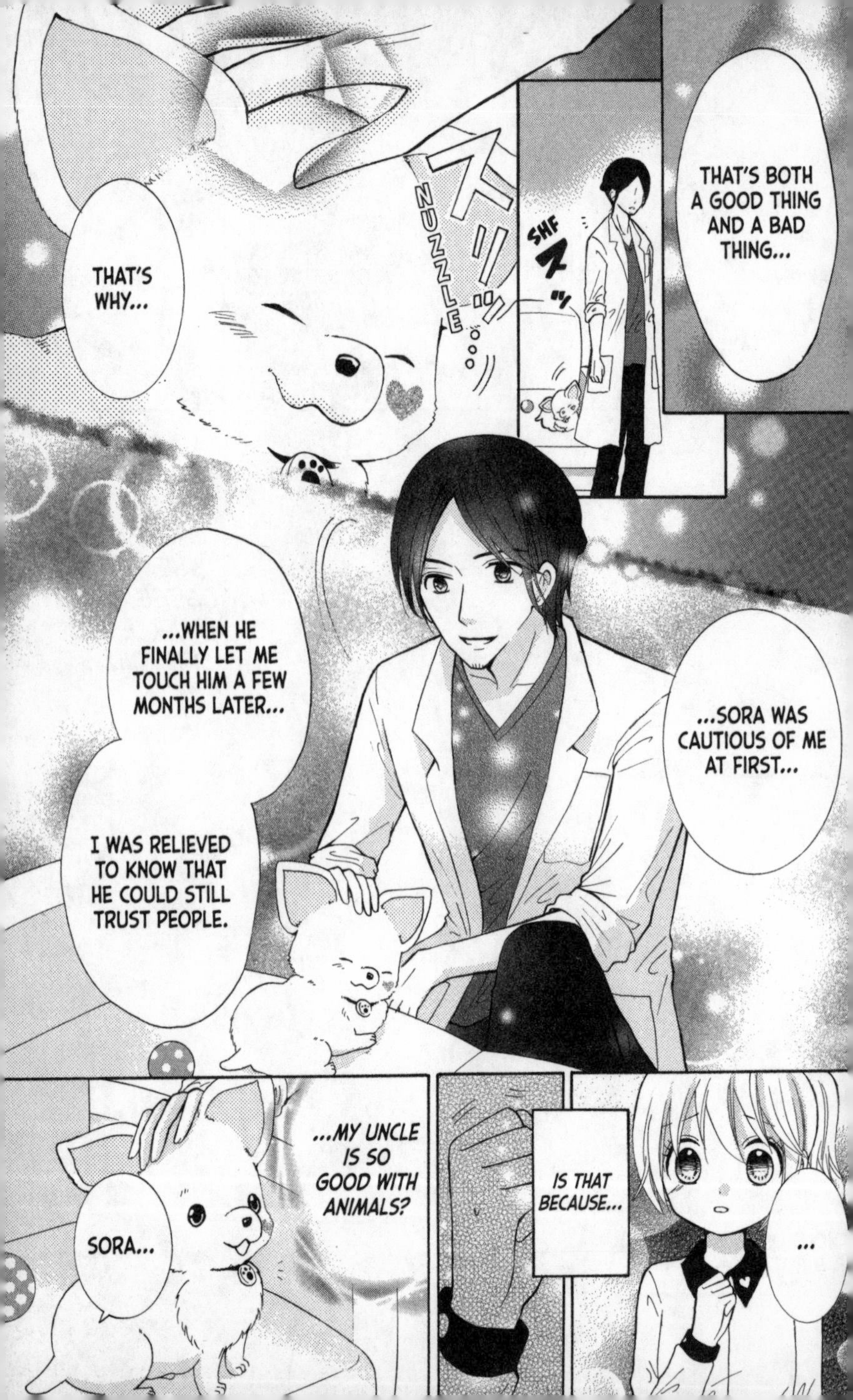
THAT'S BOTH A GOOD THING AND A BAD THING...
SHF
NUZZLE
THAT'S WHY...
...SORA WAS CAUTIOUS OF ME AT FIRST...
...WHEN HE FINALLY LET ME TOUCH HIM A FEW MONTHS LATER...
I WAS RELIEVED TO KNOW THAT HE COULD STILL TRUST PEOPLE.
...
IS THAT BECAUSE...
...MY UNCLE IS SO GOOD WITH ANIMALS?
SORA...

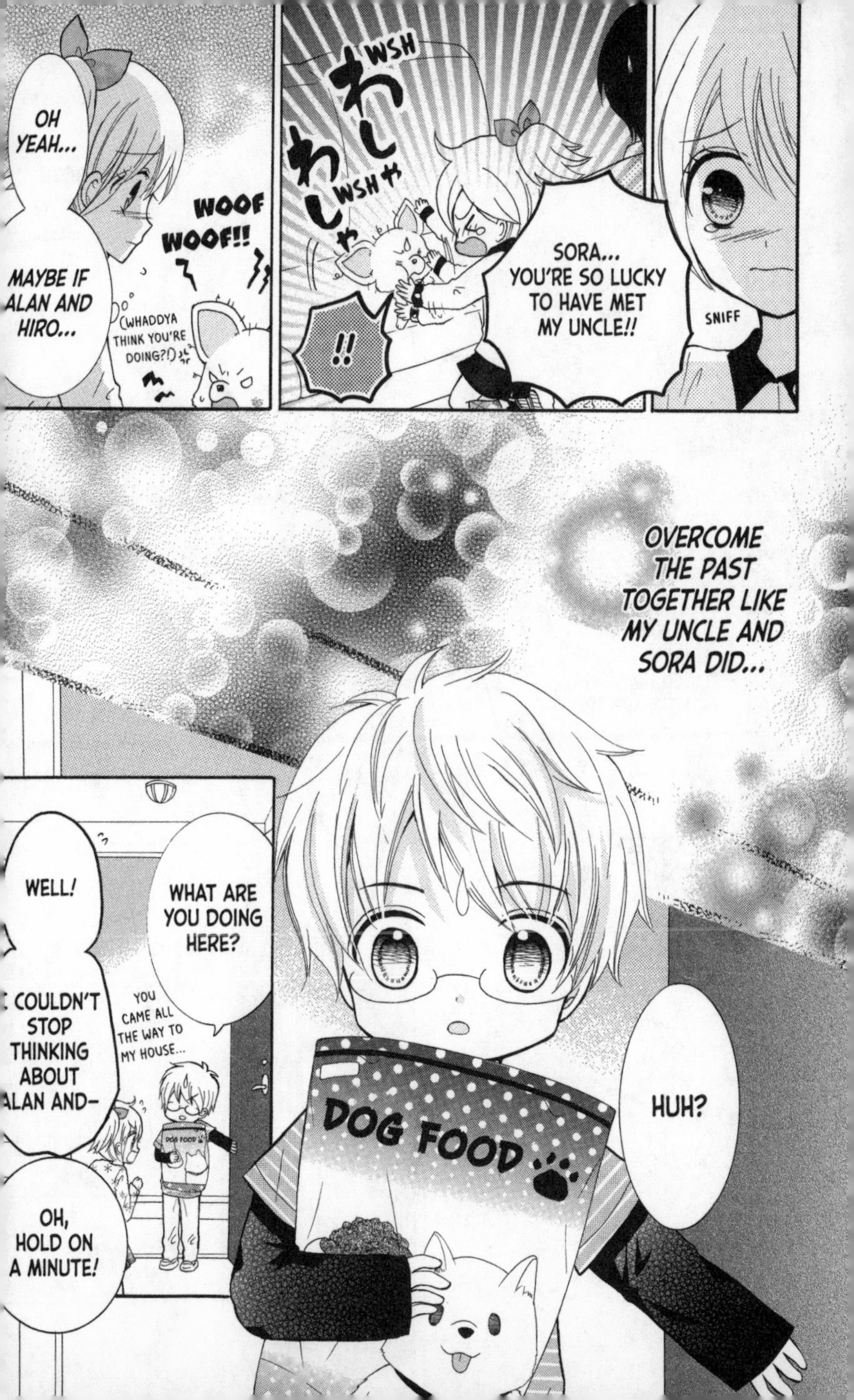
SNIFF
SORA... YOU'RE SO LUCKY TO HAVE MET MY UNCLE!!
WSH WSH
!!
OH YEAH...
WOOF WOOF!!
(WHADDYA THINK YOU'RE DOING?!)
MAYBE IF ALAN AND HIRO...
OVERCOME THE PAST TOGETHER LIKE MY UNCLE AND SORA DID...
HUH?
DOG FOOD
WHAT ARE YOU DOING HERE?
YOU CAME ALL THE WAY TO MY HOUSE...
WELL!
COULDN'T STOP THINKING ABOUT ALAN AND–
OH, HOLD ON A MINUTE!

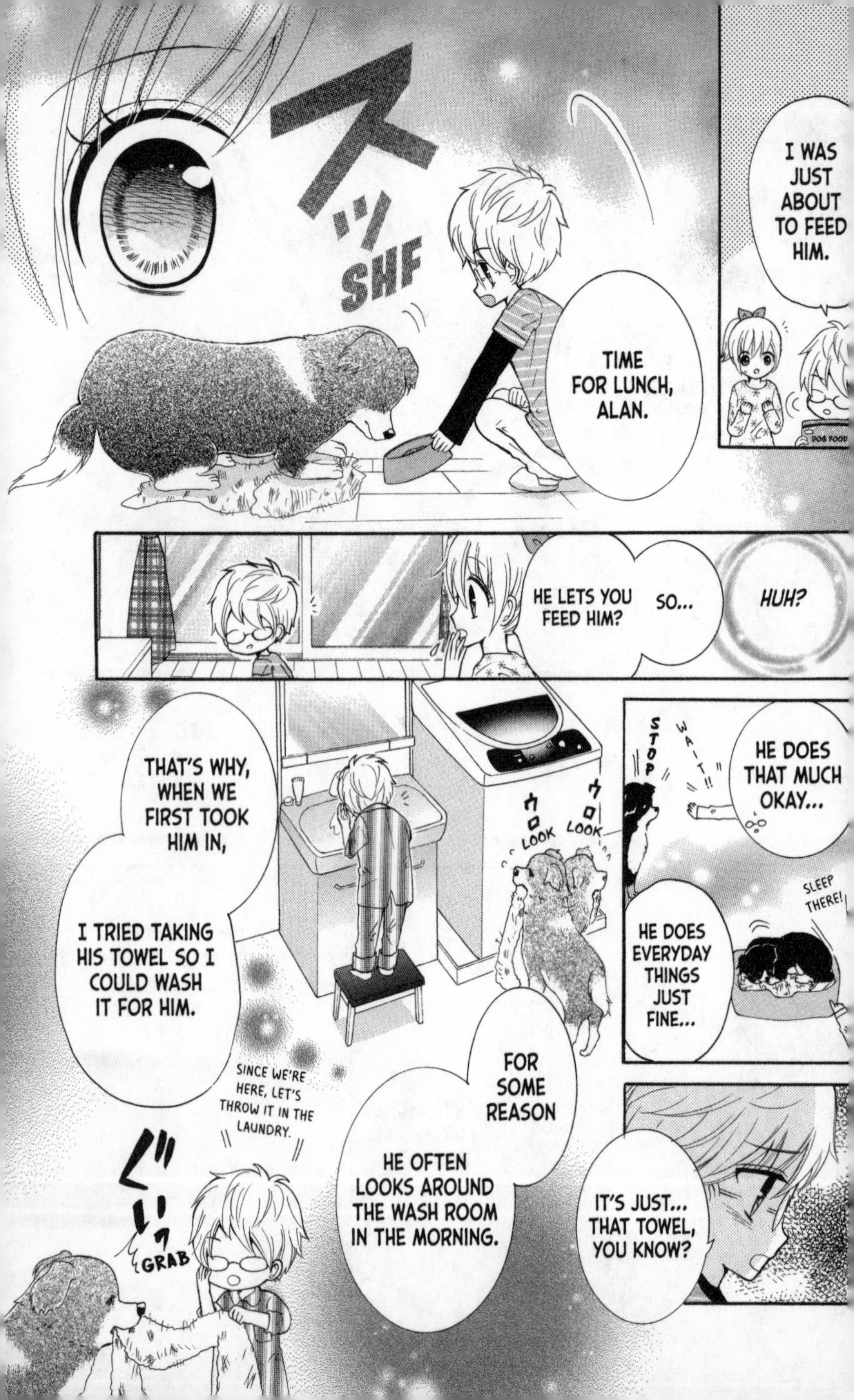
I WAS JUST ABOUT TO FEED HIM.
DOG FOOD
SHF
TIME FOR LUNCH, ALAN.
HUH?
SO...
HE LETS YOU FEED HIM?
HE DOES THAT MUCH OKAY...
STOP
WAIT!!
HE DOES EVERYDAY THINGS JUST FINE...
SLEEP THERE!
IT'S JUST... THAT TOWEL, YOU KNOW?
FOR SOME REASON
HE OFTEN LOOKS AROUND THE WASH ROOM IN THE MORNING.
LOOK
LOOK
THAT'S WHY, WHEN WE FIRST TOOK HIM IN,
I TRIED TAKING HIS TOWEL SO I COULD WASH IT FOR HIM.
SINCE WE'RE HERE, LET'S THROW IT IN THE LAUNDRY.
GRAB

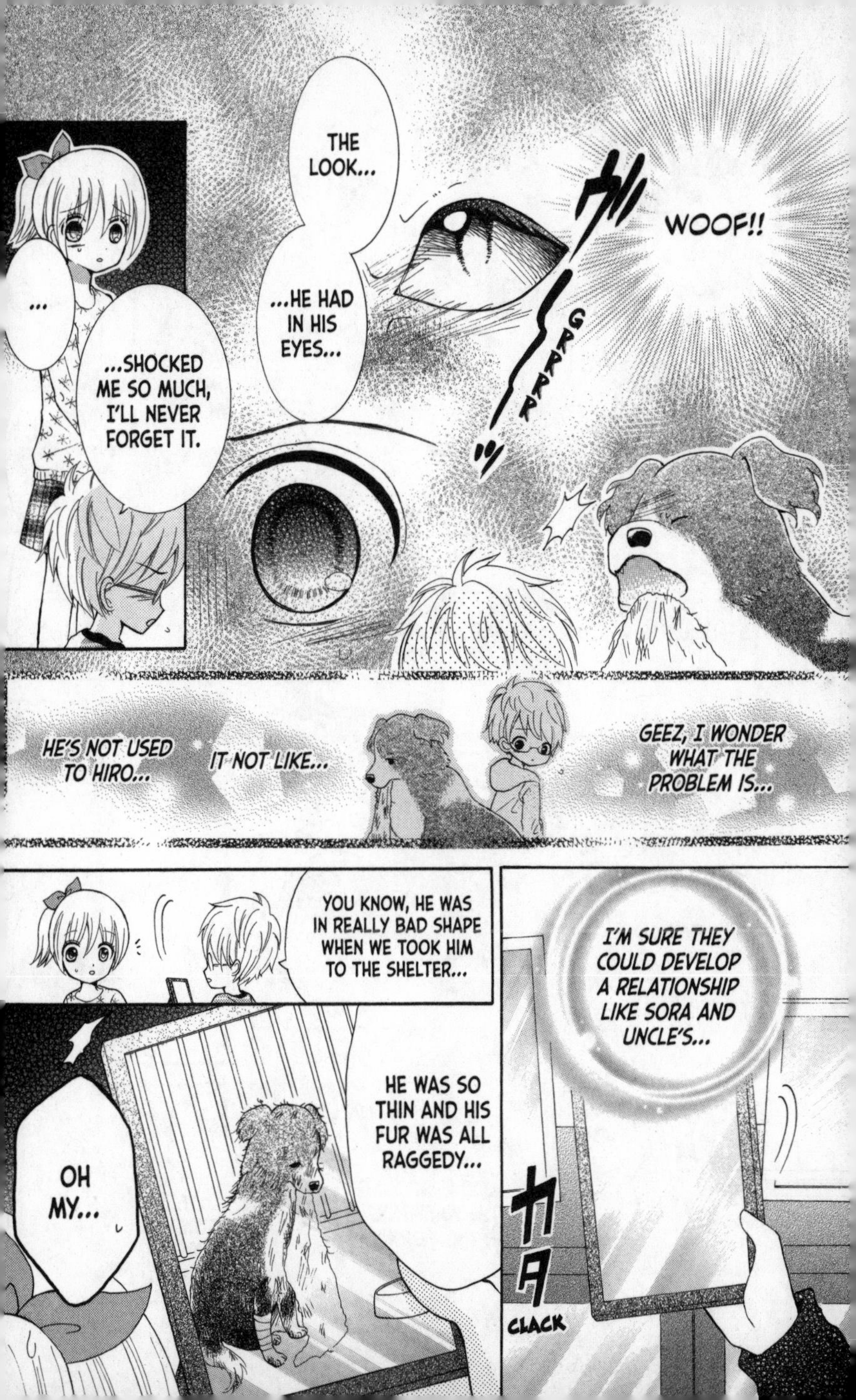
WOOF!!
GRRRR
THE LOOK...
...HE HAD IN HIS EYES...
...
...SHOCKED ME SO MUCH, I'LL NEVER FORGET IT.
GEEZ, I WONDER WHAT THE PROBLEM IS...
IT NOT LIKE...
HE'S NOT USED TO HIRO...
I'M SURE THEY COULD DEVELOP A RELATIONSHIP LIKE SORA AND UNCLE'S...
カタ
CLACK
YOU KNOW, HE WAS IN REALLY BAD SHAPE WHEN WE TOOK HIM TO THE SHELTER...
HE WAS SO THIN AND HIS FUR WAS ALL RAGGEDY...
OH MY...

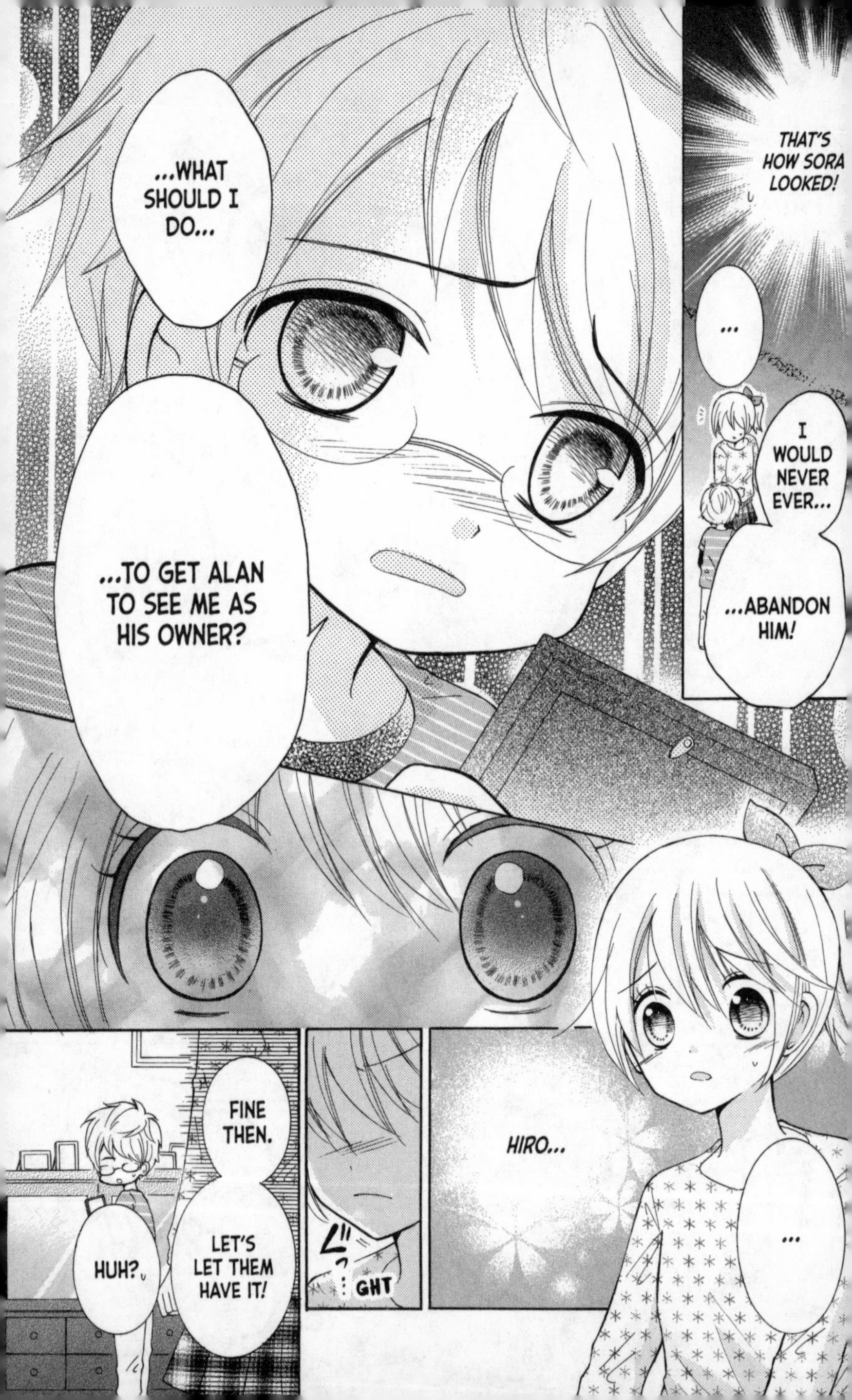
THAT'S HOW SORA LOOKED!
...
I WOULD NEVER EVER...
...ABANDON HIM!
...WHAT SHOULD I DO...
...TO GET ALAN TO SEE ME AS HIS OWNER?
HIRO...
...
GHT
FINE THEN.
LET'S LET THEM HAVE IT!
HUH?

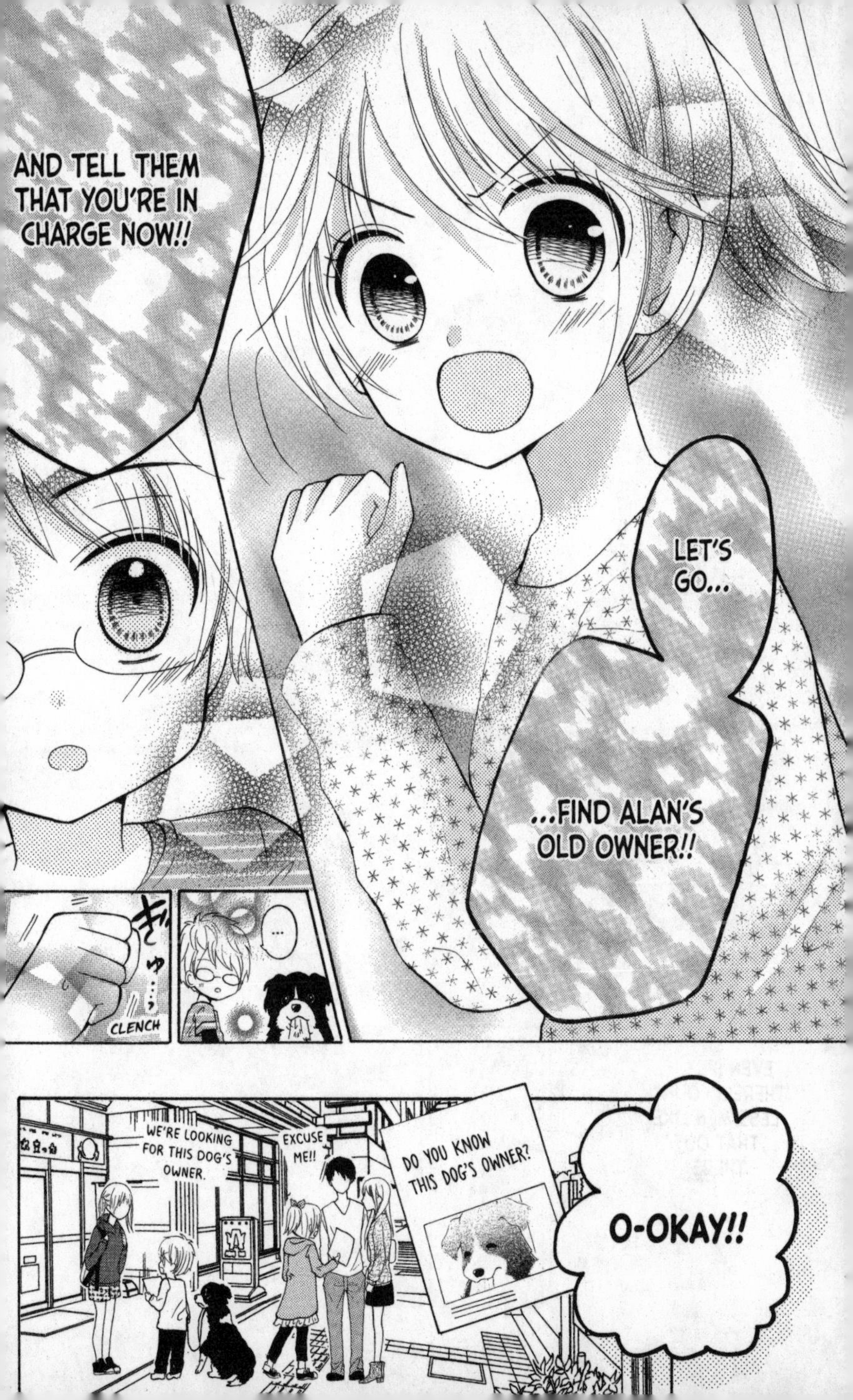
LET'S GO...
...FIND ALAN'S OLD OWNER!!
AND TELL THEM THAT YOU'RE IN CHARGE NOW!!
...
ぎゅ…っ
CLENCH
O-OKAY!!
DO YOU KNOW THIS DOG'S OWNER?
EXCUSE ME!!
WE'RE LOOKING FOR THIS DOG'S OWNER.

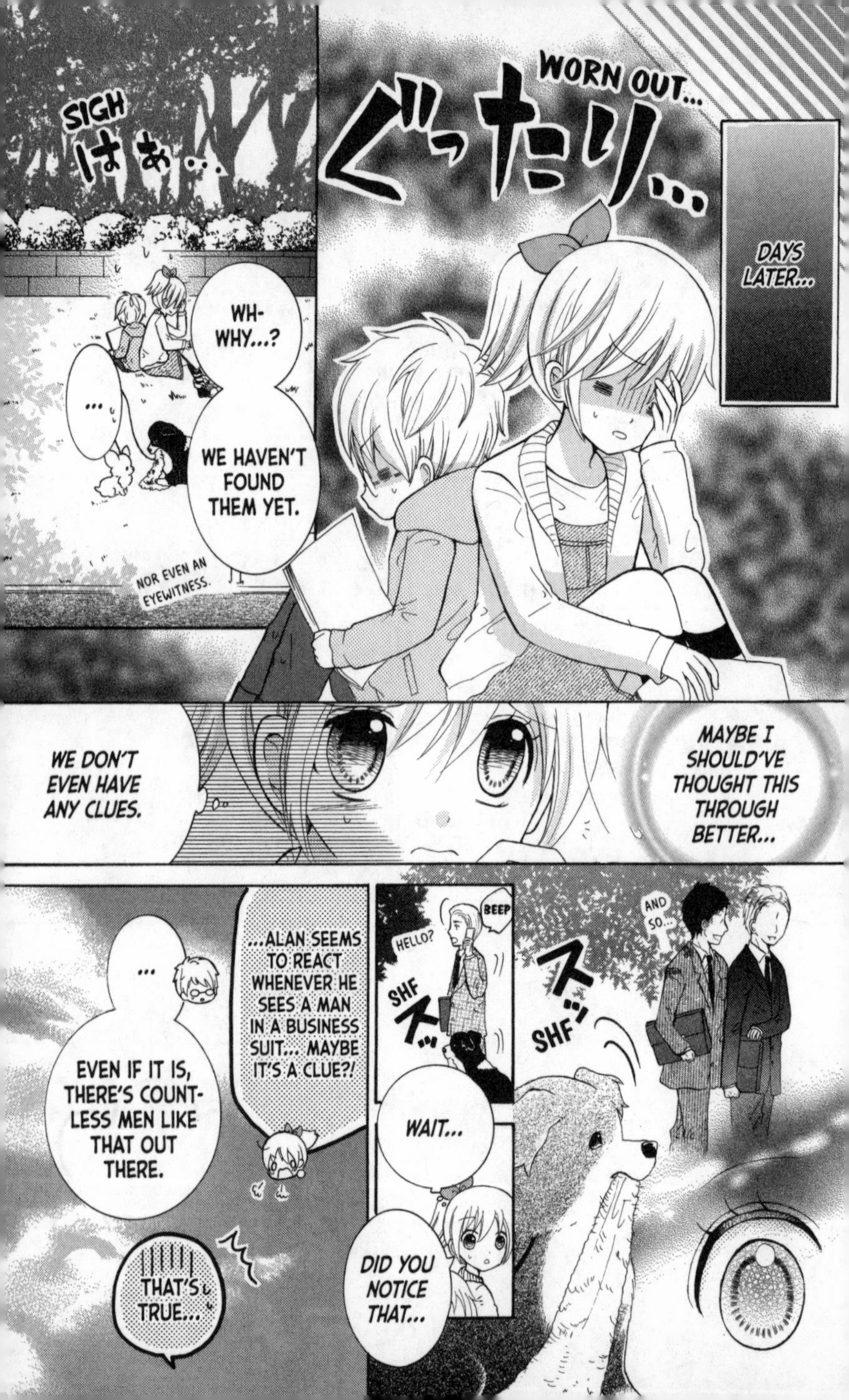

DAYS LATER...
WORN OUT...
ぐったり...
SIGH
はぁ...
WH- WHY...?
WE HAVEN'T FOUND THEM YET.
...
NOR EVEN AN EYEWITNESS.
MAYBE I SHOULD'VE THOUGHT THIS THROUGH BETTER...
WE DON'T EVEN HAVE ANY CLUES.
AND SO...
SHF
スッ
BEEP
HELLO?
SHF
スッ
WAIT...
DID YOU NOTICE THAT...
...ALAN SEEMS TO REACT WHENEVER HE SEES A MAN IN A BUSINESS SUIT... MAYBE IT'S A CLUE?!
...
EVEN IF IT IS, THERE'S COUNTLESS MEN LIKE THAT OUT THERE.
THAT'S TRUE...

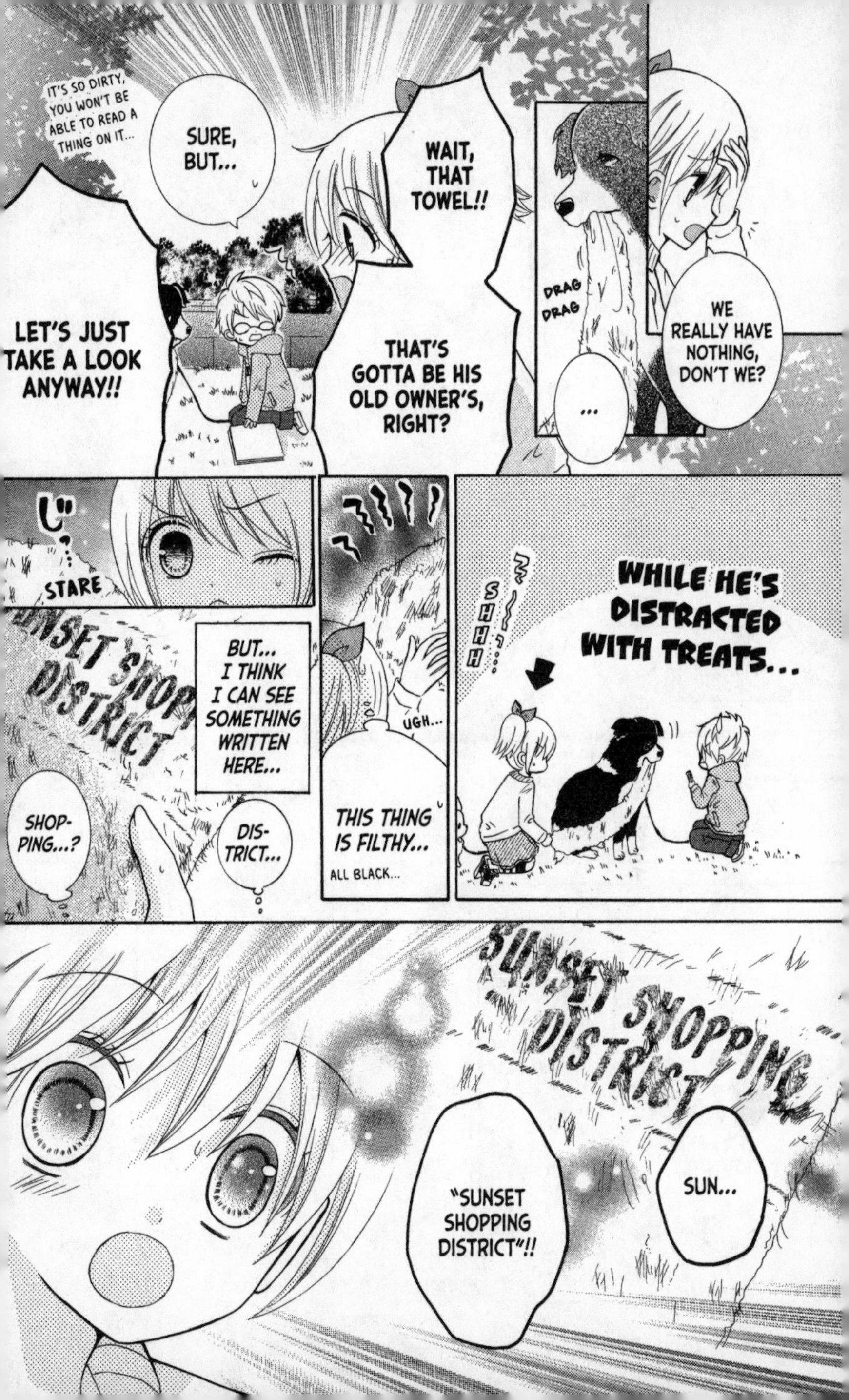
WE REALLY HAVE NOTHING, DON'T WE?
...
DRAG DRAG
WAIT, THAT TOWEL!!
THAT'S GOTTA BE HIS OLD OWNER'S, RIGHT?
SURE, BUT...
IT'S SO DIRTY, YOU WON'T BE ABLE TO READ A THING ON IT...
LET'S JUST TAKE A LOOK ANYWAY!!
WHILE HE'S DISTRACTED WITH TREATS...
SHHH...
UGH...
THIS THING IS FILTHY...
ALL BLACK...
STARE
BUT... I THINK I CAN SEE SOMETHING WRITTEN HERE...
DIS-TRICT...
SHOP-PING...?
SUNSET SHOPPING DISTRICT
SUN...
"SUNSET SHOPPING DISTRICT"!!

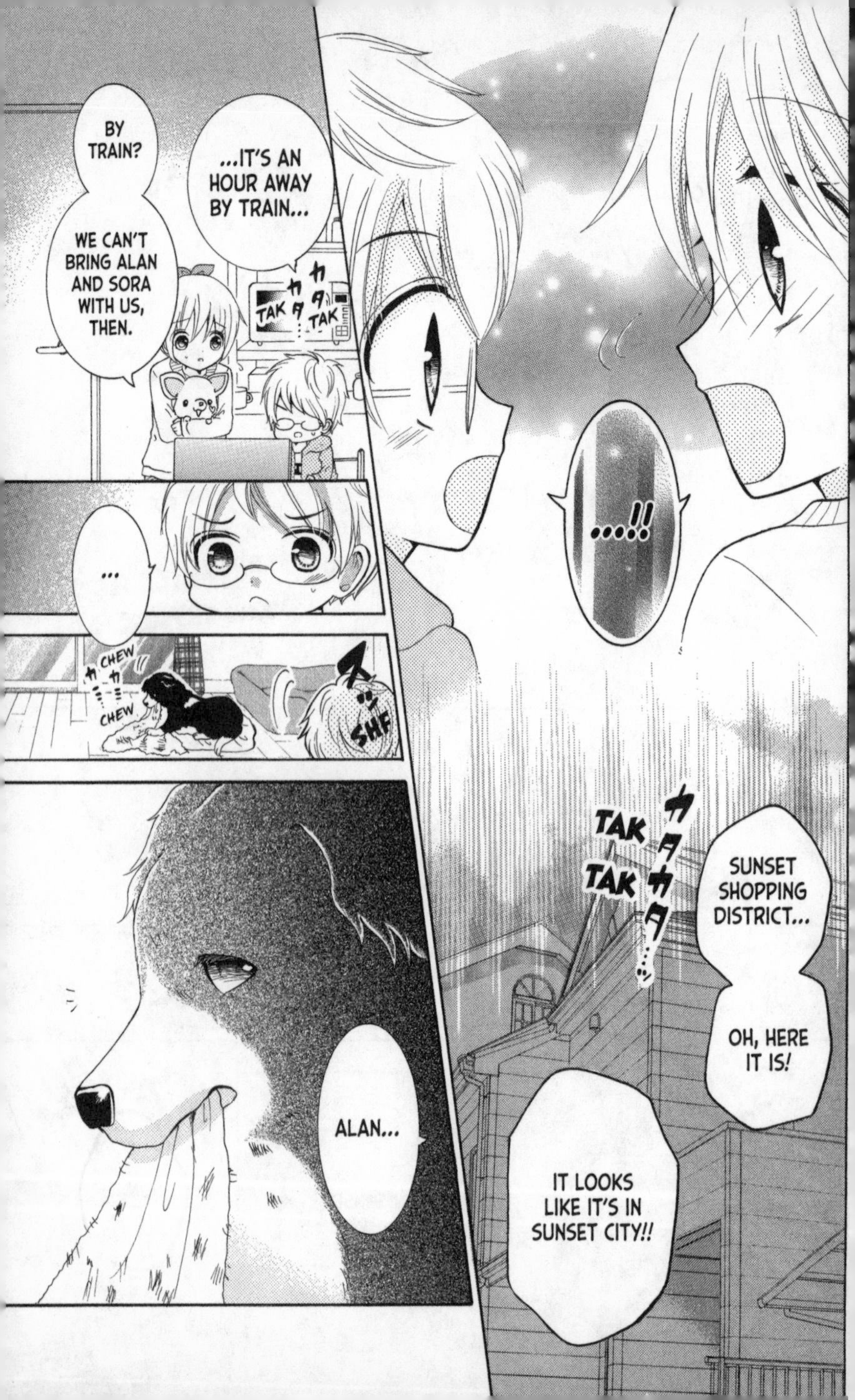
...!!
TAK TAK
SUNSET SHOPPING DISTRICT...
OH, HERE IT IS!
IT LOOKS LIKE IT'S IN SUNSET CITY!!
...IT'S AN HOUR AWAY BY TRAIN...
TAK TAK
BY TRAIN?
WE CAN'T BRING ALAN AND SORA WITH US, THEN.
...
SHF
CHEW CHEW
ALAN...

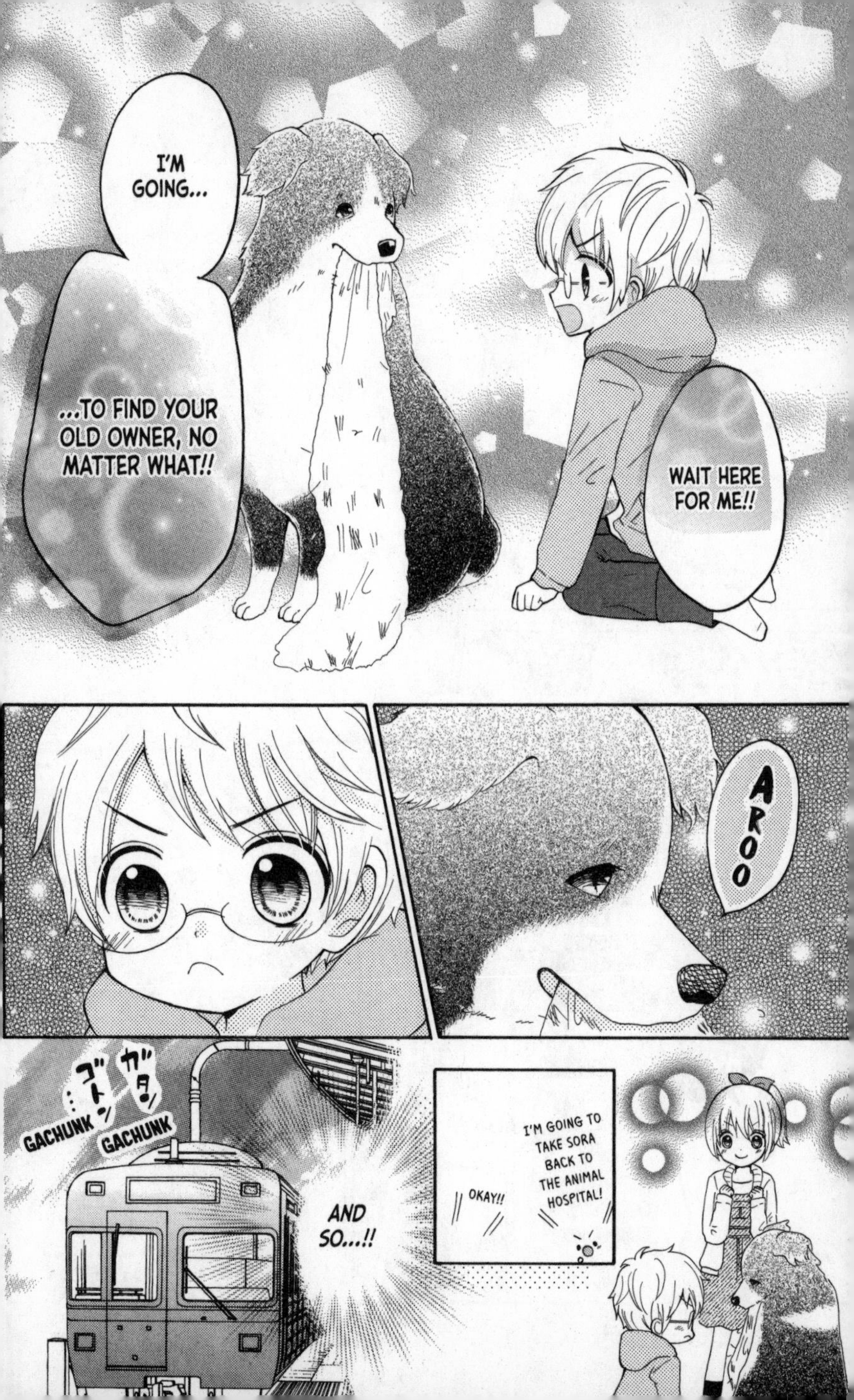
I'M GOING...
...TO FIND YOUR OLD OWNER, NO MATTER WHAT!!
WAIT HERE FOR ME!!
AROO
I'M GOING TO TAKE SORA BACK TO THE ANIMAL HOSPITAL!
OKAY!!
ガタン
ゴトン…
GACHUNK
GACHUNK
AND SO...!!

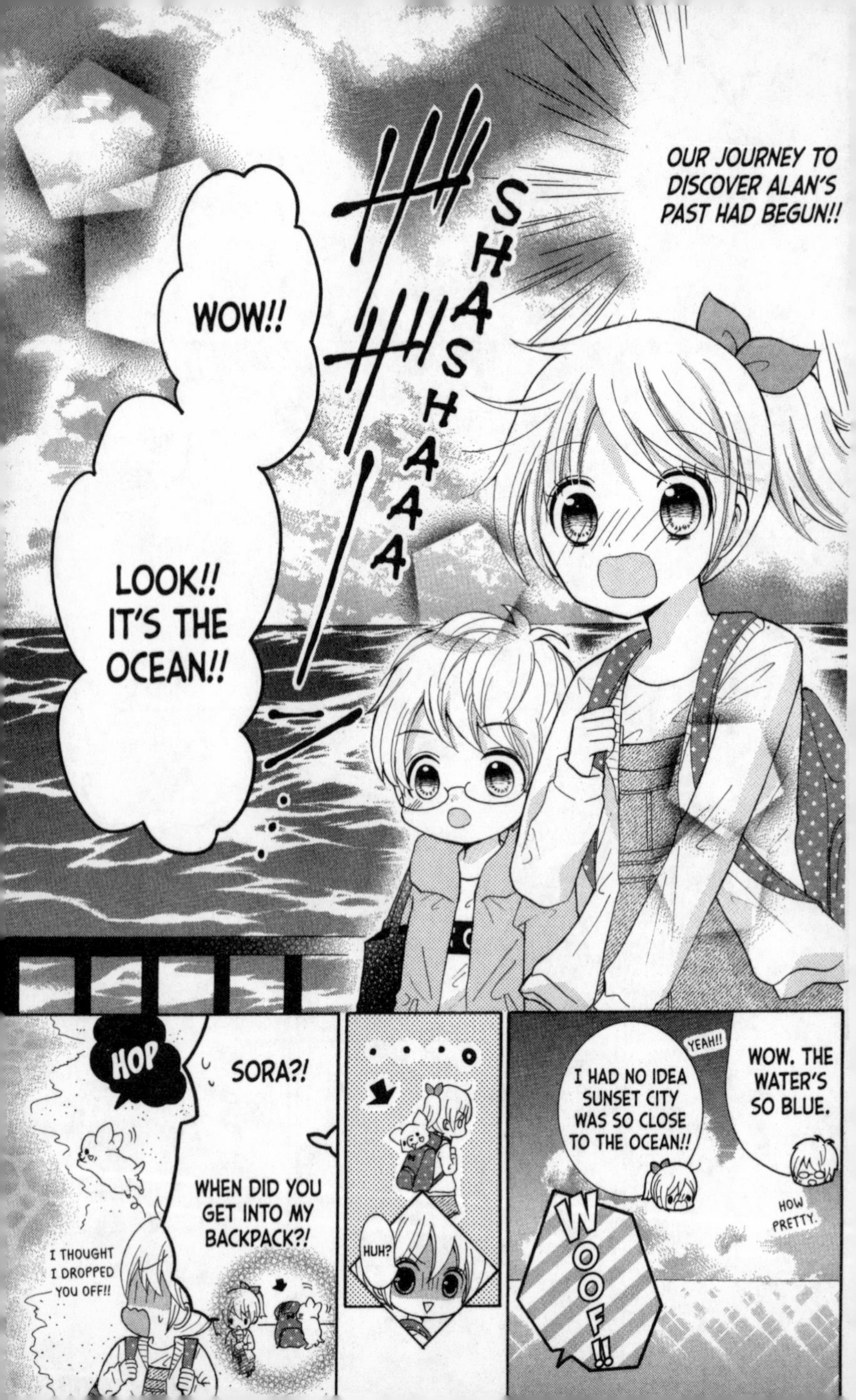
OUR JOURNEY TO DISCOVER ALAN'S PAST HAD BEGUN!!
SHASHAAAA
WOW!!
LOOK!! IT'S THE OCEAN!!
WOW. THE WATER'S SO BLUE.
HOW PRETTY.
I HAD NO IDEA SUNSET CITY WAS SO CLOSE TO THE OCEAN!!
YEAH!!
WOOF!!
....
HUH?
HOP
SORA?!
WHEN DID YOU GET INTO MY BACKPACK?!
I THOUGHT I DROPPED YOU OFF!!

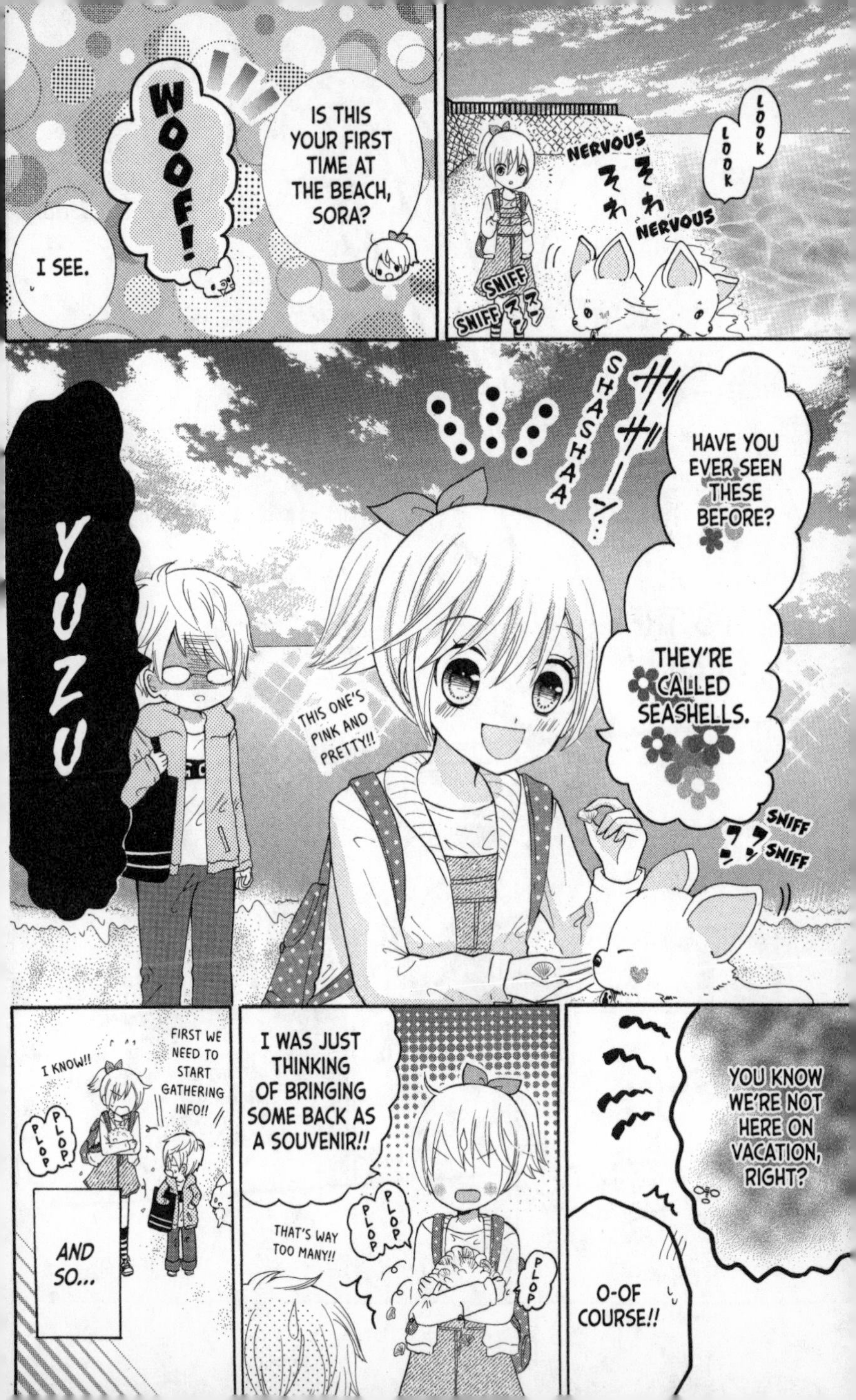
LOOK LOOK
NERVOUS
NERVOUS
SNIFF
SNIFF
IS THIS YOUR FIRST TIME AT THE BEACH, SORA?
WOOF!
I SEE.
HAVE YOU EVER SEEN THESE BEFORE?
SHASHAA
THEY'RE CALLED SEASHELLS.
SNIFF SNIFF
THIS ONE'S PINK AND PRETTY!!
YUZU
YOU KNOW WE'RE NOT HERE ON VACATION, RIGHT?
O-OF COURSE!!
I WAS JUST THINKING OF BRINGING SOME BACK AS A SOUVENIR!!
PLOP PLOP
PLOP
THAT'S WAY TOO MANY!!
FIRST WE NEED TO START GATHERING INFO!!
I KNOW!!
PLOP PLOP
AND SO...

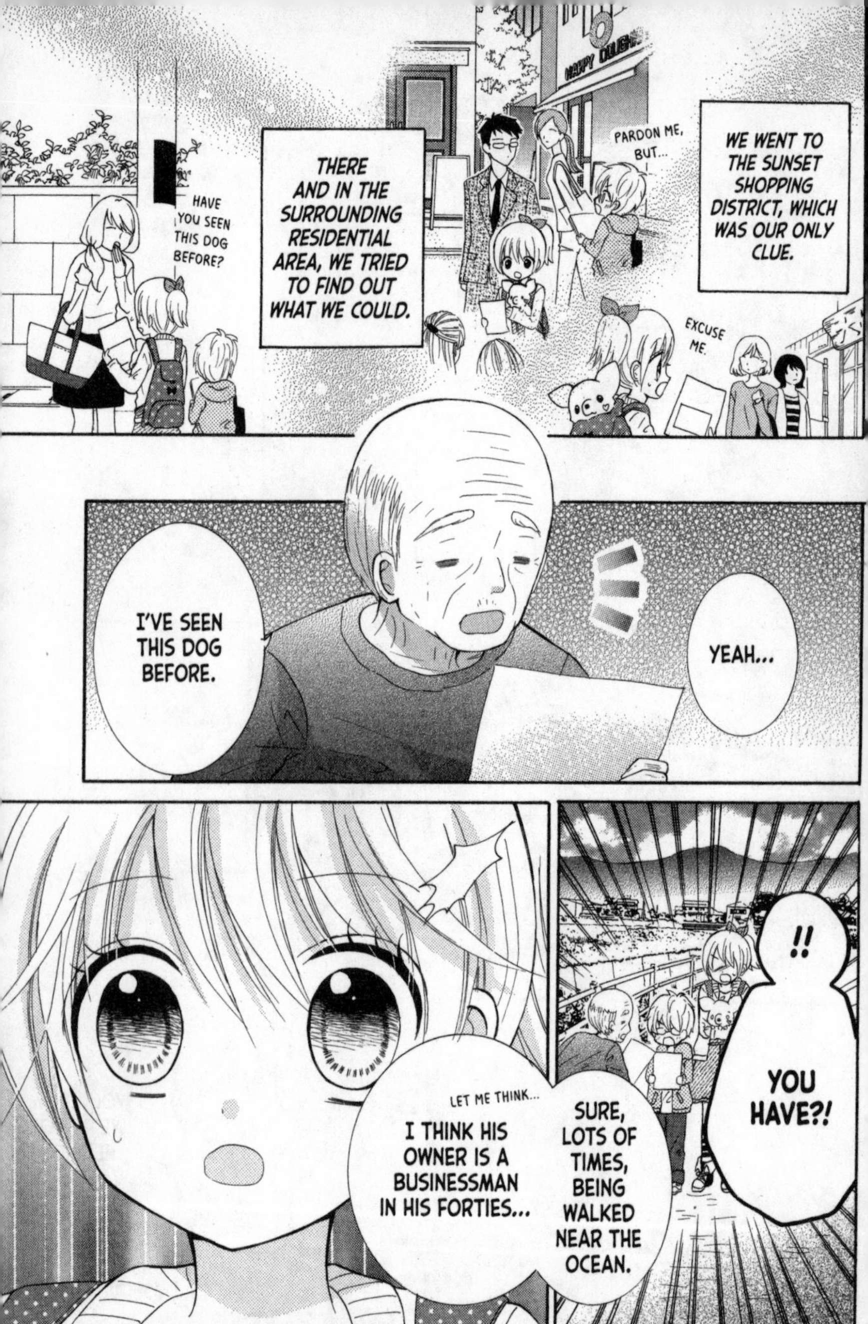
WE WENT TO THE SUNSET SHOPPING DISTRICT, WHICH WAS OUR ONLY CLUE.
EXCUSE ME.
PARDON ME, BUT...
THERE AND IN THE SURROUNDING RESIDENTIAL AREA, WE TRIED TO FIND OUT WHAT WE COULD.
HAVE YOU SEEN THIS DOG BEFORE?
YEAH...
I'VE SEEN THIS DOG BEFORE.
!!
YOU HAVE?!
SURE, LOTS OF TIMES, BEING WALKED NEAR THE OCEAN.
LET ME THINK...
I THINK HIS OWNER IS A BUSINESSMAN IN HIS FORTIES...

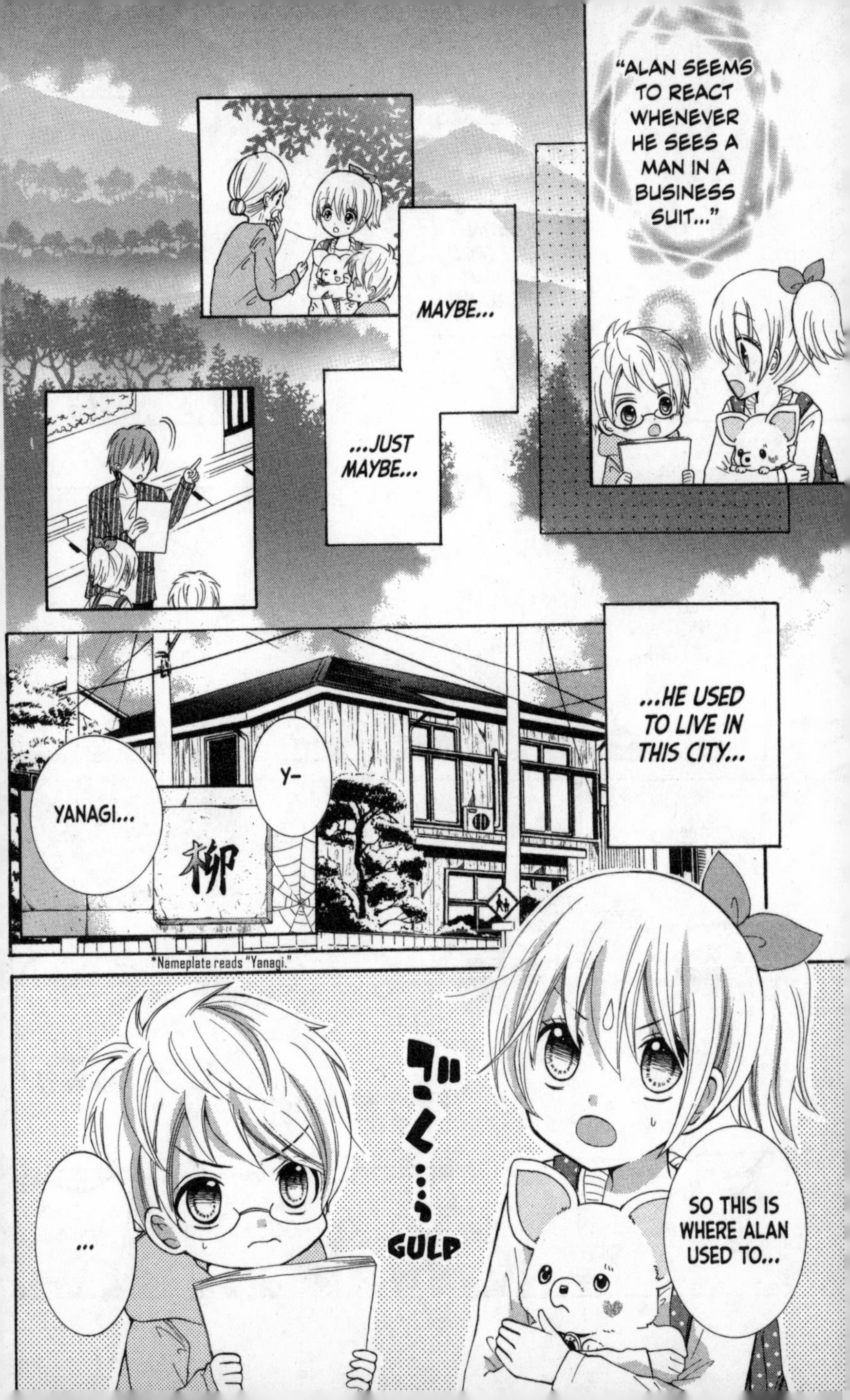
"ALAN SEEMS TO REACT WHENEVER HE SEES A MAN IN A BUSINESS SUIT..."
MAYBE...
...JUST MAYBE...
...HE USED TO LIVE IN THIS CITY...
Y-
YANAGI...
柳
SO THIS IS WHERE ALAN USED TO...
ごく...
GULP
...
*Nameplate reads "Yanagi."

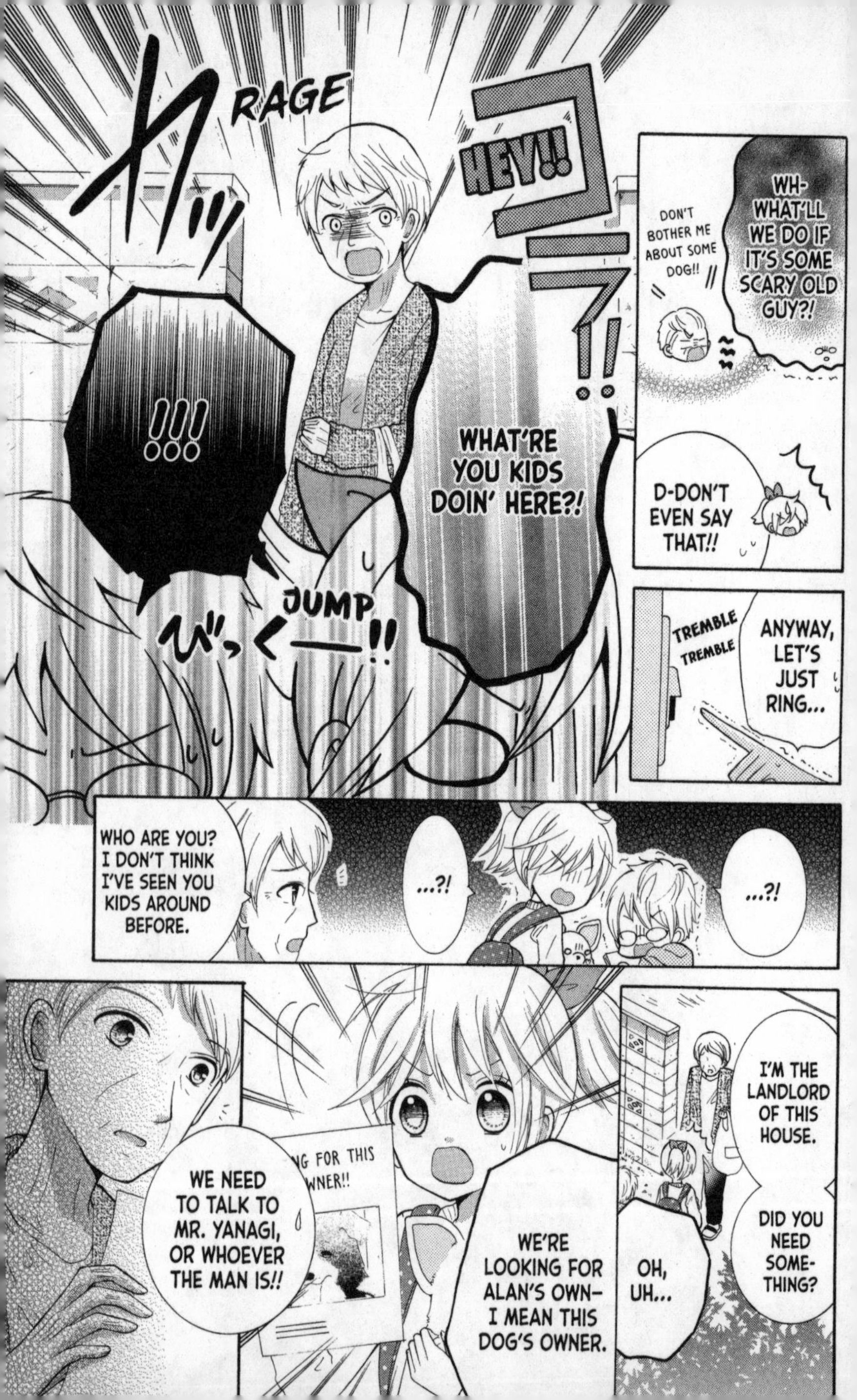
WH-WHAT'LL WE DO IF IT'S SOME SCARY OLD GUY?!
DON'T BOTHER ME ABOUT SOME DOG!!
D-DON'T EVEN SAY THAT!!
ANYWAY, LET'S JUST RING...
TREMBLE TREMBLE
HEY!!
RAGE
WHAT'RE YOU KIDS DOIN' HERE?!
!!!
JUMP
...?!
...?!
WHO ARE YOU? I DON'T THINK I'VE SEEN YOU KIDS AROUND BEFORE.
I'M THE LANDLORD OF THIS HOUSE.
DID YOU NEED SOME-THING?
OH, UH...
WE'RE LOOKING FOR ALAN'S OWN— I MEAN THIS DOG'S OWNER.
WE NEED TO TALK TO MR. YANAGI, OR WHOEVER THE MAN IS!!

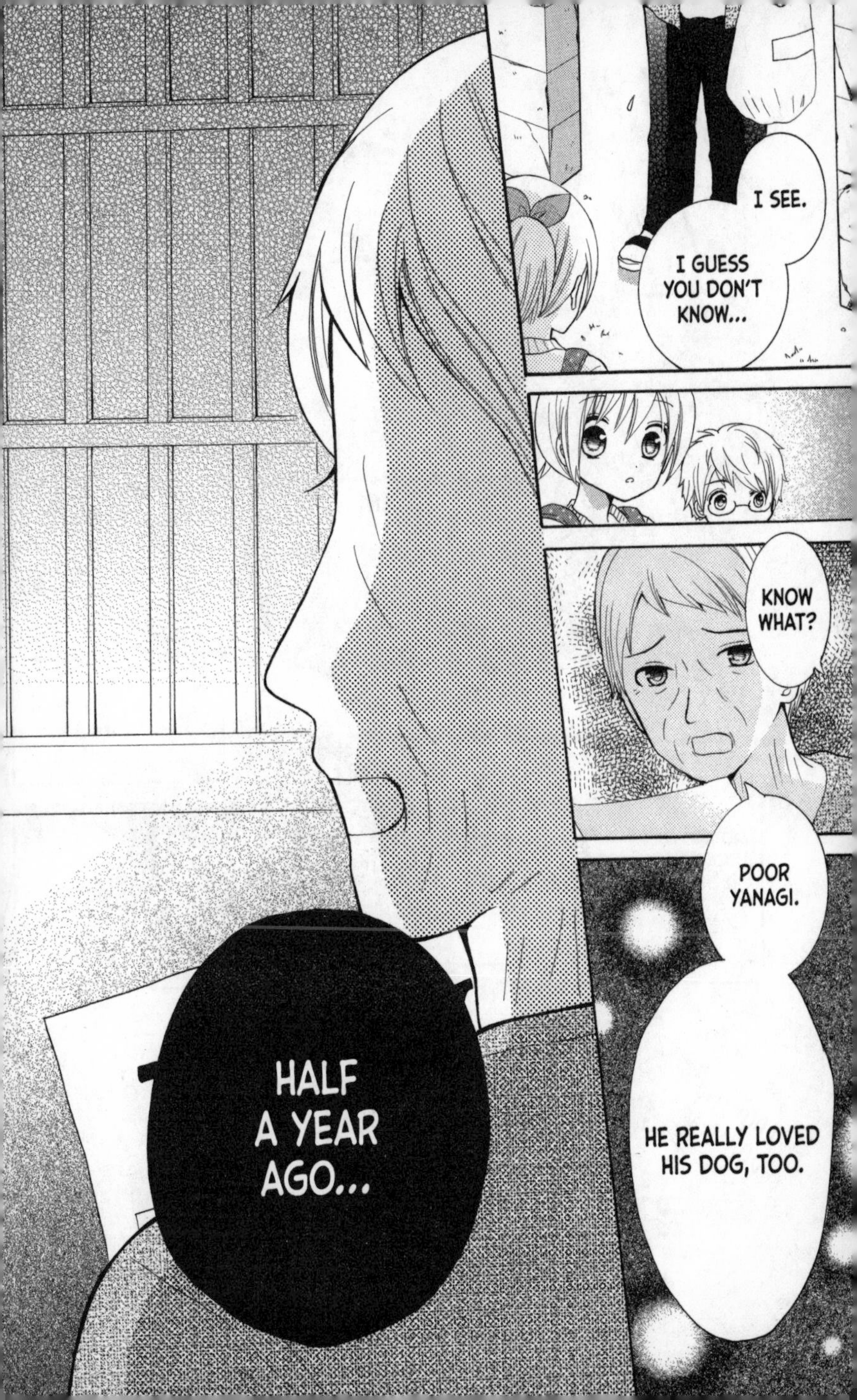
I SEE.
I GUESS YOU DON'T KNOW...
KNOW WHAT?
POOR YANAGI.
HE REALLY LOVED HIS DOG, TOO.
HALF A YEAR AGO...

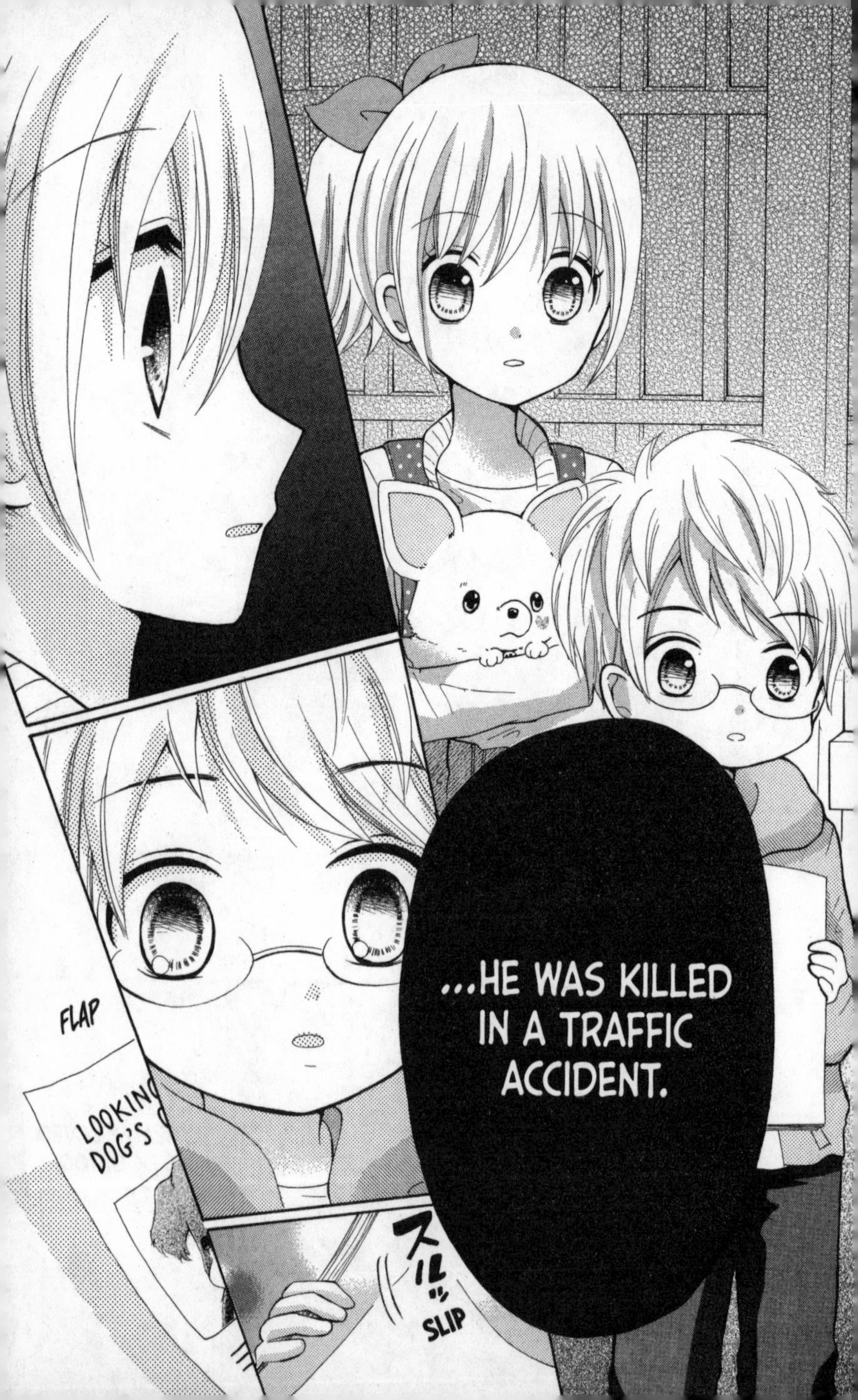
...HE WAS KILLED IN A TRAFFIC ACCIDENT.
FLAP
LOOKIN
DOG'S
スルッ
SLIP

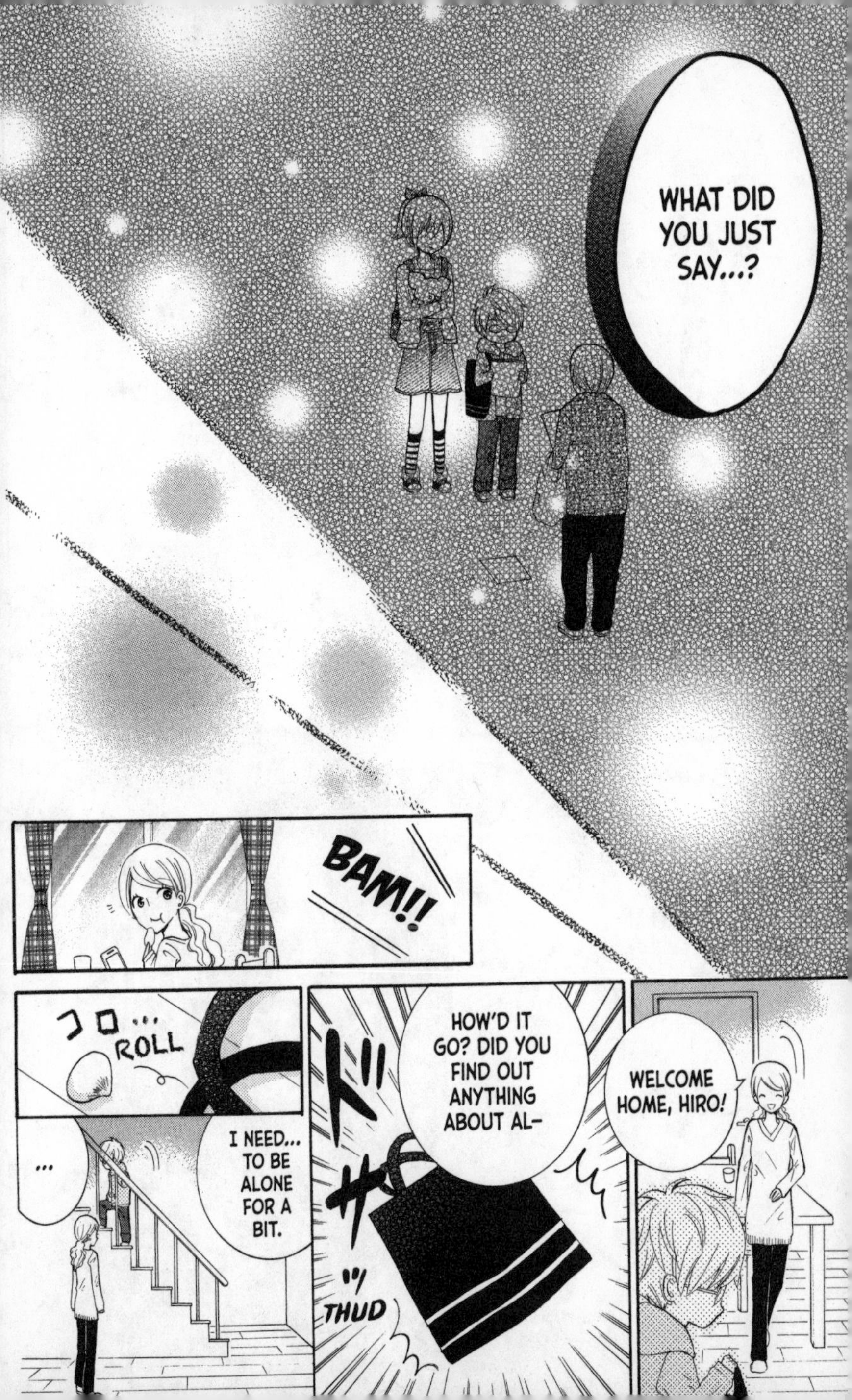
WHAT DID YOU JUST SAY...?
BAM!!
WELCOME HOME, HIRO!
HOW'D IT GO? DID YOU FIND OUT ANYTHING ABOUT AL-
ドサ
THUD
コロ... ROLL
I NEED... TO BE ALONE FOR A BIT.
...

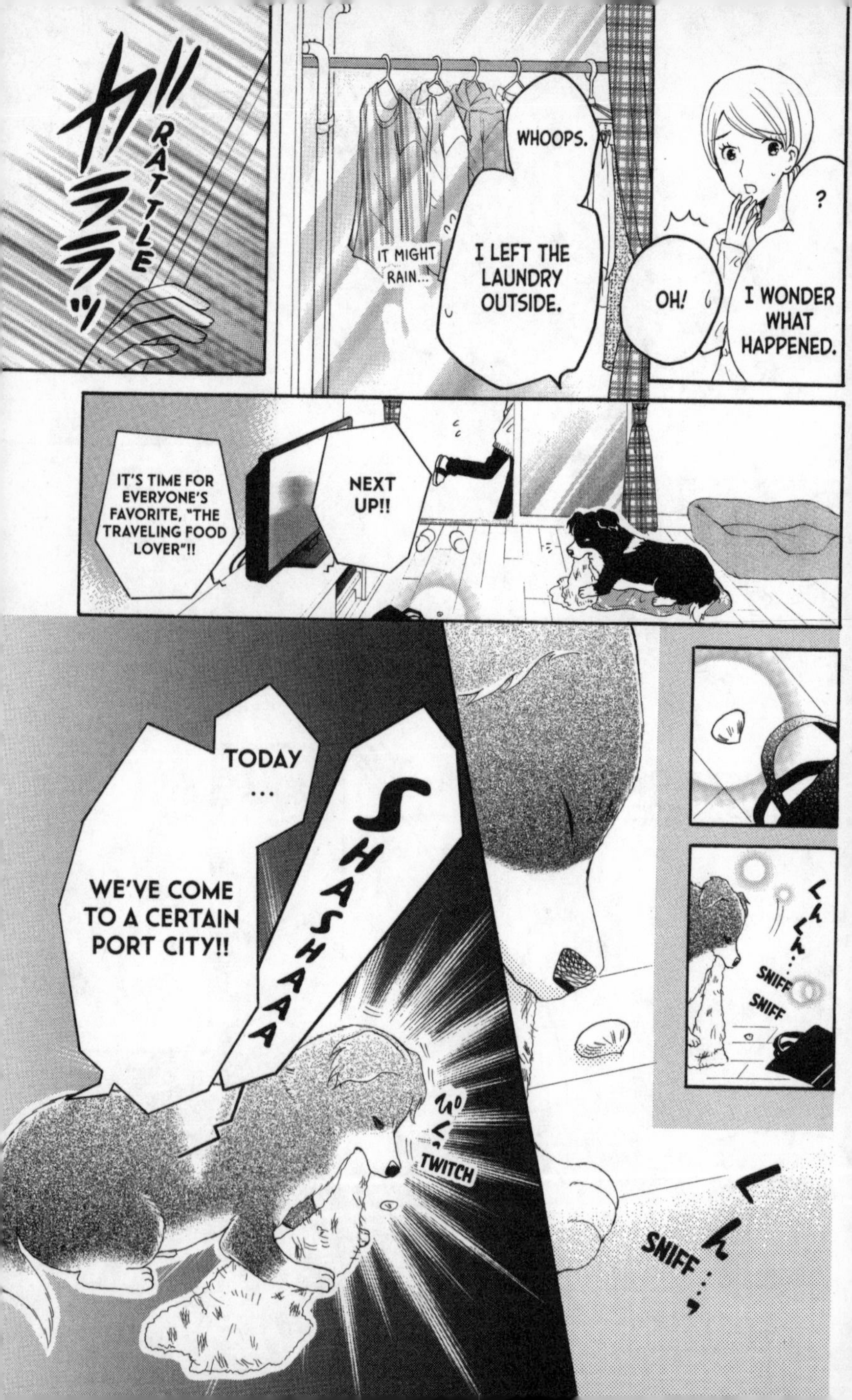
?
I WONDER WHAT HAPPENED.
OH!
WHOOPS.
I LEFT THE LAUNDRY OUTSIDE.
IT MIGHT RAIN...
ガラララッ
RATTLE
NEXT UP!!
IT'S TIME FOR EVERYONE'S FAVORITE, "THE TRAVELING FOOD LOVER"!!
くんくん...
SNIFF SNIFF
くん...
SNIFF...
ぴく
TWITCH
SHASHAAAA
TODAY ...
WE'VE COME TO A CERTAIN PORT CITY!!

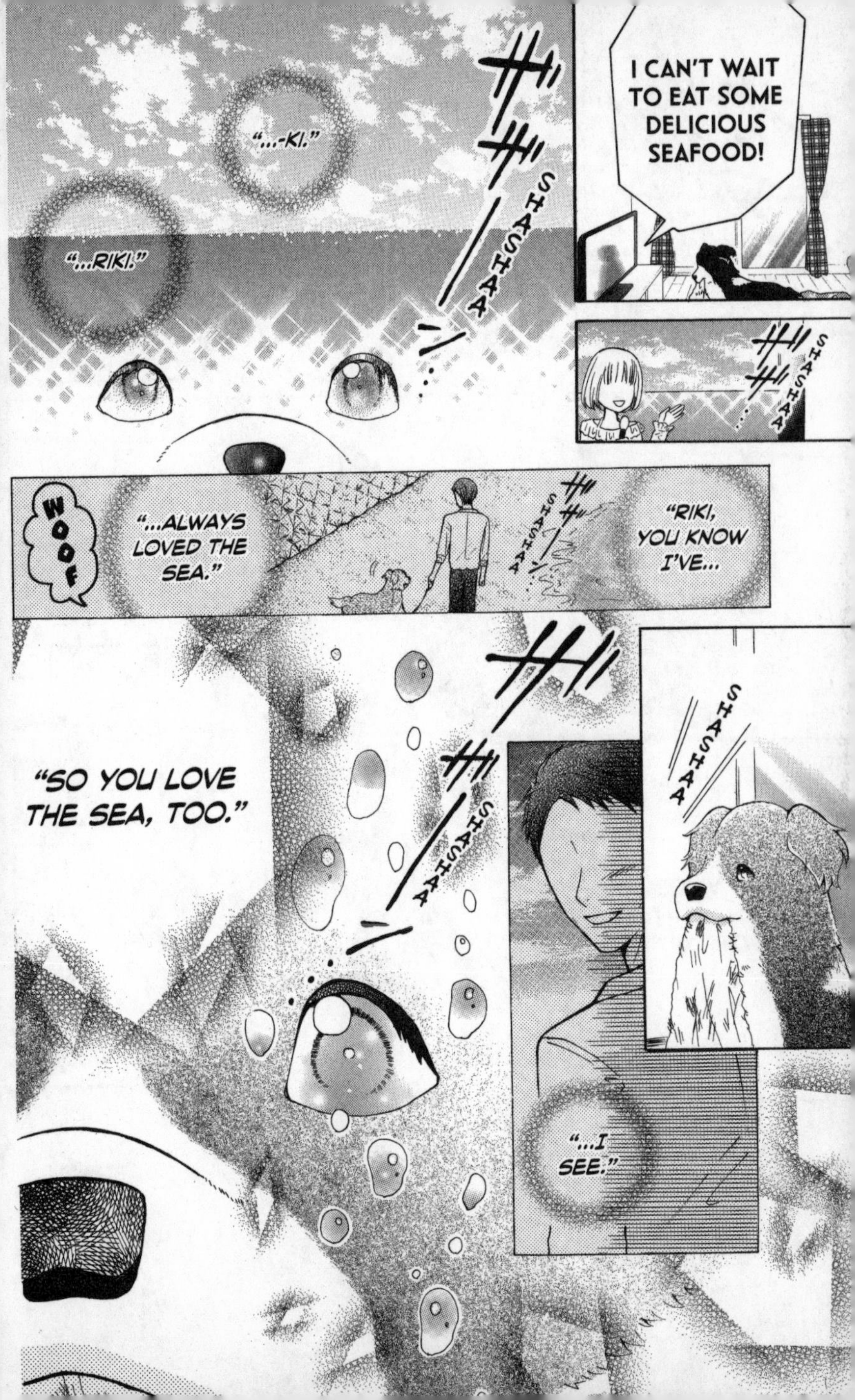
I CAN'T WAIT TO EAT SOME DELICIOUS SEAFOOD!
SHASHAA
SHASHAA
"...-KI."
"...RIKI."
"RIKI, YOU KNOW I'VE...
SHASHAA
"...ALWAYS LOVED THE SEA."
WOOF
SHASHAA
"...I SEE."
SHASHAA
"SO YOU LOVE THE SEA, TOO."

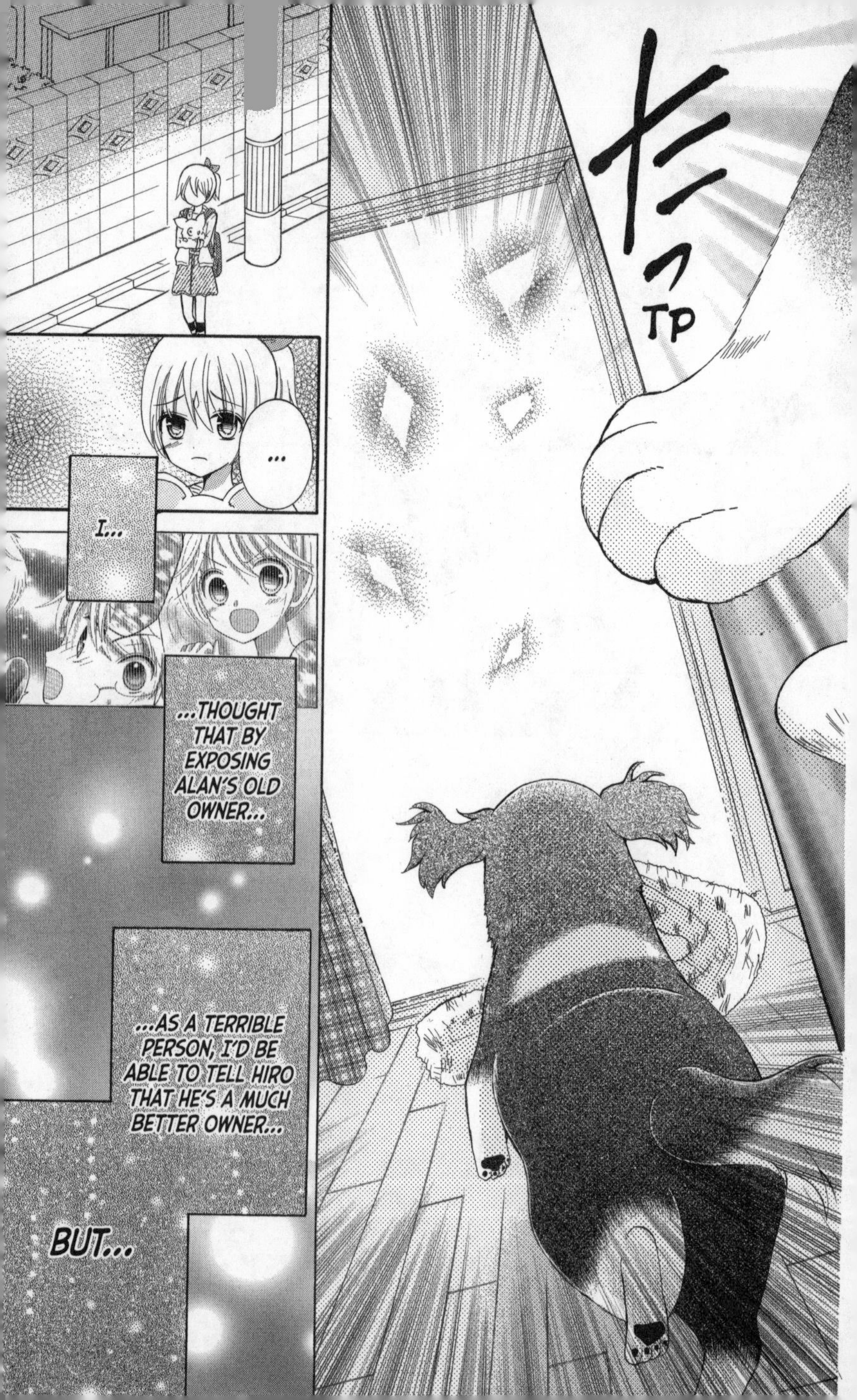
たっ
TP
...
I...
...THOUGHT THAT BY EXPOSING ALAN'S OLD OWNER...
...AS A TERRIBLE PERSON, I'D BE ABLE TO TELL HIRO THAT HE'S A MUCH BETTER OWNER...
BUT...

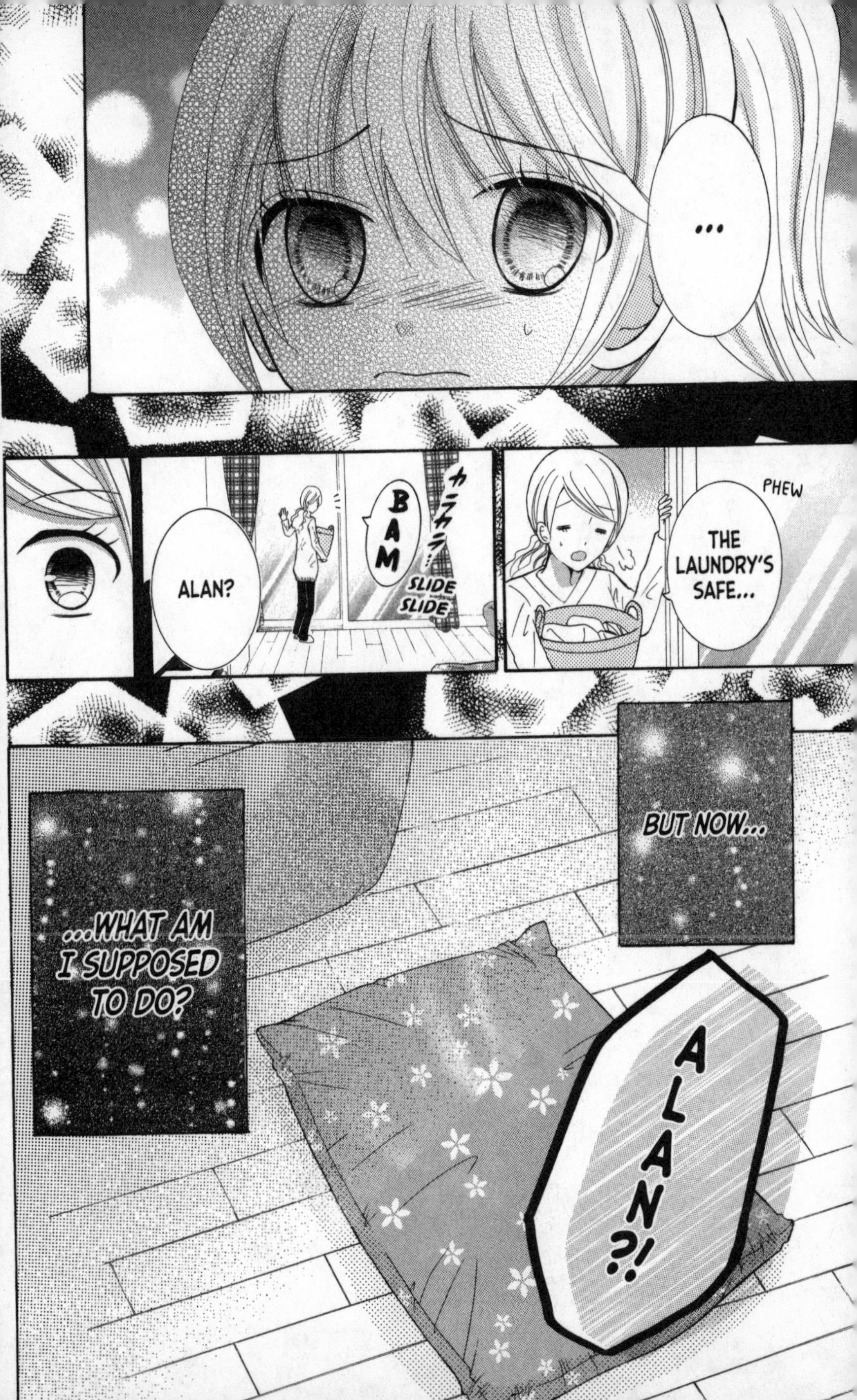
...
PHEW
THE LAUNDRY'S SAFE...
カラカラ…
SLIDE SLIDE
BAM
ALAN?
BUT NOW...
...WHAT AM I SUPPOSED TO DO?
ALAN?!

To be continued in volume 6.

MEOW ♦

• A DAY IN YUZU'S LIFE •

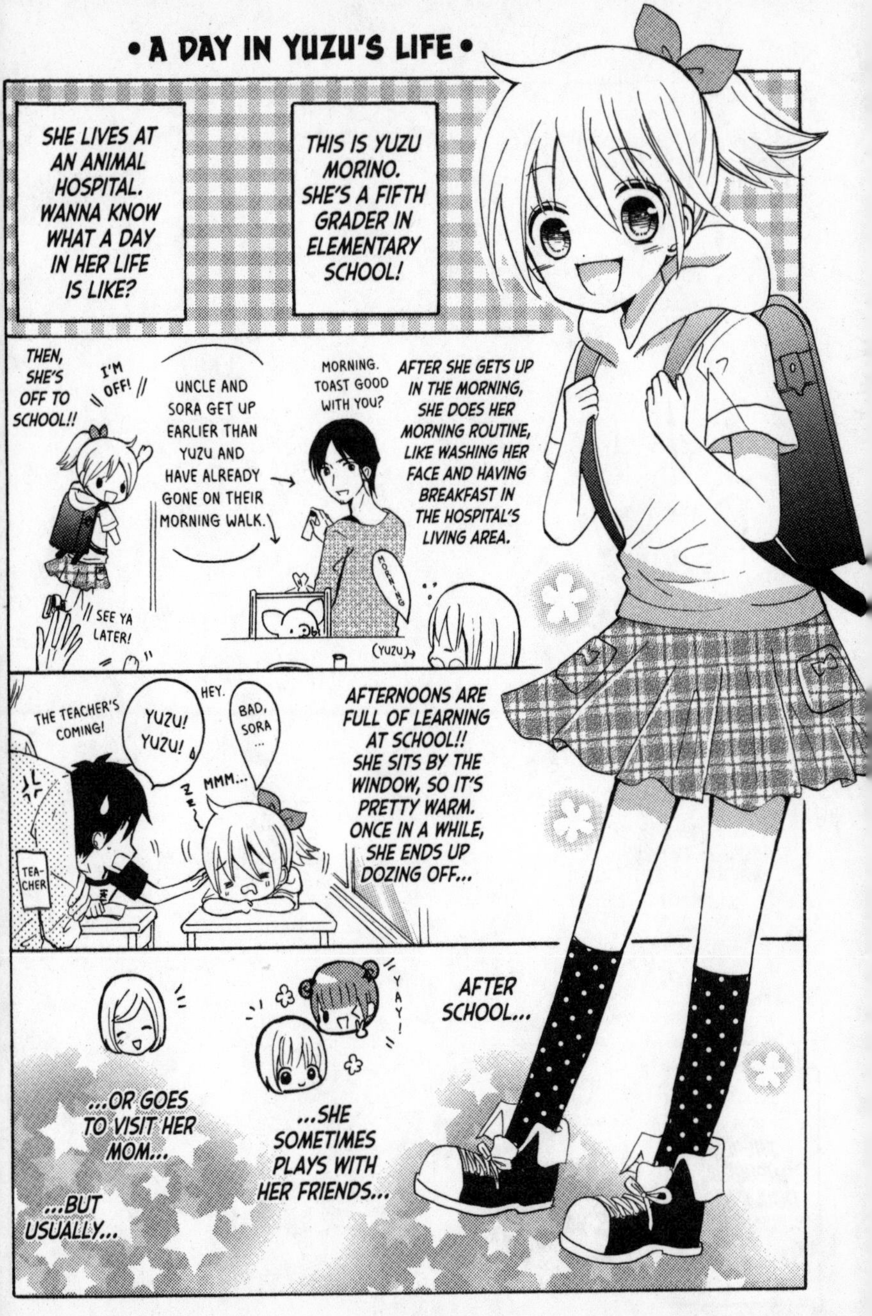

THIS IS YUZU MORINO. SHE'S A FIFTH GRADER IN ELEMENTARY SCHOOL!
SHE LIVES AT AN ANIMAL HOSPITAL. WANNA KNOW WHAT A DAY IN HER LIFE IS LIKE?
AFTER SHE GETS UP IN THE MORNING, SHE DOES HER MORNING ROUTINE, LIKE WASHING HER FACE AND HAVING BREAKFAST IN THE HOSPITAL'S LIVING AREA.
MORNING. TOAST GOOD WITH YOU?
MORNING
(YUZU)
UNCLE AND SORA GET UP EARLIER THAN YUZU AND HAVE ALREADY GONE ON THEIR MORNING WALK.
THEN, SHE'S OFF TO SCHOOL!!
I'M OFF!
SEE YA LATER!
AFTERNOONS ARE FULL OF LEARNING AT SCHOOL!! SHE SITS BY THE WINDOW, SO IT'S PRETTY WARM. ONCE IN A WHILE, SHE ENDS UP DOZING OFF...
BAD, SORA...
HEY.
MMM...
YUZU! YUZU!
THE TEACHER'S COMING!
TEA-CHER
AFTER SCHOOL...
YAY!
...SHE SOMETIMES PLAYS WITH HER FRIENDS...
...OR GOES TO VISIT HER MOM...
...BUT USUALLY...

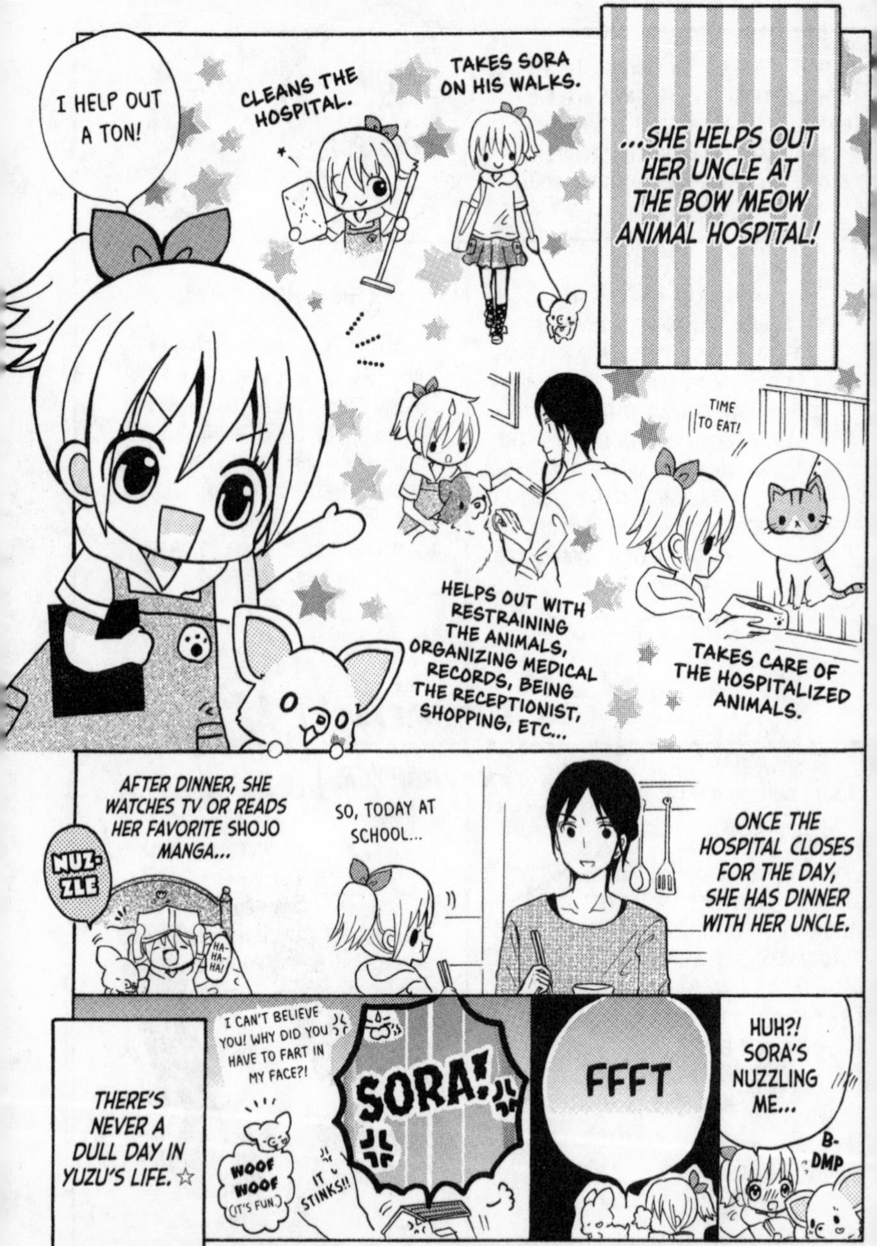
...SHE HELPS OUT HER UNCLE AT THE BOW MEOW ANIMAL HOSPITAL!
TAKES SORA ON HIS WALKS.
CLEANS THE HOSPITAL.
I HELP OUT A TON!
TIME TO EAT!
TAKES CARE OF THE HOSPITALIZED ANIMALS.
HELPS OUT WITH RESTRAINING THE ANIMALS, ORGANIZING MEDICAL RECORDS, BEING THE RECEPTIONIST, SHOPPING, ETC...
ONCE THE HOSPITAL CLOSES FOR THE DAY, SHE HAS DINNER WITH HER UNCLE.
SO, TODAY AT SCHOOL...
AFTER DINNER, SHE WATCHES TV OR READS HER FAVORITE SHOJO MANGA...
NUZ-ZLE
HA-HA-HA!
HUH?! SORA'S NUZZLING ME...
B-DMP
FFFT
SORA!
I CAN'T BELIEVE YOU! WHY DID YOU HAVE TO FART IN MY FACE?!
IT STINKS!!
WOOF WOOF
(IT'S FUN.)
THERE'S NEVER A DULL DAY IN YUZU'S LIFE. ☆

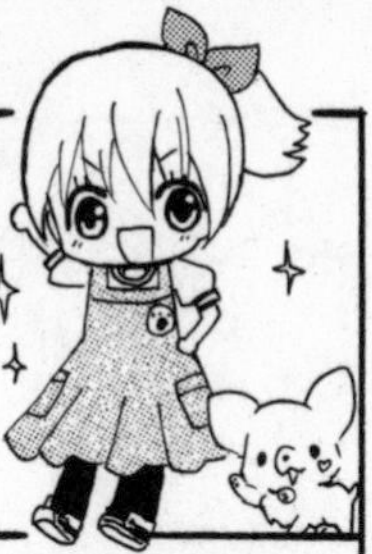

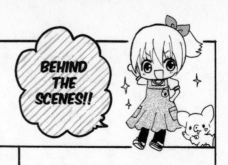

BEHIND THE SCENES!!

I HAVE A LOT OF FUN WRITING THESE BEHIND-THE-SCENES SECTIONS SINCE I GET TO REFLECT ON WHAT IT WAS LIKE WHEN I WAS DRAWING THE STORIES. PLEASE READ THIS SECTION AFTER YOU FINISH THE MAIN STORY. ✩✩ ↓↓

CHAPTER 17

<THE NAMELESS PUPS>

YUZU'S MOM MAKES HER FIRST APPEARANCE IN A WHILE. I LIKE THE EXCHANGE BETWEEN YUZU, HER MOM, AND SORA AT THE BEGINNING. SORA SEEMS CUNNING IN THAT HE CAN JUDGE WHETHER A PERSON WILL BE NICE TO HIM OR NOT (LOL). IT WAS FUN GETTING TO DRAW TINY PUPPIES. ✿

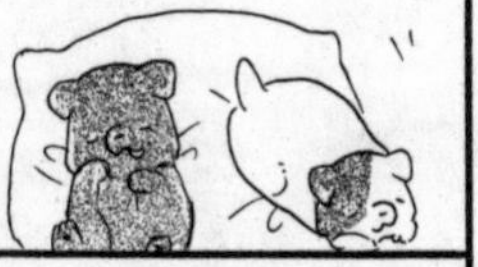

CHAPTER 18

<KENTA THE LAZY DOG>

I'M ALWAYS LOOKING FOR BOOKS AND VIDEOS TO USE AS A REFERENCE MATERIAL WHILE DRAWING MY STORIES. WHILE DOING RESEARCH ON PUGS, I TOTALLY FELL IN LOVE WITH THEIR CUTENESS! TO TELL THE TRUTH, DURING THE PLANNING STAGE FOR THIS CHAPTER, I WASN'T SURE IF I SHOULD MAKE KENTA A PUG OR ANOTHER BREED. I'M GLAD THAT IN THE END I MADE HIM A LAZY PUG!

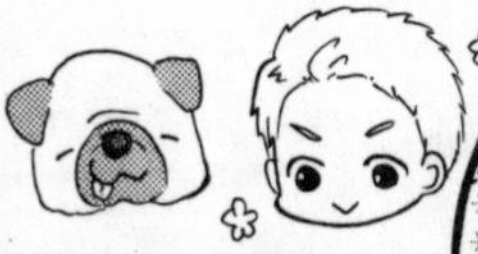

CHAPTER 19

<KANBAN THE MASCOT CAT>

WHEN COMING UP WITH THE STORY FOR THIS ONE, MY EDITOR REQUESTED I MAKE KANBAN A BIT CHUBBY AND BOLD, WHICH IS HOW HE ENDED UP LOOKING THE WAY HE DOES. I REALLY LIKE HOW HE HAS THIS IMPOSING BOSS CAT AURA TO HIM! ✧✧ I WANNA GO SHOPPING AT THE SHOP KANBAN'S AT!

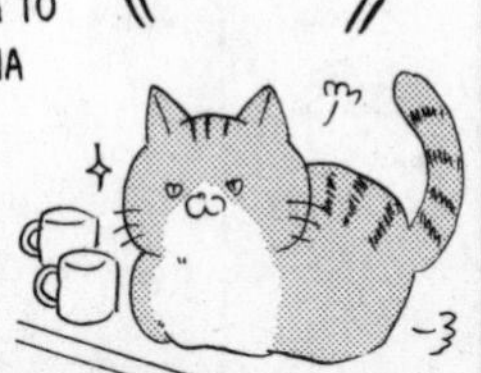

CHAPTER 20

<ALAN THE DOG WHO WON'T BOND PART 1>

MY ASSISTANTS AND FRIENDS ALL THOUGHT HIRO AND HIS SASSY SELF WAS CUTE. I DIDN'T EXPECT THAT... (LOL) THE STORY WILL CONTINUE IN VOLUME 6, SO... I GUESS I CAN'T REALLY SAY MUCH ABOUT THIS CHAPTER YET. WHAT'S GOING TO HAPPEN TO ALAN NOW THAT HE'S RUN AWAY?! PLEASE BE SURE TO READ VOLUME 6!!

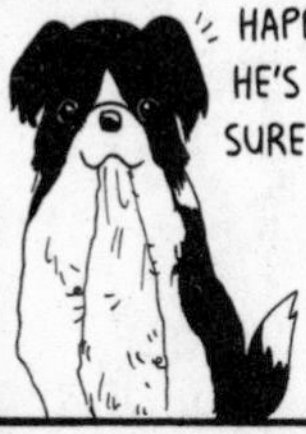

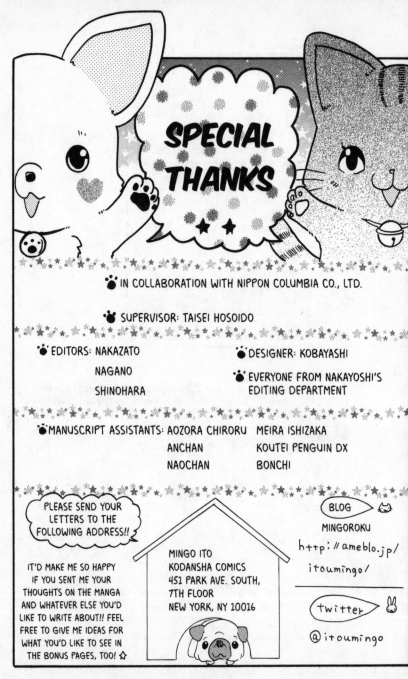

SPECIAL THANKS

🐾 IN COLLABORATION WITH NIPPON COLUMBIA CO., LTD.

🐾 SUPERVISOR: TAISEI HOSOIDO

🐾 EDITORS: NAKAZATO
NAGANO
SHINOHARA

🐾 DESIGNER: KOBAYASHI

🐾 EVERYONE FROM NAKAYOSHI'S EDITING DEPARTMENT

🐾 MANUSCRIPT ASSISTANTS: AOZORA CHIRORU   MEIRA ISHIZAKA
ANCHAN   KOUTEI PENGUIN DX
NAOCHAN   BONCHI

PLEASE SEND YOUR LETTERS TO THE FOLLOWING ADDRESS!!

IT'D MAKE ME SO HAPPY IF YOU SENT ME YOUR THOUGHTS ON THE MANGA AND WHATEVER ELSE YOU'D LIKE TO WRITE ABOUT!! FEEL FREE TO GIVE ME IDEAS FOR WHAT YOU'D LIKE TO SEE IN THE BONUS PAGES, TOO! ☆

MINGO ITO
KODANSHA COMICS
451 PARK AVE. SOUTH,
7TH FLOOR
NEW YORK, NY 10016

BLOG
MINGOROKU
http://ameblo.jp/itoumingo/

twitter
@itoumingo

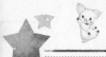

Translation Notes

Kanban, page 77

Kanban means "sign" in Japanese, but it is also a word you can use to describe a person or thing as something's star or mascot.

OPEN

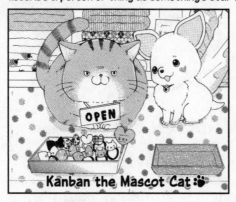

Kanban the Mascot Cat

"Kotori-Asobu...", page 116

Yuzu is struggling to read the Chinese characters (*kanji*) for Hiro's name. The same *kanji* can be read in different ways with different meanings. Names, in particular, can be difficult to read.

小鳥遊博士
"KOTORI-ASOBU-HAKASE"...?
"HAKASE" IS READ AS "HIROMORI."
"KOTORI-ASOBU" IS READ AS "TAKANASHI."
IT'S "HIROMORI TAKANASHI"!!

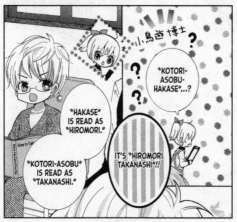

The adorable new odd-couple cat comedy manga from the creator of the beloved *Chi's Sweet Home*, in full color!

Sue & Tai-chan

Konami Kanata

Sue is an aging housecat who's looking forward to living out her life in peace... but her plans change when the mischievous black tomcat Tai-chan enters the picture! Hey! Sue never signed up to be a catsitter! *Sue & Tai-chan* is the latest from the reigning meow-narch of cute kitty comics, Konami Kanata.

KC KODANSHA COMICS

Young characters and steampunk setting, like *Howl's Moving Castle* and *Battle Angel Alita*

A boy with a talent for machines and a mysterious girl whose wings he's fixed will take you beyond the clouds! In the tradition of the high-flying, resonant adventure stories of Studio Ghibli comes a gorgeous tale about the longing of young hearts for adventure and friendship!